JUDICIAL RESPONSIBILITY AND *COUPS D'ÉTAT*

Judging Against Unconstitutional Usurpation of Power

Kriangsak Kittichaisaree

Routledge
Taylor & Francis Group
LONDON AND NEW YORK

Designed cover image: © Getty Images

First published 2023
by Routledge
4 Park Square, Milton Park, Abingdon, Oxon OX14 4RN

and by Routledge
605 Third Avenue, New York, NY 10158

Routledge is an imprint of the Taylor & Francis Group, an informa business

British Library Cataloguing-in-Publication Data
A catalogue record for this book is available from the British Library

ISBN: 978-1-032-40719-7 (hbk)
ISBN: 978-1-032-40718-0 (pbk)
ISBN: 978-1-003-35842-8 (ebk)

DOI: 10.4324/9781003358428

Typeset in Bembo
by Apex CoVantage, LLC

JUDICIAL RESPONSIBILITY AND *COUPS D'ÉTAT*

This book examines the responsibility of judges of domestic courts following unconstitutional usurpation of power of government (*coups d'état*). It explores judges' liability for failing to discharge their judicial duty independently and impartially, and the criminality of usurpers and their accomplices and collaborators for their violation of fundamental rights and freedoms or commission of crimes of international concern. Written by a highly regarded non-Western author, the book is coherent and meticulously researched, covering an approach to *coups* in an insightful and fascinating fashion. It includes a sophisticated and thorough analysis of the relevant comparative jurisprudence of domestic and international courts, with concrete examples of the best practices among decisions of domestic courts in countries that have experienced *coups d'état*. With an increasing global interest in the phenomenon of *coups*, democratic backsliding and the place and role of the judiciary as the only hope to rein in acts of unconstitutional usurpation of power, the book will be an essential reading for members of the legal profession, those cherishing democracy as well as students and researchers in constitutional law, law and political science, public international law, international human rights law, international criminal law, regime changes, transitional justice and international organizations.

Kriangsak Kittichaisaree is a Judge of the International Tribunal for the Law of the Sea. He has served as Chairperson of the UN General Assembly's Working Group on the Administration of Justice at the United Nations; member of the UN International Law Commission responsible for the topic 'The Obligation to Extradite or Prosecute (*aut dedere aut judicare*)'; and Thailand's Ambassador to Iran, Australia and Russia. He has taught international law at renowned law schools in four continents. His 11 books include the pioneering textbook *International Criminal Law* (2001); *Public International Law of Cyberspace* (2017, also translated into Chinese); *The Obligation to Extradite or Prosecute* (2018); *International Human Rights Law and Diplomacy* (2020); and *The Rohingya, Justice and International Law* (2021).

CONTENTS

Preface vii
List of Abbreviations x

1 Introduction 1
Overview 1
Scope of this book 2
Modus operandi *of unconstitutional usurpation of power 4*
Judges' roles in unconstitutional usurpation of power 7
Practical challenges 9
Methodological and related normative questions 11

2 Legal bases to assess the lawfulness of unconstitutional usurpation of power 15
Legal bases used to validate coups *16*
Legal bases used to invalidate coups *43*
Concluding remarks 72

3 Permissible parameters for judges in post-*coup* suppression of fundamental rights and freedoms 75
International conventions and rules of customary international law on the protection of fundamental rights and freedoms 75
States of emergency and derogation of fundamental rights and freedoms 89
Military tribunals 104
Law enforcement measures 114

Refusal to render judgments on 'political questions' *119*
Concluding remarks *122*

4 Availability or non-availability of defences for judges in relation to judicial responsibility post-*coups* 125
Individual criminal responsibility arising from judges' roles in an oppressive regime *127*
Independence of judiciary and allegiance to the new 'constitutional' order *139*
Superior orders *153*
Duress *155*
Judicial immunity *158*
Concluding remarks *159*

5 Amnesties, pardons, immunities and other restrictions on the prosecution of usurpers of power and their accomplices or collaborators 161
Amnesties, pardons and immunities *161*
Statutes of limitations *184*
Transitional justice *188*
A right balance *208*
Concluding remarks *216*

6 International or extra-territorial criminal prosecution of *coups*-related crimes of international concern 219
Prosecution before the International Criminal Court, ad hoc international tribunals and hybrid courts *219*
Prosecution in foreign courts exercising universal jurisdiction *238*

7 Epilogue 248

Index *261*

PREFACE

Unconstitutional usurpation of power of government either by means of a military *coup d'état* or a self-*coup* by the incumbent Head of State or Government still takes place in several parts of the world nowadays. In 2021 alone, there were military *coups* in Myanmar, Chad, Sudan, Guinea, and Mali as well as the self-*coup* by the President of Tunisia.

Unlike the Cabinet and the Legislature that are normally dissolved after the usurpation of power, the Judiciary is usually kept in operation to uphold the legitimacy of the regime installed by the usurper, sometimes with judges toeing the line and the usurper replacing those who are not. There are several writings, from a comparative constitutional law perspective, on domestic courts' decisions on the lawfulness or otherwise of 'revolutions', including *coups*, but not much has been written on judicial responsibility in this regard that spans not only comparative constitutional law, but also criminal law, public international law, international human rights law, transitional justice and international criminal law. To fill this gap, this book will analyze judicial responsibilities of domestic judges to uphold fundamental rights and freedoms usually curtailed after *coups d'état*; their liability for failing to discharge their judicial duty independently and impartially; and the criminality of usurpers, their accomplices and collaborators for the usurpation of power and consequential abuses.

Citizens whose fundamental rights and freedom are adversely affected by acts resulting from unconstitutional usurpation of power desperately look up to the Judiciary as their saviour. Should the Judiciary fail, the nation's democracy as well as the protection of its citizens' fundamental rights and freedoms also fails.

Since modern-day *coups* are staged in the non-Western world, in the Global South, Western liberal democratic principles are not cherished by *coup* leaders and there seems to be no existing book that covers all the issues just mentioned in a holistic manner. A book written by a non-Western author may be more favourably considered as not condescending on countries that have experienced *coups*, or 'neo-imperialistic' in subjugating the values and interests of these countries.

Thailand, where I come from, has experienced 12 military *coups d'état* plus one self-*coup* by the then civilian Prime Minister and quite a few failed *coup* attempts since the end of the absolute monarchy in 1932. I have heard and seen what has happened in the aftermath of each of the six *coups* and three attempted *coups* ever since I can remember. I have even had surreal experiences about two of the *coups*. When the Thai Army Chief staged the *coup* to topple the Thai Prime Minister on 19 September 2006, I was with the Premier in New York City, where he was scheduled to address the General Debate of the United Nations General Assembly. As the then Director-General of the Department of International Organizations of the Ministry of Foreign Affairs of Thailand, it was my responsibility to oversee the Premier's official trip to the United Nations as well as provide the substance of his speeches and multilateral dialogues. The secretariat's room was turned into a war room trying to challenge the *coup* in Bangkok, thousands of miles away. The Premier issued a few orders dismissing the Army Chief and instructing key armed forces personnel to return to the barracks, and it was my task to translate these orders into English to inform the international community who was still in charge of the country at that moment. The following year, in September 2007, still Director-General of that Department, I accompanied the Prime Minister installed by the *coup* to New York City, again to address the UN General Assembly and meet with his counterparts from friendly countries. In an evening, I even found myself one of the four persons having a small private dinner with the very courteous Premier. Several months later, I took up my new position as Thailand's Ambassador to the Islamic Republic of Iran and my first official guest from Thailand was, believe it or not, the former Army Chief who staged the *coup* in September 2006. He was paying an official visit to Iran in his capacity as Deputy Prime Minister in charge of national security, the position he held from 1 October 2006 to 28 January 2008. The General also visited Iran privately quite a few times after he left that position. When I was Ambassador to the Russian Federation, I organized the first-ever official visit abroad by the Thai Premier who had come into power by the military *coup* of 22 May 2014. A colleague from the Thai Judiciary who worked closely with me during the early days of my career with the Thai Government happened to be the presiding judge of the Supreme Court in a case challenging the legitimacy of the 2014 *coup*. With such unique personal contact with those directly involved in the two Thai *coups* and living in a society that has experienced so many *coups*, I assume that I can understand the ethos and mindset of *coup* leaders and their opponents. Now as an international judge, my sense of judicial responsibility compels me to look closely at the need to balance the positions of these opposing sides in an impartial, judicious manner.

It is always a great pleasure to be reunited with Alison Kirk, Senior Commissioning Editor of Routledge, and her team who have efficiently and expeditiously steered the publication of my latest two books. I very much appreciate how Anna Gallagher, Editorial Assistant/Law, has helped me through the process.

I would like to express my thanks to the following individuals who have provided invaluable information for my research: Stephen Rapp, Phani Dascalopoulo-Livada, Charles Jalloh, Renzo A. Cristaldo Garay, Sarthak Roy, Marie Anne Cyra Uy, Ayşe Güzel Öztürk, Louis Savadogo and Niki Manafa. I am also grateful to Mrs Rosa Palau, Director of the Documentation and Archive Centre for the Defence of Human Rights, or the Museum of Justice which is a unit of the Judiciary of Paraguay, where the archives related to the dictatorship in Paraguay (better known as the 'Archives of Terror') are kept. She has kindly shared with me the relevant rulings of the Supreme Court of Paraguay.

Thanks are owed to Elzbieta Mizerska-Dyba, Head of Library and Archives, and Svenja Heim, Library Assistant, of the International Tribunal for the Law of the Sea for their assistance in finding the publications I needed.

All the webpages referred to in this book are accessible as of 15 November 2022.

ABBREVIATIONS

AC	Appeal Cases
ACDEG	African Charter on Democracy, Elections and Governance
ACHPR	African Commission on Human and Peoples' Rights
ACtHPR	African Court on Human and Peoples' Rights
AFPRC	Armed Forces Provisional Ruling Council (The Gambia)
AFRC	Armed Forces Revolutionary Council (Sierra Leone)
AHRLR	African Human Rights Law Reports
AJIL	American Journal of International Law
App	Application
App Ch	Appeals Chamber
ASEAN	Association of Southeast Asian Nations
AU	African Union
BLT	Bangladesh Law Times
CAR	Central African Republic
CAT	Committee against Torture
CCPR	Human Rights Committee
CED	Committee on Enforced Disappearances
CEDAW	Committee on the Elimination of Discrimination against Women
CERD	Committee on the Elimination of Racial Discrimination
CESCR	Committee on Economic, Social and Cultural Rights
CLR	Commonwealth Law Reports
CMW	Committee on the Protection of the Rights of All Migrant Workers and Members of their Families
Comp L	Comparative Law
CRC	Committee on the Rights of the Child

Crim	Criminal
CRPD	Committee on the Rights of Persons with Disabilities
CRPH	Committee for Representing Pyidaungsu Hluttaw (Myanmar)
Ct App	Court of Appeal(s)
CUP	Cambridge University Press
Doc	Document
DR Congo	Democratic Republic of the Congo
ECOMIG	ECOWAS Mission in The Gambia
ECOWAS	Economic Community of West African States
ECtHR	European Court of Human Rights
EJIL	European Journal of International Law
ETS	European Treaty Series
EU	European Union
F3d	Federal Reports, Third Series (United States)
F Supp	Federal Supplement (United States district courts)
GA	General Assembly
GC	Grand Chamber of the European Court of Human Rights
Govt	Government
G.R.	General Register (Philippines)
HCSS	Hybrid Court for South Sudan
HRC	United Nations Human Rights Council
Hum Rts	Human Rights
IACHR	Inter-American Commission on Human Rights
IACtHR	Inter-American Court of Human Rights
IAPF	Inter-American Peace Force
ICC	International Criminal Court
ICCPR	1966 International Covenant on Civil and Political Rights
ICJ	International Court of Justice
ICLQ	International and Comparative Law Quarterly
ICRC	International Committee of the Red Cross
ICTR	International Criminal Tribunal for Rwanda
ICTY	International Criminal Tribunal for the former Yugoslavia
IIMM	Independent Investigative Mechanism for Myanmar
ILC	United Nations International Law Commission
ILJ	International Law Journal
ILM	International Legal Materials
IMT	International Military Tribunal or the 'Nuremberg Tribunal'
Int'l	International
Int'l L	International Law
ISIL	Islamic State of Iraq and the Levant
J	Journal
JIL	Journal of International Law

LJ	Law Journal
LRC	Butterworths' Law Reports of the Commonwealth
L Rep	Law Reports
L Rev	Law Review
MP	Member of Parliament, Member of the House of Representatives
NCPO	National Council for Peace and Order (Thailand)
NGO	non-governmental organization
No *or* no	Number *or* number
NUG	National Unity of Government formed by the CRPH
OAS	Organization of American States
OECS	Organization of Eastern Caribbean States
OJ	Official Journal
OPCAT	Optional Protocol to the Convention against Torture
OUP	Oxford University Press
PCA	Permanent Court of Arbitration
PCIJ	Permanent Court of International Justice
PCO	Proclamation of Emergency (Pakistan)
PDRC	People's Democratic Reform Committee (Thailand)
PLD	Pakistan Legal Decisions
PSC	African Union's Peace and Security Council
Rep	Report(s)
res	resolution
Rev	Review
Rts	Rights
SA	Storm Troopers or Brownshirts
SADC	Southern African Development Community
SAPS	South African Police Service
SC, S/C, *or* S Ct	Supreme Court
SD	Sicherheitsdienst, an intelligence service of the SS and the Nazi Party
Ser	Series
Sess	Session
SPT	Subcommittee on Prevention of Torture and other Cruel, Inhuman or Degrading Treatment or Punishment
SS	Schutzstaffel, a major paramilitary organization under Adolf Hitler and the Nazi Party
Supp	Supplement
TRRC	Truth, Reconciliation and Reparations Commission (The Gambia)
U	University
UN	United Nations
UNGA	United Nations General Assembly

UNGA OR	Official Records of the United Nations General Assembly
UNODC	United Nations Office on Drugs and Crime
UNTS	United Nations Treaties Series
U.S.	United States Reports (Supreme Court)
WLR	Weekly Law Reports
YB	Yearbook
YBIL	Yearbook of International Law

1

INTRODUCTION

Overview

In time of acute national crises, democracy is a luxury. This is the most frequently cited reason for unconstitutional usurpation of power through *coups d'état*, or overthrows of the incumbent government by armed forces or through an autocrat's exercise of extra-constitutional power.[1]

Coups have been staged from time immemorial. They happen after unsolvable internecine political and/or severe economic crises in the country, or are based on an excuse citing the existence of such crises, with the usurper claiming to be the saviour of the nation.[2] The Bible recorded, as early as in 885 BCE, the murder

1 A very exhaustive and up-to-date list of *coups* by country can be found in https://en.m.wikipedia.org/wiki/List_of_coups_and_coup_attempts_by_country. Cf. Jonathan Powell and Clayton Thyne, 'Global Instances of Coups from 1950 to 2010: A New Dataset' (2011) 48 J Peace Research 249, 252, defining *coups* as successful efforts by the military or other elites within the State apparatus to unseat the sitting executive by unconstitutional means, and a *coup* attempt is defined as successful if the perpetrators seize and hold power for at least seven days. See also Edward Luttwak, *Coup D'État: A Practical Handbook* (revised edn, Harvard U Press 2016) 1–12; Naunihal Singh, *Seizing Power: The Strategic Logic of Military Coups* (Johns Hopkins U Press 2014).

2 See, e.g., Alper Yagci, 'The Political Economy of Coups d'etat: A General Survey and a Local Theory for Turkey' (2018) 19 Turkish Studies 72; Benjamin Gourisse, 'What Politics Does to the Army: Divisions and Reconfigurations to the Military Institution in the 27 May 1960 Coup in Turkey' (2021) 58 Middle Eastern Studies 70; George Harris, 'The Causes of the 1960 Military Revolution in Turkey' (1970) 24 Middle East J 438; Tanel Demirel, 'The Turkish Military's Decision to Intervene: 12 September 1980' (2003) 29 Armed Forces & Society 253. One empirical research finds slow economic growth rates, previous *coup* experiences and other forms of political violence to be particularly conducive to inciting *coups* (Martin Gassebner, Jerg Gutmann and Stephan Voigt, *When to Expect a Coup d'état? An Extreme Bounds Analysis of Coup Determinants*, KOF Working Paper No 409 (August 2016)). A study on the phenomenon of military *coups* in Africa concludes that by addressing some core economic and socio-political problems, governments could mitigate the risk

DOI: 10.4324/9781003358428-1

of King Elah of Israel by his chariot commander, Zimri, who succeeded him as king before killing himself while under siege by Omri, the army commander who had been proclaimed king by the army.[3] During the Cold War era, foreign powers are sometimes suspected of instigating *coups* to maintain their sphere of influence.[4] *Coups* in the modern day are staged mostly in the Global South although allegations of attempted or plotted *coups* can be heard anywhere.[5] Of the 14 *coups* recorded globally since 2017, all but one—Myanmar in February 2021—have been in Africa.[6] Recent *coups* which have attracted the greatest international reaction were staged in Myanmar on 1 February 2021 and Sudan on 25 October 2021. Democracy is often perceived by modern-day usurpers of power as Western-centric, with little appreciation of non-Western values and societies facing the crises.

Scope of this book

This book aims at comprehensively analyzing the domestic and international legal regimes concerning *coups d'état*, with concrete examples of the best practices among decisions of domestic courts of countries that have experienced *coups* from around the world. It explains how judges could be criminally liable domestically

---

of a *coup* because good governance and policies that provide economic opportunities for all citizens and that create the enabling environment for poverty reduction may be the panacea to tackle political instability (Habiba Ben Barka and Mthuli Ncube, *Political Fragility in Africa: Are Military Coups d'Etat a Never-Ending Phenomenon?* (African Development Bank 2012)). Cf. Rebecca Schiel, 'An Assessment of Democratic Vulnerability: Regime Type, Economic Development, and Coups d'état' (2019) 26 Democratization 1439.

3 *Holy Bible*, New International Version, 1 Kings 16:9, 15, https://biblehub.com/niv/1_kings/16.htm. Cf. Stuart Cohen, 'How to Mount a Successful Coup d'etat: Lessons from the Bible (II Kings 11, II Chronicles 23)' (2000) 11 Diplomacy & Statecraft 1.

4 See, e.g., Kai Bird, 'Bangladesh: Anatomy of a Coup' (1979) 14 Economic & Political Weekly 1999; Stephen Kinzer, *Overthrow: America's Century of Regime Change from Hawaii to Iraq* (Times Book 2007); Raymond Bonner, *Weakness and Deceit: U.S. Policy and El Salvador* (OR Books 2016).

5 E.g., on 26 November 2021 Ukrainian President Volodymyr Zelensky alleged that Russian 'representatives' were planning to overthrow his government on 1 December 2021 ('Ukraine-Russia Conflict: Zelensky Alleges Coup Plan Involving Russians' *BBC* (26 November 2021), https://www.bbc.com/news/world-europe-59428712). Also on 26 November 2021, security services in Kyrgyzstan detained 15 'active members' of a *coup* plot involving members of parliament and former high-ranking government officials who tried to get '1,000 aggressive young people' to protest the results of the upcoming parliamentary elections and subsequently to aggravate the situation, provoke clashes with law enforcement authorities and instigate violent seizure of power ('Kyrgyzstan Detains 15 in "Coup Plot" before Vote' *Al Jazeera* (26 November 2021), https://www.aljazeera.com/news/2021/11/26/kyrgyzstan-detains-15-in-coup-plot-before-vote). On the allegation that US President Donald Trump was attempting a *coup* for him to remain in office after the November 2020 Presidential election, see 'READ: Trump Lawyer's Memo on Six-step Plan for Pence to Overturn the Election' *CNN* (21 September 2021), https://edition.cnn.com/2021/09/21/politics/read-eastman-memo/index.html; Chris Cillizza, 'Donald Trump's Hands Are All Over the Coup Attempt' *CNN* (21 January 2022), https://edition.cnn.com/2022/01/21/politics/trump-giuliani-january-6-2020/index.html.

6 Peter Mwai, 'Sudan Coup: Are Military Takeovers on the Rise in Africa?' *BBC* (3 October 2022), https://www.bbc.com/news/world-africa-46783600.

and/or internationally for failing to discharge their judicial duty independently and impartially to uphold fundamental rights and freedoms as well as punish usurpers, their accomplices and collaborators for abuses amounting to serious violations of human rights or even crimes of international concern.

Filling the existing gap in the literature that focuses on the comparative constitutional law aspect of *coups* and on tyranny, dictatorship and authoritarianism in general, the book strives to deal holistically with usurpation of power not only from the perspective of public international law, including international human rights law and international criminal law, but also from the perspectives of criminal law, transitional justice and constitutional law.

This book is not about the regime adopted by a national revolution which fundamentally transforms the system of government in a nation State, as in the case of, for example, the revolution in China that has transformed China into a Communist State under the name the People's Republic of China, the military *coup* in Afghanistan in 1973 that overthrew the monarchy and turned Afghanistan into a republic, the Islamic Revolution in Iran in 1979 that turned Iran into an Islamic Republic and the violent civil unrest known as 'the Romanian Revolution' in December 1989 that ended 42 years of Communist rule in Romania. Nor is the book about usurpation of power that leads to protracted civil wars, such as the United Somali Congress' overthrow of the President of Somalia in January 1995 which started the Somali Civil War and the power struggle in Yemen that has culminated in the ongoing civil war with foreign intervention.

This book is also not about authoritarian styles of government which has come to power by general elections—the so-called electoral authoritarianism,[7] provided that this does not amount to a de facto *coup*, or a self-*coup*, by a democratically elected President or Prime Minister, as in the self-*coup* by Chancellor Adolf Hitler who unconstitutionally assumed full power in Germany on 23 March 1933.[8] Another example of a de facto *coup* took place in the Philippines, when Ferdinand E. Marcos, elected President in 1965 and re-elected in 1969, imposed martial law and suspended the Constitution in order to keep himself in office beyond the two four-year term limits imposed by the Constitution. Yet another notorious self-*coup* took place in Peru, when, on 5 April 1992, with the support of the Peruvian military, Alberto Fujimori, who had been elected President in July 1990, revoked the Constitution, dissolved the opposition-controlled Congress and 'reorganized' the Judiciary in a purge.[9]

7 Cf. Klaus Larres (ed.), *Dictators and Autocrats: Securing Power Across Global Politics* (Routledge 2021); Steven Levitsky and Daniel Ziplatt, *How Democracy Dies* (Crown 2018); William Dobson, *The Dictator's Learning Curve: Inside the Global Battle for Democracy* (Anchor Books 2013).

8 See further Eric Kurlander, 'Adolf Hitler: From Democracy to Dictatorship' in Klaus Larres (ed.), *Dictators and Autocrats*, ch 2.

9 César Landa, *The Scales of Justice in Peru: Judicial Reform and Fundamental Rights* (Institute of American Studies, University of London, Occasional Paper 2001). More generally, see Julio Carrión (ed.), *The Fujimori Legacy: The Rise of Electoral Authoritarianism in Peru* (Penn State U Press 2006); John Crabtree,

Modus operandi of unconstitutional usurpation of power

The common features of these *coups* and their aftermath are: (a) propaganda by *coup* leaders to justify their unconstitutional usurpation of power,[10] (b) suspension or annulment of the constitution, (c) suppression of fundamental rights and freedoms, (d) drafting a new constitution and/or election law to grant a blanket amnesty or pardon to the junta and to ensure *coup* leaders will return to power by means of election, (e) holding a referendum to approve the said constitution/law and (f) setting up a new government after the general election under the new constitution, often with the continued suppression of fundamental rights and freedoms for the government to stay in power,[11] the so-called elective despotism.[12]

During phases (a) to (e), a state of emergency is declared. There is a close connection between these phases and the post-*coup* developments in phase (f). After a *coup*, the usurper often sets up an unelected legislative body to act as its de facto rubber stamp to keep it in power. Once a new constitution is drafted by those appointed by the usurper, a referendum is usually held in such a way as to ensure the constitution will be approved by the referendum, by stifling free and open public debates on and any campaign against the constitution with severe punishment imposed on violators.[13] Full democracy normally returns after successive failures of the regime propped up by the junta, as in the cases of Argentina, Benin, Chile, Greece, Indonesia and South Korea, to name just a few.[14] This transition to democracy often results from constitutional reforms to restore the democratic institutions and fundamental rights and freedoms previously abrogated by the usurper. The transition to democracy is sometimes made possible by another *coup*. Such were the case of the January 1958 *coup* following a popular uprising in Venezuela that ousted military dictator Marcos Pérez Jiménez; the one in the Philippines

'The Collapse of *Fujimorismo*: Authoritarianism and Its Limits' (2001) 20 Bulletin of Latin Amer Research 287. It is alleged that after US President Donald Trump lost his presidential re-election in November 2020 there was well-grounded fear he might stage a *coup* to keep him in power as President (Carol Leonnig and Philip Rucker, *I Alone Can Fix It: Donald J. Trump's Catastrophic Final Year* (Penguin 2021) 365–6, 432–4, 441–2, 487).

10 See further Taku Yukawa, Kaoru Hidaka and Kaori Kushima, 'Coups and Framing: How Do Militaries Justify the Illegal Seizure of Power?' (2020) 27 Democratization 816.

11 See also Tom Ginsburg and Aziz Hug, *How to Save a Constitutional Democracy* (U Chicago Press 2018) 6–34, contending that democracy cannot be reduced to the mere fact of elections since countries can still experience democratic decline even if they continue to hold elections.

12 Tom Ginsburg, 'Democratic Backsliding and the Rule of Law' (2018) 44 Ohio Northern U Law Rev 351, 355–7.

13 See, e.g., the International Federation for Human Rights, Union for Civil Liberties and Internet Law Reform Dialogue, *Joint Shadow Report (Thailand)*, submitted to the Human Rights Committee, 119th Session (6–29 March 2017) 24–5.

14 In Benin, for example, the 19-year rule of President Mathieu Kérékou, who led a military *coup* to topple the then Government in 1972, was terminated in 1991 relatively peacefully and smoothly due to the dismal economic situation in that country (Samuel Decalo, 'First of the New Democracies' in John Clark and David Gardinier (eds), *Political Reform in Francophone Africa* (Routledge 1997) 43–61). See also Einar Berntzen, 'Prospects and Dilemmas of Democratic Consolidation in Latin America' (1989) 19 Ibero-Americana, Nordic J Latin Amer Studies 21, passim and 40–1.

in February 1986 after the successful People Power Revolution and the civilian-backed military *coup* led by then Defence Minister Juan Ponce Enrile and General Fidel Ramos that toppled President Ferdinand E. Marcos' dictatorship; the February 1989 *coup* in Paraguay which ended Alfredo Stroessner's dictatorship lasting from 1954;[15] and the November 2017 *coup* to remove Zimbabwe's President Robert Mugabe from power after 47 years of his repressive rule.[16]

One empirical study[17] finds *coup* leaders generally have three options. First, there is no regime change, as in the case of the 1975 Nigerian *coup* that replaced General Yakubu Gowon with Brigadier Murtala Muhammad, without changing either the group in power or the rules for governing. Second, a new dictatorship is established in lieu of the deposed one, as in the cases of the 1971 Ugandan *coup* that toppled the civilian government led by Milton Obote and brought General Idi Amin to power and the 2008 *coup* in Guinea by Captain Dadis Camara, a day after the death of long-time dictator Lansana Conté.[18] Third, the ouster of the dictatorship is followed by democratization (as in Niger in 1999 and 2010). The third one should include the Ugandan military *coup* in May 1980, after which the junta handed over the power to the civilian government on 15 December 1980 after the general election five days earlier. Also in the third category is the bloodless *coup* in Ecuador on 11 January 1976 by the military junta of the triumvirate led by Vice Admiral Alfredo Poveda Burbano that overthrew the military regime of Guillermo Rodríguez Lara, who himself had come to power by a military *coup* in 1972. The triumvirate held power until the return to civilian rule after the general election on 29 April 1979, as irrevocably promised by Poveda.[19] Overall, the study finds the association between

15 Carlos Miranda, *The Stroessner Era: Authoritarian Rule in Paraguay* (Westview Press 1990); Cesar Insfan, 'Paraguay Celebrates New Constitution' *UPI* (20 June 1992), https://www.upi.com/Archives/1992/06/20/Paraguay-celebrates-new-constitution/5182709012800/. Andrés Rodríguez Pedotti who toppled Stroessner in the *coup* replaced the latter as President, signed a new constitution into law on 22 June 1992 that, among other things, limited the Presidency to a single five-year term with retroactive effect and stepped down as President on 15 August 1993.

16 Blessing-Miles Tendi, 'The Motivations and Dynamics of Zimbabwe's 2017 Military Coup' (2020) 119 African Affairs 39. See also Kalyani Mookherji, *20 Dictators of the World* (Oceans Book 2016) ch 19. For the arguments that *coups* are not necessarily a deplorable means to change government if it brings about a positive break with the existing order and generate a desirable regime change, particularly in States where a tyrannical government endlessly clings to power, see Jean d'Aspremont, 'Responsibility for Coups d'État in International Law' (2010) 18 Tulane J Int'l & Comp L 451, 452, 473–5. *Contra*: Oisín Tansey, 'The Fading of the Anti-Coup Norm' (2017) 28 J Democracy 144.

17 George Derpanopoulos, Erica Frantz, Barbara Geddes and Joseph Wright, 'Are Coups Good for Democracy?' (January–March 2016) Research & Politics 1–2.

18 As another example in this category, the *coup* by Idriss Déby Itno on 2 December 1990 that ousted Chadian President Hissène Habré in December 1990 was followed by the *coup* leader becoming President of Chad, re-elected every five years until he was killed by an armed rebel group in April 2021, only to be succeeded as President by his own son.

19 Cf. John Martz, *The Military Rule in Ecuador: Policies and Politics of Authoritarian Rule*, Occasional Research Paper Series No 3, Latin American & Iberian Institute, U New Mexico (June 1988) 33–40; Ozan Varol, 'The Diplomatic Coups d'État' (2012) 53 Harvard ILJ 291. There are several instances in which *coup* leaders subsequently run for office in multi-party elections, as in the case of Azali Assoumani who staged a *coup* in April 1999 and became President of Comoros up to 2002. He

coups and democratization is statistically insignificant, while that between *coups* and the establishment of new dictatorships is robust. Although democracies are occasionally established in the wake of *coups*, most frequently new authoritarian regimes emerge, along with higher levels of State-sanctioned violence since a new set of autocratic elites is installed after a *coup* and citizens are exposed to higher levels of repression.[20] Sudan might fall within the last mentioned scenario. Omar al-Bashir staged a bloodless *coup* to topple the Government of Sudan on 30 June 1989 and ruled the country until toppled by the Sudanese armed forces on 11 April 2019 after months of widespread protests and national uprisings against his rule.[21] A transitional government with the military sharing power with civilians to lead Sudan on the path back to full democracy was brought to an end by the *coup* staged by the military on 25 October 2021, just weeks before the civilians in the transitional government would take their turns leading the transitional government. The *coup* leader cited as the main reason for the *coup* the need to avoid civil war by sidelining politicians who were inciting against the armed forces. He promised to hold elections in July 2023 and hand over power to an elected civilian government then.

Fundamental rights and freedoms usually restricted or even violated after a *coup* for the junta to stay in power are the right to life; the freedom of speech; the freedom of the press; the right to peaceful assembly; the freedom of association; the right to hold opinions without interference; the right to take part in the conduct of public affairs, directly or through freely chosen representatives as well as the right to vote and to be elected at genuine periodic elections; the freedom from unreasonable search and seizure; the right to a fair trial under the due process of law, including the principle of legality according to which no one may be accused or convicted of a criminal offence on account of any act or omission which did not

---

was also President from 2002 to 2006 and, again, from 2016 after winning multi-party elections. If such elections are free and fair by international standards, those initially coming to power by means of a *coup* can be considered to have followed the path of democratization. However, elections that return former *coup* leaders to power are often controversial, as in the case of the Republic of Congo's President Denis Sassou Nguesso, who came to power by the *coup* in February 1979 and by another *coup* in October 1997. In April 2021 he was sworn in as President for another term, extending his 36-year accumulated rule after getting 88.4 per cent of the vote with the turnout of 67.55 per cent of some 2.5 million eligible voters in the 21 March 2021 election, boycotted by the main opposition and accused of widespread vote irregularities (Vava Tampa, 'Sassou Rules Like an Emperor While Congolese Die from Extreme Poverty' *Guardian* (10 April 2021), https://www.theguardian.com/global-development/2021/apr/10/denis-sassou-nguesso-rules-like-an-emperor-while-congolese-die-from-extreme-poverty-congo-brazzaville).

20 Derpanopoulos, Frantz, Geddes and Wright, 'Are Coups Good for Democracy?' 2. Another study of successful and failed *coups* from 1950 to 2015 suggests that while successfully staged *coups* lead to democratization in wealthier countries, high levels of income and State capacity allow authoritarian-leaning leaders to autocratize the country following a failed *coup* attempt (Huseyin Zengin, 'Why Do Some Coups Lead to Democratization?' (2022) 29 Democratization 798. Cf. Jonathan Powell, 'An Assessment of the "Democratic" Coup Theory' (2014) 23 African Security Rev 213.

21 Mai Hassan and Ahmed Kodouda, 'Sudan's Uprising: The Fall of a Dictator' (2019) 30 J Democracy 89; Willow Berridge, Justin Lynch, Raga Makawi and Alex de Waal, *Sudan's Unfinished Democracy: The Promise and Betrayal of a People's Revolution* (Hurst 2022).

constitute a criminal offence at the time it was committed, nor may a heavier penalty be imposed than that which was applicable at the time the criminal offence was committed; the right to liberty and security of person; the freedom from torture or to cruel, inhuman or degrading treatment or punishment; the right to liberty of movement; and the right to the protection of the law against arbitrary or unlawful interference with one's privacy, family, home or correspondence or unlawful attacks on one's honour and reputation.[22] In the era of advanced information technologies, multifarious strategies and tactics are used by the usurper to suppress Internet freedom to maintain the unconstitutional regime's iron grip on power lest a free and unregulated Internet constitute a threat to the regime's survival.[23]

Judges' roles in unconstitutional usurpation of power

Judges at times play a role in paving the way for a *coup*. The June 2009 *coup* in Honduras resulted from a constitutional crisis caused by the Honduran President's plan to change the Constitution to enable presidential re-election, contrary to the entrenched constitutional provision against such re-election, which can never be amended. The Honduran Supreme Court ordered the President to cancel the referendum on convening a constituent assembly to rewrite the Constitution for this purpose and, after he disregarded the order, ordered his removal from office. However, there were no specific procedures for removing or prosecuting an incumbent President. The Honduran military took the matter into its own hands by staging a *coup*, detaining the President, putting him on a plane bound for Costa Rica and having the Honduran National Congress name the President of Congress as President of Honduras.[24]

22 See, e.g., Nopphon Achamat, Poonsuk Poonsukcharoen, Pathanij Yaodum, Montana Duangprapa, Suppanut Boonsod and Ittipol Kotamee, *Recommendations for Dealing with the Aftermath of a Coup d'État: Law, Policy, and Judicial Process to Protect Citizens' Rights and Freedoms* (Thai Lawyers for Human Rights 2019) 41–57. The following provisions on civil and political rights under the 1966 International Covenant on Civil and Political Rights (999 UNTS 171, in force 23 March 1976) are routinely violated: Art 2 (right to an effective remedy), Art 4 (derogation during a state of emergency), Art 9 (liberty and security of person), Art 10 (humane treatment of persons deprived of their liberty), Art 12 (freedom of movement), Art 14 (right to equality before courts and tribunals and right to a fair trial), Art 19 (right to freedom of opinion and expression), Art 21 (right to freedom of peaceful assembly) and Art 25 (participation in public affairs and the right to vote). For instance, after the 22 May 2014 military *coup* in Thailand, the National Council for Peace and Order (NCPO) set up by the military junta issued 556 orders before the NCPO was dissolved in 2018. The orders were to control four areas: political activities; public information and media reports; the judicial system, such as using military courts for political cases; and natural resources management and the promotion of industrial development. Since these orders have no expiry date, new laws are needed to replace or repeal them.

23 Eda Keremoğlu and Nils Weidmann, 'How Dictators Control the Internet: A Review Essay' (2020) 53 Comparative Political Studies 1690. Cf. Olesya Tkacheva, Lowell Schwartz, Martin Libicki, Julie Taylor, Jeffrey Martini and Caroline Baxter, *Internet Freedom and Political Space* (Rand Corp 2013).

24 William Booth and Juan Ferrero, 'Honduran Military Sends President into Exile; Supportive Congress Names Successor' *Washington Post* (29 June 2009), https://www.washingtonpost.com/wp-dyn/content/story/2009/06/29/ST2009062901282.html.

In studying the role of Thai lawyers in the aftermath of the 22 May 2014 military *coup* in Thailand, an author finds these lawyers have played a critical role in the success of the *coup* either as lawyers entrusted with building a new legal regime for the usurper or as judges entrusted with supporting the power and actions of the usurper. Additionally, Thai lawyers have arguably played another, critical, role by interpreting the constitution in such a way as to destroy constitutional mechanisms for resolving political conflict to the extent that it has entailed a constitutional crisis giving rise to an opportunity for the military to stage another *coup*.[25] This phenomenon is not unique to Thailand.

It is correct to assert that law is not useless *ex ante* in deterring a *coup* and, unlike the Cabinet and the Legislature, the Judiciary is usually not dissolved after a *coup*—at least because judicial affirmation of the regime imposed by the *coup* confers legitimacy upon the *coup* and judges are needed to uphold 'law and order' imposed by the usurper of power as the 'legal façade' of tyranny.[26] Indeed, throughout the different phases of usurpation of power of government, judges are called upon to uphold the 'law' promulgated at the behest of the usurper and, subsequently, under the new constitution promulgated after the *coup*. Judges thus become the persons who are in a position to validate or invalidate the consequences of usurpation of power.[27] It is also quite normal for military courts or tribunals to take over 'national security–related' cases from civil courts post-*coups*. One of the most infamous trials after a *coup* was the trial by a special court set up by the junta on Türkiye's Yassiada Island after the first military *coup* in Türkiye, on 27 May 1960.

25 Supanut Boonsod, 'A Role of Thai Lawyers During a Non-Democratic *Coup d'État*: The Case Study of the *Coup d'État* on 22 May 2014' (2019) 12 CMU Journal of Law & Social Sciences 123, 130–50.

26 John Hatchard and Tunde Ogowewo, *Tackling the Unconstitutional Overthrow of Democracies: Emerging Trends in the Commonwealth* (Commonwealth Secretariat 2003) 12, 14; Achamat *et al.*, *Recommendations for Dealing with the Aftermath of a Coup d'État* 21–31, 40–1; Hakeem Yusuf, *Transitional Justice, Judicial Accountability and the Rule of Law* (Routledge 2010) 33–49, 68–89, 183–7; Eduardo Monteiro Burkle, *When Forgetting Is Dangerous: Transitional Justice, Collective Remembrance and Brazil's Shift to Far-Right Populism*, European Master's Degree in Human Rights and Democratization (EMA) thesis (2020) 12, 44–5. According to Aoife O'Donoghue (*On Tyranny and the Global Legal Order* (CUP 2021) Introduction, ch 1 and ch 2), tyranny enables political decisions unrestrained by law, where the legal order enables rather than restricts or holds political action to account, and the interrelationship between political choices and legal structures ensures the longevity and effectiveness of tyranny. This is because tyranny often co-opts and utilizes law in its operation, hiding its lack of legitimacy beneath rule of law, whereas it is in fact 'rule by law'. See also Robert Barros, 'Courts Out of Context: Authoritarian Sources of Judicial Failures in Chile (1973–1990) and Argentina (1976–1983)' in Tom Ginsburg and Tamir Moustafa (eds), *Rule by Law: The Politics of Courts in Authoritarian Regimes* (CUP 2008) 156–78; Anthony Pereira, *Political (In)Justice: Authoritarianism and the Rule of Law in Brazil, Chile and Argentina* (U Pittsburgh Press 2005); Hans Petter Graver, *Judges Against Justice: On Judges When the Rule of Law Is Under Attack* (Springer 2015) 15–112.

27 See also Ginsburg, 'Democratic Backsliding and the Rule of Law' 358–63. Cf. Aziz Huq and Tom Ginsburg, 'Democracy without Democrats' (2020) 6 Constitutional Studies 165, 169–84, where the authors show how unelected actors and institutions, such as high court judges, election commissions, prosecutors and military leaders may have both the incentives and the ability to stand in the way of democratic backsliding by taking actions to preserve the possibility of democratic endurance.

A series of criminal cases were brought by the military regime against the former elected government leaders from the Democrat Party, in particular, former Prime Minister Adnan Menderes, former Foreign Minister Fatin Rustu Zorlu and former Finance Minister Hasan Polatkan, all of whom were sentenced to death on 15 September 1961. Their trials commencing within months of the *coup* were efforts by the military to show to the country how corrupt the former ruling party had been and how just the new regime would be.[28]

There are instances in which ambassadors denounce *coups* staged in their respective countries and profess to continue to represent the toppled regimes, as in the cases of Myanmar's Ambassador to the United Kingdom and Myanmar's Permanent Representative to the United Nations, New York, after the 2021 *coup* in Myanmar. Subsequent to the October 2021 military *coup* in Sudan, Sudanese ambassadors to the United States, the European Union, China, France and Qatar as well as Sudan's Permanent Representative to the United Nations Offices in Geneva rejected the military takeover. These envoys were immediately sacked by the juntas. Since ambassadors are part of the executive branch of government, their roles differ from those of judges who are members of the Judiciary and the former can, at most, lobby the international community to put pressure on the juntas to cede power and return the country back to democracy. For their part, the juntas can dismiss and replace the disobedient ambassadors and the receiving host country can do little. For example, in March 2021 Kyaw Zwar Minn, Myanmar's Ambassador to the United Kingdom, who had criticized the military *coup*, was dismissed and replaced by the Myanmar junta. Although the British Foreign Secretary condemned the 'bullying actions' by the Myanmar junta against the Ambassador, the UK Government had no choice but to accept the change after the UK Foreign and Commonwealth Office received the notification by 'the sending State' of the termination of the Ambassador's appointment pursuant to Article 43(a) of the 1961 Vienna Convention on Diplomatic Relations,[29] to which both the United Kingdom and Myanmar are party.

Practical challenges

Part of the challenge, when it comes to countries experiencing *coups*, is that the relevant judicial decisions are hard to track down.[30] The official law reporting system

28 Middle East Record, Vol 1, 1960, 454–8; Walter Weiker, *The Turkish Revolution 1960–1961: Aspects of Military Politics* (Brookings Institution 1963); Reuben Silverman, 'Show (and tell) Trials: Competing Narratives of Turkey's Democrat Party Era' (2021) 22 Turkish Studies 147.

29 500 UNTS 95, in force 24 April 1964.

30 For example, since 1974 courts in Burma/Myanmar are constitutionally required to operate in Burmese, rather than English and the publication of courts decisions has often been late, sporadic and difficult to access. In 2014, the Constitutional Tribunal Law was amended so that all decisions of the Constitutional Tribunal must be announced in the Government Gazette and published as reported cases, to ensure access for the domestic audience. See Melissa Crouch, 'Dictators, Democrats, and

may have broken down completely or *coup*-related issues do not usually go to court. In some countries, such as Myanmar, trials of those deposed by a *coup* are held in closed-door proceedings, with the public and the media being denied access to the hearings and lawyers subject to gag orders. For example, on 6 December 2021 Myanmar's President Win Myin who was toppled in the February 2021 military *coup* and Aung San Suu Kyi, State Counsellor and de facto Head of the Government ousted by the *coup*, were each sentenced by the Zabuthiri Court in the capital Naypyidaw to four years' imprisonment for incitement of public dissent and violation of government measures under a natural disaster management law to contain the COVID-19 pandemic. Myanmar's State media announced on the same day that the junta leader granted a partial pardon 'on a humanitarian ground' to each of them to reduce their respective sentences to two years. According to the Assistance Association for Political Prisoners, a human rights NGO, as of 22 April 2022 no fewer than 123 opponents of the *coup* had been sentenced to jail, including Aung San Suu Kyi's aide, Win Htein, who was sentenced to 20 years in prison in October 2021.[31] Their convictions and sentences were announced by the military junta's spokesman to news outlets, and no official court judgment has been published or made available to the public. This kind of trial is a sham trial in secretive proceedings before a military controlled court that is nothing but politically motivated.

Accessible case law about unconstitutional usurpation of power of government among nation States that have experienced this phenomenon varies. Therefore, it seems difficult to compile practices among their domestic courts with a view to establishing 'a rule of customary international law governing the lawfulness or unlawfulness of unconstitutional usurpation of power' that is binding on all States. There can be no such rule unless it can be proven to have derived from 'the practice of States that contributes to the formation, or expression, of rules of customary international law' which is 'sufficiently widespread and representative, as well as consistent' and also being 'undertaken with a sense of legal right or obligation'.[32] Worse still, because judges of domestic courts in countries ruled by the regime set up by the usurper usually discharge their judicial duty in the circumstance where opposition against the regime is not tolerated, some of these judgments may give a wrong impression that *coups* are not generally unlawful and the restriction or violation of fundamental rights and freedoms by the regime may be legally permissible.

Constitutional Dialogue: Myanmar's Constitutional Tribunal' (2018) 16 Int'l J Constitutional L 421, 426.

31 https://aappb.org/.

32 Conclusions 4(1), 8(1) and 9(1) of the UN International Law Commission's topic 'Identification of customary international law', Report of the International Law Commission, 70th Sess (30 April–1 June and 2 July–10 August 2018), Official Records of the General Assembly, 73rd Sess, Suppl No 10 (A/73/10) para 65. See also Katie Johnston, 'The Nature and Context of Rules and the Identification of Customary International Law' (2021) 32 EJIL 1167; Panos Merkouris, Jörg Kammerhofer and Noora Arajärvi (eds), *The Theory, Practice, and Interpretation of Customary International Law* (CUP 2022).

Methodological and related normative questions

Several questions arise in relation to judicial responsibility post-*coups*. First, why are judges willing to uphold the 'law' made by the usurper? This necessitates an analysis of legal bases used by judges in this regard. Second, what can judges do to keep in check the restriction or suppression of fundamental rights and freedoms during the unconstitutional regime? In the context of the answers to the first and second questions comes the third question: do judges have any defence against prosecution in either domestic courts or a competent international criminal court or tribunal in respect of their conduct post-*coups*? In this connection, some nation States assert 'universal' criminal jurisdiction to punish crimes committed abroad even where neither the perpetrator nor the victim is their national and the State is not in any way injured by the crimes. The fourth question concerns the validity or otherwise of an amnesty, pardon, immunity and any other method to shield the usurper, their accomplices and collaborators from criminal prosecution at home and abroad.

A central claim in this book is that while a rule of customary international law governing the lawfulness or unlawfulness of unconstitutional usurpation of power may be difficult to ascertain or establish, there are numerous prohibitions applicable in the context of usurpation of power that have become rules of customary international law of universal application, as in the case of the proscription against crimes against humanity and torture, as will be elaborated in subsequent chapters.

In addition, the book sets out to compile reasoning of domestic courts concerning unconstitutional usurpation of power that may be considered 'best practices' for judges to emulate. As will be explained in a subsequent chapter, the decision of the Fijian Court of Appeal in *Republic of Fiji v Prasad*[33] declaring the usurper's regime which was still in power to be unlawful led to the announcement by the Prime Minister of the Interim Civilian Government set up by the *coup* that Fiji would be returned to democratic rule and his Government then resigned, followed by a general election. Judgments of domestic courts in some other countries, such as Pakistan and Chile, have served as a catalyst for the eventual downfall of military regimes. According to the best practices deriving from many jurisdictions, even when the usurper is still in power judges must uphold fundamental rights and freedoms, as will be seen in Chapters 2, 3, 4 and 5. Judges should also, as certain domestic courts have done, set a reasonable timeline for the junta to return the country back to democracy, explaining why, based on their impartial reasoning, this timeline is imperative. This in and of itself could galvanize the populace to demand and strive for the end of the junta.[34] The best practices point to the morally appropriate position for judges to take, as the alternative could be much worse (i.e., an even more arbitrary exercise of executive power).

This book's normative thinking about best practices as regards judicial responsibility after unconstitutional usurpation of power can be summarized in three

33 [2001] 2 LRC 743.
34 See also Graver, *Judges Against Justice* 275–300.

sentences. First, although judges may *not always* be in a position to rule that a *coup* is not justifiable and therefore unlawful, they must, at a minimum, discharge their judicial functions to safeguard the fundamental rights and freedoms for all under due process of law, the rule of law and the principle of legality including any international legal obligations binding upon the country. Second, the overarching considerations and the fundamental drivers behind this approach to the best practices for such judicial responsibility are to ensure that judges do not become mere tools to provide the 'legal façade' of the usurper's repressive regime. Third, judges, like any other individual, can be held liable for their roles in supporting or sustaining repressive regimes. These are the overriding legal and social commitments that arise for a judge in the case of a *coup*.

In this respect, the book avoids trying to determine categorically whether the entire collection of these best practices or part thereof constitutes 'general principles of law' insofar as the terminology 'general principles of law' has not been used consistently in the practice and in the literature.[35] Yet, readers may find the reasoning used by domestic courts which constitute the best practices 'common to the various legal systems of the world'[36] as determined from a wide and representative comparative analysis of national legal systems (i.e., national laws, decisions of national courts and other relevant materials) from the different geographical regions across the globe.[37]

The following chapters of the book will proceed as follows.

Chapter 2 explores the legal bases invoked by judges to assess the lawfulness or otherwise of usurpation of power; namely, necessity in dire situations faced by a nation, effectiveness or efficacy of the usurpation of power giving rise to a new legal order according to which the validity of the laws and correctness of judicial decisions have to be determined, sovereignty vested in the usurper as the de facto ruler of the country, the meaning of the rule of law vis-à-vis an authoritarian regime and the existence of legal vacuum should courts refuse to uphold laws promulgated by the junta. These legal bases are then assessed against criteria set by some domestic court judgments: the protection of the welfare of the people and the level of popular acceptance of a particular *coup* by the citizens of the country as well as international acceptance by the international community of nations, including the global and regional organizations to which the country belongs, bearing in

35 First Report of the Special Rapporteur of the International Law Commission on General Principles of Law, Doc A/CN.4/732 (5 April 2019) para 254; Memorandum of the Secretariat of the International Law Commission, 'General Principles of Law', Doc A/CN.4/742 (12 May 2020). Cf. Xuan Shao, 'What We Talk about When We Talk about General Principles of Law' (2021) 20 Chinese JIL 219; Mariana Clara de Andrade, 'Regional Principles of Law in the Works of the International Law Commission' (2021) 86 Questions of Int'l L 23; Yilin Wang, 'A Critical Reflection on the Gap-filling Function of General Principles of Law' (2022) 11 Cambridge ILJ 96.

36 Draft conclusion 4(a) of the International Law Commission's work on the topic 'General principles of law', Doc A/CN.4/L.955 (28 July 2021).

37 Draft conclusion 5 of the International Law Commission's work on the topic 'General principles of law', Doc A/CN.4/L.955/Add.1 (29 July 2021).

mind that popular reactions inside the country may be subjected to misinformation and nationwide censorship by the repressive regime. Without a respectable level of popular and international acceptance of the *coup*, judges should see a red flag warning them that the *coup* lacks legitimacy, and that they must exercise their judicial duty to protect fundamental rights and freedoms inside the country even more vigilantly.

Chapter 3 explains legally permissible parameters for judges faced with a repressive regime's demand for them to suppress rights and freedoms in the country as well as the declaration of the state of emergency underpinning the suspension or even complete annulment of rights and freedoms. These measures must be scrutinized under applicable treaties and/or rules of customary international law and, where applicable, by competent international bodies such as regional human rights courts and human rights treaty bodies monitoring the implementation by States Parties to the relevant human rights treaties. The role and (il)legitimacy of military tribunals usually utilized by the usurper to sustain its rule are critically examined. The chapter also explains the proscription of crimes of international concern that has attained the status of peremptory norm (*jus cogens*) under customary international law of universal application. It criticizes as unjustifiable the hands-off stance adopted in some jurisdictions which considers that judicial scrutiny of the usurper's acts raises 'political questions' not justiciable in a court of law.

Chapter 4 analyzes whether judges exercising their duty to sustain the usurper's regime have any valid defence against any potential prosecution in a domestic court of their own country after a regime change, a competent international/ad hoc/hybrid criminal court or a foreign domestic court exercising universal jurisdiction. After extra-constitutional usurpations, judges may be required to take a new oath of allegiance to the new 'constitutional' order and the judges who refuse to do so are removed from office. The question is how taking the new oath impacts judicial responsibility, including the well-established doctrine of the independence of judiciary. The chapter also considers whether the judges can claim they act under superior orders and/or under duress, and whether the doctrine of judicial immunity is applicable to the situation brought about by a *coup*. The judgment of the post–Second World War US Military Tribunal in the *Justice* case[38] is illustrative of how judges could be held criminally liable for their respective judicial roles in a repressive regime.

Chapter 5 looks closely at amnesties and pardons for as well as other restrictions on the prosecution of unconstitutional usurpers of power and their accomplices or collaborators, including immunities for certain office holders and the applicability of a statute of limitations, or a prescriptive period that imposes a maximum time after an event within which criminal prosecution may be initiated. Judges

38 *In re Josef Altstoetter and Others*, Military Tribunal III Case 3, Report of the Trials of War Criminals before the Nuremberg Military Tribunals under Control Council Law No 10, October 1946–April 1949 vol III.

of domestic courts have two roles in this respect. First, they have to determine whether they are required by domestic law and/or applicable rules of international law to uphold or invalidate the amnesties, pardons, immunities and/or statute of limitations. Second, the judges themselves may benefit from such restrictions on the prosecution of acts of the usurper's regime in which they are co-perpetrators or accomplices. The chapter then examines the role of transitional justice after the country's return to democracy. Transitional justice has been cited as the main reason not to prosecute members of repressive regimes of the past so as to prevent their still powerful supporters from revolving against democratic governments now in power and/or so as to achieve national reconciliation post-conflicts. In many countries, full-scale accountability for past wrongs without any compromise is the rule, however. The chapter thus seeks to strike a delicate balance in this matter.

Chapter 6 explores the issue of international and extra-territorial criminal prosecution of the usurper and their accomplices/collaborators, including judges of domestic courts, for acts that are crimes of international concern.

The epilogue provides additional food for thought and constructive recommendations as regards judicial responsibility and accountability in the aftermath of unconstitutional usurpation of power and in light of what has been elucidated in the preceding chapters.

2

LEGAL BASES TO ASSESS THE LAWFULNESS OF UNCONSTITUTIONAL USURPATION OF POWER

After unconstitutional usurpation of power, judges are called upon to enforce decrees, laws, orders, regulations and other acts promulgated by the usurper or its regime. This raises the question concerning the legal validity of the aforesaid. The judges are placed in a logically incoherent situation in which the reality demands them to adjudicate cases before them by exercising supra-constitutional jurisdiction at the time when the constitution from which they derive their jurisdiction is either abrogated or suspended by the usurper.[1] Judgments in various jurisdictions confronting this situation proceed to determine the issue according to numerous doctrines.

The doctrine of necessity is often invoked to legitimize *coups*. Indeed, all *coups* are staged thanks to the reason or excuse that it is necessary for the usurper to seize power to save the country from national calamity, be it political, economic, social or otherwise. Domestic courts in some jurisdiction applies the doctrine of effectiveness or efficacy of the usurpation of power—a *fait accompli* giving rise to a new legal order according to which the validity of the laws and correctness of judicial decisions have to be determined. Closely related to effectiveness/efficacy is the doctrine of sovereignty being vested in the usurper as the de facto ruler of the country and that there must not be a legal vacuum after a *coup*. The meaning of the 'rule of law' is not synonymous with 'rule by law' under an authoritarian regime, though.

1 George Williams, 'The Case That Stopped a Coup? The Rule of Law and Constitutionalism in Fiji' (2001) 1 Oxford U Commonwealth LJ 73 at 73. According to Leslie Wolf-Phillips ('Constitutional Legitimacy: A Study of the Doctrine of Necessity' (1979) 1 Third World Quarterly 97), special constitutional courts might be more suitable than Supreme Courts to adjudicate cases challenging the lawfulness of unconstitutional usurpation of power.

DOI: 10.4324/9781003358428-2

Certain domestic courts also resort to the tests of protection of the welfare of the people, genuine popular acceptance and international acceptance by the international community of nations to determine the legitimacy of a *coup*. International oversight mechanisms in relation to unconstitutional usurpation of power can be multilateral or bilateral, judicial or diplomatic.

This chapter will first analyze the doctrines used to validate *coups* before proceeding to examine those used to invalidate them unless certain stringent conditions are fulfilled.

Legal bases used to validate *coups*

Necessity

A famous invocation of necessity in an exceptionally dire situation is that by Thomas Jefferson, a Founding Father and third President of the United States of America (1801–9). He wrote in 1810:

> The question . . . whether circumstances do not sometimes occur, which make it a duty in officers of high trust, to assume authorities beyond the law, is easy of solution in principle, but sometimes embarrassing in practice. A strict observance of the written laws is doubtless one of the high duties of a good citizen, but it is not the highest. *The laws of necessity, self-preservation and saving the country when in danger are of higher obligation.* To lose our country by a scrupulous adherence to written law, would be to lose the law itself, with life, liberty, property and all those who are enjoying them with us; thus absurdly sacrificing the end to the means. When, in the battle of Germantown, General Washington's army was annoyed from Chew's house, he did not hesitate to plant his cannon against it, although the property of a citizen. When he besieged Yorktown, he leveled the suburbs, feeling that *the laws* of property *must be postponed to the safety of the nation.* While the army was before York, the Governor of Virginia took horses, carriages, provisions and even men by force, to enable that army to stay together till it could master the public enemy; and he was justified. A ship at sea in distress for provisions, meets another having abundance, yet refusing a supply; *the law of self-preservation* authorizes the distressed to take a supply by force. In all these cases, *the unwritten laws of necessity, of self-preservation and of the public safety control the written laws of [mine and yours]. . . .*
>
> In these, the example of overleaping the law is of greater evil than a strict adherence to its imperfect provisions. It is incumbent on those only who accept of great charges, to risk themselves on great occasions, *when the safety of the nation, or some of its very high interests are at stake.* An officer is bound to obey orders; yet he would be a bad one who should do it in cases for which they were not intended, and which involved the

> most important consequences. The line of discrimination between cases may be difficult; but the good officer is bound to draw it at his own peril, and throw himself on the justice of his country and the rectitude of his motives.[2]

Necessity is a defence in Common Law jurisdictions.[3] It was accepted by English courts as early as 1551 in *Reninger v Fagossa*, citing the New Testament (Matthew 12:3–4) example of eating sacred bread through necessity of hunger or taking another's corn to reach the conclusion that 'A man may break the words of the law, and yet not break the law itself . . . where the words of them are broken to avoid greater inconvenience, or through necessity, or by compulsion'.[4] The rule in the 1609 judgment of an English court in *Mouse's Case*[5] that a man may sacrifice the property of another to save his own life, or that of another, may be considered the starting point of most of the earlier decisions in the law of cases of necessity.[6] In 1792 Judge Buller summarized the English judgments on the law of necessity as follows:

> There are many cases in which individuals sustain an injury, for which the law gives no action; for instance, pulling down houses, or raising bulwarks, for the preservation and defence of the Kingdom against the King's enemies. . . . This is one of those cases to which the maxim applies, *salus populi suprema est lex*.[7]

In other words, as one learned author puts it, the defence of overriding necessity flowed directly from the assumptions of *salus populi* (welfare of the people) and sovereign prerogative—if the common welfare and safety of society were the highest law, it followed that when the preservation of that society was at stake lesser rules and conventions gave way.[8]

Another legal scholar succinctly explains there are two different forms of the defence of necessity in situations of emergency or natural disaster. The first is 'justificatory necessity defence' or 'lesser evil defence'—the actor commits no offence

2 Thomas Jefferson's Letter to John Colvin (20 September 1810) as reproduced in Paul Leicester Ford (ed.), *The Writings of Thomas Jefferson* (G.P. Putnam's Sons 1898) vol 9, 279 (emphasis added).

3 P.R. Glazebrook, 'The Necessity Plea in English Criminal Law' (1972) 30 Cambridge LJ 87. See also Lawrence Tiffany and Carl Anderson, 'Legislating the Necessity Defense in Criminal Law' (1975) 52 Denver LJ 839; Mark Stavsky, 'The Doctrine of State Necessity in Pakistan' (1983) 16 Cornell ILJ 341, 347–58, 364–9.

4 [1551] 75 Eng Rep 1, 29–30, quoted in Edward Arnolds and Norman Garland, 'The Defense of Necessity in Criminal Law: The Right to Choose the Lesser Evil' (1974) 65 J Crim L & Criminology 289, 291.

5 77 Eng Rep 1341, 1342 (K.B. 1609).

6 Frederick McKean Jr., 'The Law of Necessity' (1932) 36 Dickinson L Rev 237, 248.

7 *British Cast Plate Manufacturers v Meredith* 100 Eng Rep 1306 (K.B. 1792) 1307–8.

8 William Novak, 'Common Regulation: Legal Origins of State Power in America' (1994) 45 Hastings LJ 1061, 1092.

because the conduct was the right thing to do and the harm caused was proportionate to the benefits intended to be gained. The other is 'excusatory necessity', often called 'duress of circumstances', where although the actor's conduct is recognized as involving the commission of a criminal offence, the law excuses the conduct because no person faced with the peril or threat confronting the actor could have been expected to act differently.[9]

Necessity as applied in the Western World, or the 'Global North', does not uphold the legitimacy or lawfulness of unconstitutional usurpation of power—it merely protects the rights and interests of citizens affected by such usurpation. This is substantiated by US judgments invoking necessity in the context of the American Civil War (12 April 1861–9 May 1865) fought between the federal states of the Union, or 'the North', and the federal states of the Confederacy, or 'the South', that had voted to secede from the Union.

Let's assume for the purpose of our discussion that the rebellious South was the unconstitutional usurper of power. The following are three pertinent examples of the US Supreme Court's judgments in this context.

In *Texas v White*, decided in 1868, the US Supreme Court recognized the 'historical fact' that the Government of Texas, then in full control of the state of Texas, was its only actual, de facto, government in the exercise of the ordinary functions of administration. The Supreme Court held that acts of the de facto government which were *necessary* to peace and good order among citizens, such as acts sanctioning and protecting marriage and the domestic relations, governing the course of descents, regulating the conveyance and transfer of property, real and personal, and providing remedies for injuries to person and estate and other similar acts, which would be valid if emanating from a lawful government, must be regarded in general as valid when proceeding from an actual, though unlawful government. However, acts in furtherance or support of rebellion against the United States, or intended to defeat the just rights of citizens, and other acts of like nature were held to be, in general, invalid and void.[10]

In *Horn v Lockhart*, decided by the US Supreme Court in 1873, the legatees in a will brought a lawsuit to compel an executor to account for moneys received by him from sales of property belonging to the estate of his testator and to pay to them their distributive shares. The executor invested such funds in the bonds of the Confederate government by authority of a law of the state of Alabama in which he was executor, and such investment was approved by the decree of the probate court having settlement of the estate. The Supreme Court held that laws in the Confederate states between the citizens thereof, during the Civil War, *except such as were directly in aid of the rebellion*, ought to stand good because of a '*political necessity* required by the dignity of the Government of the United States, and by every

9 Jeremy Finn, 'Emergency Situations and the Defence of Necessity' (2016) 34 Law Context: A Socio-Legal J 100 at 100, 103–4, 108. See also Jerome Bickenbach, 'The Defence of Necessity' (1983) 13 Canadian J Philosophy 79.

10 74 US (7 Wall.) 700, 733 (1868).

principle of fidelity to the Constitution and laws of our common country'. The Supreme Court did not invalidate the action of the probate court of Alabama in the settlement of the accounts of the executor, except insofar as it approved the investment of funds received by him in Confederate bonds which directly contributed to the resources of the Confederate government. The executor was therefore directed to pay to the legatees their distributive shares in those bonds.[11]

In its 1898 judgment in *Baldy v Hunter*, the US Supreme Court held that transactions between persons actually residing within the territory dominated by the government of the Confederate states were not invalid for the reason only that they occurred under the sanction of the laws of that government or of any local government recognizing its authority. Justice Harlan delivering the opinion of the Supreme Court dealt with the doctrine of necessity as follows. First, in the whole territory controlled by the Confederacy the power of the insurgent government could not be questioned and it made obedience to its authority in civil and local matters not only a *necessity*, but a duty. Without such obedience, civil order was impossible. It was by this government exercising its power throughout an immense territory that the Confederate notes were issued. As a necessary consequence from this actual supremacy of the insurgent government as a belligerent within the territory where it circulated, and from the *necessity* of civil obedience on the part of all who remained in it, this currency had to be considered in courts of law in the same light as if it had been issued by a foreign government temporarily occupying a part of the territory of the United States. Contracts stipulating for payments in this currency could not be regarded for that reason only as made in aid of the foreign invasion in the one case, or of the domestic insurrection in the other. They were transactions in the ordinary course of civil society, and though they might indirectly and remotely promote the ends of the unlawful government, were without blame, except when proved to have been entered into with actual intent to further invasion or insurrection. Such contracts had to be enforced in the courts of the United States, after the restoration of peace, to the extent of their just obligation. Citing *Horn v Lockhart*, Justice Harlan reasoned that the existence of a state of insurrection and war did not loosen the bonds of society, or do away with civil government or the regular administration of the laws. Order was to be preserved, police regulations maintained, crime prosecuted, property protected, contracts enforced, marriages celebrated, estates settled and the transfer and descent of property regulated precisely as in time of peace. No one seriously questioned the validity of judicial or legislative acts in the insurrectionary states touching these and kindred subjects where they were not hostile in their purpose or mode of enforcement to the authority of the national government, and did not impair the rights of citizens under the Constitution. It was only when, in the use of these powers, substantial aid and comfort were given or intended to be given to the rebellion, when the functions necessarily reposed in the state for the maintenance of civil

11 84 US 570, 575–6 (1873) (emphasis added).

society were perverted into the manifest and intentional aid of treason against the government of the Union, that their acts were void.[12]

As a matter of general principle, it may be questioned whether these US judgments on necessity could be emulated in cases concerning *coups d'état* covered by this book. A note of caution concerning any general application of the principle enunciated in these US cases is sounded by the Privy Council in *Madzimbamuto v Lardner Burke*, on appeal from the High Court of Southern Rhodesia, which was then a British colony. The case concerns the (un)lawfulness of South Rhodesian Prime Minister Ian Smith's taking control of the government and promulgation of the unilateral declaration of independence from Great Britain and a new constitution in November 1965. The appellant's husband was kept in detention under emergency regulations promulgated by the Smith regime. The Privy Council concluded, Lord Pearce dissenting, that as the United Kingdom still retained full sovereignty over Southern Rhodesia, acts done by the de facto government of the territory were not to be recognized. The Respondent argued that according to the doctrine of 'necessity', when a usurper was in control of a territory, loyal subjects of the lawful British sovereign who resided in that territory had to recognize, obey and give effect to commands of the usurper insofar as necessary to preserve law and order and the fabric of civilized society. The Privy Council, Lord Pearce dissenting, treated with caution judgments of the US Supreme Court as to the position in the federal states which attempted to secede during the American Civil War. This was because of the very different constitutional position in the United States. The US Supreme Court had held that during the rebellion the seceding federal states continued to exist as federal states of the Union, but that, by reason of their having adhered to the Confederacy, members of their Legislatures and Executives had ceased to have any lawful authority although they had continued to make laws and carry out executive functions and the inhabitants of those states could not avoid carrying on their ordinary activities on the footing that these laws and executive acts were valid. So, after the end of the Civil War a wide variety of questions arose as to the legal effect of transactions arising out of that state of affairs. The majority of the Privy Council distinguished these US judgments from the case at bar. In particular, the US decisions were concerned with the legal effect, as regards the civil claims of individuals, after the end of the American Civil War, of acts done during it. *None of them were cases of courts called upon, during the rebellion, to pass upon the lawfulness of the governments of the rebelling federal states or of their legislation.* In any event, *none* of these US cases conferred any validity upon laws or decrees of the Confederate States which were *contrary to the* US *Constitution.*[13]

How has necessity become a legal justification to uphold the lawfulness of a *coup d'état*, which is a rebellion contrary to the constitution in force, or an unconstitutional usurpation of power?

12 171 US 388 (1898).

13 [1969] 1 AC 645. For a detailed analysis of this case, see Herman Hahlo, 'The Privy Council and the Gentle Revolution' (1970) 16 McGill LJ 92.

Necessity forms the main basis of the judgment of the Supreme Court of Pakistan in *Jilani v Government of the Punjab*.[14] Unable to quell civil unrest and mass uprising in East Pakistan, President Ayub Khan ceded power to the Army's Commander-in-Chief, General Yahya Khan, on 24 March 1969. The latter imposed martial law two days later, abrogated the 1962 Constitution and appointed himself President and Chief Martial Law Administrator.

Asma Jilani came to court to seek the release of her father whereas Zarina Gohar came to court for the release of her husband, both of whom had been detained under Martial Law Regulation No 78 of 1971 issued by General Yahya Khan as Chief Martial Law Administrator.

According to the Supreme Court of Pakistan, where the civil courts are sitting and civil authorities are functioning the establishment of martial law cannot be justified, and its validity is always a judicial question, for courts of law have always claimed and have in fact exercised the right to say whether the *necessity* for the imposition of martial law in this limited Common Law sense exists.[15] On necessity, probably because there was no foreign court decision concerning the situation similar to the *coup* in Pakistan, the Pakistani Supreme Court alluded to the lone dissenting opinion of Lord Pearce in *Madzimbamuto* for guidance. Lord Pearce in that case applied the doctrine of necessity in the reasoning of the US Supreme Court cases related to the American Civil War to the situation in Rhodesia under the Ian Smith regime, to the effect that judges had to give recognition to certain of the acts, orders and legislation of the illegal regime, otherwise chaos would certainly result. In Lord Pearce's view, there were questions to be asked. First, did the ordinary orderly running of the country reasonably require it? Second, did the declaration of emergency and the order impair the citizen's rights under the Constitution? In one sense, any recognition of an unlawful order adverse to a citizen impaired his rights under the Constitution, since he would be better off if the unlawful order were not recognized. But this was not the true sense. If it had been, the doctrine of *necessity* or implied mandate would have never applied when anyone's interest was adversely affected. The true question was whether the act, if done by the lawful authorities, would conflict with his rights under the Constitution. Third, was this declaration of emergency intended directly to help or did it directly help the usurpation or did it run counter to the policy of the lawful government? The problem had to be approached with common sense and with a reasonable margin of tolerance. Judges could not carry on without acknowledging some formalities and acts that had an illegal origin. The difficulty lied in deciding the scope of the intended margin of tolerance and whether in fact it covered a particular case.[16]

The Supreme Court of Pakistan then held in *Jilani* that acts done by those actually in control without lawful authority might be recognized as valid or acted upon by the courts within certain limitations, on '*principles* [sic] *of necessity*'. According to

14 [1972] PLD SC 139.
15 Ibid 187.
16 [1969] 1 AC 645, 737, 739–41.

the Pakistani Supreme Court, such principle has also been adopted in the United States in various cases which came up after the suppression of the rebellion of the Southern federal states and US courts too adopted the policy that where the acts done by the usurper were 'necessary to peace and good order among citizens and had affected property or contractual rights they should not be invalidated', not because they were legal but because they would cause inconvenience to innocent persons and lead to further difficulties. Recourse has to be taken to the doctrine of necessity where ignoring it would result in disastrous consequences to the body politic and upset the social order itself but *this doctrine can be invoked in aid only after a court of law has come to the conclusion that the acts of the usurper were illegal and illegitimate.* It is only then that the question arises as to how many of his acts, legislative or otherwise, should be condoned or maintained, notwithstanding their illegality, in the wider public interest.[17]

Applying this test, the Supreme Court in *Jilani* condones all transactions which are past and closed, for no useful purpose can be served by re-opening them; all acts and legislative measures which are in accordance with, or could have been made under, the abrogated Constitution or the previous legal order; all acts which tend to advance or promote the good of the people; all acts required to be done for the ordinary orderly running of the State; and all such measures as would establish, or lead to the establishment of, the objectives mentioned in the fundamental constitutional principles approved by the Constitutional Assembly in 1954. But the Supreme Court would *not* condone any act intended to entrench the usurper more firmly in his power or to directly help him to run the country contrary to the usurper's legitimate objectives, or anything which seriously impairs the rights of the citizens except insofar as they may be designed to advance the *social welfare* and national solidarity.[18]

In conclusion, the Supreme Court struck down the impugned Martial Law Regulation since the assumption of power by General Yahya Khan was wholly unconstitutional and could not be recognized as valid. When the General was in effective control of governmental power, only those of his legislative and administrative acts could be recognized by the courts which might be found to be absolutely necessary on the doctrine of necessity within the limitations of the doctrine to be adjudged by the courts.

Of importance is the commendable and brave pronouncement by the Supreme Court in *Jilani* that the *coup* was illegal and illegitimate, but as a matter of pragmatism the Court hesitantly had to ensure that life in the society carry on as usual as possible after the *coup*, provided that certain strict conditions were fulfilled.[19] The Court's willingness to condone acts designed to advance the social welfare and national solidarity seems to mirror the assumption of *solus populi*, or welfare of the people, recognized in other jurisdictions as forming part and parcel of the doctrine of necessity. At the time of the Supreme Court's judgment in 1972 General Yahya

17 [1972] PLD SC 139, 204–6, 229–30, 243.

18 Ibid 207. Also discussed in Stavsky, 'The Doctrine of State Necessity in Pakistan' 372–5.

19 See also Po Jen Yab, *Courts and Democracies in Asia* (CUP 2017) 135–56.

Khan was no longer in power, however, having resigned on 20 December 1971, a few days after Pakistan's military defeat in the war over East Pakistan which has since become a new sovereign State named the People's Republic of Bangladesh.

Pakistan's Supreme Court also resorted to the doctrine of necessity five years later in *Bhutto v Chief of Army Staff*,[20] a case concerning martial law imposed by General Zia ul Haq, Chief of Army Staff, who staged the *coup* in July 1977. Zulfiqar Ali Bhutto and the ten other leaders of the Pakistan People's Party were arrested on 17 September 1977 under Martial Law Order No 12 of 1977 and detained in various prisons. Ali Bhutto's wife challenged their detention in the Supreme Court of Pakistan by filing a Constitutional Petition. The Supreme Court dismissed the plaintiff's challenge to the validity of the Chief of Army Staff's promulgation of martial law as well as the detention of Ali Bhutto and the other political party leaders. The Supreme Court held that the legal consequences of an abrupt political change, by imposition of martial law, had to be *judged by consideration of the total milieu preceding the change*; namely, the 'objective' political situation prevailing at the time, its historical imperatives, compulsions, motivations of persons bringing the change and the extent of preservation of suppression of the old legal order. The 1973 Constitution of Pakistan still remained the supreme law of the land, subject to the condition that certain parts thereof had been suspended. The Chief of Army Staff assuming power by means of an extra-constitutional step was held to be a matter of *State necessity* and a step taken *for the welfare of the people*. Therefore, he was entitled to perform all acts and promulgate all legislative measures. In view of the events during and after the 7 March 1977 general elections and the allegations of poll rigging, the broken state of law and order and the shattered economy the usurper took over government administration *for a short duration* to arrange for fresh elections within the shortest possible time. The new arrangements dictated by consideration of *State necessity and welfare of the people* had acquired its effectiveness owing to its moral content and promise of restoration of democratic institutions, and was therefore justified on the basis of doctrine of necessity.[21]

The Supreme Court in *Bhutto* did not rule that the *coup* was illegal, probably because, unlike the usurper in *Jilani*, the usurper in *Bhutto* was still in power. It proceeded instead to determine whether the usurpation was necessary. This was a departure from the cases discussed earlier, although the *Bhutto* judgment added to the conditions enunciated in *Jilani* the reasonable timeline requirement for the usurper to return the country to democracy after the total milieu preceding the necessity for the *coup*, as an extra-constitutional step avowedly taken for the welfare of the people, was neutralized. Any positive aspect of the application of the doctrine of necessity in *Bhutto* has to be balanced against the sad fact that martial law continued until March 1985 when the 1973 Constitution was eventually restored, and that General Zia ul Haq ruled Pakistan with ruthlessness until his death in a plane crash in August 1988.

20 [1977] PLD SC 657.

21 See also Stavsky, 'The Doctrine of State Necessity in Pakistan' 376–94.

The Pakistani military staged another *coup* in October 1999. In *Zafar Ali Shah* v *General Pervez Musharraf*,[22] decided in May 2000, the Supreme Court of Pakistan went one step further by explicitly upholding the legitimacy of the military regime installed by General Pervez Musharraf after the *coup* that was still in power at the time of the judgment, invoking, inter alia, the doctrine of *necessity*. Nevertheless, it added the requirement of *implied consent of the populace* for the junta to fulfil. As will be seen in Chapters 3 and 4, the Supreme Court retained its judicial power to review laws and decrees enacted by the military regime on the ground that on no principle of necessity could powers of the judicial review vested in Pakistan's Superior Courts under the 1973 Constitution of Pakistan be taken away, and, therefore, any provision purporting to restrain the power of judicial review of the Superior Courts was to be ignored altogether.

The Supreme Court in *Zafar Ali Shah*, after an extensive analysis, concluded that the doctrine of State necessity was recognized not only in Islam and other religions of the world but also accepted by the eminent international jurists including Hugo Grotius and some Superior Courts from foreign jurisdictions to fill a political vacuum and bridge the gap. However, the 1973 Constitution of Pakistan still remained the supreme law of the land subject to the condition that certain parts thereof had been held in abeyance on account of State necessity. The usurper was empowered to amend the 1973 Constitution, provided that no amendment was to be made in the salient features of the Constitution; namely, the independence of judiciary, federalism and the parliamentary form of government blended with Islamic provisions. The Supreme Court reached this conclusion after finding the machinery of the government at the centre and the provinces had completely broken down, been corrupted and become privy to the one-man rule by the then Prime Minister;[23] the 1973 Constitution had been rendered unworkable; and a situation had arisen for which the Constitution provided no solution and the Armed Forces had to intervene to save the State from further chaos, to maintain peace and order, economic stability, justice and good governance, and to safeguard integrity and sovereignty of the country dictated by highest considerations of State necessity and *salus populi est suprema lex* (the welfare of the people is the supreme law). The Supreme Court held that all the elements (namely, inevitable necessity, exceptional circumstances, no other applicable remedy, and the measures taken being proportionate to the necessity and of temporary character limited to the duration of exceptional circumstances) were present, inasmuch as the Constitution provided no solution to meet the extraordinary situation prevailing on 12 October 1999 when the Armed Forces took over the affairs of Pakistan.

22 [2000] PLD SC 869.

23 According to the Supreme Court, all institutions of the State including the Judiciary were being systematically destroyed in the pursuit of self-serving policies. Furthermore, attempts were made to politicize the army, destabilize it and create dissension within its ranks, and had the toppled Prime Minister been successful in his designs, there would have been chaos and anarchy—a situation of civil war where some factions of the Armed Forces would be fighting against others.

The Supreme Court in *Zafar Ali Shah* concluded that although initially the status of the junta-installed government was de facto, the validation by the Supreme Court through its order accorded to the government the status of a de jure government.[24] Nonetheless, stressed the Supreme Court, it was for the representatives of the people to see to it that everything was in line with the fundamental principles of the Constitution and the law had the support of the Superior Courts. Superior Courts were firmly committed to the governance of the country by the people's representatives and the definition of the term 'democracy' to the effect that 'it [was] government of the people, by the people and for the people' and not by the Army rule for an indefinite period. Here there was *an implied consent of the governed* (i.e., the people of Pakistan in general including politicians/parliamentarians and so on) to the Army takeover, in that *no protests worth the name or agitations* had been launched against the Army takeover and/or its continuance. The Supreme Court could take *judicial notice* of the fact that the people of Pakistan had generally welcomed the Army takeover due to their avowed intention to initiate the process of across-the-board and transparent accountability against those alleged of corruption in every walk of life, of abuse of national wealth and of not taking appropriate measures to stabilize the economy and democratic institutions. However, prolonged involvement of the Army in civil affairs ran a grave risk of politicizing it, which would not be in national interest and civilian rule in Pakistan had to be restored within the shortest possible time after achieving the declared objectives as reflected in General Musharraf's speeches on 13 and 17 October 1999 in which he explained what had necessitated the military takeover on 12 October 1999. The Supreme Court observed that although the Court was not in favour of an Army rule in preference to a democratic rule, there were evils of such grave magnitude that the civilian government could not continue to run the affairs of the country in the face of complete breakdown. The remedy to the said evils was the holding of fair and impartial elections by the Chief Election Commissioner at the earliest possible time, but the same could not be achieved till the electoral rolls were updated. Ordinarily, the Court would have allowed minimum time for holding of fresh elections as contemplated under the Constitution, but the Attorney-General submitted that, according to a report of the Chief Election Commissioner, updating of the electoral rolls could not be done before two years and thereafter objections, an electoral district designation process and so forth were to be attended to. In the absence of proper and authentic electoral rolls, millions of people would be disenfranchised. Since this submission by the Attorney-General was not rebutted, there was no choice but to grant reasonable time to enable General Musharraf, as Chief Executive of Pakistan under martial law, to restore the democratic institutions to the rightful holders of the office of public

24 Cf. the argument that, in one sense, the doctrine of necessity gives de facto but not de jure recognition of the regime that comes into power unconstitutionally (Nang Mo Kham Hom, '"Revolutionary Legality": The Coup d'Etat of 1962 and the Burmese Military Regime' (2000) 4 Southern Cross U Law Rev 60, 62)).

representatives under the Constitution. The Supreme Court, after having regard to all the relevant factors involved, allowed a three-year period to the Chief Executive of Pakistan with effect from the date of the Army takeover for achieving his declared objectives. The Chief Executive of Pakistan was to appoint a date, not later than 90 days before the expiry of three years, for holding a general election to the National Assembly, Provincial Assemblies and Senate of Pakistan.

All these three judgments of the Supreme Court of Pakistan were consistent in ruling that the Constitution of Pakistan in force at the time of the *coups* continued to apply and remained the supreme law of the land, subject to the condition that certain parts thereof had been suspended. The Supreme Court has, in effect, subjected the doctrine of necessity to scrutiny in three dimensions. It first examines the *raison d'être* for the *coup*. Second, irrespective of whether the *coup* is staged out of the dire necessity of circumstances, such necessity is limited in duration and the return to democracy shall take place in the shortest reasonable time. Third, necessity for the *coup* is also limited in space, or the room for the unconstitutional usurper to manoeuvre. On no principle of necessity could powers of the judicial review vested in Pakistan's Superior Courts under the Constitution be taken away, and the Superior Courts did not condone acts which would seriously impair the rights and freedom of the citizens except insofar as they might be designed to advance the social welfare and national solidarity.

For its part, the Court of Appeal of Grenada in *Mitchell and Others v Director of Public Prosecutions and Another* imposed a high threshold in ascertaining the legitimacy of a *coup*. The case concerns the homicide of the late Grenadian Prime Minister Maurice Bishop of the People's Revolutionary Government which was heard and determined by the former Court of Appeal and the former Supreme Court set up by law promulgated in March 1979 by the Revolutionary Government after the *coup* by Bishop to oust the then Government of Grenada. The Court of Appeal in *Mitchell* held that laws enacted by the People's Revolutionary Government which was a de facto sovereign, even though unlawful, were valid under the principle of necessity or implied mandate. Several of the conditions imposed by the Grenadian Court of Appeal resonate well with those imposed by the Pakistani Supreme Court in the various cases discussed earlier. The Grenadian Court of Appeal held the doctrine of necessity could be applied in the following circumstances to justify an intervention by the President in a crisis. First, an imperative necessity must arise because of the existence of exceptional circumstances not provided for in the Constitution, for immediate action to be taken to protect or preserve some vital function of the State. Second, there must be no other course of action reasonably available. Third, any such action must be reasonably necessary in the interest of preserving peaceful order. Fourth, it must not impair the just rights of the citizens under the Constitution. Fifth, it must not be one the sole effect and intention of which is to consolidate or strengthen the revolution as such.[25] Moreover, the

25 [1986] Law Reports of the Commonwealth 35, 88.

general population's conformity and obedience with the new regime must be due to *genuine popular acceptance and support* and not mere tacit submission to coercion or fear of force exerted by the usurper; and it must not appear that the regime installed by the usurper is oppressive and undemocratic.[26]

Any use of the doctrine of necessity to validate a *coup d'état* or other revolutionary alteration of the government is criticized as inappropriate and incorrect for at least four reasons. First, the assumption that the court can influence the military regime by using the doctrine in this manner is not realistic.[27] Second the court's action validating the junta-installed regime gives it the appearance of legitimacy sanctioned by a supposedly impartial judiciary.[28] Third, although courts may insist on the junta returning the country back to democracy within a shortest possible reasonable time, the *coup* leader usually finds ways and means to stay in power long after such 'reasonable time', as in the case of General Zia ul Haq who retained power after the *coup* in 1977 until his death in 1988 and that of General Musharraf who became President from 20 June 2001 up to 18 August 2008, when he was forced into self-imposed exile abroad. Fourth, what is necessity cannot be objectively determined for all nations and peoples. Perceptions of how citizens trade off civil liberties during major crises varies from one country to another and, even within the same country, from one group to another, as attested by one study analyzing how citizens around the world trade off health security and civil liberties throughout one of the most challenging crises in recent history, the COVID-19 pandemic. The result of two large-scale online surveys, from March 2020 to January 2021, of more than 550,000 people in 15 countries—Australia, Canada, China, France, Germany, India, Italy, Japan, the Netherlands, Singapore, Spain, South Korea, Sweden, United Kingdom and United States—paints a complicated picture. Willingness to sacrifice rights and freedom during crises is shaped by different exposure to the health risks, diverse socio-economic background and distinct perceptions of the potential long-term erosion of civil liberties.[29] Therefore, courts validating the usurper's legitimacy on the principle of necessity are frequently accused by those opposed to the *coup* of condoning the *coup* that cannot be genuinely justified by the exigencies of the situation.[30]

26 Ibid 72. The Fijian Court of Appeal in *Prasad* considered the criterion against the oppressive and undemocratic nature of the regime as going too far, however (*Republic of Fiji v Prasad* [2001] New Zealand Administrative Reports 385 (CA Fiji) at 414).

27 Stavsky, 'The Doctrine of State Necessity in Pakistan' 393–4.

28 Ibid.

29 Marcella Alsan, Luca Braghieri, Sarah Eichmeyer, Minjeong Joyce Kim, Stefanie Stantcheva and David Yang, *Civil Liberties in Times of Crisis*, National Bureau of Economic Research Working Paper 27972 (July 2021).

30 The Supreme Court of Pakistan in *Bhutto*, after conceding it was in no position to determine 'the factual correctness or otherwise of the several allegations and counter-allegations made by the parties against each other', relied on 'the broad trends and circumstances' leading to the *coup* to reach its conclusion in that case ([1977] PLD SC 657, 693).

Effectiveness/efficacy

According to a school of thought, one of the primary considerations in assessing the lawfulness of a regime unconstitutionally installed is the efficacy of the change brought by that new regime.

As early as in 1953, the Thai Supreme Court held that the military junta which had *effectively* succeeded in unconstitutional usurpation of power of government in November 1947 had the power to change, annul and enact law 'according to a revolutionary system' in order to run the country, otherwise there would be no peace in the nation. The (Interim) Constitution promulgated by the junta in 1947 was, therefore, held to be valid *ab initio* and the second defendant had legally been appointed Finance Minister thereunder with the necessary ministerial authority to dismiss the plaintiff, a senior Finance Ministry official, on the ground of the latter's serious dereliction of duty that had caused grave damage to the government.[31] The usual brevity of Thai courts' judgments, directly addressing the legal question to be settled, is relatively unhelpful compared to the more elaborated reasoning found in the judgments of most of their foreign counterparts.

The 1953 precedent relying on the doctrine of effectiveness has been followed in subsequent cases decided by Thai courts.

Prosecutor v Sombat Boon-ngamanong decided by the Thai Supreme Court in 2017 concerns the 22 May 2014 military *coup* in Thailand. Prior to 20 May 2014 in Bangkok and its surrounding provinces as well as in many parts of Thailand, there were several political protests and alleged *agents provocateurs* with the intention to stir up widespread unrest with the use of war weapons against unarmed citizens and important government buildings, causing several deaths and injuries as well as property damage. The events seemed to have escalated to the extent there would be riots and unrest in many locations. The Army Commander-in-Chief declared a nationwide state of emergency as of 20 May 2014. Thereafter, on 22 May 2014, the National Council for Peace and Order (NCPO) took over the government, declaring the termination of the Constitution of 2007 except for Chapter II (the King). Subsequently, the NCPO issued announcements ordering named individuals including the defendant to report in person to the NCPO at specified locations by specified time, failing which they would be subject to imprisonment of up to two years or a fine of not exceeding 40,000 Baht (approximately US$1,250) or both. The defendant failed to report to the NCPO in person without giving any explanation. The case went all the way to the Supreme Court. The defendant argued that at the time when the NCPO issued the relevant announcements ordering the defendant to report to the NCPO in person the NCPO had not yet succeeded in acquiring the power to govern the country. Also, continued the defendant, since he was exercising his rights under Section 69 of the 2007 Constitution[32] to resist the *coup* he could not be found guilty as charged.

31 *Daokrajai Lilamian v Ministry of Finance and Others*, Thai Supreme Court Case No 45/2496 (1953).

32 Section 69: A person shall have the right to resist peacefully an act committed for the acquisition of the power to rule the country by a means which is not in accordance with the modes stipulated in this Constitution.

In its judgment, the Supreme Court referred to Sections 68 and 70 of the 2007 Constitution. Section 68 stipulates in its pertinent part that no person shall exercise the rights and liberties prescribed in the Constitution to overthrow the democratic regime of government with the King as Head of State or to acquire the power to rule the country by any means not in accordance with the modes stipulated in this Constitution. Where a person or a political party commits the said proscribed act, the person knowing of such act shall have the right to request the Prosecutor General to investigate its facts and submit a motion to the Constitutional Court to order the cessation of such act without, however, prejudice to the institution of a criminal action against such person. By virtue of Section 70, every Thai person shall have a duty to uphold the nation, religions, Monarchy and democratic regime of government with the King as Head of State. The Thai Supreme Court held that Sections 69 and 70 of the 2007 Constitution could be enforceable only when the acquisition of power to rule the country was not yet successful. In the present case, *the acquisition of power to rule the country had already been accomplished* because the NCPO had declared a state of emergency throughout the Kingdom and announced the termination of the 2007 Constitution except for Chapter II (The King) thereof. Moreover, the NCPO had issued many announcements and orders to exercise power to govern the country as a result of which the defendant's rights under the said provisions of the 2007 Constitution were thereby extinguished as of the date of the NCPO's annulment of the 2007 Constitution.[33]

Effectiveness was once an accepted doctrine in Pakistan. In 1958 Pakistan's President Iskander Mirza imposed martial law and appointed General Ayub Khan, Commander-in-Chief of Pakistan's Army, as Chief Martial Law Administrator. All of the government apparatuses including Legislatures, central and provincial, were dissolved. Mirza was toppled by a *coup* staged by Ayub Khan 13 days later. In *State v Dosso*, Pakistan's Chief Justice Mohammad Munir stated that if the attempt to usurp the Constitution failed, those who sponsored or organized it were judged by the existing Constitution as guilty of the crime of treason, but if the usurpation was successful this in itself became a law-creating fact since thereafter its own lawfulness was no longer judged by the annulled Constitution. The latter constituted 'the *efficacy* of change' giving rise to a new legal order according to which the validity of the laws and the correctness of judicial decisions had to be determined.[34] The Court referred to the writings of Austrian-Hungarian born legal theorist Hans Kelsen. As one learned commentator succinctly summarizes Kelsen's work in this respect, Kelsen portrays the legal order of a nation as a pyramid of norms derived through successive levels of derivation from the norm-creating powers conferred by the constitution, which, in turn, derives its validity from any earlier constitutional arrangements pursuant to which it was adopted, and ultimately from a *Grundnorm* or 'basic norm' embodying the axiomatic assumption that the legal order is to be obeyed. According to Kelsen, a legal system is based upon the presupposition or basic norm

33 *Prosecutor v Sombat Boon-ngamanong*, Thai Supreme Court Case No 3578/2560 (2017).
34 (1958) PLD SC 533. Also discussed in Stavsky, 'The Doctrine of State Necessity in Pakistan' 370–2.

that one ought to behave according to the actually established and *effective* constitution, and where there has been a revolution or other event that has overthrown the existing constitution and put another in its place, this presupposition may allow the new constitution to become recognized as lawful.[35] Ironically, the military regime in Pakistan collapsed the very day after the *Dosso* judgment was rendered.

Dosso was overruled by the Supreme Court of Pakistan in *Jilani* in 1972, on the ground that the principle laid down in *Dosso* was wholly unsustainable and could not be treated as good law either on the principle of *stare decisis* or otherwise. Kelsen's theory alluded to in *Dosso* was considered not a universally accepted theory nor was it a theory which could claim to have become a basic doctrine of the science of modern jurisprudence, nor did Kelsen ever attempt to formulate any theory which 'favours totalitarianism'.[36] Instead, as already explained earlier, the Supreme Court in *Jilani* applied the doctrine of necessity. In *Bhutto*, the Supreme Court found Kelsen's theory to be irrelevant to a situation where the breach of legal continuity of the Constitution was purely temporary in nature and for a specified limited purpose.

Yet, the doctrine of efficacy/effectiveness has been applied in several other jurisdictions.

The reasoning in *Dosso* was followed by the Ugandan High Court sitting as Constitutional Court in *Uganda v Commissioner of Prison, ex parte Matovu*[37] and by the Nigerian Supreme Court in *Attorney-General of the Federation v Guardian Newspaper Limited*.[38]

In the Nigerian case just mentioned, the Nigerian Supreme Court upheld the validity of a Decree signed by the Commander-in-Chief of the Armed Forces who was then Nigeria's Head of State after the military *coup* of 17 November 1993. Previously, in *Lakanmi v Attorney-General, Western State*,[39] the Nigerian Supreme Court had invalidated the Constitution (Suspension and Modification) Decree No 1 of 1966 promulgated by the junta after the *coup* on 29 July 1966 that suspended Nigeria's Constitution and ousted the jurisdiction of courts to review this and other decrees issued by the junta. The Court in *Lakanmi* added that the powers of the military government to make laws were not absolute, and that the *coup* was not a revolution; hence, it did not overthrow the pre-existing legal order. The military regime responded by issuing the Federal Military Government (Supremacy and Enforcement of Powers) Decree No 28 of 1970 to affirm its right to unfettered and unlimited legislative competence and that the 1966 military *coup* was a revolution

35 Williams, 'The Case That Stops a Coup?'. See also Mahmud, 'Jurisprudence of Successful Treason' 106–16; Alexandre Travessoni Gomes Trivisonno, 'On the Continuity of the Doctrine of the Basic Norm in Kelsen's Pure Theory of Law' (2021) 12 Jurisprudence 321.

36 [1972] PLD SC 139, 183. See also Adam Holden, 'Succeeding at Succeeding: Revolutions, Courts and the Limits of Legality' (2014) 20 Auckland U L Rev 195, 209–16, 219–22.

37 [1966] East African L Rep 514, 539.

38 [1999] 9 Nigeria Weekly L Rep 187.

39 (1971) 1 U Ife Law Rep 201.

which *effectively* abrogated the whole pre-existing legal order except as preserved by Decree No 1 of 1966. In *Adejumo v Johnson*, decided in 1972, the Supreme Court acknowledged the military takeover of 1966 as a revolution.[40] Thereafter, the Nigerian Supreme Court held that military decrees constituted the basic norm in Nigeria from which the validity of all other laws, including the Constitution, had to be sourced.[41]

Ex parte Matovu concerns the unilateral suspension on 22 February 1966 by the then Ugandan Prime Minister Milton Obote of Uganda's Independence Constitution of 1962, which had established a federal system of government. On 15 April 1966 Uganda's National Assembly passed a resolution to abolish the 1962 Constitution and replace it with a new Constitution vesting all executive authority in Obote, who became President of Uganda. In the unanimous judgment of the Ugandan High Court in this case, Chief Justice Udo Udoma enunciated the following criteria whereby a new order could be recognized as replacing an old order: there must be an abrupt political change (i.e., a *coup d'état* or a revolution) not within the contemplation of an existing constitution, the change must destroy the entire legal order except what is preserved, and the new constitution and government must be *effective*.[42] In particular, the Court found the impugned 1966 Constitution to be valid for a number of reasons including the political reality in which the 1966 Constitution had been *accepted by the people of Uganda and the international community* (in the sense that recognition had been accorded to the new Ugandan Government by all foreign countries with which Uganda dealt) and had been firmly established and implemented throughout Uganda without opposition.[43] This judgment of the Ugandan Court in 1966 was the first among decisions of domestic courts around the world that accords importance to the dual test of popular acceptance by the people of the country that has experienced the *coup* together with the approval by the international community.

The 1988 decision of the High Court of Lesotho in *Mokotso and Others v King Motshoeshoe II and Others* deals with the question: To what extent, and on what basis, may courts recognize the legitimacy of a government which has come to power by the *coups* in 1970 and 1986? Chief Justice Cullinan opines that a court may hold a revolutionary government to be lawful and its acts to have been legitimated *ab initio* where it is satisfied that (a) the government is firmly established, there being no other government in opposition thereto; and (b) the government's

40 (1972) 1 All Nigerian Law Rep 159.

41 *See, e.g., Military Governor, Ondo State v Adewumi* (1988) 3 Nigeria Weekly L Rep (Pt 82) 280; *Labiyi v Anretiola* (1992) 8 Nigeria Weekly L Rep (Pt 258) 139; and *Attorney-General of the Federation v Sade* (1993) 6 Nigeria Weekly L Rep (Pt 302) 692, discussed in Ambrose Ekpu, 'Judicial Response to Coup D'etat: A Reply to Tayyab Mahmud (From a Nigerian Perspective)' (1996) 13 Arizona J Int'l & Comp L 1, 19–21.

42 [1966] East African Law Rep 514, 543.

43 Ibid 539.

administration is *effective*, in that the majority of the people are behaving, by and large, in conformity therewith.[44]

A possible overlap between the doctrine of necessity and that of effectiveness/efficacy was considered by the Fijian Court of Appeal in 2001.

In May 2000, in a quest to disenfranchise Fiji's ethnic Indian minority a group of hard-line ethnic Fijian nationalists held Indo-Fijian Prime Minister Mahendra Chaudhry and several Cabinet members hostage. The Commander of the Royal Fiji Military Force, Commodore Josaia Voreqe (Frank) Bainimarama, staged a counter-*coup* against the rebels by declaring martial law and abrogating the 1997 Constitution,[45] with Commodore Bainimarama assuming executive authority over Fiji. On 4 July 2000, an interim civilian government was set up by Bainimarama, with Laisenia Qarase as Prime Minister. Also on 4 July 2000, Chandrika Prasad brought a legal action in the High Court of Fiji against the Republic of Fiji Islands and the Attorney-General of the Interim Civilian Government. Prasad, a farmer who had been forced from his home as well as suffered property damage in the aftermath of the *coup*, said he brought the case to inform the international community of the human rights violations occurring in Fiji and because he believed an affirmation of the rule of law and the 1997 Constitution might enable him to live peacefully in his own home and be treated with respect. Prasad did not seek damages for his physical suffering, but instead a declaration that the 1997 Constitution abrogated by the junta still remained in force and that the elected government of Fiji had not been lawfully dismissed.[46] The High Court's judgment on 15 November 2000 found for Prasad and affirmed that Prasad possessed the standing to bring the matter. The High Court made several orders, including that the revocation of the 1997 Constitution was *not* made within the Common Law doctrine of *necessity* as raised by the defendants. It reasoned that *necessity* permits emergency action to be taken validly in times of extreme crisis, such action being in normal circumstances illegal, provided that such action taken must be transient and a proportionate response to the crisis in order to uphold the rule of law and the existing Constitution. Necessity cannot be resorted to so as to justify or support the abrogation of the existing legal order. Therefore, the doctrine of necessity could come to aid Commodore Bainimarama in resolving the hostage crisis, allowing him to impose curfews, maintaining roadblocks and ensuring law and order on the streets. Once the hostage crisis was resolved on 14 July 2000 and all other law and order matters contained if not entirely eradicated, the Constitution, previously temporarily abrogated or suspended, would re-emerge as the supreme law demanding

44 [1989] Law Reports of the Commonwealth 24, 133. Lesotho's Court of Appeal in *Makenete v Lekhanya* [1993] Law Reports of the Commonwealth 13, esp at 65 endorsed the validity of the revolutionary regime in *Mokotso*. See also Taslim Olawale Elias, *Africa and the Development of International Law* (Martinus Nijhoff 1988) ch 6 (The Legality of Illegal Regimes in Africa).

45 Constitution Amendment Act 1997 (Fiji Islands).

46 See the detailed analysis of this case in George Williams, 'Republic of Fiji v Prasad: Introduction' (2001) 2 Melbourne JIL 144. Professor Williams represented Prasad in this case.

his support and that of the military to uphold it and to buttress it against any other usurpers. The doctrine of necessity could not be used to give sustenance to a new extra-constitutional regime.[47]

On appeal by the Interim Civilian Government, on 1 March 2001 the Fijian Court of Appeal unanimously dismissed the appeal,[48] holding, inter alia, that the 1997 Constitution remained the supreme law of the Republic of the Fiji Islands and had not been abrogated, and that Parliament had not been dissolved but was prorogued on 27 May 2000 for six months. The Court of Appeal agreed with the High Court that the doctrine of *necessity* authorizes *temporary* extra-constitutional actions but does not permit permanent changes to a written Constitution, let alone its complete abrogation. With regard to the lawfulness or otherwise of the Interim Civilian Government, the Court of Appeal developed *a test for the efficacy or effectiveness* of a revolution as a new legal order, based on whether a new regime is in fact established based on the *factual criteria of the absence of a rival government and acceptance by the people in the sense of popular support by (or the acquiescence of) the people for the new regime*. On the evidence before it, this test was not satisfied by the Interim Civilian Government for two reasons. First, there was a rival (or opposition) government striving for power ready and willing to assume office under the 1997 Constitution. Second, the Fijian people had made their opposition clear in many forms, signifying that passive compliance was hardly a persuasive indication of true acquiescence in a government which had been in power for only about seven months and severely restricted public protest. The Court of Appeal expressed concern that Kelsen's 'principle of effectiveness' might too readily reward a usurping regime. Therefore, the Court required a new regime to prove its rule was based on 'popular acceptance and support' as distinct from 'tacit submission to coercion or fear of force', and the holding of elections would be 'powerful evidence of efficacy'. Nonetheless, it rejected the plaintiff's submission to require the new regime to acknowledge basic human rights as evidenced by international obligations assumed by Fiji. In the Court's view, such criterion was not necessary since the 1997 Fijian Constitution already contains many of the rights and freedoms mandated by international instruments. Importantly, the Court considered the unfavourable reaction of the 'international community' as a reason for concluding that the Fijian military had failed to execute a successful revolution.[49] Put another way, the doctrine of necessity is used to assess the legitimacy of *temporary* extra-constitutional actions, whereas the continuation of the regime set up extra-constitutionally is subjected to the test of efficacy/effectiveness.

47 *Prasad v Republic of Fiji* [2001] New Zealand Administrative Reports 21, 48.

48 *Republic of Fiji v Prasad* [2001] 2 Law Report of the Commonwealth 743.

49 See further Michael Head, 'The Doctrines of Necessity and Revolution—A Critical Review of *Republic of Fiji Islands and Attorney General v Prasad*' (2001) 8 Australian ILJ 259, 268–9; id, 'A Victory for Democracy?: An Alternative Assessment of Republic of Fiji v. Prasad' (2001) 2 Melbourne JIL 535, 547–9; John Hatchard and Tunde Ogowewo, *Tackling the Unconstitutional Overthrow of Democracies: Emerging Trends in the Commonwealth* (Commonwealth Secretariat 2003) 50–164.

What is amazing about the Fijian Court of Appeal's judgment in *Prasad* is that the Court dared to declare the usurper's regime which was still in power to be unlawful. Immediately after this judgment, the Prime Minister of the Interim Civilian Government announced Fiji would be returned to democratic rule under the 1997 Constitution and his Government then resigned, followed by a general election under the 1997 Constitution held from 25 August to 5 September 2001.

Sovereignty

Some courts proceed to give legitimacy to unconstitutional usurpation of power on the ground that sovereign authority is vested in the usurper as the de facto ruler of the country during the usurpation of power of government.

This is the well-established jurisprudence of the Thai Supreme Court, as early as in 1962.[50] It was held that, in 1958, after the junta succeeded in taking over the government, the head of the junta thus had the *sovereign authority* to govern the country. Any words ordered by the junta leader for citizens to obey had to be deemed to have the force of law although His Majesty the King did not promulgate it with advice and consent of the Legislature. In a subsequent case decided in 1980, the plaintiff contended that once a post-*coup* constitution was promulgated, announcements or orders by the junta or the reform council set up by the junta immediately ceased to be enforceable since they trampled upon the *sovereignty* belonging to the Thai population. The Supreme Court held in this latter case that when the junta which had staged a *coup* or a body set up to reform national governance had succeeded in usurping government power, the leader of the junta or the body set up by the junta had the power to issue announcements or orders enforceable against the general population. Even though a new constitution had been promulgated but when it did not annul such announcements or orders, they continued to have the force of law.[51]

In Prosecutor v Sombat Boon-ngamanong, the Thai Supreme Court equates effectiveness/efficacy with sovereignty when it reasons that when the acquisition of power to rule the country is successful, the junta becomes a *sovereign* with the authority to issue announcements and orders with the force of law and any rights the defendant in that case may have under the 2007 Constitution which has been annulled by the *coup* of May 2014 are thereby extinguished.[52]

The Thai Supreme Court's recognition of the usurper as the entity vested with sovereign authority is somewhat at variance with that of the Supreme Court of Pakistan in *Zafar Ali Shah*, whereby the latter Court deems the welfare of the people to be the supreme law (*salus populi est suprema lex*) for the Court to uphold and the Court must subject the usurper to judicial scrutiny, as explained earlier. As will be explained in more detail in Chapter 4, the Pakistani Supreme Court in that

50 Thai Supreme Court Case No 1662/2505 (1962).
51 Thai Supreme Court Case No 1234/2523 (1980).
52 Thai Supreme Court Case No 3578/2560 (2017).

case stresses that the Objectives Resolution contained in the Preamble to the Constitution of Pakistan, which now forms a substantive part thereof, recognizes the 'Islamic doctrine of sovereignty' as expounded in the Holy Book (Qur'an) according to which sovereignty belongs neither to the ruler nor the ruled but Almighty Allah alone which is to be exercised by the people of Pakistan through their chosen representatives. It is a fundamental principle of jurisprudence that courts in Pakistan must always endeavour to expand their jurisdiction to safeguard the rights of the people against arbitrary violations by the Executive.

The High Court Division of the Supreme Court of Bangladesh in *Bangladesh Italian Marble Works Ltd v Bangladesh*[53] also approaches the concept of sovereignty differently from the Thai Supreme Court's aforesaid judgments. According to the Bangladeshi Court, it does not mean that for the sake of continuity of the sovereignty of the State, the Constitution has to be soiled with illegalities; rather, the perpetrators of such illegalities via unconstitutional usurpation of power should be suitably punished and condemned so that in future no adventurist, no usurper, would have the audacity to defy the people, their Constitution, their Government, established by them with their consent. What is illegal and wrong must always be condemned as illegal and wrong till eternity. In the context of the August 1975 *coup* and its consequences, the illegality and gravest wrong were committed against the People's Republic of Bangladesh and its people as a whole. But, the Bangladeshi Court in exceptional circumstances, in order to avert the resultant evil of illegal legislations, may condone such illegality on the greater interest of the community in general but on condition that those acts could have been legally done at least by the proper authority.[54] This condition is thus the same as the one imposed by the US Supreme Court, Pakistani Supreme Court and courts in several other jurisdictions as discussed earlier.

The Bolivian Supreme Court has treated sovereignty differently from the treatment given to it by its Thai counterpart. In its judgment of 21 April 1993, the Bolivian Supreme Court convicted and imposed heavy sentences on General Luis García Meza Tejada and his collaborators, who staged the *coup* in Bolivia on 17 July 1980. This judgment[55] marked the first time in Latin American legal history that members of a de facto military government including a former de facto

53 (2006) BLT (Special) (HCD) 1.

54 Po Jen Yab, *Courts and Democracies in Asia* 157–78. In May 2011, the Appellate Division of the Supreme Court of Bangladesh, in its brief decision, upheld the decision of the High Court in *Siddique Ahmed v Bangladesh* ((2011) 33 Bangladesh Legal Decisions 84) declaring all proclamations, Martial Law Regulations and Martial Law Orders made/promulgated during the period between 24 March 1982, the day of the *coup* by General Hussain Mohammed Ershad, and the date of commencement of the Constitution (Seventh Amendment) Act 1986 'illegal and void'. However, the Appellate Division provisionally condoned all acts, things, deeds and transactions and proceedings during the military rule of Ershad between 24 March 1982 and 10 November 1986, the day before the enactment of the Act 1986, as remaining effective until their fate would be decided by Parliament. It also condoned forever the international treaties concluded by Bangladesh during that period.

55 www.derechos.org/nizkor/bolivia/doc/meza.html.

President were held to account for usurping power and violating constitutional norms. The Court proceeds, inter alia, on the basis that sovereignty is inalienable, not subject to limitation, imprescriptible and indivisible according to the Constitution. By organizing unconstitutional armed groups to overthrow the government, the defendants undermined the rights of the Bolivian people for illicit purposes. In accordance with the provisions of the Constitution, sovereignty resides in the people and its exercise is delegated to the legislative, executive and judicial branches whose functions cannot be brought together in the same body. Consequently, every de facto government installed by the junta is, in principle, unconstitutional and its 'legal provisions' (that is, decrees and orders made by it) completely illegal. Therefore, those who violate the legal order in force at the time by usurping public power or violating the fundamental rights and guarantees of people are criminally responsible and must be held accountable therefor. The Bolivian Supreme Court held that the Bolivian Armed Forces is entrusted with constitutional obligation to defend and preserve national independence, security and stability of the Republic as well as honour and national sovereignty; protect the rules of the Constitution; and discharge the inexcusable and imperative duty to guarantee the stability of the legally constituted government, and obeying superior orders is not a legitimate defence to free the authors and/or co-authors of impugned acts from these responsibilities.[56]

In a similar vein, the Greek court trying several defendants accused of the bloody suppression of student demonstrators at the Athens Polytechnic in November 1973 dismissed the motion from Colonel Georgios Papadopoulos, head of the Greek junta who had come to power by a military *coup*, asserting Presidential immunity because he was President of Greece during the time of the event. The court ruled that the *coup* on 21 April 1967 by a group of military officers usurped the authority and the 'sovereign rights of the people', thereby making the consequent governments installed by the junta 'governments of violence' and anyone who exercised duties of governmental authority under any office, including that of the Head of State, did not in reality exercise legal authority and consequently they had no immunity for their actions during the exercise of such authority.[57]

In a judgment in 2009, the Supreme Court of Uruguay held, inter alia, that the current regulation of human rights is not based on the position of sovereign States,

56 Cf. also Judgment No 11/2562 of 18 August 2019 in which the Thai Constitutional Court held that the Commander-in-Chief of the Army who staged the May 2014 *coup* was not barred from becoming Prime Minister while also keeping onto his position of Army Chief. In reaching this conclusion, the Court merely focused on his position as the head of the National Council for Peace and Order set up by the junta, who exercised 'the supreme sovereign authority' after accomplishing the acquisition of power to rule the country, 'without being subject to any government command or oversight'. Therefore, held the Court, he was not an 'employee' or 'official' of the government or a State enterprise whom the Constitution prohibits from holding a political office while still in that position.

57 www.primidi.com/greek_junta_trials/the_polytechnic/trial_of_the_polytechnic.

but in the individual person as holder, given his or her status as such, of essential rights that cannot be ignored.[58]

On the whole, the doctrine of sovereignty is not invoked outside Thailand to validate unconstitutional usurpation of power.

Rule of law

The rule of law is not to be confused with the need to maintain 'law and order', or the need to 'rule by law', frequently invoked by the usurper as justification for it to take measures to maintain and strengthen its grip on power.

The third preambular paragraph of the 1948 Universal Declaration of Human Rights[59] cogently declares: 'it is essential, if man is not to be compelled to have recourse, as a last resort, to rebellion against tyranny and oppression, that human rights should be protected by the rule of law'. This principle is also enshrined in the 1950 European Convention for the Protection of Human Rights and Fundamental Freedoms, or the European Convention on Human Rights,[60] as interpreted by the European Court of Human Rights[61] and is extensively referred to in the 1992 Treaty of the European Union,[62] including in Article 21(1), which delimits the European Union's action in the international sphere. Although the 1966 International Covenant on Civil and Political Rights (ICCPR)[63] does not expressly refer to the rule of law as such, the Human Rights Committee entrusted with monitoring compliance with the ICCPR has held that the safeguards in relation to the derogation under Article 4 of the ICCPR allowing measures in response to a public emergency are 'based on the principle of legality and the rule of law inherent in the [ICCPR] as a whole'.[64]

With respect to the principle of legality, it is a rule of customary international law binding on all States according to which no one may be accused or convicted of a criminal offence on account of any act or omission which did not constitute a criminal offence under national or international law at the time it was committed, nor may a heavier penalty be imposed than that which was applicable at the time the criminal offence was committed.[65] Its close connection to the rule of law is

58 *Nibia Sabalsagaray*, Sentencia No 365/2009, Judgment of 19 October 2009, quoted by the Inter-American Court of Human Rights in *Gomes Lund et al. ('Guerrilha Do Araguaia') v Brazil*, Judgment of 24 October 2010, Ser C no 219 para 167.

59 UNGA res 217A (III), UNGA OR, 3rd Sess, Supp No 13, UN Doc A/810 (1948) 71.

60 213 UNTS 221, in force 3 September 1953.

61 See, e.g., *Engel and Others v The Netherlands*, App nos 5100/71, 5101/71, 5354/72 and 5370/72 (ECtHR, 8 June 1976) para 69.

62 OJ C 326/43, in force 1 November 1993.

63 999 UNTS 171, in force 23 March 1976.

64 General Comment No 29, States of Emergency (Art 4), Human Rights Committee, CPR/C/21/Rev.1/Add.11, 31 August 2001.

65 International Committee of the Red Cross, Rule 101, *ICRC International Humanitarian Law Database on Customary International Law*. See also Jason Varuhus, 'The Principle of Legality' (2020) 79

also affirmed, for instance, by the Bolivian Supreme Court in *Meza*, a case arising from a military *coup*. The Court held that, in applying the principle of legality that governs legally organized societies, the Constitution and laws oblige everyone to protect the rule of law, as well as to respect the rights and guarantees enshrined in our legal system and the universal declaration of the rights of man.[66]

What is the exact meaning of 'rule of law'? In one of its research reports, the European Commission for Democracy through Law (Venice Commission) finds that although the British concept 'Rule of Law', the German concept '*Rechtsstaat*' and the French concept '*État de droit*' have different origins, their underlying standards are the same. The necessary elements are: (a) legality (in the sense of supremacy of the law), including a transparent, accountable and democratic process for enacting law; (b) legal certainty; (c) prohibition of arbitrariness; (d) access to justice before independent and impartial courts, including judicial review of administrative acts; (e) respect for human rights; and (f) non-discrimination and equality before the law.[67] This is similar to the idea of rule of law famously posited by A. V. Dicey that it signifies predominance of regular laws as opposite to arbitrariness, equality before the law and institutional protection of rights.[68]

The annual Rule of Law Index prepared by the World Justice Project measures the rule of law based on the experiences and perceptions of the general public and in-country legal practitioners and experts worldwide. The index uses multifarious factors in ranking the state of the rule of law in each country. They essentially include the following that are pertinent to our discussion here.

First, government powers must be effectively limited by the Legislature, with legislative bodies having the ability in practice to exercise effective checks on and oversight of the government. Government powers must be effectively limited by the Judiciary which has the independence and the ability in practice to exercise effective checks on the government. Government powers must be effectively limited by independent comptrollers or auditors, as well as national human rights ombudsman agencies, which have sufficient independence and the ability to

---

Cambridge LJ 587; Talita Dias, *Beyond Imperfect Justice: Legality and Fair Labelling in International Criminal Law* (Brill 2022) 35–84.

66 On the interrelationship between the principle of legality and the rule of law as well as due process, see Theodore Meron, *Standing Up for Justice: The Challenges of Trying Atrocity Crimes* (OUP 2021) 69–102.

67 European Commission for Democracy through Law (Venice Commission), 'Report on the Rule of Law' (4 April 2011) 512/2009, CDL-AD(2011)003rev, para 41.

68 A.V. Dicey, *Introduction to the Study of the Law of the Constitution* (10th edn, Macmillan 1959) 201–3. For formal and substantive conceptions of the rule of law, see Jack Beatson, *Key Ideas in Law: The Rule of Law and the Separation of Powers* (Hart 2021) 17–22. Another study identifies non-arbitrariness, consistency and predictability as the core and minimum requirements of the international rule of law deriving from the practice of States at the international level (Noora Arajärvi, 'The Core Requirements of the International Rule of Law in the Practice of States' (2021) 13 Hague J Rule of Law 173). Cf. Stephen Humphreys, *Theatre of the Rule of Law: Transnational Legal Intervention in Theory and Practice* (CUP 2010); Matthieu Burnay, *Chinese Perspectives on the International Rule of Law: Law and Politics in the One-Party State* (Edward Elgar Publishing 2018) 11–44, 64–131.

exercise effective checks on and oversight of the government. Government officials must be sanctioned for misconduct, whether they are members of the Executive, Legislature, Judiciary or the police. Government powers must be subject to checks by an independent media, civil society organizations, political parties and individuals who are free to report and comment on government policies without fear of retaliation. Transition of power must be subject to the law in the sense that government officials are elected or appointed in accordance with the rules and procedures set forth in the constitution. Where elections take place, the index also measures the integrity of the electoral process, including access to the ballot, the absence of intimidation and public scrutiny of election results. The index measures the effectiveness of civic participation mechanisms, including the protection of the freedoms of opinion and expression, assembly and association, and the right to petition the government. It also measures whether people can voice concerns to various government officers and whether government officials provide sufficient information and notice about decisions affecting the community.

Second, the right to life and security of the person must be effectively guaranteed. The index thus measures whether the police inflict physical harm upon criminal suspects during arrest and interrogation, and whether political dissidents or members of the media are subjected to unreasonable searches, arrest, detention, imprisonment, threats, abusive treatment or violence.

Third, in the context of due process of law and rights of the accused, the index measures whether the basic rights of criminal suspects are respected, including the presumption of innocence and the freedom from arbitrary arrest and unreasonable pre-trial detention. It also measures whether criminal suspects are able to access and challenge evidence used against them, whether they are subject to abusive treatment, and whether they are provided with adequate legal assistance. In addition, it measures whether the basic rights of prisoners are respected once they have been convicted of a crime.

Fourth, in relation to freedom of opinion and expression, the index measures whether an independent media, civil society organizations, political parties and individuals are free to report and comment on government policies without fear of retaliation.

Fifth, the index measures the freedom from arbitrary interference with privacy by assessing whether the police or other government officials conduct physical searches without warrants or intercept electronic communications of private individuals without judicial authorization.

Sixth, the guarantee of the freedom of assembly and association is assessed by examining whether people can freely attend community meetings, join political organizations, hold peaceful public demonstrations, sign petitions and express opinions against government policies and actions without fear of retaliation.[69]

69 World Justice Project, *Rule of Law Index 2020*, https://worldjusticeproject.org/sites/default/files/documents/WJP-ROLI-2020-Online_0.pdf. See also Paul Gowder, *The Rule of Law in the Real World* (CUP 2016).

In light of the aforementioned, domestic judges must understand that the rule of law is not synonymous with 'rule by law' or maintaining 'law and order' to support the continued governing of the country by the unconstitutional usurper of power.[70]

Legal vacuum

In *Re Manitoba Language Rights*, the Canadian Supreme Court evoked *necessity* to temporarily suspend a constitutional requirement for all laws to be enacted, printed and published in English and French so that all Manitoban laws which were mostly enacted in English only could be re-enacted, reprinted and republished bilingually by the Manitoba Legislature. This suspension on the basis of necessity avoided exposing Manitoba to a *legal vacuum* during this process.[71]

Judges post-*coups* may try to avoid a legal vacuum after the annulment or suspension of the constitution by the junta. This may be a rationale behind the decision of Mali's Constitutional Court on 28 May 2021 which appointed the colonel who had, four days earlier, ousted the transitional government set up after the August 2020 *coup* to lead Mali back to democracy, with the colonel being given the official title of 'President of the transition, Head of State' due to the 'vacancy in the Presidency'.[72]

In 2018, the Thai Supreme Court in *Punsak Sritape and 14 Others v General Prayuth Chan-o-cha and four others* invokes the need to uphold the junta's announcements and orders essentially because there must not be a *legal vacuum* after the Constitution is annulled and the three branches of government are suspended. Otherwise, reasons the Court, there would be no *sovereign* and the Kingdom of Thailand would lack a qualification to be a nation State. In the Court's opinion, a State must possess a defined territory, a population residing within the territory, a government and its own sovereignty. Importantly, interpretation of law must be in such a way as to make the law enforceable and for the benefit of purpose of the existence of statehood or nationhood.[73]

The need to avoid a legal vacuum is thus linked to the doctrines of necessity and sovereignty/Statehood. The doctrine of necessity has already been discussed at length in this chapter. With respect to its reasoning in *Punsak Sritape and 14 Others*, the Thai Supreme Court apparently relies on the following definition of statehood as defined in Article 1 of the 1933 Montevideo Convention on the Rights and Duties of States:[74] 'A State as a person of international law should possess the following

70 See also Anthony Pereira, *Political (In)justice: Authoritarianism and the Rule of Law in Brazil, Chile, and Argentina* (U Pittsburgh Press 2005); Tom Ginsburg, 'Democratic Backsliding and the Rule of Law' (2018) 44 Ohio Northern U L Rev 351, 358–63.

71 [1985] 1 Supreme Court Rep 721 paras 86–95.

72 'Mali Court Appoints Assimi Goita as Interim President' *Al Jazeera* (29 May 2021), https://www.aljazeera.com/news/2021/5/29/malis-court-appoints-assimi-goita-as-interim-president.

73 Thai Supreme Court Case No 1688/2561 (27 March 2018).

74 165 League of Nations Treaty Series 19, in force 26 December 1934.

qualifications: (a) a permanent population; (b) a defined territory; (c) government and (d) capacity to enter into relations with the other States'. The Convention has been ratified by 15 States in the Americas. As a matter of international law, there seems to be no settled definition of what constitutes a nation State, however.[75] For its part, the International Law Association's Committee on Recognition and Non-Recognition in International Law agrees that although the Montevideo Convention's criteria continue to provide the basic framework for assessing statehood controversies, where competing regimes have sought recognition as a State's Government, the various approaches taken have not reflected firmly established criteria for assessing governmental legitimacy.[76] The Thai Supreme Court's reasoning may seem to echo the writing in 1945 by the famous legal theorist Hans Kelsen who treats a State as the personification of a single, total and unified national legal order.[77] Such treatment of a State is only one of the many theories proffered by jurists of multifarious schools of law[78] and it essentially ignores the constitutional concept of the State as a complex social group comprising institutions, people and territory united together by rules, with the primary purpose of promoting citizens' well-being.[79]

What sets the aforesaid case law of the Thai Supreme Court apart from that of its counterparts in other jurisdictions is the fact that the Thai Court never examines the *raison d'être* for the *coups*; it merely accepts the *fait accompli* post-*coups*. As of this writing, there have been 12 military *coups* and one civilian self-*coup* in Thailand since 1932 and they were staged in different contexts and under different reasons or excuses.

The *coup* on 24 June 1932 overthrew Thailand's absolute monarchy and transformed the country into a constitutional monarchy. This can be considered a 'revolution', and not merely unconstitutional usurpation of government. The civilian Prime Minister who staged a self-*coup* on 1 April 1933 to seize power from the junta that had overthrown the absolute monarchy was toppled in a military *coup* by that junta 81 days later.

The *coups* in June 1933, November 1947, November 1951, September 1957, October 1958 and November 1971 were staged for the purpose of purging those opposed to the juntas. They were 'internal' *coups* among the military elites vying for power over the country.

The *coup* on 6 October 1976 was staged following a massacre of a large number of university students demonstrating in Bangkok against the return from exile abroad

75 See, e.g., the analysis in Derek Wong, 'Sovereignty Sunk? The Position of "Sinking States" at International Law' (2013) 14 Melbourne JIL 1, 7–46.

76 Paras 1 and 6 of Resolution 3/2018 of the Committee on Recognition and Non-Recognition in International Law, 78th Conference of the International Law Association, Sydney, Australia, 19–24 August 2018.

77 Hans Kelsen, *General Theory of Law & State* (Routledge 2005) 181–2 and see his treatment of sovereignty at 383–5. The work was originally published by Harvard University Press in 1945.

78 See Alexander Orakhelashvili, *International Law and International Politics: Foundations of Interdisciplinary Analysis* (Edward Elgar Publishing 2020) 1–38.

79 As elaborated in N.W. Barber, *The Constitutional State* (OUP 2010) ch 2 ff.

of a former Thai Prime Minister ousted by the popular uprising against his Government that had left 77 deaths and 857 persons injured on 14 October 1973. The main reason for the *coup* was apparently to prevent a Vietnamese-backed communist plot to turn Thailand into a Communist State in the wake of the Communist takeover in Vietnam, Laos and Cambodia.[80] This *coup* reflected the suppression of leftists elsewhere during the then ongoing Cold War, especially under Operation Condor implemented by right-wing dictatorships in the Southern Cone of South America.

The October 1977 *coup* was staged on the grounds that the Government had divided the country and had virtually no public support, the economic situation had worsened and people generally disagreed with the toppled Government's long-term suspension of democracy.

The 24 February 1991 military *coup* cited five justifications: widespread corruption by the Government, politicians' abuse of power to persecute career public officials, the Government's abuse of its absolute control of Parliament, the Government's attempt to destroy the military and the Government's distortion of criminal proceedings against those accused of overthrowing the monarchy.

In the new millennium, two overwhelmingly elected governments were deposed by two *coups* after a series of interconnected events. Thaksin Shinawatra, a telecommunications businessman, became Thailand's Prime Minister in 2001 and was re-elected by an overwhelming majority of voters in 2005 thanks to his populist agenda and empowerment of the rural mass as well as the subsidized universal health care initiated by his Government. He was accused by his opponents of abusing his political party's absolute majority, or 'parliamentary dictatorship', in the House of Representatives for his own personal gains. Growing public opposition against Thaksin led to political crises culminating in the *coup* on 19 September 2006 while he was on an official trip to the United Nations in New York.[81] Since August 2008, Thaksin has been living in self-imposed exile abroad after facing a plethora of criminal charges against him as well as being sentenced *in absentia* by the Thai Supreme Court's Criminal Division for Holders of Political Offices to a combination of several years of imprisonment for abusing his power as Prime Minister and/or abuse of power through acts constituting a conflict between personal and public interests. Yingluck Shinawatra, Thaksin's younger sister, became Thailand's Prime Minister in August 2011. In November 2013, her political party which was in control of the House of Representatives passed an amnesty bill to grant amnesty to any person charged with offences committed during the political turmoil following the September 2006 *coup*. The bill's critics opposed it for fear that the amnesty would allow Thaksin's return to Thailand a free man. Less than two weeks later, the Senate voted 141–0 to reject the bill. By then demonstrations against the bill

80 Marian Mallet, 'Causes and Consequences of the October '76 Coup' (1978) 8 J Contemporary Asia 80, 91.

81 See also Ukrist Pathmanand, 'A Different *Coup d'état*?' (2008) 38 J Contemporary Asia 124; Michael Connors, 'Liberalism against the People: Learning to Live with Coups d'état' (2019) 24 J Political Ideologies 11.

had spread across the country leading to one political crisis after another, culminating in the 22 May 2014 *coup*. As chairperson of Thailand's National Rice Policy Committee, Yingluck was investigated by Thailand's anti-corruption agency about her role in the rice-pledging scheme.[82] Two of her former Cabinet Ministers were also investigated and later sentenced to decades in prison. Yingluck's trial started on 15 January 2016 but she did not appear in court on 25 August 2017 when the Court was scheduled to render its verdict. It transpired that she had skipped bail and left Thailand to live in exile abroad. On 27 September 2017 the Thai Supreme Court's Criminal Division for Holders of Political Offices sentenced her *in absentia* to five years' imprisonment for dereliction of duty by failing to stop fake and corruption-plagued government-to-government sales of rice under her Government's rice-pledging scheme. The two Shinawatra brother and sister have been claiming innocence, insisting their prosecutions are all politically motivated. Hard-line supporters of the media savvy Thaksin are convinced their hero and his sister are victims of vindictive prosecutions devised to deliver injustice as punishment for their political parties' landslide parliamentary election victories against the old establishment in Thailand.[83] Critics of Thaksin and Yingluck Shinawatra vehemently disagree with the views of the pro-Shinawatra camp, however.

By omitting to scrutinize the reasons for the *coups*, the judges of the Thai Supreme Court in these cases may have avoided exercising their subjective value judgment to determine whether the *coups* are good or bad and risk being seen as passing political judgments, all the more so after a new government is set up following a general election that gives the leadership of the *coups* an apparently democratic mandate to continue to govern the country. Nevertheless, unlike several of their counterparts in, say, Pakistan, they have omitted to subject the unconstitutional usurpation of power to limitations in 'duration' and 'space' as they should have.

Legal bases used to invalidate *coups*

Several judgments discussed previously impose conditions before an impugned act resulting from a *coup* can be upheld in courts of law. Some of these conditions are so crucial that they may negate the lawfulness of the *coup* itself.

Welfare of the people

It may be recalled that the maxim '*salus populi suprema est lex*' was referred to as early as in 1792.

82 The Yingluck Shinawatra Government implemented the rice-pledging scheme immediately after winning the 2011 election to give Thai rice farmers the opportunity to pledge and then provide an unlimited supply of their rice to the Government at a higher price for their rice than they would obtain by selling it at market rates set by rice traders and middlemen. The Government then released the rice supplied by the farmers onto the market or sold it to foreign governments.

83 See also Po Jen Yab, *Courts and Democracies in Asia* 125–34.

As already explained, the Pakistani Supreme Court in *Jilani, Bhutto* and *Zafar Ali Shah* accord importance to the welfare of the people after a *coup*. In *Zafar Ali Shah*, it even specifically deems the welfare of the people to be the supreme law (*salus populi est suprema lex*) for courts to uphold. Clearly, fundamental rights and freedoms of the people must be protected even during the *coup* and the regime installed by it. As the Court of Appeal of Grenada in *Mitchell* has put it, the *coup* must not impair the just rights of the citizens under the Constitution.

Popular acceptance

The 'popular acceptance' test was alluded to in the Ugandan case of *Matovu* and even more clearly in *Liasi v Attorney-General*,[84] decided in 1975, where the Cypriot Supreme Court considered whether the regime installed by the *coup* of 15 July 1974 had legal validity. During the eight days that the usurpers held office, a number of public officials were removed from their jobs and others appointed in their place. Some police constables whose service was terminated by an officer appointed by the usurpers challenged their dismissal in this case. According to the Cypriot Supreme Court, the first, substantial, test of legitimacy of the usurper's regime is 'popular acceptance', even if a tacit one, of the change and the legal values thereby invoked, whereas the second, the formal test, is the legalization of the *coup d'état* Government through the recognition of its actions by the next lawful Government. Popular acceptance requires submission to the new regime followed by active acceptance or a persistently long and conscious silence under the appropriate conditions. The Court held that the *coup* failed to meet the substantial test of legitimacy since the violence accompanying the *coup* caused many persons to be killed and injured, a curfew was imposed and maintained and there was strong resistance to the *coup* among State agencies and the general public. As for the formal test, the next lawful Government had reinstated many public officials dismissed by the usurpers and the Legislature had enacted a new law which expressly provided that the *coup* and the Government installed by it had no legal basis whatsoever.

The legitimacy of acts deriving from the *coup d'état* of 5 June 1977 in Seychelles was the issue before the Court of Appeal of Seychelles in *Valabhaji v Controller of Taxes*.[85] The Court reasons that central to nearly all thinking on this subject is the belief that *sovereignty* ultimately depends on *consent or acceptance by the people*, manifested by obedience to the precepts of those claiming authority. Most of the disputes have turned on whether that acceptance had been established or at what point it had been established, but once firmly established there appears to have been little dispute as to its consequences. In order to ascertain such consent or acceptance, what is required is that once the new regime is *firmly or irrevocably in*

84 (1975) 3 CLR 558 (Cyprus). Discussed in Tayyab Mahmud, 'Jurisprudence of Successful Treason: Coup d'Etat & Common Law' (1994) 27 Cornell ILJ 49, 76–8.

85 (1981) 7 Commonwealth Law Bulletin 1249. Discussed in Mahmud, 'Jurisprudence of Successful Treason' 82–4.

control it becomes a lawful or legitimate government and entitled to the authority that goes with that status and this legitimation is extended retroactively to cover legislation enacted by the regime from the inception of its control.

Valabhaji seems to endorse the notion of 'might makes right' where there is no genuine consent or acceptance by the people. It is not followed by the 1986 judgment of the Court of Appeal of Grenada in *Mitchell* which stresses the general population's conformity and obedience with the new regime must be due to genuine popular acceptance and support and not mere tacit submission to coercion or fear of force exerted by the usurper, and it must not appear that the regime installed by the usurper was oppressive and undemocratic. *Mitchell* goes one step further than *Liasi* where the Cypriot Court is willing to recognize *tacit* popular acceptance of the usurper's regime.

Mitchell was extensively cited by the 1988 decision of the High Court of Lesotho in *Mokotso*. The latter Court departs somewhat from the reasoning in *Mitchell* by acknowledging that although judges should not be blind to the unpopularity of a new regime that comes to power by unconstitutional means, or to any factors affecting issues of morality or justice, these are not necessarily vital considerations as regards the question in *Mokotso*. In the opinion of the Lesothian Court, it may be that the unpopularity of a new regime or any factors affecting issues of morality or justice are relevant to a judge's own personal decision to accept the change, that is, to resign or to decide to 'join the revolution'. However, if the judge is satisfied that *the new regime is firmly established and there is no opposition thereto*, and that the people are acting by and large in conformity with the new legal order, signifying their acceptance thereof *for whatever reason*, the judge cannot hold that regime to be other than legitimate.[86] This is because the judge's function in this matter goes no further than to give effect to *the will of the people, however motivated*—be it based on weakness or even fear—which creates a new legal order and the judge must recognize this fact and give effect thereto.[87]

If the usurper follows *Valabhaji* or *Mokotso* he would use all means, including repressive ones, to ensure the people accept his regime however reluctant or unwilling they are. This is precisely the worst part of unconstitutional usurpation of power and the seed of evil of dictatorship. Therefore, neither *Valabhaji* nor *Mokotso* should be followed. These two judgments are in any event odd ones out among all the judgments discussed in this chapter. For example, Fiji's case law after *Mokotso* has not followed such extreme reasoning. The Fijian Court of Appeal in *Prasad* denied the legitimacy of the *coup* in question because the Interim Civilian Government set up by the *coup* could not prove it had the acquiescence generally of the people of Fiji, as witnessed by suppression of public demonstrations of dissent, several affidavits expressing disapproval of the Government and the declared readiness of the ousted Government to resume office.[88] In the same vein, according to

86 (1990) 90 Int'l L Rep 427, 518.

87 Ibid 519. See also Brad Roth, *Governmental Illegitimacy in International Law* (OUP 1999) 137–42.

88 Cf. *Matanzima v President of the Republic of Transkei* [1989] 4 South African L Rep 989, 999, where the High Court of Transkei, a territory granted independence from South Africa in 1976 which

the Pakistani Supreme Court in *Zafar Ali Shah*, in order to satisfy the test of popular acceptance it must be conclusively proven that no protests worth the name or agitations have been launched against the *coup* and/or its continuance.

Numerous acts of unconstitutional usurpation of power of the present days just do not pass this test of popular acceptance.

This is true in the case of all the military *coups* in Burma, which changed its name to Myanmar in 1989. Reasons cited in support for the necessity of these military takeovers have been domestically and internationally discredited. The 2 March 1962 military *coup* staged by General Ne Win to depose the then Burmese Government was resisted by a large portion of the Burmese population, as evidenced by the widespread popular uprising in 1988, among others, culminating in Ne Win's resignation from the post of Chairman of the Burmese Socialist Programme Party, which was the de facto ruler of Burma, on 23 July 1988. The *coup* by the Burmese military in August 1988 installed the State Law and Order Restoration Council under the chairmanship of the Chief of Staff of the Armed Forces, Senior General Saw Maung, intent on quelling the ongoing unrest and retaining the military rule. In deciding to award the Nobel Peace Prize for the year 1991 to Aung San Suu Kyi, the Norwegian Nobel Committee cogently rebutted any presumption that the junta had ever passed the popular acceptance test. Suu Kyi was lauded for her non-violent struggle for democracy and human rights in Myanmar after becoming the leader of a democratic opposition which employed non-violent means to resist 'a regime characterized by brutality'. She also emphasized the need for conciliation between the sharply divided regions and ethnic groups in her country. Although the election held in May 1990 resulted in a conclusive victory for the opposition, the military regime ignored the election results. Suu Kyi refused to leave the country and was kept under strict house arrest. Suu Kyi's struggle was praised as being one of the most extraordinary examples of civil courage in Asia in recent decades. She had become 'an important symbol in the struggle against oppression'.[89]

As for the Myanmar military regime installed after the *coup* on 1 February 2021, it has met with sustained internal armed resistance as well as widespread civil disobedience[90] and the junta has been using lethal force against those opposed to it. In March 2021, those opposed to the *coup* set up a National Unity Government (NUG) aiming at weakening the governance mechanisms of the military

---

suffered a military *coup* in September 1987, held that isolated strikes in some professions were not sufficient to infer a lack of public acceptance of the usurper's regime, and that, on the contrary, there was no sign of civil disobedience among public servants or members of the public of the new government installed by the *coup*. This case is discussed in Mahmud, 'Jurisprudence of Successful Treason' 93–6.

89 Norwegian Nobel Committee, Press Release (14 October 1991). See also Nang Mo Kham Hom, 'Revolutionary Legality' 70–7, 97–106.

90 For example, the streets in towns and cities across Myanmar were deserted on the Human Rights Day on 10 December 2021, as the public held a 'silent strike' to protest against the military government with businesses closed between 10 am and 4 pm.

government, supporting the civil disobedience movement and making arrangements for national defence. Armed groups who call themselves 'People's Defence Forces' have sprung up across the country to fight the military government and have drawn the troops into a bloody stalemate of clashes and reprisals. According to the report dated 15 March 2022 by the UN High Commissioner for Human Rights, Myanmar's military and security forces have committed crimes against humanity in their flagrant disregard for human life, mass killings, bombarding populated areas with airstrikes and heavy weapons and deliberately targeting civilians, many of whom have been shot in the head, burned to death, arbitrarily arrested, subjected to sexual violence including rape, tortured or used as human shields. The report cites the unbroken determination of Myanmar's people in their opposition to the *coup*. More than 1,600 people have been killed by security forces and their affiliates, more than 12,500 people detained, more than 440,000 others displaced and 14 million in need of urgent humanitarian assistance, the delivery of which has largely been blocked by the military in new and pre-existing areas of need.[91] The violence committed by the military regime after this *coup* was much worse than the dark decades of previous military regimes in Burma/Myanmar when most atrocities happened behind closed doors, and not in plain view as in the case of the latest *coup*. Finding any trace of credible popular acceptance of the military regime was out of the question insofar as the military regularly shut down the Internet, routinely blocked social media platforms and censored online information, all in the name of securing national stability.

International acceptance

It may be recalled that the Fijian Court of Appeal in *Prasad* considered the unfavourable reaction of the 'international community' as a reason for concluding the Fijian military had failed to execute a successful revolution. Comparing Fiji in 2001 with Lesotho in 1986, the Court found the latter *coup* had international approval whereas rather the opposite applied to Fiji. Although there are conflicting views concerning the international approval of the 1986 *coup* in Lesotho,[92] the principle

91 Report of the UN High Commissioner for Human Rights, 'Situation of human rights in Myanmar since 1 February 2021', A/HRC/49/72 (15 March 2022). While most of the gross human rights violations documented were carried out by security forces, the report finds that no fewer than 543 individuals—including local administrators, their families and alleged informants—were also reportedly killed due to their perceived support of the military, and that anti-*coup* armed elements claimed responsibility for 95 of the incidents.

92 See Ned Temko, 'Coup in Lesotho Delights Citizens—and Neighboring South Africa' *Christian Science Monitor* (21 January 1986), https://www.csmonitor.com/1986/0121/oles.html; John D'Oliveira, 'Lesotho: 20 Years of Iron-fisted Rule Comes to an End' (1986) 16 Africa Focus 6; M.L. Pherudi and S.L. Barnard, 'Lesotho Coups d'État: Political Decay and Erosion of Democracy' (2001) 26 Southern J Contemporary History 69. For a criticism of the factual 'international approval' of the *coup* at issue in *Prasad* itself, see Head, 'A Victory for Democracy?' 263–4, 269, where Head also expresses some concern that a logical conclusion of this test would mean that courts should quite openly endorse regimes that seize power with diplomatic and economic support in the West.

of approval by the international community of the *coup* alluded to by the Ugandan Court in *Matovu* and further enunciated in *Prasad* is sound and substantiated in international practice.

One issue after a military *coup* concerns the unwillingness of other States to have international intercourse with the junta-installed government.[93] With the fall of the Soviet Union and the resultant end of the Cold War, the United States and other Western powers have apparently recommitted themselves to upholding democracy instead of turning a blind eye to human rights abuses and atrocities in dictatorship regimes that were their allies against the onslaught of Communism.[94] One empirical study finds that from 1950 to 1989, 14 per cent of successfully staged *coups* against dictatorships led to democracy within two years, while 40 per cent did so from 1990 to 2015, either because of the altruistic desire of the usurpers of power to save their countries from autocratic incumbents, because they value free and fair elections, or because of the incentives created by international pressure and sanctions in the post–Cold War era, including international threats to suspend foreign aid.[95]

International reaction to a *coup* can be unilateral reaction vis-à-vis the usurper and his regime or through a competent international organization. It is axiomatic that for a foreign State to be able to make any difference to the political situation in another nation State the former must have sufficient leverage and resources to significantly influence the latter. Therefore, only a handful of States fall into the former category—they may, on their own or jointly with some other States, impose sanctions against the junta-installed government as well as those involved

93 On the complexity of the modern-day recognition or non-recognition of government, see Brad Roth, *Government Illegitimacy in International Law* (OUP 2000); Federica Paddeu and Alonso Gurmendi Dunkelberg, 'Recognition of Governments: Legitimacy and Control Six Months after Guaidó' *Opinio Juris* (18 August 2019). Cf. Jean d'Aspremont, 'Legitimacy of Government in the Age of Democracy' (2006) 38 NYU JIL & Policy 877, 901–6, 909–17; Naomi Wiener, 'The Gap between International Legitimacy and Legality of Transitional Regimes' in Emmanuel de Groof and Micha Wiebusch (eds), *International Law and Transitional Governance: Critical Perspectives* (Routledge 2020) ch 6. See also the judgment of 20 December 2021 of the UK Supreme Court in *'Maduro Board' of the Central Bank of Venezuela v 'Guaidó Board' of the Central Bank of Venezuela* [2021] UKSC 57, where the UK Supreme Court unanimously reaffirms that courts in this jurisdiction is bound to follow a certificate from the UK executive branch clarifying which of the competing governments in a foreign State the UK Government recognizes and where there were no formal statement by the UK executive branch on recognition of a foreign government, recognition ceases to be the determinative criterion and the court must identify who may be the Government or Head of State by making its own findings of fact (paras 98 and 110).

94 David Schmitz, *The United States and Right-Wing Dictatorships: 1965–1989* (CUP 2006); Elizabeth Schmidt, *Foreign Intervention in Africa: From the Cold War to the War on Terror* (CUP 2013) 16–192; Neovi Karakatsanis and Jonathan Swarts, *American Foreign Policy Towards the Colonels' Greece: Uncertain Allies and the 1967 Coup d'État* (Palgrave Macmillan 2018); Barbara Keys and Roland Burke, 'Human Rights' in Richard Immerman and Petra Goedde (eds), *The Oxford Handbook of the Cold War* (OUP 2013) 486–502.

95 George Derpanopoulos, Erica Frantz, Barbara Geddes and Joseph Wright, 'Are Coups Good for Democracy?' (January–March 2016) Research & Politics 2. See also Niccolò Ridi and Veronika Fikfak, 'Sanctioning to Change State Behaviour' (2022) 13 J Int'l Dispute Settlement 210.

in usurpation of power by unconstitutional means. For instance, in response to the 1 February 2021 *coup* in Myanmar, leading junta members, some members of their families and businesses associated with them have been subjected to sanctions imposed by the United States, United Kingdom, Canada, New Zealand and the European Union, among others.[96] In February 2022, the United States halted US$158.6 million in US aid to Burkina Faso after determining the 24 January 2022 unconstitutional usurpation of power in that country constituted a military *coup*, triggering aid restrictions under US law under which US foreign aid, except for funds to promote democracy, must be stopped to a country whose elected Head of Government is deposed by military *coup* or in a *coup* in which the military plays a decisive role.[97] Separately, Millennium Challenge Corporation, a US Government foreign assistance agency paused activity related to an agreement signed in August 2020 for US$450 million in funding to Burkina Faso. As another example, in February 2022 the European Union imposed travel bans and asset freezes on five senior members of Mali's military junta which staged the *coup* in August 2020 and failed to organize presidential and legislative elections by February 2022 as demanded by the Economic Community of West African States, of which Mali is one of its 15 Member States.

The lawfulness of unilateral sanctions has been subject to extensive debates and is usually disputed by targeted States.[98] Sanctions imposed by competent international organizations, where feasible, may be more justifiable since they represent the collective will of their members and within the limit of their respective constituent instruments.[99] It is beyond the scope of this chapter to dwell on the

96 See Kriangsak Kittichaisaree, *The Rohingya, Justice and International Law* (Routledge 2021) 282–3. See also id, *International Human Rights Law and Diplomacy* (Edward Elgar Publishing 2020) 28–31.

97 Public Law 116–260, Division K, Section 7008. See Congressional Research Service, *Coup-Related Restrictions in US Foreign Aid Appropriations* (26 October 2021).

98 See, e.g., Mohamed Helal, 'On Coercion in International Law' (2019) 52 NYU JIL & Politics 1; Surya Subedi, *Unilateral Sanctions in International Law* (Hart 2021); Charlotte Beaucillon, *Research Handbook on Unilateral and Extraterritorial Sanctions* (Edward Elgar Publishing 2021); Eirik Borge, Dapo Akande and Payam Akhavan, 'Economic Sanctions, International Law, and Crimes against Humanity: Venezuela's ICC Referral' (2021) 105 AJIL 493; Kittichaisaree, *The Rohingya, Justice and International Law* 245–8; European Commission, Proposal for a regulation of the European Parliament and of the Council on the protection of the European Union and its Member States from economic coercion by third countries, 2021/0406(COD) 8 December 2021; Sienho Yee, 'Unilateral Sanctions: Kind and Degree; Long-arm and Strong-arm Jurisdiction; Real Intent and "Could-be" Intent' (2021) 20 Chinese JIL 817. See also Nikolay Marinov and Shmuel Nili, 'Sanctions and Democracy' (2015) 41 Int'l Interactions 765, arguing that some sanctions policies to secure democratization when used under specific conditions are more justifiable, but there are other sanctions policies that are less justifiable.

99 For an exhaustive analysis of United Nations sanctions, see Enrico Carisch, Loraine Rickard-Martin and Shawna Meister, *The Evolution of UN Sanctions: From a Tool of Warfare to a Tool of Peace, Security and Human Rights* (Springer 2017) 17–481. See also Jeremy Matam Farrall, *United Nations Sanctions and the Rule of Law* (CUP 2007); Guglielmo Verdirame, *The UN and Human Rights: Who Guards the Guardian?* (CUP 2011) 300–19; Rebecca Barber, 'An Exploration of the General Assembly's Troubled Relationship with Unilateral Sanctions' (2021) 70 ICLQ 343.

legitimacy or otherwise of the sanctions. The focus of this chapter is on international acceptance of *coups* so that domestic judges can bear in mind when ruling on the lawfulness or otherwise of the usurpation and the consequential repression of rights and freedom.

When a State resorts to unilateralism, its ulterior motive vis-à-vis the State targeted by it is always questioned. When the use of force or threat thereof is involved, this is usually in violation of international law. An example is the US Government's use of armed forces to intervene in the military *coup* and counter-*coup* in Grenada on 14 and 19 October 1983 that toppled and summarily executed the then Prime Minister Maurice Bishop. The US invasion culminated in deposing and replacing the military junta by an interim advisory council until the 1984 general elections. A resolution of the UN General Assembly in November 1983 deeply deplores the armed invasion which was a flagrant violation of international law and of the independence, sovereignty and territorial integrity of Grenada contrary to Article 2(4) of the UN Charter,[100] according to which all UN Member States are obliged to refrain in their international relations from the threat or use of force against the territorial integrity or political independence of any State or in any other manner inconsistent with the principles of the Charter. The resolution also deplores the death of innocent civilians resulting from the armed intervention; calls upon all States to show the strictest respect for the sovereignty, independence and territorial integrity of Grenada; calls for an immediate cessation of the armed intervention and the immediate withdrawal of the foreign troops from Grenada; requests that free elections be organized as rapidly as possible to enable the people of Grenada to choose its government democratically; and requests the UN Secretary-General as a matter of urgency to assess the situation and to report back to the General Assembly within 72 hours.[101]

On the whole, although reaction against a *coup* by as many nation States as possible is indicative of the disapproval by some members of the international community, it is reaction in competent international organizations that is more credible.

United Nations

At the United Nations and its agencies, there have been challenges as to who are entitled to represent the Government after a *coup*—those appointed by the ousted Government or those appointed by the *coup*-installed Government.[102] For example,

100 1 UNTS XVI, in force 24 October 1945.

101 A/RES/38/7 (2 November 1983), adopted by a recorded vote of 108 in favour (including Grenada) to 9 against, with 27 abstentions. Therefore, the unilateral armed intervention by France to reverse the bloodless military *coup* in Gabon, which had gained independence from France in 1960, even without the deposed Gabonese President's official request for assistance would not be lawful under the UN Charter.

102 See also Larry Johnson, 'Expert Background: How Can the Taliban Be Prevented from Representing Afghanistan in the United Nations' *Just Security* (18 August 2021), https://www.justsecurity.org/77806/

Andry Nirina Rajoelina, 'President of the High Transitional Authority of the Republic of Madagascar', was not allowed to address the UN General Assembly's general debate in 2009 because he had 'gained power through a *coup*'. The opposition to his address to the General Assembly was tabled by 15 of the 16 members of the Southern African Development Community (SADC), of which Madagascar was a member. Twenty-three countries rejected the 'President' of Madagascar taking the floor, four countries accepted he could take the floor, and six countries abstained.[103] As a general principle, UN General Assembly resolution 396 of 14 December 1950 recommends that, whenever more than one authority claims to be the government entitled to represent a Member State in the United Nations and this question becomes the subject of controversy in the United Nations, the question should be considered in light of the Purposes and Principles of the UN Charter and the circumstances of each case. When any such question arises, it should be considered by the UN General Assembly, or by the Interim Committee if the General Assembly is not in session, and the attitude adopted by the General Assembly or its interim committee concerning any such question should be taken into account in other organs of the United Nations and in the specialized agencies.[104]

The UN General Assembly condemns *coups d'état* from times to times, as in the case of the *coup d'état* in Honduras on 28 June 2009 in which the General Assembly demanded the immediate and unconditional restoration of the legitimate and Constitutional Government of the President of Honduras, José Manuel Zelaya Rosales, and of the legally constituted authority in Honduras as well as decided to call firmly and unequivocally upon States to recognize no Government other than that of the Constitutional President and expressed the General Assembly's firm support for the regional efforts being undertaken to resolve the political crisis in Honduras.[105] As another example, by a vote of 119 to 1 (Belarus), with 36 abstentions and 37 UN Member States not voting, the General Assembly adopted a resolution on 18 June 2021 to, among other things, call upon the Myanmar armed forces to respect the result of the 8 November 2020 general election; to end the state of emergency; to respect all human rights of all the people of Myanmar and to allow the sustained democratic transition of Myanmar, including the opening of the democratically elected Parliament and by working towards bringing all national institutions, including the armed forces, under a fully inclusive civilian government representative of the will of the people. It also called upon the Myanmar armed forces to

---

expert-backgrounder-how-can-the-taliban-be-prevented-from-representing-afghanistan-in-the-united-nations/.

103 UNGA OR, 64th Sess, 8th Plenary Mtg (25 September 2009), A/64/PV.8, 18–22. SADC comprises Angola, Botswana, Comoros, DR Congo, Lesotho, Madagascar, Malawi, Mauritius, Mozambique, Namibia, Seychelles, South Africa, Swaziland, Tanzania, Zambia and Zimbabwe.

104 A/RES/5/396 (14 December 1950). See also the UN Secretary-General's memorandum on the legal aspects of the problems of representation in the United Nations, UN Doc S/1466 (9 March 1950).

105 A/RES/63/301 (30 June 2009).

immediately and unconditionally release President Win Myint, State Counsellor and de facto Head of Government Aung San Suu Kyi, other government officials and politicians and all those arbitrarily detained, charged or arrested, including to ensure their rightful access to justice. The resolution further called upon the Myanmar armed forces to immediately stop all violence against peaceful demonstrators, as well as members of civil society, women, youth, children and others and to end restrictions on medical personnel, civil society, labour union members, journalists and media workers and restrictions on the Internet and social media.[106]

Where the UN Security Council, comprising 15 members, has on its agenda the situation in a particular country and that country subsequently experiences a military *coup*, the UN plays a direct and active leading role as well as coordinates efforts to pressure the junta to restore the constitutional order and the transition process to transfer power back to the civilian government.

After Haitian President Jean-Bertrand Aristide had been toppled by a military *coup* on 30 September 1991, the UN Security Council adopted a resolution in July 1994 to authorize a multinational force under unified command and control to restore the legitimately elected President and authorities of the Government of Haiti. The resolution, among other things, expressed the Council's grave concern as regards the significant further deterioration of the humanitarian situation in Haiti, in particular the continuing escalation by the illegal de facto regime of systematic violations of civil liberties, and the desperate plight of Haitian refugees. It reaffirmed the goal of the international community was the restoration of democracy in Haiti and the prompt return of the legitimately elected President Aristide. It also recognized the unique character of the ongoing situation in Haiti and its deteriorating, complex and extraordinary nature, requiring an exceptional response. Acting under Chapter VII (Action with respect to threats to the peace, breaches of the peace and acts of aggression) of the UN Charter, the Council authorized UN Member States to form a multinational force under unified command and control and, in this framework, to use all necessary means to facilitate the departure from Haiti of the military leadership, the prompt return of the legitimately elected President and the restoration of the legitimate authorities of the Government of Haiti, and to establish and maintain a secure and stable environment in the country, on the understanding that the cost of implementing this temporary operation would be borne by the participating UN Member States.[107] Joseph Raoul Cédras, head of the junta, was pressured by the US Government to leave Haiti in October 1994 for Panama, where he has since been living in exile, and the potential invasion by a multinational force authorized by the Security Council resolution was eventually averted. This was the first time the Security Council authorized the use of force to restore democracy.

On 29 February 2004, also acting under Chapter VII of the UN Charter, the Security Council adopted another resolution, on the appeal of Haiti's interim

106 A/RES/75/287 (18 June 2021).
107 S/RES/940 (1994) 31 July 1994.

President for the urgent support of the international community to assist in restoring peace and security in Haiti and to further the constitutional political process then under way after a three-week rebellion had forced President Aristide to resign and leave Haiti for exile abroad. This latter resolution authorized the immediate deployment of a Multinational Interim Force for a period of not more than three months from the adoption of the resolution. Such force was entrusted with, among other things, contributing to a secure and stable environment pursuant to the interim Haitian President's request for international assistance to support the constitutional political process under way in Haiti as well as facilitating the provision of international assistance to the Haitian police and the Haitian Coast Guard to establish and maintain public safety and law and order and to promote and protect human rights.[108]

The UN Security Council can only adopt a resolution and/or take concrete action in response to a *coup* insofar as any one of the Council's five permanent members—China, France, Russia, the United States and the United Kingdom—does not cast a veto against the tabled course of action.[109] For instance, in the case of the *coup* in Myanmar, the Security Council only managed to issue statements without condemning the *coup*, merely expressing, among other things, the Security Council members' deep concern at the declaration of the state of emergency imposed in Myanmar by the military, the arbitrary detention of members of the deposed Government and the escalation of armed violence in Myanmar as well as encouraging the pursuit of dialogue and reconciliation in accordance with the will and interests of the people of Myanmar.[110] In the same vein, in the aftermath of the October 2021 military *coup* in Sudan the Security Council only managed to issue a press statement three days later and without condemning the *coup*. The Council's statement expressed serious concern about the *coup*, called upon all parties in Sudan to exercise the utmost restraint and refrain from the use of violence,

108 S/RES/1529 (2004) 29 February 2004.

109 Since the founding of the United Nations up to 25 February 2022, Russia cast vetoes 119 times, United States 82 times, United Kingdom 29 times, China 16 times and France 16 times ('UN Approves Measure Requiring States to Justify Veto' *Al Jazeera* (26 April 2022), https://www.aljazeera.com/news/2022/4/26/un-approves-measure-requiring-states-to-justify-veto). For the Security Council's inconsistency in countering military *coups*, see Oisín Tansey, 'The Fading of the Anti-Coup Norm' (2017) 28 J Democracy 144, 148–9. Jennifer Trahan, *Existing Legal Limits to Security Council Veto Power in the Face of Atrocity Crimes* (CUP 2020) contends that the right of veto by permanent members of the UN Security Council in the face of genocide, crimes against humanity or war crimes needs to be measured against the legal obligations within the remainder of the system of international law, including obligations to respect overriding peremptory norms (*jus cogens*), obligations to respect the UN Charter (including its 'Purposes and Principles') and other treaty obligations. See also Olivier de Frouville, *From Cosmopolitanism to Human Rights* (Hart 2022) ch 14.

110 Cf. Martin Mennecke and Ellen Stensrud, 'The Failure of the International Community to Apply R2P and Atrocity Prevention in Myanmar' (2021) 13 Global Responsibility to Protect 111; Tamsin Phillipa Paige, 'The Bear and the Dragon: Pragmatism and State-centric International Law in the UN Security Council' (2021) 90 Nordic JIL 446.

and emphasized the importance of full respect for human rights, including the right to peaceful assembly and freedom of expression, as well as demanded the immediate release of all those detained. It also affirmed the Council's readiness to support efforts to realize Sudan's democratic transition and the peoples' aspirations for an inclusive, peaceful, stable, democratic and prosperous future.

The fact that due to geopolitics the UN Security Council cannot take action against a *coup* because one or more of the Council's permanent member casts a veto does not mean the international community approves of the *coup*. On 26 April 2022, the UN General Assembly adopted, by consensus, a resolution titled 'Standing mandate for a General Assembly debate when a veto is cast in the Security Council'[111] aimed at holding the five permanent Council members accountable for their use of veto. Pursuant to this resolution, the President of the UN General Assembly shall convene a formal meeting of the General Assembly within ten working days of the casting of a veto by one or more permanent members of the Security Council, to hold a debate on the situation as to which the veto was cast, provided that the General Assembly does not meet in an emergency special session on the same situation. It invites the Security Council to submit a special report on the use of the veto in question to the General Assembly at least 72 hours before the relevant discussion in the General Assembly. The reaction to a *coup* by the UN General Assembly, where all UN Member States participate on an equal footing, when the UN Security Council fails to take action concerning the *coup* can thus reflect whether the international community approves of or opposes the *coup*.

Regional organizations

Regional organizations and other non-UN organizations also address usurpation of power within their respective competences and/or human rights mechanisms.[112]

Europe

The Council of Europe, set up in 1949 to uphold human rights, democracy and the rule of law in Europe, has 46 Member States, including all the 28 Members of the European Union (EU) and all Eastern European States except Russia and Belarus. All the members of the Council of Europe are parties to the 1950 European Convention on Human Rights.[113] The European Court of Human Rights (EctHR) established by the 1950 Convention has contributed significantly to the development of norms protecting human rights under that Convention. The

111 A/RES/76/262.

112 See also Jacob Wobig, 'Defending Democracy with International Law: Preventing Coup Attempts with Democracy Clauses' (2015) 22 Democratization 631.

113 See further Martyn Bond, *The Council of Europe and Human Rights: The European Convention on Human Rights* (Council of Europe Publishing 2018); William Schabas, *The European Convention on Human Rights: A Commentary* (OUP 2015).

European Commission of Human Rights, which became obsolete in 1998 with the restructuring of the EctHR, played an important role in assisting the EctHR from 1953 to 1998 by considering if a petition was admissible before the EctHR, and, if so, by examining the petition to determine the facts of the case and look for parties to help settle the case in a friendly manner. If a friendly settlement was not reached, the Commission would issue a report on the established facts with an opinion on whether or not a violation had taken place.[114]

The Report of the Human Rights Sub-Commission on the applications against Greece brought by Norway, Sweden, Denmark and the Netherlands on 20 September 1967,[115] or the *Greek Case*, an inter-State application before the European Commission of Human Rights,[116] details the violation of several provisions of the European Convention on Human Rights, especially Article 3 which prohibits torture, by the military junta that seized power in Greece on 21 April 1967.

After determining the issue of admissibility of the applications, the Sub-Commission addressed the junta's declaration of state of emergency. The Report reaffirmed the Commission's competence to examine the acts of governments in political situations of an extraordinary character, such as after a revolution, and that a revolution did not absolve the State concerned from its obligations under the European Convention. On the other hand, a revolutionary government established in a High Contracting State, and recognized as representing this State in international relations, was in principle entitled to take measures derogating from its obligations under this Convention in time of emergency 'threatening the life of the nation' as provided in Article 15 where the conditions thereunder were fulfilled. The Sub-Commission was not convinced by the evidence that there was on 21 April 1967, when the junta staged the *coup*, a public emergency threatening the life of the Greek nation. Although the junta-installed Government had annulled or relaxed certain measures of derogation since then, the state of siege continued and the Government pointed out two new factors; namely, the bomb incidents and acts of sabotage, which were often repeated since the summer of 1967, and the formation and activities of a number of illegal organizations since April l967. However, the Sub-Commission did not find, on the evidence before it, either factor was beyond the control of the public authorities exercising normal measures, or they were on a scale threatening the organized life of the country. In November 1969 the Commission adopted the Report submitted to it by the Sub-Commission in the preceding month. On 12 December 1969, the Committee of Ministers of the

114 See further John White, 'The European Commission of Human Rights: An Analysis and Appraisal' (1977) 3 Brooklyn JIL 119.

115 App nos 3321/67 (*Denmark v Greece*), 3322/67 (*Norway v Greece*), 3323/67 (*Sweden v Greece*) and 3344/67 (*Netherlands v Greece*). They were declared admissible in 1968. A second application was submitted by Denmark, Norway and Sweden for additional violations, mainly of Art 3 on the prohibition of torture, which was also declared admissible in 1968.

116 At that time Greece had not accepted the 'individual application' procedure before the ECtHR, so only an inter-State application was possible.

Council of Europe met to consider a resolution on Greece, when Greece's foreign minister denounced the European Convention and walked out.[117] Greece is the first State to leave the Council of Europe;[118] it returned to the Council's membership after the transition to democracy with the fall of the junta in 1974.

Africa

As of this writing, 13 of the 14 *coups* recorded globally since 2017 have been in Africa.[119]

Article 4(m) of the 2000 Constitutive Act of the African Union (AU)[120] lists as one principle of the AU 'respect for democratic principles, human rights, the rule of law and good governance'. Pursuant to Article 30 of the Constitutive Act, 'Governments which shall come to power through unconstitutional means shall not be allowed to participate in the activities of the Union'. On 30 January 2007, the AU adopted the African Charter on Democracy, Elections and Governance (ACDEG),[121] which entered into force on 15 February 2012 after ratification by 15 States. As of this writing, the ACDEG has been ratified by 34 States out of the AU's 55 Member States.[122] Some of the ACDEG's pertinent provisions include Article 14(1), requiring States Parties to strengthen and institutionalize constitutional civilian control over the armed and security forces to ensure the consolidation of democracy and constitutional order. Articles 17 through 22 deal with democratic elections.[123] Articles 23 through 26 cover sanctions in case of unconstitutional changes of government, broadly defined as illegal means of accessing or maintaining power and including any amendment or revision of the constitution or legal instruments, which is an infringement on the principles of democratic change of government.[124] Article 25 provides, inter alia, that where there has been

117 See also James Becket, 'The Greek Case Before the European Human Rights Commission' (1970) 1 Human Rights 91.

118 The Committee of Ministers of the Council of Europe formally decided on 16 March 2022 that, because of Russia's invasion of Ukraine starting from 24 February 2022, Russia ceased to be a member of the Council of Europe, which Russia had joined on 28 February 1996.

119 Peter Mwai, 'Sudan Coup: Are Military Takeovers on the rise in Africa?' *BBC* (3 October 2022), https://www.bbc.com/news/world-africa-46783600.

120 2158 UNTS 3, in force 6 May 2001.

121 https://au.int/en/treaties/african-charter-democracy-elections-and-governance.

122 Algeria, Benin, Burkina Faso, Cameroon, Central African Republic, Chad, Comoros, Côte d'Ivoire, Djibouti, Ethiopia, The Gambia, Ghana, Guinea, Guinea-Bissau, Lesotho, Liberia, Madagascar, Malawi, Mali, Mozambique, Mauritania, Namibia, Niger, Nigeria, Rwanda, Sahrawi Arab Democratic Republic (aka Western Sahara), Seychelles, Sierra Leone, São Tomé and Príncipe, South Africa, South Sudan, Sudan, Togo and Zambia.

123 Cf. Eki Yemisi Omorogbe, 'The AU and Disputed Presidential Elections' in Olufemi Amao, Michèle Olivier and Konstantinos Magliveras (eds), *The Emergent African Union Law: Conceptualization, Delimitation, and Application* (OUP 2021) 189–207.

124 See also Erika de Wet, 'The African Union's Struggle Against Unconstitutional Change of Government: From a Moral Protection to a Requirement under International Law' (2021) 32 EJIL 199, 202–3.

an unconstitutional change of government in a State Party and diplomatic initiatives have failed, the State Party shall be suspended from the exercise of its right to participate in the AU's activities until the situation leading to the suspension is resolved. However, the suspended State Party shall continue to fulfil its obligations to the AU, in particular with regard to those relating to respect for human rights. The perpetrators of unconstitutional change of government shall not be allowed to participate in elections held to restore the democratic order or hold any position of responsibility in political institutions of their State and they may also be tried before the competent court of the AU. In addition, the Assembly of Heads of State and Government of the AU may decide to apply other forms of sanctions on perpetrators of unconstitutional change of government, including punitive economic measures.

A notable outcome of the ACDEG is the development of the African Governance Architecture as the overall political and institutional framework mechanism for dialogue between stakeholders mandated to promote and strengthen democracy, good governance and human rights in Africa. According to one study published in 2017, while the ACDEG has led to changes in some AU Member States' approach to democracy and governance, in other AU Member States it has had limited impact. The level of acceptance and implementation of the ACDEG remains highly uneven across the African continent.[125]

The AU at times suspends Member States over *coups d'état*, readmitting them when they return or are on the path back to constitutional democracy. For example, it suspended Madagascar after the *coup* in March 2009 until January 2014 when the newly elected Government was sworn in. The AU suspended Mali after the *coup* in March 2012 until October of that year after the AU had endorsed a roadmap for fresh elections and the return of law and order in Mali.

Yet, there is inconsistency in enforcing compliance with the ACDEG. According to one research, there are several reasons for this phenomenon. Signing and ratifying the ACDEG does not seem to be directly linked to good governance parameters since several African nations with 'illiberal democracies' (i.e., formal democracies by regime type, but authoritarian in nature) are also parties to the ACDEG. Some of the 15 members of the Peace and Security Council (PSC), the most important day-to-day decision-making body of the AU outside the meetings of the AU Assembly of Heads of State and Government, are nation States with illiberal democracies which demonstrate poorer scores in their quality of democracy than the average AU Member State. When it comes to the more general issue

125 Chika Charles Aniekwe, Lutz Oette, Stef Vandeginste and Micha Wiebusch, *The 10th Anniversary of the African Charter on Democracy, Elections and Governance* (Institute of Development Studies 2017). Cf. Wobig, 'Defending Democracy with International Law' 613; Solomon Ayele Dersso, 'Defending Constitutional Rule as a Peacemaking Enterprise: The Case of the AU's Ban of Unconstitutional Changes of Government' (2017) 24 Int'l Peacekeeping 639; Tom Ginsburg, 'International Courts and Democratic Backsliding' (2019) 37 Berkeley JIL 265, 285–7; Sören Stapel, *Regional Organizations and Democracy, Human Rights, and the Rule of Law: The African Union, Organization of American States, and the Diffusion of Institutions* (Palgrave Macmillan 2022) 237–75; Dawn Nagar, *Challenging the United Nations Peace and Security Agenda in Africa* (Palgrave Macmillan 2022) 319–51.

of dominant decision-making within the AU, particularly in the PSC, there are numerous reasons for the implementation gap of the ACDEG. First of all, there is a strong organizational culture of non-implementation—an obvious disconnect between collective, consensual expressions of political will and the actual concrete political desire of individual AU Member States to follow through. This is partly due to the culture of political consensus dominating the AU's decision-making: there is a tacit understanding that other Member States will not enforce compliance with a position which a particular Member State does not support in principle. This is linked to another reason: even African States with liberal democracies have adopted a 'do not rock the boat' mentality towards their illiberal fellow AU members, probably owing to the need of the former to rely on the latter's support in regional or global relations, for instance, in the UN General Assembly.[126]

As concluded by another learned author, the AU has not consistently prevented *coup* perpetrators from standing in subsequent elections, as provided for in Article 25 of the ACDEG and reaffirmed in the 2009 decision of the PSC as well as the 2010 decision of the AU Assembly of Heads of State and Government. The AU's ambivalent relationship with military *coup* regimes is reflective of the fact that at the time of the AU's founding in 2000 several Member States were represented by Governments that had previously come to power through *coups*, such as Libya and Sudan. Since the AU's creation, swift suspension of AU membership followed *coups* on nine occasions, while in five instances the AU either imposed suspension in a delayed fashion or not at all. According to that author, the instances in which the AU responded with swift suspension include Togo (2005), Guinea (2008), Mauritania (2005 and 2008), Madagascar (2009), Niger (2010), Guinea-Bissau (2012), Mali (2012) and Egypt (2013).[127]

The aforesaid suspensions of both Mali and Egypt were limited in duration. The AU suspended Mali until the junta was accommodated in the transitional government that took office in August 2012 and was swiftly recognized by the AU and remained in power until presidential elections were held a year later. This brief suspension might have served the purpose of returning Mali to democracy. Unfortunately, Mali suffered another *coup* when, in August 2020, Mali's elected President Ibrahim Boubacar Keita was ousted by the military led by Colonel Assimi Goita following mass protests over perceived corruption and a bloody insurgency. In early

126 Ulf Engel, 'The 2007 African Charter on Democracy, Elections and Governance: Trying to Make Sense of the Late Ratification of the African Charter and Non-Implementation of Its Compliance Mechanism' (2019) 54 African Spectrum 127, 131–46. Cf. Alison Duxbury, *The Participation of States in International Organisations: The Role of Human Rights and Democracy* (CUP 2011) 265–310, arguing that human rights and democracy criteria, including a criterion for determining the application of membership sanctions, have not been consistently applied within an organization or across organizations with similar mandates or membership policies, but nevertheless have influenced decisions on participation. Individual Member States and groups of States have also used the language of human rights and democracy in membership decisions to fulfil their own political objectives or to advance their ideological views.

127 de Wet, 'The African Union's Struggle Against Unconstitutional Change of Government' 205.

June 2021, the AU's Peace and Security Council suspended Mali's membership in the AU until normal constitutional order was restored in the country. The PSC asked the Malian military to urgently and unconditionally return to the barracks and refrain from further interference in the political processes in Mali, or else the PSC would impose targeted sanctions and other punitive measures.

As far as Egypt was concerned, the AU acted contrary to its own guiding principles as it condoned the participation of a *coup* perpetrator in elections conducted to return to constitutional order. The AU explained it lifted Egypt's suspension because of: (a) the progress made and the steps taken by the Egyptian authorities to formally restore constitutional order in Egypt, (b) the fact that the suspension of Egypt for almost one year had sent a strong signal to the Egyptian stakeholders about the AU's commitment to its principles and instruments and (c) the need for the AU to remain engaged with Egypt and to accompany the efforts of the Egyptian authorities for the full implementation of the roadmap to restore full democracy. The AU underscored this should not be a precedent in terms of adherence to Article 25 of the ACDEG, but 'should only be viewed in light of the unique set of circumstances'. It also suggested Egypt was to be persuaded to speedily sign and ratify all relevant AU instruments on democracy, elections and governance, notably the ACDEG, and to take concrete steps towards the implementation of the provisions contained therein.[128] Moreover, despite lifting the suspension, the AU would continue to keep human rights and democracy in Egypt on the PSC's agenda. In view of the difficulties encountered in applying the AU norms on unconstitutional changes of government, particularly in the context of popular uprisings, the AU adopted a guideline for determining the compatibility of popular uprisings with AU norms on unconstitutional changes of government. Taking into account recent experiences in North Africa, including in Egypt, the following elements should be considered together: (a) the descent of the government into total authoritarianism to the point of forfeiting its legitimacy, (b) the absence or total ineffectiveness of constitutional processes for effecting change of government, (c) popularity of the uprisings in the sense of attracting a significant portion of the population and involving people from all walks of life and ideological persuasions, (d) the absence of involvement of the military in removing the government and (e) peacefulness of the popular protests.[129] The AU's stance could have been influenced by the prevarication among the United States and other Western powers who were concerned about the undemocratic change of government in Egypt but happy to see the ouster of democratically elected President Mohamed Morsi, an Islamist affiliated with the Muslim Brotherhood organization. The US Government even publicly

128 As of this writing, Egypt has not yet become party to the ACDEG.

129 Final Report of the African Union High-Level Panel for Egypt, 22 July 2014 paras 75–83, www.peaceau.org/en/article/final-report-of-the-african-union-high-level-panel-for-egypt. Cf. Solomon Dersso, 'The Status and Legitimacy of Popular Uprisings in the AU Norms on Democracy and Constitutional Governance' (2019) 63(S1) J African Law 107.

declined to call the usurpation a *coup*.[130] In any event, the significance of popular acceptance discussed earlier in this chapter in this context should be duly noted.

Coups provoking delayed responses from the AU included the one in Burkina Faso in 2014 and another one in Sudan in 2019, both of which were parties to the ACDEG at the time of the *coups*. In the case of Burkina Faso, on 1 November 2014 the military led by Lt Col Isaac Zida staged a *coup* and declared himself President after President Blaise Compaore was forced to resign and fled to a neighbouring country amid protests against Compaore's plan to amend the constitution to allow him to run for the Presidency for another term after 27 years in office since 1987 when he led a *coup* to oust the government then in power. On 2 November 2014, the AU issued a two-week deadline for the military to restore civilian rule or face sanction, thereby leading to an agreement, by the deadline, among the country's military, civil and political leaders on transitional government under an interim President who would not be eligible to run for office in the election to be held in 2015.[131] The AU's suspension of Burkina Faso only occurred after a second military *coup* in September 2015 when the presidential guard overthrew the interim President one month before the scheduled general elections. The *coup* collapsed one week later and the ousted interim President was re-installed. The AU was much quicker in suspending Burkina Faso, on 31 January 2022, from all AU activities until the effective restoration of constitutional order in the country after the 24 January 2022 military *coup*. In the case of Sudan, the Defence Minister took control in April 2019, establishing a two-year transitional military government and suspending Sudan's Constitution. The AU did not punish Sudan right away probably because the military takeover toppled President Omar al-Bashir, a pariah of the international community who was being sought by the International Criminal Court to stand trial for genocide, war crimes and crimes against humanity. Only after a paramilitary crackdown on protests in Khartoum in early June 2019 that left more than 120 people dead did the AU suspend Sudan from participating in its activities until the effective establishment of a civilian-led Transitional Authority. In August 2019, negotiations were concluded regarding the establishment of a three-year transitional government which, although civilian-led, would also include military leaders. Shortly thereafter, the AU's suspension of Sudan was lifted.[132] On 27 October 2021, the AU swiftly suspended Sudan from its membership after the Sudanese military's *coup* on 25 October 2021.

There were instances in which the AU did not sanction its Member States for an unconstitutional change of government at all, as in the case of the *coup* in São Tomé and Príncipe in July 2003, since the constitutional order was restored through

130 Dan Roberts, 'US in Bind over Egypt after Supporting Morsi But Encouraging Protesters' *Guardian* (3 July 2013), https://www.theguardian.com/world/2013/jul/03/egypt-obama-us-mohamed-morsi-crisis.

131 'Burkina Faso Leaders Agree Transitional Framework' *BBC* (13 November 2014), https://www.bbc.com/news/world-africa-30046413.

132 de Wet, 'The African Union's Struggle Against Unconstitutional Change of Government' 206–7.

mediation within a few weeks, including the return of the elected President. After a military *coup* led to the resignation of Zimbabwe's President Robert Mugabe in November 2017, the AU did not condemn the *coup*; nor in fact did any AU Member State seem eager to refer to the military takeover as a *coup*. The AU instead chose to praise President Mugabe for stepping down, recognizing the expressed will of the Zimbabwean people for a peaceful transfer of power in a manner which secured the democratic future of their country.[133] It could be that the AU considered the latter a good *coup* because it enjoyed both extensive popular support and international approval, especially since the Mugabe Government had forfeited its legitimacy by engaging in widespread and systematic human rights abuses.[134] The AU refrained from sanctioning the July 2021 self-*coup* by the Tunisian President and even elected Tunisia as a member of its Peace and Security Council in February 2022, apparently preferring to focus its scant resources on countries experiencing military *coups*.

Idriss Déby, who came to power in Chad in the 1990 *coup d'état*, was killed on the frontline fighting an armed rebel group on 19 April 2021. Soon after his death, the Chadian military took over the government and installed his son, a military commander, as interim President who would lead an 18-month Transitional Military Council to maintain national stability and ensure a peaceful and democratic transition of power. The Council 'provisionally' dissolved both the Executive and Legislature as well as 'provisionally' suspended the Chadian Constitution, which provides, inter alia, that upon the death of the President of Chad his duties are to be provisionally exercised by the President of the National Assembly. The Council's action was therefore unconstitutional usurpation of power. On 14 May 2021, the PSC of the AU issued its decision on the situation in Chad, endorsing Chad's Transitional Military Council, subject to conditions including the immediate review of the draft transition charter and the rejection of any potential extension of the 18-month transition. The PSC also called for the establishment of a national transition council as the interim legislative body, inclusive national dialogue and respect for human rights and fundamental freedoms. The AU's special envoy would work closely with the transition government leading to the organization of free, fair and credible elections. To justify its decision, the PSC considered Chad was justified in suspending its constitutional rules because it was under attack from foreign mercenaries (allegedly from Libya) with terrorist ambitions.[135]

On the whole, even if there were agreement within the AU that an unconstitutional change of government has taken place, the obligation to suspend the perpetrators may be outweighed by economic or security interests and/or geopolitical power relationships that may involve other regional or external actors.[136]

133 Ibid 208.

134 Ibid 209.

135 Communiqué of the 996th meeting of the PSC of the AU on the consideration of the Report of the Fact Finding Mission to the Republic of Chad, 14 May 2021.

136 de Wet, 'The African Union's Struggle Against Unconstitutional Change of Government' 209–12.

Besides the AU, the Economic Community of West African States (ECOWAS)[137] has imposed sanctions on usurpers of power in Africa, sometimes in concert with the AU.

On 8 September 2021, for example, ECOWAS suspended Guinea's membership and demanded the military junta return Guinea to the constitutional order and immediately release President Alpha Condé who had been overthrown by the military *coup* three days earlier. A week later, on 16 September 2021, ECOWAS imposed sanctions against the military government in Guinea by freezing the financial assets and imposing travel bans on Guinea's military leaders and their relatives, insisting on the release of President Condé and the holding of the general election in six months' time. The military government refused an ECOWAS mediator and announced in May 2022 a 39-month transition to democracy, which period was shortened in late July 2022 to 24 months. Both of these proposals were rejected by the ECOWAS Summits of Heads of State who told Guinea's military to propose a reasonable timeline or else Guinea would face additional sanctions.

After the *coup* in Mali in August 2020, ECOWAS suspended Mali from its membership until February 2022 when the transitional government headed by the military-appointed interim civilian President and Prime Minister would be expected to transfer their power to those elected in a general election. On 7 November 2021, ECOWAS imposed sanctions on Mali's transitional leaders after they had informed ECOWAS they would not be able to hold presidential and legislative elections in February 2022. On 9 January 2022, an extraordinary summit of the leaders of ECOWAS rejected the proposal from Mali's transitional authorities to hold elections in December 2025 instead of February 2022 as originally agreed. The summit imposed additional sanctions with immediate effect, including the closure of ECOWAS members' land and air borders with Mali, the suspension of non-essential financial transactions and the freezing of Malian State assets in ECOWAS central and commercial banks. Meanwhile, the West African Economic and Monetary Union, the customs and currency union among eight ECOWAS Member States,[138] instructed all financial institutions under its umbrella to suspend Mali with immediate effect, severing the country's access to regional financial markets.[139] On 3 July 2022 the ECOWAS Summit of Heads of State lifted the economic and financial sanctions after the Malian military regime had proposed a 24-month transition to democracy and published a new electoral law. Yet, they decided to maintain individual sanctions against members of the military government and the transitional council and the suspension of Mali from ECOWAS until

137 ECOWAS comprises 15 Member States: Benin, Burkina Faso, Cabo Verde, Côte d'Ivoire, The Gambia, Ghana, Guinea, Guinea-Bissau, Liberia, Mali, Niger, Nigeria, Senegal, Sierra Leone and Togo. As a regional trading union, ECOWAS aims to create a single, large trading block through economic cooperation and integration.

138 Benin, Burkina Faso, Côte d'Ivoire, Guinea-Bissau, Mali, Niger, Senegal and Togo.

139 On 6 June 2022 the Malian *coup* leader signed a decree to restore civilian rule within 24 months from 26 March 2022.

its return to democracy. This carrot-and-stick strategy came after there was some tangible progress on returning the country to democracy while the economic and financial sanctions were crippling Mali's economy, causing widespread humanitarian suffering.

On 28 January 2022, ECOWAS suspended Burkina Faso from its membership after the *coup* four days previously. However, ECOWAS decided a few days later not to impose 'maximum sanctions' against the country since ECOWAS had engaged the junta and the latter had shown interest in working with ECOWAS towards the restoration of constitutional order within a reasonable time. The ECOWAS Summit of Heads of State on 3 July 2022 accepted the junta's pledge to return the country to democratic rule in 24 months instead of the 36 months previously proposed by the junta. However, there was another military *coup* in Burkina Faso on 30 September 2022 to oust the said junta on the ground of its inability to deal with a worsening Islamic insurgency. ECOWAS immediately issued its strong condemnation of the latest *coup*, which came at an inopportune time when progress was being made towards the country's return to constitutional order. ECOWAS also reaffirmed its unreserved opposition to any taking or maintaining of the power by unconstitutional means.

The UN Security Council also supports the AU and ECOWAS in this regard when the Security Council finds it appropriate to do so and no veto is cast by any of the Council's permanent members. For instance, during the post-election crisis in Côte d'Ivoire in 2011 the Security Council urged all the Ivorian parties and other stakeholders to respect the will of the people and the election of Alassane Dramane Ouattara as President of Côte d'Ivoire, as recognized by ECOWAS, the AU and the rest of the international community, and imposed targeted sanctions against those individuals obstructing the aforesaid.[140] In April and May 2012, the Security Council expressly supported the efforts by the AU, ECOWAS, the Community of Portuguese Speaking Countries and the EU in response to the political crisis in Guinea-Bissau and the mediation efforts led by ECOWAS in response to the military *coup* on 12 April 2012 in that country. The Security Council demanded that the military junta take immediate steps to restore and respect constitutional order, including a democratic electoral process, by ensuring that all soldiers return to the barracks, and that members of the junta relinquish their positions of authority. The Security Council also decided that all UN Member States were to impose travel bans on leading members of the junta.[141] A few months later, in July 2012, the Security Council unanimously adopted a resolution to condemn the March 2012 seizure of power by some members of the Malian armed forces and called for the creation of a roadmap for the restoration of constitutional order and State authority throughout Malian territory. In this connection, the Security Council expressed its full support to the coordinated efforts of ECOWAS, the AU

140 S/RES/1975 (2011) 30 March 2011 paras 1, 12.
141 S/RES/2048 (2012) 18 May 2012.

and the transitional authorities of Mali to face the country's multiple challenges, which, besides the *coup* in the capital, Bamako, and fighting in the north, also included threats from Al-Qaida in the Islamic Maghreb. The Security Council expressed its readiness to further examine the request of the two regional organizations for a United Nations mandate authorizing the deployment of an ECOWAS stabilization force in Mali to support a political process and support security sector reform and strengthening.[142] As another example, in January 2017 the Security Council passed a resolution welcoming the decisions of the AU's Peace and Security Council declaring the inviolable nature of the outcome of the Presidential elections held on 1 December 2016 in The Gambia, calling upon former President Yahya Jammeh to keep his promise to honour the elections' outcome and declaring further that, as of 19 January 2017, outgoing President Jammeh would cease to be recognized as the legitimate President of The Gambia. The Security Council thus endorsed the decisions of ECOWAS and the AU to recognize Adama Barrow as the newly elected President of The Gambia and called upon the countries in the region and the relevant regional organizations to cooperate with President Barrow in his efforts to realize the transition of power.[143] Thereafter, approximately 7,000 troops from Ghana, Mali, Nigeria, Senegal and Togo, as well as aircraft and naval assets from Nigeria, entered The Gambia as part of the ECOWAS Mission in The Gambia, or ECOMIG, entrusted with ensuring former President Jammeh would not disrupt the handover of power. ECOMIG was an unprecedented African peace operation deployed as part of an international effort to prevent an unconstitutional usurpation of power of government.

In a commendable effort, the AU has endeavoured to criminalize unconstitutional change of government. Article 25 of the ACDEG stipulates, inter alia, that perpetrators of unconstitutional change of government may also be tried before the competent court of the AU. On 1 July 2008, the AU resolved to merge the African Court on Human and Peoples' Rights with the African Court of Justice to become the African Court of Justice and Human Rights by means of the Protocol on the Statute of the African Court of Justice and Human Rights (the Single Protocol).[144] In June 2014 the AU adopted the Protocol on Amendments to the Protocol on the Statute of the African Court of Justice and Human Rights (Malabo Protocol)[145] to extend the jurisdiction of the yet-to-be-established African Court of Justice and Human Rights to 14 different crimes under international law and transnational crimes; namely, the crime of unconstitutional change of government, piracy,

142 S/RES/256 (2012) 5 July 2012. On 20 December 2012 the Security Council adopted a resolution (S/RES/2085) to authorize the African-led International Support Mission to Mali, an ECOWAS-organized military mission to support Mali in its fight against terrorist and criminal groups in northern Mali.

143 S/RES/2337 (2017) 19 January 2017.

144 https://au.int/sites/default/files/treaties/36396-treaty-0035_-_protocol_on_the_statute_of_the_african_court_of_justice_and_human_rights_e.pdf.

145 https://au.int/sites/default/files/treaties/36398-treaty-0045_-_protocol_on_amendments_to_the_protocol_on_the_statute_of_the_african_court_of_justice_and_human_rights_e.pdf.

corruption, money laundering, illicit exploitation of natural resources, trafficking in drugs, trafficking in persons, trafficking in hazardous wastes, mercenarism, terrorism, war crimes, crimes against humanity, genocide and the crime of aggression. Article 28E of the Malabo Protocol proscribes the crime of 'unconstitutional change of government', defined as

> committing or ordering to be committed the following acts, with the aim of illegally accessing or maintaining power: (a) a putsch or *coup d'état* against a democratically elected government; (b) an intervention by mercenaries to replace a democratically elected government; (c) any replacement of a democratically elected government by the use of armed dissidents or rebels or through political assassination; (d) any refusal by an incumbent government to relinquish power to the winning party or candidate after free, fair and regular elections; (e) any amendment or revision of the constitution or legal instruments, which is an infringement on the principles of democratic change of government or is inconsistent with the constitution; (f) any substantial modification to the electoral laws in the last six months before the elections without the consent of the majority of the political actors.[146]

The Malabo Protocol has not been implemented by any State and appears to have been an attempt to reinforce the political argument that the International Criminal Court's prosecutions of Africans for war crimes, crimes against humanity, genocide and/or the crime of aggression are unnecessary[147] (even though the Malabo Protocol also immunizes incumbent Heads of State or Government and senior State officials).[148]

The Americas

The Santiago Commitment to Democracy and the Renewal of the Inter-American System, adopted by the Organization of American States (OAS) General Assembly in June 1991, gives special priority to representative democracy as an expression of the legitimate and free manifestation of the will of the people.[149]

146 See also Harman van der Wilt, 'Unconstitutional Change of Government: A New Crime within the Jurisdiction of the African Criminal Court' in Charles Jalloh, Kamari Clarke and Vincent Nmehielle (eds), *The African Court of Justice and Human and Peoples' Rights in Context* (CUP 2019) 619–42.

147 See also Eki Yemisi Omorogbe, 'The Crisis of International Criminal Law in Africa: A Regional Regime in Response?' (2019) 66 Netherlands Int'l L Rev 287; Ben Chigara, 'The Quasi-Supranational AU and the International Criminal Court' in Amao, Olivier and Magliveras (eds), *The Emergent African Union Law* 248–67.

148 Art 46A *bis* of the Malabo Protocol reads: 'No charges shall be commenced or continued before the Court against any serving AU Head of State or Government, or anybody acting or entitled to act in such capacity, or other senior State officials based on their functions, during their tenure of office'.

149 OAS Doc OEA/SerP/AG Doc 2734/91, 4 June 1991, Preamble para 4. See also Stephen Schnably, 'Constitutionalism and Democratic Governance in the Inter-American System' in Gregory Fox

Under Article 9 of the 1948 OAS Charter, as amended by the Washington Protocol of 1992,[150] in force since 1997, an OAS Member State whose democratically constituted government has been 'overthrown by force' may be suspended from the exercise of the right to participate in the sessions of the OAS General Assembly, Meeting of Consultation, Councils and Specialized Conferences as well as in the commissions, working groups and any other bodies established. The power to suspend shall be exercised only when diplomatic initiatives undertaken by the OAS to promote the restoration of representative democracy in the affected Member State have been unsuccessful. The decision to suspend or lift the suspension shall be adopted at a special session of the OAS General Assembly by an affirmative vote of two-thirds of the Member States. The suspension notwithstanding, the OAS shall endeavour to undertake additional diplomatic initiatives to contribute to the re-establishment of representative democracy in the affected Member State and the Member which has been subject to suspension shall continue to fulfil its obligations to the OAS.

On 11 September 2001, the OAS adopted the Inter-American Democratic Charter[151] binding on all OAS Member States. Its preamble refers, inter alia, to the 1948 American Declaration on the Rights and Duties of Man[152] and the 1969 American Convention on Human Rights,[153] which contain the values and principles of liberty, equality and social justice that are intrinsic to democracy. The Preamble reaffirms the promotion and protection of human rights as a basic prerequisite for the existence of a democratic society and recognizes the importance of the continuous development and strengthening of the Inter-American human rights system for the consolidation of democracy. Articles 7 through 10 of the Democratic Charter cover the issue of democracy and human rights. Article 7 stipulates that democracy is indispensable for the effective exercise of fundamental freedoms and human rights in their universality, indivisibility and interdependence, embodied in the respective constitutions of States and in Inter-American and international human rights instruments. Article 8 requires OAS Member States to, inter alia, reaffirm their intention to strengthen the Inter-American system for the protection of human rights for the consolidation of democracy in the hemisphere. Article 9 then elaborates that the elimination of all forms of discrimination (especially gender, ethnic and racial discrimination as well as diverse forms of intolerance), the promotion and protection of human rights of indigenous peoples and migrants and the respect for ethnic, cultural and religious diversity in the Americas contribute to the strengthening of democracy and citizen participation. According to Article 10, the promotion and strengthening of democracy require the full and

---

and Brad Roth (eds), *Democratic Governance and International Law* (CUP 2000) 155, 162–7; Stapel, *Regional Organizations and Democracy* 201–36.

150 (1994) 33 ILM 1005, in force 25 September 1997.

151 (2001) 40 ILM 1289.

152 (1949) 43(S3) AJIL 133.

153 1144 UNTS 123, in force 18 July 1978.

effective exercise of workers' rights and the application of core labour standards and democracy is strengthened by improving standards in the workplace and enhancing the quality of life for workers in the hemisphere.

Pursuant to Articles 19 through 21 of the Inter-American Democratic Charter, when a special session of the OAS General Assembly determines there has been an unconstitutional interruption of the democratic order or unconstitutional alteration of the constitutional regime that seriously impairs the democratic order in a Member State and diplomatic initiatives have failed, the special session shall take the decision to suspend the Member State, with immediate effect, from the exercise of its right to participate in the OAS by an affirmative vote of two-thirds of the Member States. However, the suspended Member State shall continue to fulfil its obligations to the OAS, in particular its human rights obligations. Notwithstanding the suspension of the Member State, the OAS will maintain diplomatic initiatives to restore democracy in that State. Article 22 provides for the possibility of lifting the suspension once the situation that led to suspension has been resolved.[154]

Since the entry into force of the OAS 'democratic clauses', there have been two *coups* in the Americas: the eight-hour bloodless military takeover in Ecuador in January 2000 and the military *coup* in Honduras in June 2009.[155] In August 2009 the OAS suspended Honduras' membership before readmitting it two years later after elections were held in that country. Apart from this collective action in response to a *coup*, the OAS has been expressing its collective concern about the deteriorating

154 See also Rubén Perina, 'The Role of the Organization of American States' in Morton Halperin and Mirna Galic (eds), *Protecting Democracy: International Response* (Lexington Books 2005) 127–73.

155 It is debatable whether Bolivia's constitutional crisis in November 2019 was a *coup* when Bolivian President Evo Morales was told by the military and the police to step down subsequent to 21 days of civil unrest following the disputed October 2019 general election. His resignation came hours after the OAS said it had found 'clear manipulation' of the vote, with the OAS Electoral Observation Mission having identified serious irregularities in the conduct of the election and conclusive proof of election fraud, such as forged signatures in electoral records and the presence of an unauthorized Internet server interfering with the vote count. Jeanie Áñez, Second Vice President of the Senate who was the highest-ranking official who had not resigned along with the Cabinet members and leaders of the Legislature, assumed the Presidency with support of the Bolivian Armed Forces despite the fact that the Legislative Assembly that confirmed her Presidency did not have the quorum required by the Bolivian Constitution. After the October 2020 general election, the new President, Luis Arce from Morales' political party, declared Áñez's Presidency a result of a *coup* and illegitimate and had her prosecuted for the crimes of violating laws related to constitutional and legislative procedures for the appointment of a Head of State as well as genocide over two incidents in November 2019 in which 22 supporters of Morales were killed during clashes with the police. Áñez argued that her Presidency was a legitimate constitutional succession during a political crisis pending a new general election. On 10 June 2022, Áñez was convicted by a Bolivian court of making decisions contrary to the constitution and of dereliction of duty. She was sentenced to ten years' imprisonment. Former Armed Forces commander Williams Kaliman and former police commander Vladimir Calderon was each sentenced to ten years in prison, whereas four other former military chiefs received lighter sentences. On 1 May 2021, El Salvador's Legislative Assembly voted to remove several judges of the Supreme Court and the Attorney-General who were opposed to the President of El Salvador. This was considered a *coup* by the President's opponents and was condemned by the OAS.

state of democracy in its Member States. Constant international pressure from the OAS regarding the allegedly undemocratic, autocratic rule and fraudulent elections in Venezuela and Nicaragua has led the former to indicate, in April 2017,[156] and the latter to indicate, in November 2021, their intention to withdraw from the OAS.

The Washington DC-based Inter-American Commission on Human Rights (IACHR), comprising seven independent members serving in their personal capacity, is a permanent principal organ of the OAS mandated to promote and protect human rights in the Americas.

For instance, in 1979 the IACHR conducted a 17-day on-site inquiry in Argentina, with the grudging consent of the Argentine military government. The IACHR recorded thousands of denunciations of the regime's exterminatory assault on left-wing insurgents and anyone suspected of assisting them, whether materially or intellectually. After privately interviewing hundreds of political prisoners and securing testimony from torture victims, among others, the IACHR submitted a report which began the process of regime de-legitimation that culminated in the restoration of democracy four years later. The IACHR's report helped to highlight the military junta's failures especially in the aftermath of Argentina's humiliating defeat in the Falklands/Malvinas War waged by the junta in its attempt to play a popular nationalist card in a desperate effort to restore public support at the time of national economic crisis besetting Argentina.[157]

The IACHR's work is bolstered by the jurisprudence of the Inter-American Court of Human Rights (IACtHR). As early as in 1988, the IACtHR rules that States Parties to the 1969 American Convention on Human Rights have the obligation to investigate, prosecute, punish and rectify grave human rights violations.[158] The IACtHR's judgments have been extensively cited by several domestic courts in the Americas to punish the usurpers of power, as will be discussed in Chapter 5.

ASEAN

The Association of Southeast Asian Nations (ASEAN), set up on 8 August 1967, has ten members: Brunei, Cambodia, Indonesia, Laos, Malaysia, Myanmar, the Philippines, Singapore, Thailand and Vietnam. The most recent *coups* in the ASEAN region as of this writing happened in Thailand on 22 May 2014 and in Myanmar on 1 February 2021.

The principle of non-interference in international affairs of ASEAN Member States is rooted in the fourth preambular paragraph of the 1967 ASEAN Declaration

156 See Antonio Perez, 'Democracy Clauses in the Americas: The Challenges of Venezuela's Withdrawal from the OAS' (2017) 33 American U Int'l L Rev 391, 426–76.

157 Tom Farer, 'I Cried for You, Argentina' (2016) 38 Hum Rts Quarterly 851, 899–906. Farer was a member of the IACHR, helped write its report, presented it to the OAS foreign ministers, testified at the 1985 trial of the junta leaders and then returned periodically to appreciate the evolution of Argentina's transition back to democracy.

158 *Velásquez-Rodríguez v Honduras*, IACtHR, Judgment (29 July 1988) Ser C no 4 para 166. See also *Gomes Lund et al.* para 137.

(or Bangkok Declaration)[159] and Article 2(2)(e) of the 2007 ASEAN Charter.[160] Since ASEAN works on the basis of the 'comfort level' of the ASEAN Member States concerned, bearing in mind their different political systems, ASEAN does not adopt punitive measures such as sanctions against an ASEAN Member State. The ASEAN way of working on the basis of consensus has, at least until 2021, resulted in not naming, shaming or censuring any ASEAN Member State or Government, but in trying instead to help it find a way out of the problem without anybody losing face. ASEAN also does not have either a regional human rights court or an international mechanism to hear individual complaints about human rights violations despite the fact that the ASEAN Charter specifically mentions among its purposes and principles the promotion and protection of, as well as respect for, human rights and fundamental freedoms in its Member States.[161]

Although Article 1(7) of the ASEAN Charter stipulates that one of the purposes of ASEAN is 'to strengthen democracy, enhance good governance and the rule of law', ASEAN took a hands-off stance in the case of *coups* in Thailand. Things are different as regards the most recent *coup* in Myanmar due to the widespread opposition to the junta inside Myanmar and abroad, especially in light of the junta's ruthless suppression of fundamental rights and freedom as well as the high number of deaths and injuries reportedly inflicted by the junta on those opposed to it. The special ASEAN Summit convened on 24 April 2021 at the ASEAN Secretariat in Jakarta, chaired by Brunei, reached the following Five-Point Consensus. First, there shall be immediate cessation of violence in Myanmar and all parties shall exercise utmost restraint. Second, constructive dialogue among all parties concerned shall commence to seek a peaceful solution in the interests of the people. Third, a special envoy of the ASEAN Chair shall facilitate mediation of the dialogue process, with the assistance of the Secretary General of ASEAN. Fourth, ASEAN shall provide humanitarian assistance through the ASEAN Coordinating Centre for Humanitarian Assistance on Disaster Management. Fifth, the ASEAN special envoy and his delegation shall visit Myanmar to meet with all parties concerned.

On 15 October 2021, an online emergency meeting of the ASEAN Foreign Ministers took an unprecedented step to exclude any 'political representative' of Myanmar from future ASEAN Summits and Related Summits, citing insufficient progress in the implementation of the Five-Point Consensus by Myanmar and concerns over Myanmar's commitment, in particular in establishing constructive dialogue among all concerned parties in Myanmar. They noted the importance of the principles enshrined in the ASEAN Charter while at the same time acknowledging that the situation in Myanmar was having an impact on regional security as

159 (1967) 6 ILM 1233.

160 2624 UNTS 223, in force 15 December 2008.

161 Arts 1(7) and 2(i) of the ASEAN Charter. One internationally renowned scholar of constitutional law considers ASEAN's regionalism to be 'sovereignty reinforcing' because of its emphasis on the traditional principles of non-interference, sovereignty and independence, and because international legal cooperation within ASEAN has been increasingly utilized to defend authoritarianism in the Member States (Tom Ginsburg, 'Authoritarian International Law?' (2020) 114 AJIL 221, 243–5).

well as the unity, credibility and centrality of ASEAN as a rule-based organization. There were competing claims between the junta and the 'National Unity Government' set up by those opposed to the junta to represent Myanmar at the upcoming ASEAN Summits. The emergency meeting, therefore, reaffirmed the principle of non-interference in political affairs of another ASEAN Member State and, after noting the 'reservations' (that is, the dissenting vote) from the Myanmar representative to that emergency meeting, decided to invite only a 'non-political representative' from Myanmar to the upcoming Summits so as to allow Myanmar the space to restore its internal peace and stability and return to normalcy. The 'non-political representative' is understood to mean a senior career civil servant in the relevant Ministry of Myanmar who is not a political appointee. Myanmar has refused to send any non-political representative to attend the Summits and, as a consequence, has been excluded from meetings in which 'political representatives' from Myanmar were normally invited to attend before the *coup*.[162]

Commonwealth

The Commonwealth is a voluntary association of 54 'independent and equal countries'—19 of them are in Africa, eight in Asia, 13 in the Americas and the Caribbean, three in Europe (i.e., Cyprus, Malta and the United Kingdom) and 11 in the Pacific and Oceania. Although the Commonwealth's roots go back to the British Empire, today any country can join the modern Commonwealth, and the latest country to join the Commonwealth was Rwanda, in 2009.

On 12 November 1995 the Commonwealth Heads of Government meeting in New Zealand issued the Millbrook Commonwealth Action Programme on the Harare Declaration.[163] They recalled that at Harare, Zimbabwe, in 1991, they had pledged to work for the protection and promotion of the fundamental political values of the Commonwealth; namely, democracy, democratic processes and institutions which reflect national circumstances, fundamental human rights, the rule of law and the independence of judiciary and just and honest government. During their Retreat at Millbrook, New Zealand, they decided to adopt this Commonwealth Action Programme to fulfil more effectively the commitments contained in the Harare Commonwealth Declaration. This Programme is in three parts: advancing Commonwealth fundamental political values; promoting sustainable development; and facilitating consensus building, the first of which is relevant to our

162 However, the Myanmar junta's Minister of Defence participated in person at the meeting of ASEAN Defence Ministers, held in Cambodia on 22 June 2022, despite the fact that Singapore, the Philippines, Indonesia and Malaysia had urged Cambodia, ASEAN's chair for the year 2022, to exclude the Myanmar junta until there was progress in implementing the Five-Point Consensus. This was the first and, as of this writing, only participation by a 'political representative' from Myanmar in an ASEAN meeting since the October 2021 decision by the ASEAN Foreign Ministers.

163 https://thecommonwealth.org/sites/default/files/inline/Millbrook-Commonwealth-Action-Programme-on-Harare-Declaration.pdf.

discussion here. The Programme states unequivocally that in the event of an unconstitutional overthrow of a democratically elected government, appropriate steps should be taken to express the collective concern of Commonwealth countries and to encourage the restoration of democracy within a reasonable time frame. These include: immediate public expression by the Commonwealth Secretary-General of the Commonwealth's collective disapproval of any such infringement of the Harare principles; early contact by the Secretary-General with the de facto government, followed by continued good offices and appropriate technical assistance to facilitate an early restoration of democracy; encouraging bilateral démarches by Member States, especially those within the region, both to express disapproval and to support early restoration of democracy; appointment of an envoy or a group of eminent Commonwealth representatives where, following the Secretary-General's contacts with the authorities concerned, such a mission is deemed beneficial in reinforcing the Commonwealth's good offices role; stipulation of up to two years as the time frame for the restoration of democracy where the institutions are not in place to permit the holding of elections within, say, a maximum of six months; pending restoration of democracy, exclusion of the Government concerned from participation at ministerial-level meetings of the Commonwealth; suspension of participation at all Commonwealth meetings and of Commonwealth technical assistance if acceptable progress is not recorded by the Government concerned after a period of two years; and consideration of appropriate further bilateral and multilateral measures by all Member States (e.g., limitation of government-to-government contacts, people-to-people measures, trade restrictions, and, in exceptional cases, suspension from the Commonwealth), to reinforce the need for change in the event that the Government concerned chooses to leave the Commonwealth and/or persists in violating the principles of the Harare Commonwealth Declaration even after two years. A Commonwealth Ministerial Action Group on the Harare Declaration is established to deal with serious or persistent violations of the principles contained in that Declaration. The Group will be convened by the Secretary-General and will comprise the Foreign Ministers of eight countries, supplemented as appropriate by one or two additional ministerial representatives from the region concerned. It will be the Group's task to assess the nature of the infringement and recommend measures for collective Commonwealth action aimed at the speedy restoration of democracy and constitutional rule. The composition, terms of reference and operation of the Group will be reviewed by the Heads of Government every two years.

Since the adoption of the Millbrook Commonwealth Action Programme, the Commonwealth has twice suspended Pakistan—from 19 October 1999, after the 12 October 1999 *coup*, to 22 May 2004 and from 22 November 2007 to 22 May 2008. The second suspension came after Pakistan had failed to meet a deadline for restoration of democracy and rule of law in the country. The Commonwealth has also suspended Fiji twice—from 6 June 2000, after the 19 May 2000 *coup*, to 20 December 2001 and from 8 December 2006, after the 5 December 2006 *coup*, to 26 September 2014. Fiji's suspension imposed in December 2006 merely excluded Fiji from Commonwealth ministerial meetings. On 1 September 2009 the suspension was extended in full, to include the exclusion of Fiji from all Commonwealth meetings, sporting events and the technical assistance programme (with an exception for assistance in re-establishing democracy). This full suspension resulted from Fiji's failure to meet the deadline set by the Commonwealth on taking steps toward holding 'credible elections' by October 2010. The Fijian *coup* leader insisted Fiji would adhere to its so-called roadmap to elections in 2014, four years later than the deadline.[164]

The Commonwealth interceded when there was an allegation of unconstitutional change of government in the Maldives in 2012. It signed an agreement with the Government of the Maldives on 15 May 2012 for the latter to set up a national commission of inquiry entrusted with the independent and impartial investigations of the following issues: the events that transpired in the Maldives from 14 January 2012 to 8 February 2012, the change of government on 7 February 2012, whether the resignation of the then President Nasheed was illegally coerced and whether the government changed legally on 7 February 2012. The final report of the National Commission of Inquiry concluded that the change of President on 7 February 2012 was legal and constitutional; the events on 6 and 7 February 2012 were, in large measure, reactions to the actions of President Nasheed; the resignation of President Nasheed was voluntary and of his own free will, and was not caused by any illegal coercion or intimidation; and there were acts of police brutality on 6, 7 and 8 February 2012 that had to be investigated and pursued further by the relevant authorities. With regard to the idea that there was a '*coup d'état*', nothing in the Maldives changed in constitutional terms—indeed, the Constitution was precisely followed as prescribed. Moreover, in terms of the democratic intent and legitimacy of the authority of the Presidency, as foreseen in the Constitution, President Waheed properly succeeded President Nasheed.[165] The UN Secretary-General urged all parties to accept the findings of the Commission and begin the process of national dialogue aimed at national reconciliation to resolve the political problems facing the country.

Concluding remarks

Judges of domestic courts called upon to rule on legal issues concerning unconstitutional usurpation of power have resorted to various doctrines/principles to reach judgments in these cases. Some of them proceed with judicial audacity, others with judicial pragmatism and yet others with the combination of both.

164 The general elections were held on 17 September 2014. Apart from the Commonwealth, Fiji had been suspended from the 16-nation Pacific Islands Forum in May 2009 after the Fijian *coup* leader had broken an earlier promise to hold elections by March 2009. Fiji was also subjected to sanctions from the EU, United States, Australia and New Zealand. See also Rognvald Leask, '"The Commonwealth Walks Alongside You": Supporting Democracy in the South-West Pacific' (2008) Round Table 839.

165 Report of the Commission of National Inquiry, Maldives, 30 August 2012, https://maldivesindependent.com/files/2015/03/CONI-Report-20121.pdf.

When the courts in *Jilani, Liasi* and *Mitchell* held that the respective *coups* were unlawful, the usurpers were no longer in power.

The Court of Appeal of Fiji in *Prasad* was unexceptionably brave to declare the 29 May 2000 military *coup* at issue in that case unlawful although the usurper was still in power. The *Prasad* judgment did lead to the immediate return to democracy in Fiji. However, it may be impractical to expect every domestic court to follow *Prasad*. In fact, after the Fijian Court of Appeal's ruling in *Qarase v Bainimarama*[166] that the December 2006 military *coup* was unlawful, as will be discussed in Chapter 4, and refused leave by the Interim Government installed by the *coup* to appeal to the Fijian Supreme Court, on the very next day Fiji's President abrogated the Constitution and revoked the commission of all judges.

As a pragmatic alternative, when the usurper is still in full control of the country judges should at least, as some courts have done, set a reasonable timeline for the country to return to democracy, explaining why, based on their impartial reasoning, this timeline is imperative. They must also exert their utmost efforts to uphold fundamental rights and freedoms in spite of the junta's directives to the contrary. An excellent example is the Pakistani Supreme Court's insistence in *Zafar Ali Shah* that the Court retained its judicial power to review laws and decrees enacted by the military regime because powers of the judicial review vested in Pakistan's Superior Courts under the 1973 Constitution of Pakistan could not be taken away even by a *coup*.

Judgments of domestic courts which may be considered as representing best practices do not treat necessity, effectiveness/efficacy and so forth as stand-alone tests of legitimacy of a *coup*. Several of them demand, for instance, that the regime must have genuine popular acceptance and widespread international approval, and that the constitution is only partially held in abeyance by the usurper without also nullifying fundamental rights and freedoms of citizens, which constitute the welfare of the people. Although *Matovu* and *Prasad* seem to be the only known judgments requiring that, for a *coup* to be validated, it must, among other things, receive the approval of the international community, in practice States on their own and/or collectively through international organizations react to *coups* in such a way that international approval plays a significant role in this respect. Despite the fact that international reaction reflects *realpolitik* in international relations, the widespread international opposition to a *coup*, especially in a competent international organization, negates any presumption that the *coup* is legitimate and alerts domestic judges in the country concerned to ensure they exert their utmost efforts to judicially scrutinize the regime's conduct. For instance, judges of domestic courts in the country where a *coup* takes place cannot simply ignore the UN Security Council's condemnations of and demands for accountability regarding atrocities perpetrated by the junta, as in the Statement of the President of the UN Security Council on 29 December 2021 condemning the reported killing of no fewer than 35 people,

166 [2009] Fiji Law Rep (Court of Appeal) 9.

including four children and two staff members of Save the Children, in Kayah State, Myanmar, on 24 December 2021, for which the Security Council stressed 'the need to ensure accountability'.[167]

By and large, it is not necessarily a crime for judges to uphold the legitimacy of the unconstitutional usurpation of power. They can invoke a variety of justifiable reasons and oft-cited doctrines/principles in their discharge of judicial duties in this matter. Besides, there are practical considerations for judges to bear in mind during the time when the nation faces a national crisis, real or conjured up by the usurper, the *fait accompli* of the taking over of the government and the need for the Judiciary to stay in power to keep the usurper's acts under strict judicial scrutiny. Only when judges fail to discharge their judicial duty to protect the fundamental rights and freedoms and punish perpetrators of crimes of international concern, as will be explained in the following chapters, may they be held accountable for their respective roles in the repressive regime.

167 UN Security Council Press Statement on Situations in Myanmar, SC/14754 (29 December 2021).

3

PERMISSIBLE PARAMETERS FOR JUDGES IN POST-*COUP* SUPPRESSION OF FUNDAMENTAL RIGHTS AND FREEDOMS

This chapter begins by discussing the permissible parameters for a post-*coup* regime to suppress fundamental rights and freedoms protected under international conventions and rules of customary international law binding on the country in question. In this connection, the proscription of crimes of international concern that has attained the status of peremptory norm (*jus cogens*) under customary international law of universal application is explained.

The chapter then discusses the lawfulness or otherwise of the declaration of state of emergency underpinning the suspension or even complete annulment of fundamental rights and freedoms, as determined by competent international bodies such as regional human rights courts and human rights treaty bodies monitoring the implementation by States Parties to the relevant human rights treaties. The role and legitimacy of military tribunals as well as law enforcement measures usually utilized by the regime to sustain its rule are also critically examined. The chapter ends by criticizing as unjustifiable the hands-off stance adopted in some jurisdictions which considers that judicial scrutiny of the usurper's acts gives rise to 'political questions' not justiciable in a court of law.

International conventions and rules of customary international law on the protection of fundamental rights and freedoms

Nation States become parties to various human rights treaties for certain reasons. Some want to belong to, and be recognized as members of, a club of States with respectable human rights reputations.[1] For others, their national constituencies are

1 See the acculturation analysis in the context of human rights promotion in Ryan Goodman and Derek Jinks, *Socializing States: Promoting Human Rights through International Law* (OUP 2013) 25–9, 187–8.

DOI: 10.4324/9781003358428-3

influential enough to demand they accept the obligations arising from the human rights treaties in question. When States do not comply with their international human rights obligations, enforcing these obligations, like enforcing other areas of international law, is quite different from enforcing domestic law. Officially, there is no world police to enforce international law, and, in reality, the more politically powerful a nation State, the more likely it can escape punishment for violation of international law. A State Party to an international human rights treaty may bring the violation of the treaty by another State Party before a competent international court, such as the International Court of Justice (ICJ),[2] where the court has jurisdiction. There are also numerous non-judicial mechanisms, either individually or in combination, to enforce human rights treaty obligations. A State may be held *accountable* before an international body, such as an international human rights treaty body with competent jurisdiction. The State could be *induced* to comply with its human rights treaty obligations in return for conditional foreign aid. Domestic movements may *pressure* the government of the State to be more responsive to human rights treaty obligations. The State may find it necessary to *adapt* itself *to external factors*, such as the policies of foreign States or the positions of international organizations, concerning human rights under the treaties by which it has expressed consent to be bound. The most drastic form of enforcement is the use of *coercive means* like economic sanctions or even the use of force by a foreign State or group of States in the name of 'humanitarian intervention' against the State accused of serious violations of human rights.[3] Most of the efforts by other States

2 Nigel Rodley, 'The International Court of Justice and Human Rights Treaty Bodies' in Mads Andenas and Eirik Bjorge (eds), *A Farewell to Fragmentation: Reassertion and Convergence in International Law* (CUP 2015) 87–108; Vera Gowlland-Debbas, 'The ICJ and the Challenges of Human Rights Law' ibid 105–45.

3 Charles Beitz, *The Idea of Human Rights* (OUP 2009) 33–42; Christian Tomuschat, *Human Rights: Between Idealism and Realism* (3rd edn, OUP 2014) 326–7; Courtney Hillebrecht, *Domestic Politics and International Human Rights Tribunals* (CUP 2014). On humanitarian intervention, see Edward Kwakwa, 'Internal Conflicts in Africa: Is There a Right of Humanitarian Action' (1994) 2 African YBIL 9, 12–22; Fernando Tesón, *Humanitarian Intervention: An Inquiry into Law and Morality* (2nd edn, Transnational Publishers 1997); Simon Chesterman, *Just War or Just Peace?: Humanitarian Intervention and International Law* (OUP 2001); J.L. Holzgrefe and Robert Keohane (eds), *Humanitarian Intervention: Ethical, Legal and Political Dilemmas* (CUP 2003); Anne Orford, *Reading Humanitarian Intervention: Human Rights and the Use of Force in International Law* (CUP 2003); Aidan Hehir, *Humanitarian Intervention: An Introduction* (2nd edn, Palgrave Macmillan 2013); Fernando Tesón and Bas van der Vossen, *Debating Humanitarian Intervention: Should We Try to Save Strangers?* (OUP 2017); Christine Chinkin and Mary Kaldor, *International Law and New Wars* (CUP 2017) 175–226; Christine Gray, *International Law and the Use of Force* (4th edn, OUP 2018) 40–64; Samuel Moyn, *Human Rights and the Uses of History* (Verso 2014) ch 3; Sabine Carey, Mark Gibney and Steven Poe, *The Politics of Human Rights: The Quest for Dignity* (CUP 2010) 165–93; Fabian Klose, 'Humanitarian Intervention as an Entangled History of Humanitarianism and Human Rights' in Michael Barnett (ed.), *Humanitarianism and Human Rights: A World of Differences?* (CUP 2020) 127–39; Dapo Akande and Katie Johnston, 'Implications of the Diversity of the Rules on the Use of Force for Change in the Law' (2021) 32 EJIL 679; Andrew Clapham, *War* (OUP 2021) 161–8; Simona Ross, 'US Justifications for the Use of Force in Syria through the Prism of the Responsibility to Protect' (2021) 8 J Use of Force & Int'l Law 233.

to promote and defend human rights elsewhere are perceived to be political and pragmatic rather than legal in nature.[4]

There are ten bodies entrusted with monitoring the implementation of the nine major international human rights treaties; namely, the Human Rights Committee (CCPR), the Committee on Economic, Social and Cultural Rights (CESCR), the Committee on the Elimination of Racial Discrimination (CERD), the Committee on the Elimination of Discrimination against Women (CEDAW), the Committee Against Torture (CAT), the Subcommittee on Prevention of Torture (SPT), the Committee on the Rights of the Child (CRC), the Committee on the Protection of the Rights of all Migrant Workers and Members of their Families (CMW), the Committee on the Rights of Persons with Disabilities (CRPD) and the Committee on Enforced Disappearances (CED).[5] Unlike the other nine treaty bodies, the SPT discharges its preventive mandate pursuant to the 2002 Optional Protocol to the Convention against Torture[6] by visiting places of detention and advising National Preventive Mechanisms of States Parties to the Convention against Torture. As of this writing, the other treaty bodies except the CMW are competent to receive and consider petitions from individuals. The treaty monitoring bodies except the SPT issue General Comments and recommendations addressed to all State Parties; concluding observations and concluding comments addressed to a particular State Party; and views/decisions, suggestions and recommendations in response to individual communications or petitions, where applicable.[7]

General Comments of treaty bodies inform States Parties how each treaty body interprets the conventions under its competence. The other mechanisms require cooperation of the States Parties concerned and therefore resemble dialogues between the treaty body and the States in question, with the former providing constructive feedback at the end of the process. The substance of the findings, concluding observations or comments, views or decisions, suggestions or recommendations as well as General Comments of these human rights treaty-monitoring

4 Beitz, *The Idea of Human Rights* 33–42; Tomuschat, *Human Rights* 326–7; Kriangsak Kittichaisaree, *International Human Rights Law and Diplomacy* (Edward Elgar Publishing 2020) 205–57. Cf. Mark Burgstaller, *Theories of Compliance with International Law* (Martinus Nijhoff 2005).

5 The respective international human rights treaties monitored by them are: the 1966 International Covenant on Civil and Political Rights (999 UNTS 171); 1966 International Covenant on Economic, Social and Cultural Rights (993 UNTS 3); 1965 International Convention on the Elimination of All Forms of Racial Discrimination (660 UNTS 195); 1979 Convention on the Elimination of All Forms of Discrimination Against Women (1249 UNTS 13); 1984 Convention against Torture and Other Cruel, Inhuman or Degrading Treatment or Punishment (1465 UNTS 85); 1989 Convention on the Rights of the Child (1577 UNTS 3); 1990 International Convention on the Protection of the Rights of All Migrant Workers and Members of their Families (2220 UNTS 3); 2006 Convention on the Rights of Persons with Disabilities (2515 UNTS 3); and 2006 International Convention for the Protection of All Persons from Enforced Disappearance (2716 UNTS 3).

6 2375 UNTS 237.

7 For a general overview of the human rights treaty body system, see Sarah Cleveland, 'Human Rights Treaty Bodies in the Age of Connectivity' in Olivier de Frouville (ed.), *Le système de protection des droits de l'homme des Nations Unies* (A. Pedone 2018) 79; Kittichaisaree, *International Human Rights Law and Diplomacy* 83–9.

bodies has been duly taken into consideration by domestic courts dispensing internal justice in the context of repression of freedoms and rights, including acts amounting to crimes of international concern, in the aftermath of unconstitutional usurpation of power.[8]

The ICJ notes that the CCPR set up under the 1966 International Covenant on Civil and Political Rights (ICCPR) has, since its inception, built up a considerable body of interpretative case law. Although the ICJ is in no way obliged, in the exercise of its judicial functions, to model its own interpretation of the ICCPR on that of the CCPR, the ICJ believes it should ascribe great weight to the interpretation adopted by this independent body set up specifically to supervise the application of the ICCPR. The point here is to achieve the necessary clarity and the essential consistency of international law, as well as legal security, to which both the individuals with guaranteed rights and the States obliged to comply with treaty obligations are entitled.[9]

The treaty bodies that are the most directly relevant in the context of unconstitutional usurpation of power are the CCPPR, CAT and CED, although repression by the usurper frequently violates the rights of the child and adversely discriminates against women based on their gender as well.

Rights and freedoms under threat by the state of emergency are essentially those protected under the ICCPR,[10] which has 173 parties as of this writing. Civil and political rights comprise the rights of physical and spiritual autonomy, rights of fair treatment and rights to participate meaningfully in the political process. Within these three broad categories are the rights to life and freedom from torture, inhuman or degrading treatment or punishment; freedom of movement; right to privacy; freedom of religion, belief and thought; right to a fair trial and equal protection of the law; freedom from discrimination; right to vote and to stand for election; and freedom of assembly and association, to name but a few.[11]

Article 2 of the ICCPR obligates States Parties to undertake to respect and to ensure to all individuals within its territory and subject to its jurisdiction the rights recognized in the ICCPR, without distinction of any kind, such as race, colour, sex, language, religion, *political or other opinion*, national or social origin, property, birth or other status. In this regard, each State Party undertakes: (a) to ensure that any person whose rights or freedoms as herein recognized are violated shall have an effective remedy, notwithstanding that the violation has been committed by persons acting in an official capacity; (b) to ensure that any person claiming such a remedy

8 Cf. Machiko Kanetake, 'Giving Due Consideration: A Normative Pathway between UN Human Rights Treaty-Monitoring Bodies and Domestic Courts' in Nico Kirsch (ed.), *Entangled Legalities Beyond the State* (CUP 2021) 133, 134, 138–52, 156–9.

9 *Ahmadou Sadio Diallo (Republic of Guinea v Democratic Republic of the Congo)* [2010] ICJ Rep 639, 664 [66].

10 See also Khalifa Alfadhel, *The Right to Democracy in International Law Between Procedure, Substance and the Philosophy of John Rawls* (Routledge 2017) ch 3.

11 Sarah Joseph, 'Civil and Political Rights' in Mashood Baderin and Manisuli Ssenyonjo (eds), *International Human Rights Law: Six Decades after the UDHR and Beyond* (Ashgate 2010) 90.

shall have his right thereto determined by competent judicial, administrative or legislative authorities, or by any other competent authority provided for by the legal system of the State, and to develop the possibilities of judicial remedy; and (c) to ensure that the competent authorities shall enforce such remedies when granted.

Article 6 of the ICCPR protects the inherent right to life of every human being, which shall be protected by law. No one shall be arbitrarily deprived of his life. It adds, inter alia, that in countries which have not abolished the death penalty, sentence of death may be imposed only for the most serious crimes in accordance with the law in force at the time of the commission of the crime and not contrary to the provisions of the ICCPR and to the 1948 Convention on the Prevention and Punishment of the Crime of Genocide.[12] This death penalty can only be carried out pursuant to a final judgment rendered by a competent court.

As for torture which is often used by repressive regimes, Article 7 of the ICCPR provides that no one shall be subjected to torture or to cruel, inhuman or degrading treatment or punishment. In particular, no one shall be subjected without his free consent to medical or scientific experimentation.

Pursuant to Article 9 of the ICCPR, everyone has the right to liberty and security of person. No one shall be subjected to arbitrary arrest or detention. No one shall be deprived of his liberty except on such grounds and in accordance with such procedure as are established by law. Anyone who is arrested shall be informed, at the time of arrest, of the reasons for his arrest and shall be promptly informed of any charges against him. Anyone arrested or detained on a criminal charge shall be brought promptly before a judge or other officer authorized by law to exercise judicial power and shall be entitled to trial within a reasonable time or to release. It shall not be the general rule that persons awaiting trial shall be detained in custody, but release may be subject to guarantees to appear for trial, at any other stage of the judicial proceedings, and, should occasion arise, for execution of the judgment. Anyone who is deprived of his liberty by arrest or detention shall be entitled to take proceedings before a court, in order that that court may decide without delay on the lawfulness of his detention and order his release if the detention is not lawful. Anyone who has been the victim of unlawful arrest or detention shall have an enforceable right to compensation.

Article 10 of the ICCPR requires all persons deprived of their liberty to be treated with humanity and with respect for the inherent dignity of the human person.

Article 12 protects the freedom of movement. Everyone lawfully within the territory of a State shall, within that territory, have the right to liberty of movement and freedom to choose his residence. Everyone shall be free to leave any country, including his own. The said rights shall not be subject to any restrictions except those which are provided by law, are necessary to protect national security, public order (*ordre public*), public health or morals or the rights and freedoms of others, and

12 8 UNTS 277, in force 12 January 1951. This will be discussed next.

are consistent with the other rights recognized in the ICCPR. Nonetheless, no one shall be arbitrarily deprived of the right to enter his own country.

Article 14 of the ICCPR has a long list of measures to protect the right to equality before courts and tribunals and the right to a fair trial. By virtue of Article 14(1), all persons shall be equal before the courts and tribunals. In the determination of any criminal charge against him, or of his rights and obligations in a suit at law, everyone shall be entitled to a fair and public hearing by a competent, independent and impartial tribunal established by law. The press and the public may be excluded from all or part of a trial for reasons of morals, public order (*ordre public*) or national security in a democratic society, or when the interest of the private lives of the parties so requires, or to the extent strictly necessary in the opinion of the court in special circumstances where publicity would prejudice the interests of justice; but any judgment rendered in a criminal case or in a suit at law shall be made public except where the interest of juvenile persons otherwise requires or the proceedings concern matrimonial disputes or the guardianship of children. Article 14(2) provides that everyone charged with a criminal offence shall have the right to be presumed innocent until proved guilty according to law. Pursuant to Article 14(3), in the determination of any criminal charge against him, everyone shall be entitled to the following minimum guarantees, in full equality: (a) to be informed promptly and in detail in a language which he understands of the nature and cause of the charge against him; (b) to have adequate time and facilities for the preparation of his defence and to communicate with counsel of his own choosing; (c) to be tried without undue delay; (d) to be tried in his presence, and to defend himself in person or through legal assistance of his own choosing; to be informed, if he does not have legal assistance, of this right; and to have legal assistance assigned to him, in any case where the interests of justice so require, and without payment by him in any such case if he does not have sufficient means to pay for it; (e) to examine, or have examined, the witnesses against him and to obtain the attendance and examination of witnesses on his behalf under the same conditions as witnesses against him; (f) to have the free assistance of an interpreter if he cannot understand or speak the language used in court; and (g) not to be compelled to testify against himself or to confess guilt. Article 14(4) requires, in the case of juvenile persons, the procedure to be such as will take account of their age and the desirability of promoting their rehabilitation. Under Article 14(5), everyone convicted of a crime shall have the right to his conviction and sentence being reviewed by a higher tribunal according to law. According to Article 14(6), when a person has by a final decision been convicted of a criminal offence and when subsequently his conviction has been reversed or he has been pardoned on the ground that a new or newly discovered fact shows conclusively that there has been a miscarriage of justice, the person who has suffered punishment as a result of such conviction shall be compensated according to law, unless it is proved that the non-disclosure of the unknown fact in time is wholly or partly attributable to him. Article 14(7) stipulates that no one shall be liable to be tried or punished again for an offence for which he has already been finally convicted or acquitted in accordance with the law and penal procedure of each country.

The principle of legality is enshrined in Article 15 of the ICCPR. Article 17 of the ICCPR provides that no one shall be subjected to arbitrary or unlawful interference with his privacy, family, home or correspondence, nor to unlawful attacks on his honour and reputation, and that everyone has the right to the protection of the law against such interference or attacks. According to Article 19, everyone shall have the right to hold opinions without interference, as well as the right to freedom of expression which includes freedom to seek, receive and impart information and ideas of all kinds, regardless of frontiers, either orally, in writing or in print, in the form of art, or through any other media of his choice. The exercise of the right to freedom of expression carries with it special duties and responsibilities. It may therefore be subject to certain restrictions, but these shall only be such as are provided by law and are necessary: (a) for respect of the rights or reputations of others; (b) for the protection of national security or of public order (*ordre public*), or of public health or morals.

The right to freedom of peaceful assembly is recognized in Article 21 of the ICCPR. No restrictions may be placed on the exercise of this right other than those imposed in conformity with the law and which are *necessary in a democratic society* in the interests of national security or public safety, public order (*ordre public*), the protection of public health or morals or the protection of the rights and freedoms of others. Peaceful protests are also protected by the right to freedom of association, the right to freedom of expression and the right to participate in public affairs (Articles 19, 22 and 25 of the ICCPR). The CCPR's General Comment No 37 on the right to peaceful assembly clarifies that violent conduct by some individuals is not sufficient to declare an assembly non-peaceful in general, nor may the violent acts of particular individuals be attributed to other participants in the assembly. Violence against participants in a peaceful assembly by the authorities, or by *agents provocateurs* acting on their behalf, does not render the assembly non-peaceful, either. The same applies to violence by members of the public aimed at the assembly, or by participants in counterdemonstrations. The conduct of specific participants in an assembly may be deemed violent if authorities can present credible evidence that, before or during the event, those participants are inciting others to use violence, and such actions are likely to cause violence; that the participants have violent intentions and plan to act on them; or that violence on their part is imminent. Isolated instances of such conduct will not suffice to taint an entire assembly as non-peaceful, but where it is manifestly widespread within the assembly, participation in the gathering as such is no longer protected under Article 21 of the ICCPR.[13]

Article 25 of the ICCPR protects not only the right of participation in public affairs, but also the right to vote. Every citizen shall have the right and the opportunity, without any of the distinctions mentioned in Article 2 and without unreasonable restrictions: (a) to take part in the conduct of public affairs, directly or through

13 CCPR/C/GC/37 (17 September 2020) paras 17–19.

freely chosen representatives; (b) to vote and to be elected at genuine periodic elections which shall be by universal and equal suffrage and shall be held by secret ballot, guaranteeing the free expression of the will of the electors; and (c) to have access, on general terms of equality, to public service in his country.

Table 3.1 shows which States are party to the ICCPR when unconstitutional usurpation of power takes place in the respective States.

TABLE 3.1 Unconstitutional usurpation of power in States Parties to the ICCPR

Date of accession/ratification	*Unconstitutional usurpation(s) of power*
Algeria: 12 Sept 1989	11 Jan 1992
Azerbaijan: 13 Aug 1992	9 June 1993
Burkina Faso: 4 Jan 1999	30 Oct 2014; 24 Jan 2022; 30 Sept 2022
Cambodia: 26 May 1992	5 July 1997
Chad: 9 Jun 1995	Apr 2021
Central African Rep: 8 May 1981	1 Sept 1981; 15 Mar 2003; 24 Mar 2013
Chile: 10 Feb 1972	11 Sept 1973
Côte d'Ivoire: 26 Mar 1992	24 Dec 1999
Cyprus: 2 Apr 1969	15 July 1974
DR Congo: 1 Nov 1976	16 May 1997
Ecuador: 6 Mar 1969	Feb 1972; Jan 2000
Egypt: 14 Jan 1982	3 Jul 2013
The Gambia: 22 Mar 1979	22 Jul 1994
Guinea: 24 Jan 1978	3 Apr 1984; 24 Dec 2008; 5 Sept 2021
Guinea-Bissau: 1 Nov 2010	12 Apr 2012
Haiti: 6 Feb 1991	30 Sept 1991; Feb 2004
Honduras: 25 Aug 1997	28 Jun 2009
Madagascar: 21 June 1971	11 Oct 1972; 5 Feb 1975; 17 Mar 2009
Mali: 16 Jul 1974	26 Mar 1991; 22 Mar 2012; 18 Aug 2020; 24 May 2021
Mauritania: 17 Nov 2004	3 Aug 2005; 6 Aug 2008
Nepal: 14 May 1991	Feb 2005
Niger: 7 Mar 1986	27 Jan 1996; 9 Apr 1999; 18 Feb 2010
Nigeria: 19 Jul 1993	17 Nov 1993
Peru: 28 Apr 1978	5 Apr 1992
Poland: 18 Mar 1977	13 Dec 1981
Rep Congo: 5 Oct 1983	25 Oct 1997
Sierra Leone: 23 Aug 1996	25 May 1997
Somalia: 24 Jan 1990	26 Jan 1991
Sudan: 18 Mar 1986	30 June 1989; 11 Apr 2019; 25 Oct 2021
Suriname: 28 Dec 1976	25 Feb 1980; 13 Aug 1980; 24 Dec 1990
Syria: 21 Apr 1969	13 Nov 1970
Thailand: 29 Oct 1996	19 Sept 2006; 22 May 2014
Tunisia: 18 Mar 1969	7 Nov 1987; 25 Jul 2021
Uruguay: 1 Apr 1970	27 Jun 1973
Yemen: 9 Feb 1987	2014–15; 2018
Zimbabwe: 13 May 1991	14 Nov 2017

A majority of States Parties to the ICCPR have become parties to the Optional Protocol to the ICCPR[14] by a separate expression of consent to be bound. This Optional Protocol enables the CCPR to receive and consider communications from individuals claiming to be victims of violations of any of the rights under the ICCPR. If the CCCPR finds a violation in a particular case, the State Party to the Optional Protocol is asked to remedy that violation, pursuant to its obligations in Article 2 of the ICCPR. The recommended remedy may be in the form of payment of compensation, repeal or amendment of legislation and/or the release of a detained person. The CCPR's designated Special Rapporteur for follow-up on Views will then pursue the implementation of the CCPR's finding in the case, including visits to the State Party in question.

Table 3.2 shows the States that have experienced unconstitutional usurpation of power which accepted this individual complaint mechanism at the time of the usurpation and during the junta-installed regimes.

In addition to the proscription against torture in Article 7 of the ICCPR, torture is covered in a discrete convention, the Convention against Torture, which defines 'torture' as

> any act by which severe pain or suffering, whether physical or mental, is intentionally inflicted on a person for such purposes as obtaining from him

TABLE 3.2 *Coup*-installed regimes that have accepted the individual complaint mechanism under the Optional Protocol to the ICCPR

Date of ratification/accession to the Optional Protocol to the ICCPR	*Date(s) of usurpation of power*
Algeria: 12 Sept 1989	Jan 1992
Chad: 9 Jun 1995	April 2021
Central African Rep: May 1981	Sept 1981; Mar 2003; Mar 2013
Congo (Rep of): Oct 1983	Nov 1989; Sept 1995; Apr 1999
DR Congo: Nov 1976	May 1997
Ecuador: Mar 1969	1972; 2000
The Gambia: Jun 1988	Jul 1994
Guinea: Jun 1993	Dec 2008; Sept 2021
Honduras: Jun 2005	2009
Madagascar: Jun 1971	Oct 1972; Feb 1975; Mar 2009
Mali: Oct 2001	Mar 2012; Aug 2020; May 2021
Niger: Mar 1986	Jan 1996; Apr 1999; Feb 2010
Peru: Oct 1980	1992
Sierra Leone: Aug 1996	May 1997
Somalia: Jan 1990	Jan 1991
Suriname: Dec 1976	Feb 1980; Aug 1980; Dec 1990
Tunisia: Jun 2011	Jul 2021
Uruguay: Apr 1970	Jun 1973

14 999 UNTS 171, in force 23 March 1976.

> or a third person information or a confession, punishing him for an act he or a third person has committed or is suspected of having committed, or intimidating or coercing him or a third person, or for any reason based on discrimination of any kind, when such pain or suffering is inflicted by or at the instigation of or with the consent or acquiescence of a public official or other person acting in an official capacity.

However, it does not include pain or suffering arising only from, inherent in or incidental to lawful sanctions. The proscription of torture under the 1984 Convention is without prejudice to any international instrument or national legislation which does or may contain provisions of wider application.

Pursuant to Article 20 of the Convention against Torture, if CAT receives *reliable information* which appears to it to contain well-founded indications that torture is being systematically practised in the territory of a State Party, CAT shall invite that State Party to cooperate in the examination of the information and, to this end, to submit observations with regard to the information concerned. Thereafter, CAT may, if it decides this is warranted, designate one or more of its members to make a confidential inquiry and to report to CAT with the cooperation of the State Party concerned, including a visit to its territory. After examining the findings of its member(s), CAT shall transmit these findings to the State Party together with any comments or suggestions which seem appropriate in view of the situation. All the aforesaid CAT proceedings shall be confidential, and at all stages of the proceedings the cooperation of the State Party shall be sought. After such proceedings have been completed with regard to an inquiry made, CAT may, after consultations with the State Party concerned, decide to include a summary account of the results of the proceedings in its annual report to all States Parties to the Convention against Torture.

By virtue of Article 21 of the Convention against Torture, a State Party may at any time declare that it recognizes CAT's competence to receive and consider *communications from a State Party* claiming that another State Party is not fulfilling its obligations under this Convention. Such communications may be received and considered according to the procedures laid down in Article 21 only if submitted by a State Party which has made a declaration recognizing in regard to itself CAT's competence. CAT shall deal with a matter referred to it under Article 21 only after it has ascertained that all domestic remedies have been invoked and exhausted in the matter, in conformity with the generally recognized principles of international law. This shall not be the rule where the application of the remedies is unreasonably prolonged or is unlikely to bring effective relief to the person who is the victim of the violation of this Convention.

CAT may consider *complaints from individuals* alleging violations of rights under the Convention against Torture by States Parties that have made the necessary declaration under Article 22 thereof. However, CAT shall consider inadmissible any communication under Article 22 which is anonymous or which it considers to be an abuse of the right of submission of such communications or to be incompatible with the provisions of this Convention. CAT shall not consider any communications from an individual under Article 22 unless it has ascertained that: (a) the same matter has not been, and is not being, examined under another procedure of international investigation or settlement; (b) the individual has exhausted all available domestic remedies; this shall not be the rule where the application of the remedies is unreasonably prolonged or is unlikely to bring effective relief to the person who is the victim of the violation of this Convention. Within six months after being notified by CAT, the State Party concerned shall submit to CAT written explanations or statements clarifying the matter and the remedy, if any, that may have been dealt with by that State. CAT will then hold closed meetings to examine communications under Article 22 and forward its views to the State Party concerned and to the individual complainant.

According to the latest information provided by CAT,[15] there are only 11 States Parties to the Convention against Torture that have accepted CAT's competence under Article 20, as at 23 May 2014; namely, Afghanistan, China, Equatorial Guinea, Israel, Kuwait, Laos, Mauritania, Pakistan, Saudi Arabia, Syria and the United Arab Emirates. States Parties to the Convention against Torture that have experienced usurpation of power after making the declarations provided for in Articles 21 and 22 of the said Convention, as at 23 May 2014, are Algeria (as of 12 October 1989), Ecuador (as of 29 April 1988) and Tunisia (as of 23 October 1988).

The Optional Protocol to the Convention against Torture (OPCAT),[16] adopted by the UN General Assembly on 18 December 2002 and in force since 22 June 2006, sets up the SPT, whose mandate is explained previously. Only three States that have experienced unconstitutional usurpation of power have become parties to OPCAT at the time of the usurpation of power and during the regimes installed by the usurper; namely, Burkina Faso (party since July 2010, before the *coup* in October 2014 and the ones in January and September 2022); Mali (party since May 2005, before the *coups* in March 2012, August 2020 and May 2021); and Tunisia (party since June 2011, before the self-*coup* by the President in July 2021).

As of 4 May 2020, Mali is the only State that has experienced a *coup* which is also a State Party to the International Convention for the Protection of All Persons from Enforced Disappearance and recognizes CED's competence to receive individual complaints under Article 31 and/or inter-State complaints under Article 32 of that Convention. Mali accepted CED's competence on 23 December 2010 before the military *coups* in March 2012, August 2020 and May 2021.[17] On 20 September 2020, CED adopted a six-page list of issues for Mali to provide information thereon in the absence of the report from Mali which was due within two years after the entry into force of this Convention for Mali in 2009. CED

15 Report of the Committee against Torture, Fifty-first session (28 October–22 November 2013) and fifty-second session (28 April–23 May 2014), UNGA Official Records, Sixty-ninth session, Supp no 44 (A/69/44) Annexes II and III.

16 2375 UNTS 237, in force 22 June 2006.

17 Report of the Committee on Enforced Disappearances Seventeenth session (30 September–11 October 2019) Eighteenth session (4 May (online) and 7 September 2020), UNGA Official Records, Seventy-fifth Session, Supp no 56, Annex.

asks Mali to clarify the status of the Convention vis-à-vis domestic law, including the Constitution, and indicate whether the provisions of the Convention can be directly invoked before and applied by courts or other competent authorities for purposes other than providing information. CED also asks Mali to indicate the measures taken to bring Mali's National Human Rights Commission into full compliance with the principles relating to the status of national institutions for the promotion and protection of human rights (the Paris Principles).[18] In addition, Mali is requested to, among other things, describe the databases on disappeared persons that currently exist and indicate the types of information that are entered into them for each case reported; provide updated statistical data, disaggregated by the victims' sex, age, nationality, ethnic origin, religious affiliation and occupation, on the number of persons who have been reported disappeared in Mali since the entry into force of the Convention for Mali; indicate whether any complaints have been lodged with respect to acts prescribed by the Convention and their outcomes; indicate whether Mali applies a statute of limitations in respect of enforced disappearance; describe the procedure and measures put in place to allow allegations of enforced disappearance to be examined promptly and investigated thoroughly and impartially and a determination to be reached as to the fate of the disappeared persons; and explain measures to prevent enforced disappearances and to provide reparation to victims.[19]

With respect to peremptory norms of international law (*jus cogens*), they completely prohibit violations of a number of fundamental rights and freedoms irrespective of whether the State in question is party to the treaties protecting such rights and freedoms.

The CCPR's General Comment No 29 singles out the proscription of crimes against humanity as peremptory norms (*jus cogens*) under customary international law of universal application from which no derogation is permitted even during the state of emergency.

Crimes against humanity are distinguished from ordinary crimes in their respective contexts.[20] Crimes against humanity are serious crimes committed in the context of widespread *or* systematic attacks, and not just random acts of violence, against civilian population.[21] Article 7(1) of the 1998 Rome Statute of the International Criminal Court[22] comprehensively enumerates a crime against humanity as any of the following acts when committed as part of a widespread or

18 Adopted by the UN General Assembly on 20 December 1993 (A/RES/48/134 (4 March 1994) Annex).
19 CED/C/MLI/QAR/1 (25 September 2020).
20 See, generally, Egon Schwelb, 'Crimes against Humanity' (1946) 23 British YBIL 178; Mark Lattimer and Philippe Sands, *Justice for Crimes Against Humanity* (Hart 2003); Larry May, *Crimes against Humanity: A Normative Account* (CUP 2004); M. Cherif Bassiouni, *Crimes against Humanity: Historical Evolution and Contemporary Application* (CUP 2011); Guénaël Mettraux, *International Crimes: Law and Practice*, vol II (Crimes against Humanity) (OUP 2020).
21 *Prosecutor v Tadic*, Case IT-94-1-A, ICTY Appeals Chamber Judgment, 15 July 1999 para 271.
22 2187 UNTS 3, in force 1 July 2002.

systematic attack directed against any civilian population, with knowledge of the attack: (a) murder; (b) extermination; (c) enslavement; (d) deportation or forcible transfer of population; (e) imprisonment or other severe deprivation of physical liberty in violation of fundamental rules of international law; (f) torture; (g) rape, sexual slavery, enforced prostitution, forced pregnancy, enforced sterilization or any other form of sexual violence of comparable gravity; (h) persecution against any identifiable group or collectivity on political, racial, national, ethnic, cultural, religious, gender or other grounds that are universally recognized as impermissible under international law, in connection with any act referred to in this paragraph or any crime within the ICC's jurisdiction; (i) enforced disappearance of persons; (j) the crime of apartheid; and (k) other inhumane acts of a similar character intentionally causing great suffering, or serious injury to body or to mental or physical health.

Other crimes under international law proscribed by peremptory norms that may be committed by the usurper include war crimes when the usurper and the opposition engage in armed conflicts, the prohibition of torture, and, in the extreme case, the prohibition of genocide.[23]

Genocide means any of the following acts committed with intent to destroy, in whole or in part, a national, ethnical, racial or religious group, as such: (a) killing members of the group; (b) causing serious bodily or mental harm to members of the group; (c) deliberately inflicting on the group conditions of life calculated to bring about its physical destruction in whole or in part; (d) imposing measures intended to prevent births within the group; (e) forcibly transferring children of the group to another group.[24] The proscription of genocide has been confirmed

23 A non-exclusive list of peremptory norms of international law encompasses the prohibition of aggression, the prohibition of genocide, the prohibition of crimes against humanity, the basic rules of international humanitarian law, the prohibition of racial discrimination and apartheid, the prohibition of slavery, the prohibition of torture and the right to self-determination (UN International Law Commission, 'Peremptory norms of general international law (*jus cogens*)', Text of the draft conclusions and Annex provisionally adopted by the Drafting Committee on second reading, A/CN.4/L.967 (11 May 2022)). See also Alexander Orakhelashvili, *Peremptory Norms in International Law* (OUP 2006) 36–66, 104–31; Daniel Costelloe, *Legal Consequences of Peremptory Norms in International Law* (CUP 2017); Dire Tladi (ed.), *Peremptory Norms of General International Law (Jus Cogens): Disquisitions and Disputations* (Brill 2021). For the debate in the UN International Law Commission on the list of 'core crimes' under international law in its 1996 Draft Code of Crimes against the Peace and Security of Mankind, see Kriangsak Kittichaisaree, *The Obligation to Extradite or Prosecute* (OUP 2018) 99–109. See also Douglas Guilfoyle, *International Criminal Law* (OUP 2016) chs 7–11. Mohsen Abdollahi and Keyvan Behzadi ('Regional *Jus Cogens*: Conceptual Difficulties and Practical Challenges' (2020) 3 Iranian Rev for UN Studies 33) argue that under positive international law (particularly regional human rights conventions), there exists special non-derogable norms (such as the prohibition of death penalty in the European regime of human rights) which are capable of performing functions assigned to regional *jus cogens*.

24 Art 2 of the Convention on the Prevention and Punishment of the Crime of Genocide; Art 6 of the Rome Statute of the ICC. See also William Schabas, *Genocide in International Law: The Crime of Crimes* (2nd edn, CUP 2009); Paola Gaeta (ed.), *The UN Genocide Convention: A Commentary* (OUP 2009); Payam Akhavan, *Reducing Genocide to Law: Definition, Meaning, and the Ultimate Crime* (CUP

by the International Court of Justice and other international courts to form part of the body of such peremptory norms.[25]

War crimes are crimes committed during an armed conflict in violation of a body of rules known collectively as 'international humanitarian law', '*jus in bello*' or 'international law of armed conflict'.[26] An armed conflict is deemed to exist whenever there is a resort to armed forces between nation States or protracted armed violence between governmental authorities and organized armed groups or between such groups fighting with a certain level of intensity within a nation State.[27] A war crime may be committed when the junta and those who oppose the junta are engaged in armed conflicts as in the case of the ongoing armed conflicts between the Myanmar junta and those opposed to its rule in the aftermath of the 1 February 2021 military *coup*.

The UN Security Council has reaffirmed the peremptory norm status of genocide, crimes against humanity and war crimes when it refers the situation in Darfur, Sudan, which is not party to the Rome Statute, to the ICC Prosecutor to investigate and prosecute those responsible.[28]

Even when torture does not fall under the ambit of a crime against humanity because it is not committed as part of a widespread or systematic attack against the civilian population, the ICJ has held in *Questions relating to the Obligation to Prosecute or Extradite (Belgium v Senegal)* that the prohibition of torture is part of customary international law and it has become a peremptory norm (*jus cogens*).[29] According to the Trial Chamber of the International Criminal Tribunal for the former Yugoslavia in *Prosecutor v Anto Furundzija*, because of the importance of the values it protects the principle proscribing torture has evolved into a peremptory norm or *jus cogens* with a higher rank in the international hierarchy than treaty law and even 'ordinary' or 'general' customary rule not endowed with the same normative force. Furthermore, this prohibition against torture is designed to produce a deterrent effect, in that it signals to all members of the international community and the individuals over whom they wield authority that the prohibition of torture is an absolute value from which nobody must deviate and every State is entitled to

---

2012); Christian Tams, Lars Berster and Björn Schiffbauer (eds), *Convention on the Prevention and Punishment of the Crime of Genocide: A Commentary* (Beck/Hart 2014); Etienne Ruvebana, *Prevention of Genocide under International Law* (Intersentia 2014).

25 *Case Concerning Armed Activities on the Territories of the Congo (New Application: 2002) (DR Congo v Rwanda)* [2006] ICJ Rep 6, 31–2 [64]; *Prosecutor v Goran Jelisic*, Case no IT-90–10, ICTY Trial Chamber I, Judgment (14 December 1999) para 60; and the Judgment of the European Court of Human Rights in *Jorgić v Germany*, Case 74613/01 para 68, ECHR 2007III.

26 Not to be confused with *jus ad bellum*, which regulates justifications or reasons for war or its prevention.

27 *Prosecutor v Dusko Tadic*, Case IT-94–1-AR72, ICTY Appeals Chamber, Decision of 2 October 1995 on the Defence Motion for Interlocutory Appeal on Jurisdiction paras 70, 562.

28 S/RES/1595 (2005) of 31 March 2005.

29 [2012] ICJ Rep 422, 457 [99]. See also the findings about the rejection of the use of torture by an overwhelming number of States in Peter Miller, 'Torture Approval in Comparative Perspective' (2011) 12 Hum Rts Rev 441.

investigate, prosecute and punish or extradite individuals accused of torture, who are present in a territory under its jurisdiction. Torture may not be covered by a statute of limitations, and must not be excluded from extradition under any 'political offence' exemption.[30]

States of emergency and derogation of fundamental rights and freedoms

A state of emergency, or state of siege or martial law, is usually declared by the junta before, during and/or after a *coup*.

Resorting to declaration of public emergency may be traced to Roman times, where countries nominated a 'dictator' with exceptional power to issue decrees with the force of law in exceptional circumstances of external attack or internal rebellion when there was a need to suspend the law so as to safeguard the life of the nation. The Roman dictatorship was limited in duration and for well-defined and limited purposes with the ultimate goal of upholding constitutional order rather than replacing it.[31] How thing were during the Roman time are not what they are in the modern world. For instance, Carl Schmitt, a German jurist and political theorist who was a prominent member of the Nazi Party during the Third Reich, argued that in a matter of an extreme emergency—the 'state of exception'—the content of the jurisdictional competence of the sovereign must by necessity remain unlimited in deciding whether there is an extreme emergency as well as what should be done to counter it.[32]

In Paraguay during the 1954–89 dictatorship under General Alfredo Stroessner, although both the Paraguayan Constitutions of 1940 and 1967 had provisions that broadly guaranteed civil rights, the main tool of the dictatorship was the successive declarations of a state of siege to deny them. A state of siege could be declared unilaterally by the President of the Republic in accordance with both Constitutions. The Supreme Court of Paraguay upheld the validity of the state of siege to suspend constitutional guarantees such as *habeas corpus*, allowing arbitrary detentions without a judicial order and all kinds of human

30 Case no ICTY-95–17/1-T, Judgment (10 December 1998) paras 154–7. The political offence exception to extradition is based on a two-fold rationale of maintaining a neutral position in internal political conflicts in another State and preventing the surrender of an offender to a jurisdiction where there is a risk that his trial or punishment might be unfairly influenced by political considerations (*per* Lord Diplock in the UK House of Lords' judgment in *Cheng v Governor of Pentonville Prison* [1973] AC 931, 945).

31 Mark Klamberg, 'International Human Rights Law and States of Emergency' in Damien Rogers (ed.), *Human Rights in War* (Springer 2022) 105–63.

32 Carl Schmitt, *Political Theology: Four Chapters on the Concept of Sovereignty* (MIT Press 1934) 5–7. See also Richard Wolin, 'Carl Schmitt, Political Existentialism, and the Total State' (1990) 19 Theory & Society 389; Leila Brännström, 'Carl Schmitt's Definition of Sovereignty as Authorized Leadership' in Matilda Arvidsson, Leila Brännström and Panu Minkinnen (eds), *The Contemporary Relevance of Carl Schmitt: Law, Politics, Theology* (Routledge 2016) 19–33; Douglas Howland, 'Carl Schmitt's Turn to Sovereignty in Jurisprudence' (2018) 9 Beijing L Rev 211.

rights abuses.[33] The repression was furthered by the enactment of two laws. Law No 294 of 1955, titled 'Defence of Democracy', made mere dissemination of a particular political ideology a criminal offence punishable by imprisonment. This law allowed the military government to accuse anyone who opposed it as a communist and every government official was obligated by that law to denounce his neighbour at the slightest suspicion that he was a communist, or else the official himself could be charged with collusion with the suspect.[34] Under Law No 209 of 1970, titled 'Defence of Public Peace and the Physical Liberty of the Individual', inciting violence or urging people to disobey laws was punishable by imprisonment of one month to three years, whereas 'preaching hate between Paraguayans' was punishable by one to six years' imprisonment. Law No 209 also proscribed defaming the President or his Cabinet Ministers.[35] These laws were often used to detain opposition leaders for several days and sometimes for months. Only after the bloody and violent *coup d'état* of February 1989 that toppled Stroessner did Paraguay ratify the main international human rights treaties of both the United Nations system and the regional system of the Organization of American States (OAS) and the Judiciary, in a period of complex transitional justice, begin to recognize and guarantee rights as well as prosecute violators. Although the cases tried were few, some more significant than others, the main civil, criminal, constitutional and supra-national judicial rulings sought to do justice to the victims of the dictatorship.[36]

In the Philippines, President Ferdinand E. Marcos declared martial law on 21 September 1972 to keep him in power beyond the constitutional limit of two terms of Presidency. The martial law granted to Marcos himself the power to maintain law and order, prevent or suppress all forms of lawless violence as well as any act of insurrection or rebellion, and enforce all the laws, decrees, orders and regulations promulgated by him personally or upon his direction. Marcos gradually increased his own power to such an extent there were no limits to his orders for the human rights violations. He promulgated an order appointing himself Commander-in-Chief of the Armed Forces of the Philippines as well as authorizing him to govern the nation and direct the operation of the entire Government, including all its agencies and instrumentalities. By two orders signed by Marcos immediately after

33 These cases are compiled into the file named 'Resoluc' at the Documentation and Archive Centre for the Defence of Human Rights or Museum of Justice, a unit of the Judiciary of Paraguay. The file can be accessed at www.pj.gov.py/contenido/132-museo-de-la-justicia/388.

34 Inter-American Commission on Human Rights, Report on the Situation of Human Rights in Paraguay, OEA/Ser.L/V/II.71, Doc 19 rev 1 (28 September 1987) ch 1.

35 https://paraguay.justia.com/nacionales/leyes/ley-209-sep-18-1970/gdoc/.

36 Perhaps one of the most high-profile cases is that of the annulment of the trial and conviction of Modesto Napoleón Ortigoza, considered Paraguay's 'Nelson Mandela' for having been perhaps the longest-incarcerated political prisoner in South America, having been jailed for 25 years (*Action of Unconstitutionality: Napoleón Ortigoza*, Case no 585, Supreme Court (Constitutional Chamber), Judgment, 31 December 1996). In civil matters, Law No 838 of 1996 compensates victims of human rights violations during the 1954–89 dictatorship.

proclaiming martial law, Marcos authorized the arrest, by the military, of a long list of dissidents. By another order, Marcos maintained, as captive, the executive and judicial branches of all political entities in the Philippines until otherwise ordered by himself personally. Immediately after the declaration of martial law, the issuance of the aforesaid orders caused arrests of persons accused of subversion, apparently because of their real or apparent opposition to the Marcos Government. These arrests were made pursuant to orders issued by the Secretary of Defence or Marcos himself. During the detentions of those arrested under the orders, the detainees experienced human rights violations amounting to various forms of torture. The more the detainees resisted, whether purposefully or out of lack of knowledge, the more serious the torture used.[37]

The state of emergency or martial law of the type described previously underpins the suspension or even complete annulment of fundamental rights and freedoms. When, in performing a judicial review, judges validate it, they contribute to the suspension or annulment of these rights and freedoms. Whether judges are in the wrong in turn depends on its lawfulness under international law and the judges' exercise in good faith of all necessary judicial protection against abuses in the country in question. Should domestic judges uphold the lawfulness of the declaration of state of public emergency/martial law but fail to protect citizens against abuses, domestic judicial remedies are not usually available, leaving it to competent international institutions, if any, to order the State to provide them to those deprived of their rights and freedoms. When there is no remedy available either domestically or internationally, the citizens often join forces to protest against the government, as in the case of the 'Arab Spring' in the early 2010s, when popular uprisings in Tunisia, Egypt, Libya, Syria, Bahrain and Yemen demanded the respective Governments to repeal abusive emergency laws associated with political repression.

In *Zafar Ali Shah* v *General Pervez Musharraf*,[38] the Supreme Court of Pakistan analyzes in detail the state of emergency declared by General Musharraf as justifications for the military *coup* in October 1999. The state of emergency includes 'regimes of exception'; that is, regimes which have overthrown and not merely suspended the previous constitutional order and have assumed legislative and executive powers analogous to those under a formal state of emergency. The Court rules that the Government is to take steps to ensure the fundamental rights of citizens are not affected and derogation must be proportionate to the emergency, while adopting constitutional as well as extra-constitutional means. For their part, Pakistani courts shall exert efforts to minimize emergencies and to induce the authorities concerned to respect the fundamental rights. As Pakistan is never party to the ICCPR, the Pakistani Supreme Court appears to consider this rule a rule of universal application.

37 As narrated by the US District Court for the District of Hawaii, *In re Estate of Marcos Human Rights Litigation*, 910 F Supp 1460, 1462–3 (D Haw 1995) 30 November 1995. See also Raissa Robles, *Marcos Martial Law: Never Again* (Filipinos for a Better Philippines, Inc. 2016).
38 [2000] PLD SC 869.

With regard to the ICCPR itself, its Article 4 reads:

> 1. In time of public emergency which threatens the life of the nation and the existence of which is officially proclaimed, the States Parties to the present Covenant may take measures derogating from their obligations under the present Covenant to the extent strictly required by the exigencies of the situation, provided that such measures are not inconsistent with their other obligations under international law and do not involve discrimination solely on the ground of race, colour, sex, language, religion or social origin.
>
> 2. No derogation from Articles 6 [right to life], 7 [prohibition of torture or to cruel, inhuman or degrading treatment or punishment], 8 [prohibition of slavery, slave trade or servitude], 11 [prohibition of imprisonment because of inability to fulfil a contractual obligation], Article 15 [the principle of legality], Article 16 [the recognition of everyone as a person before the law] and Article 18 [freedom of thought, conscience and religion] may be made under this provision.
>
> 3. Any State Party to the present Covenant availing itself of the right of derogation shall immediately inform the other States Parties to the present Covenant, through the intermediary of the Secretary-General of the United Nations, of the provisions from which it has derogated and of the reasons by which it was actuated. A further communication shall be made, through the same intermediary, on the date on which it terminates such derogation.

Derogations of human rights differ from *limitations* or *restrictions* of human rights. The former are only permitted in exceptional circumstances where States face a danger that threatens the life of the nation, whereas the latter may be invoked by States even in normal times, albeit for a limited and exhaustive number of reasons. Phrased differently, derogation clauses in treaties provide for the complete or partial elimination of a right as an international obligation, while limitations/restrictions clauses are based on the recognition that most human rights are not absolute but rather reflect a balance between individual and community interests.[39] An example of the balance struck in the limitation/restrictions clauses under the ICCPR appears in Article 19(3) of the ICCPR, stipulating that the exercise of the right to freedom of expression carries with it special duties and responsibilities and, as such, it may be subject to certain *restrictions*, as are provided by law and are necessary: (a) for respect of the rights or reputations of others; (b) for the protection of national security or of public order (*ordre public*), or of public health or morals.

39 Diane Desierto, *States of Emergency in International Human Rights Treaties: Sovereignty in Modern Treaty Interpretation* (Brill 2012) 237; Gemmo Bautista Fernandez, 'Within the Margin of Error: Derogations, Limitations, and the Advancement of Human Rights' (2019) 92 Philippine LJ 1, 4–11; Henry Steiner, Philip Alston and Ryan Goodman, *International Human Rights in Context: Law, Politics, Morals: Texts and Materials* (3rd edn, OUP 2008) 154.

The CCPR has adopted General Comment No 29 (Article 4: Derogation during a state of emergency), as follows.[40]

A *fundamental requirement* for any measures derogating from the ICCPR, as set forth in Article 4(1), is that such measures are limited to the extent strictly required by the exigencies of the situation. This requirement relates to the duration, geographical coverage and material scope of the state of emergency and any measures of derogation resorted to because of the emergency. This reflects the principle of *proportionality* which is common to derogation and limitation powers. Moreover, specific measures taken pursuant to the derogation must also be shown to be required by the exigencies of the situation. In practice, this will ensure no provision of the ICCPR, however validly derogated from, will be entirely inapplicable to the behaviour of a State party.

The *condition* that any measures derogating from a State Party's obligations under the ICCPR must be limited 'to the extent strictly required by the exigencies of the situation' means States Parties must provide careful justification not only for their decision to proclaim a state of emergency but also for any specific measures based on such a proclamation.

The fact that some ICCPR provisions have been listed in Article 4(2) as not being subject to derogation does not mean that other ICCPR provisions may be subjected to derogation at will, *even where a threat to the life of the nation exists.* The legal obligation to narrow down all derogations to those strictly required by the exigencies of the situation imposes a duty on both States Parties and the CCPR to conduct a careful analysis under each ICCPR provision based on an objective assessment of the actual situation.

Article 4(2) of the ICCPR *explicitly prohibits* derogation from the Articles listed therein. Conceptually, the qualification of an ICCPR provision as a non-derogable one does not mean that no *limitations or restrictions* would ever be justified. The reference in Article 4(3) to Article 18, a provision that includes a specific clause on restrictions in its paragraph 3, demonstrates that the permissibility of restrictions is independent of the issue of derogability. Even in times of most serious public emergencies, States that interfere with the freedom to manifest one's religion or belief must justify their actions by referring to the requirements specified in Article 18(3); namely, freedom to manifest one's religion or beliefs may be subject only to such limitations as are prescribed by law and are necessary to protect public safety, order, health, or morals or the fundamental rights and freedoms of others.

The enumeration of non-derogable provisions in Article 4 is related to, but not identical with, the question whether certain human rights obligations bear the nature of *peremptory norms of international law.* The proclamation of certain ICCPR provisions as being of a non-derogable nature in Article 4(2) is to be seen partly as recognition of the peremptory nature of some fundamental rights ensured in

40 CCPR/C/21/Rev.1/Add.11 (31 August 2001). See further, Oren Gross and Fionnuala Ní Aoláin, *Law in Times of Crisis: Emergency Powers in Theory and Practice* (CUP 2006) 247–325.

treaty form in the ICCPR (e.g., Articles 6 and 7).[41] However, some other ICCPR provisions were included in the list of non-derogable provisions apparently because it can never become necessary to derogate from these rights during a state of emergency (e.g., Articles 11 and 18). Furthermore, the category of peremptory norms extends beyond the list of non-derogable provisions as given in Article 4(2). States Parties may in no circumstances invoke Article 4 as justification for acting in violation of international humanitarian law or peremptory norms of international law, for instance by taking hostages, abductions or unacknowledged detention, imposing collective punishments, arbitrary deprivations of liberty or deviating from fundamental principles of fair trial, including the presumption of innocence.

In assessing the scope of legitimate derogation from the ICCPR, one criterion can be found in the definition of certain human rights violations as *crimes against humanity*. If action conducted under the authority of a State constitutes a basis for individual criminal responsibility for a crime against humanity by the persons involved in that action, Article 4 of the ICCPR cannot be used as justification that a state of emergency exempts the State in question from its responsibility in relation to that same conduct.

In those ICCPR provisions not listed in Article 4(2), there are elements that cannot be made subject to lawful derogation under Article 4. For example, all persons deprived of their liberty shall be treated with humanity and with respect for the inherent dignity of the human person although this right, prescribed in Article 10, is not separately mentioned in the list of non-derogable rights in Article 4(2). This right is a norm of general international law not subject to derogation, since it is supported by the reference to the inherent dignity of the human person in the preamble to the ICCPR and by the close connection between Articles 7 and 10. Furthermore, the international protection of the rights of persons belonging to minorities includes elements that must be respected in all circumstances. Also, no declaration of a state of emergency made pursuant to Article 4(1) may be invoked as justification for a State Party to the ICCPR to engage itself, contrary to Article 20, in propaganda for war or in advocacy of national, racial or religious hatred that would constitute incitement to discrimination, hostility or violence.

Article 2(3) of the ICCPR requires its States Parties to provide *remedies for any violation* of the ICCPR provisions. Even if a State Party, during a state of emergency, and to the extent that such measures are strictly required by the exigencies of the situation, may introduce adjustments to the practical functioning of its procedures governing judicial or other remedies, the State Party must comply with the fundamental obligation under Article 2(3) to provide a remedy that is effective.

The *protection of rights explicitly recognized as non-derogable* in Article 4(2) *must be secured by procedural guarantees*, including, often, judicial guarantees. Article 4 may not be resorted to in a way that would result in derogation from non-derogable

41 Article 6(3) even expressly stipulates that when deprivation of life constitutes the crime of genocide, it is understood that nothing in Article 6 shall authorize any State Party to the ICCPR to derogate in any way from any obligation assumed under the provisions of the Genocide Convention.

rights. Thus, for example, as the right to life under Article 6 of the ICCPR is non-derogable in its entirety, any trial leading to the imposition of the death penalty during a state of emergency must conform to the provisions of the ICCPR, including all the requirements of Articles 14 (right to equality before courts and tribunals and to fair trial) and 15 (the principle of legality).

Safeguards related to derogation, as embodied in Article 4 of the ICCPR, are based on *the principles of legality and the rule of law* inherent in the ICCPR as a whole which require that *fundamental requirements of fair trial* must be respected during a state of emergency. Only a court of law may try and convict a person for a criminal offence. The presumption of innocence must be respected. In order to protect non-derogable rights, the right to take proceedings before a court to enable the court to decide without delay on the lawfulness of detention must not be diminished by a State Party's decision to derogate from the ICCPR.

Article 4(3) of the ICCPR requires a State Party availing itself of the right of derogation to immediately inform the other States Parties, through the UN Secretary-General, of the provisions it has derogated from and of the reasons for such measures. The CCPR will assess whether the measures taken by the State Party were strictly required by the exigencies of the situation, and other States Parties can monitor compliance with the provisions of the ICCPR. The notification by States Parties should include full information about the measures taken and a clear explanation of the reasons for them, with full documentation attached regarding their law. Additional notifications are required if the State Party subsequently takes further measures under Article 4, for instance by extending the duration of a state of emergency. The requirement of immediate notification applies equally in relation to the termination of derogation. The CCPR's duty to monitor the law and practice of a State Party for compliance with Article 4 does not depend on whether that State Party has submitted a notification, however.

The term 'threat to the life of the nation' was inserted during the Drafting Committee's eighth session in 1952 as a result of the United Kingdom's proposal. Uruguay would prefer the term 'people' to 'nation' in order to allow derogation not only when the life of a nation is endangered, but also during calamities such as floods and earthquakes, which might affect only a section of the population. While Chile found it difficult to give a precise legal definition of the life of the nation, Chile noted that the text did *not relate to the life of the government or of the State*.[42] In any event, Article 4 of the ICCPR is not intended to justify the acts of persons, such as the usurpers of power of government, who themselves create the state of emergency.[43] *Derogation under Article 4 of the ICCPR must be owing to threats that are not self-inflicted by usurpers of power.*

42 Ignatius Yordan Nugraha, 'Human Rights Derogation during *Coup* Situations' (2018) 22 Int'l J Hum Rts 194, 197–8, citing UN Commission on Human Rights, Summary Record, 330th Mtg, 8th Sess, 10 June 1952, E/CN.4/SR.330 (1952) 11–12 and 4.

43 Nugraha, 'Human Rights Derogation During *Coup* Situations' 199, quoting the report of the Human Rights Committee to the General Assembly, A/34/40 (1979) para 78, in the context of

A most common measure taken by a regime to curb opposition or resistance to its rule is by declaring a state of emergency during which mass rallies and demonstrations are criminalized. The CCPR's General Comment No 29 foresees this possibility and clarifies that for a State Party to derogate from the ICCPR during a mass demonstration the demonstration must include instances of violence that constitutes '*a threat to the life of the nation*', and all their measures derogating from the ICCPR are *strictly required by the exigencies of the situation.* The possibility of *restricting* certain ICCPR rights under the terms of, for instance, freedom of movement (Article 12) or freedom of assembly (Article 21) is generally sufficient during such situations and *no derogation* from the provisions in question would be justified by the exigencies of the situation. This guidance by the CCPR has been correctly followed by Thailand's Dusit District Court in its judgment of 13 December 2021 in *Prosecutor (Dusit District) v Pasrawalee Thanakijvibulpol.*

On 21 October 2020, the defendant joined a public demonstration to march to the Government House to submit a petition to the Thai Prime Minister asking him to resign from office. The defendant was charged with violating the declaration of a serious emergency situation in the Bangkok Metropolitan and restrictions imposed under Sections 9 and 11 of the Emergency Decree on Public Administration in Emergency Situation, B.E. 2548 (2005), as well as the announcement of the Prime Minister to resolve serious emergency situations dated 15 October 2020. Under Section 9 of the Decree, when it is necessary to rectify and promptly resolve an emergency situation or to prevent the worsening of such situation, the Prime Minister shall have the power to issue regulations to, inter alia, prohibit the assembly or gathering of persons at any place or the commission of any act which may cause unrest. Pursuant to Section 11, where an emergency situation involves terrorism, use of force, harm to life, body or property or where there are reasonable grounds to believe there exists an act affecting the security of the State or the safety of life or property of the State or person and it is necessary to resolve the problem in an efficient and timely manner, the Prime Minister, upon the approval of the Cabinet, shall have the power to declare that such emergency situation is a serious situation. The Prime Minister's announcement of 15 October 2020 prohibits public rallies as the Government has reason to believe that several groups of persons have invited, incited and organized such rallies in Bangkok, in contravention of the law on peaceful assembly, so as to cause violence, turbulence, chaos and public unrest. Such gatherings, adds the announcement, will not be 'peaceful' and protected under the Constitution, but will adversely affect national security and the safety of life of persons or government property as well as directly undermine the effectiveness of government measures to contain the COVID-19 pandemic, thereby directly undermining the already fragile national economy.

The Dusit District Court dismissed the case against the defendant on the ground that the Decree was enforceable only when there existed an emergency

---

the Committee's consideration of the report of the junta of Chile under General Pinochet after the overthrow of the democratically elected President Salvador Allende.

situation of a serious degree. Since the public assembly the defendant took part in on that day did not have any malicious intent to perpetrate or threaten to perpetrate an act of violence or anything to cause a breach of the peace, it was a peaceful assembly to which every citizen has a right under Section 44 of the 2017 Constitution of Thailand. The Prosecutor failed to discharge the burden of proving that the exigencies of the situation justified the Government's *derogation* of the right of peaceful assembly. The Government could have legitimately imposed certain *restrictions* on the public gathering, for example by requiring the participants to wear face masks and keep certain distance to avoid COVID-19 infection; checking they were not armed or had explosive devices in their possession; and directing the participants to follow a particular route to reach their destination at the Government House.[44]

Regional human rights treaties are in harmony with the ICCPR in this respect. Article 15 of the 1950 European Convention on Human Rights[45] permits derogations '[i]n time of war or other public emergency threatening the life of the nation' to the extent strictly required by the exigencies of the situation, provided that such measures are not inconsistent with its High Contracting Party's other obligations under international law. The term 'other public emergency threatening the life of the nation' has been interpreted as 'an exceptional situation of crisis or emergency which affects the whole population and constitutes a threat to the organized life of the community of which the State is composed'.[46] The crisis or danger must be actual or imminent; its effect must involve the whole nation; the continuance of the organized life of the community must be threatened and the crisis or danger must be exceptional, in that the normal measures of restrictions, permitted by the 1950 Convention for the maintenance of public safety, health and order, are plainly inadequate.[47] Article 15 has been authoritatively construed to mean that a junta's declaration of the state of emergency is subject to scrutiny in light of this Article, and that a public emergency threatening the life of the nation must go beyond unrest such as a series of bomb incidents, acts of sabotage and activities of a number of illegal organizations which are not beyond the control of the public

44 It has been argued that the declaration of the state of emergency, in effect, turned a coronavirus into a public enemy equivalent to terrorists and rioters and it allows the Thai Government to take hard-line measures against people or ideologies labelled as public enemies (Rawin Leelapatana and Chompunoot Tangthavorn, 'Thailand: Emergency Responses or More Social Turbulence?' in Victor Ramraj (ed.), *COVID-19 in Asia: Law and Policy Contexts* (OUP 2021) 161, 167). See also Tom Ginsburg and Mila Versteeg, 'The Bound Executive: Emergency Powers During the Pandemic' (2021) 19 Int'l J Constitutional L 1498; Report of the Special Rapporteur on the rights to freedom of peaceful assembly and of association, *Protection of human rights in the context of peaceful protests during crisis situations*, A/HRC/50/42 (16 May 2022) paras 19–20, 79(c).

45 ETS 5, in force 3 September 1953.

46 *Lawless v Ireland (No 3)*, ECtHR, Judgment on Merits, App no 332/57 (A/3), [1961] ECHR 2 para 28.

47 App nos 3321/67 (*Denmark v Greece*), 3322/67 (*Norway v Greece*), 3323/67 (*Sweden v Greece*), and 3344/67 (*Netherlands v Greece*), Report of the Sub-Commission of the European Commission of Human Rights, vol I Part I para 113.

authorities exercising normal measures or on a scale threatening the organized life of the community.[48]

As regards the 1969 American Convention on Human Rights,[49] Article 27 (Suspension of Guarantees) reads:

> 1. In time of war, public danger or other emergency that threatens the independence or security of a State Party, it may take measures derogating from its obligations under the present Convention to the extent and for the period of time strictly required by the exigencies of the situation, provided that such measures are not inconsistent with its other obligations under international law and do not involve discrimination on the ground of race, color, sex, language, religion or social origin.
>
> 2. The foregoing provision does not authorize any suspension of the following articles: Article 3 (Right to Juridical Personality), Article 4 (Right to Life), Article 5 (Right to Humane Treatment), Article 6 (Freedom from Slavery), Article 9 (Freedom from *Ex Post Facto* Laws), Article 12 (Freedom of Conscience and Religion), Article 17 (Rights of the Family), Article 18 (Right to a Name), Article 19 (Rights of the Child), Article 20 (Right to Nationality) and Article 23 (Right to Participate in Government), or of the judicial guarantees essential for the protection of such rights.
>
> 3. Any State Party availing itself of the right of suspension shall immediately inform the other States Parties, through the Secretary General of the Organization of American States, of the provisions the application of which it has suspended, the reasons that gave rise to the suspension, and the date set for the termination of such suspension.

According to the preparatory work of this Convention, the term 'security' in paragraph 1 was intended to include situations such as a real and imminent danger to the existence of the people as a nation, the survival of the State as a sovereign and independent political entity, territorial integrity, respect for the Constitution in force and the exercise of the legitimate powers by the constitutional authorities.[50]

Nevertheless, very much like the ICCPR, emergency situations caused by the usurpation of power from a democratically elected government are excluded from the scope of permissible derogations.

This is explained by the Inter-American Court of Human Rights (IACtHR) in its Advisory Opinion on *Habeas Corpus in Emergency Situations (Arts 27(2), 25(1) and 7(6) American Convention on Human Rights)*.[51] The IACtHR recognizes that under certain circumstances the suspension of guarantees may be the only way to deal with emergency situations and, thereby, to preserve the highest values of a

48 Ibid paras 26–8, 49–50, 112–25, 142–4.
49 Treaty Series no 36, OAS, 1969, in force 18 July 1978.
50 Nugraha, 'Human Rights Derogation During *Coup* Situations' 200.
51 Advisory Opinion OC-8–87, IACtHR Ser A no 8 (1987) paras 20–44.

democratic society. However, abuses may result from the application of emergency measures not objectively justified in light of the requirements prescribed in Article 27 and the principles contained in other relevant international instruments. Given the principles upon which the Inter-American system is founded, the IACtHR emphasizes the suspension of guarantees cannot be disassociated from the 'effective exercise of representative democracy' referred to in Article 3 of the 1948 Charter of the Organization of the American States.[52] The soundness of this conclusion gains special validity given the context of the American Convention, whose Preamble reaffirms the intention of the American States 'to consolidate in this hemisphere, within the framework of democratic institutions, a system of personal liberty and social justice based on respect for the essential rights of man'. *The suspension of guarantees lacks all legitimacy whenever it is resorted to for the purpose of undermining the democratic system*, which establishes limits that may not be transgressed, thus ensuring certain fundamental human rights remain permanently protected. By virtue of Article 27 of the American Convention, all rights are to be guaranteed and enforced unless very special circumstances justify the suspension of certain rights, but some rights may never be suspended, however serious the emergency. The lawfulness of the measures taken to deal with each of the special situations referred to in Article 27(1) will depend, moreover, upon the character, intensity, pervasiveness and particular context of the emergency and upon the corresponding proportionality and reasonableness of the measures. Article 27(2) limits the powers of the State Party to suspend rights and freedoms by establishing a certain category of specific rights and freedoms from which no derogation is permitted under any circumstances and it includes in that category 'the judicial guarantees essential for the protection of such rights'. Any suspension of guarantees does not imply a temporary suspension of the *rule of law*, nor does it authorize those in power to act in disregard of the *principle of legality* by which they are bound at all times. When guarantees are suspended, some legal restraints applicable to the acts of public authorities may differ from those in effect under normal conditions. These restraints may not be considered to be non-existent, however, nor can the government be deemed thereby to have acquired absolute powers that go beyond the circumstances justifying the grant of such exceptional legal measures.

The determination as to what judicial remedies are 'essential' for the protection of the rights which may not be suspended will differ depending upon the rights at stake. The 'essential' judicial guarantees necessary to guarantee the rights that deal with the physical integrity of the human person must of necessity differ from those that seek to protect the right to a name, for example, which is also non-derogable. The judicial remedies that must be considered essential within the meaning of Article 27(2) are those that ordinarily will effectively guarantee the full exercise of the rights and freedoms protected by that provision and whose denial or restriction would endanger their full enjoyment. The guarantees must be not

52 119 UNTS 3, in force 13 December 1951.

only essential but also judicial in the sense of providing those judicial remedies that are truly capable of protecting these rights. Implicit in this conception is *the active involvement of an independent and impartial judicial body having the power to pass on the lawfulness of measures adopted in a state of emergency*. *Amparo* comprises a whole series of remedies, whereas *habeas corpus* is but one of its components. In some instances *habeas corpus* functions as an independent remedy when its primary purpose is to protect the personal freedom of those who are being detained or who have been threatened with detention. In other circumstances, *habeas corpus* is viewed either as the '*amparo* of freedom' or as an integral part of *amparo*. In order for *habeas corpus* to achieve its purpose, which is to obtain a judicial determination of the lawfulness of a detention, it is necessary for the detained person to be brought before a competent judge or tribunal with jurisdiction over him to ensure a person's life and physical integrity are respected, to prevent his disappearance or to keep his whereabouts secret and to protect him against torture or other cruel, inhumane or degrading punishment or treatment. Any action on the part of the public authorities that goes beyond the limits strictly required to deal with the emergency, which must be specified with precision in the decree promulgating the state of emergency, would also be unlawful notwithstanding the existence of the emergency situation. Such violation would occur, for example, if the measures taken infringed the legal regime of the state of emergency, if they lasted longer than the time limit specified, if they were manifestly irrational, unnecessary or disproportionate, or if, in adopting them, there was a misuse or abuse of power. If this is so, *an autonomous and independent judicial order must exercise control over the lawfulness of such measures*. In this context, *habeas corpus* acquires a new dimension of fundamental importance. In conclusion, given the provision of Article 27(2), the legal remedies guaranteed in Articles 7(6)[53] and 25(1)[54] of the American Convention may not be suspended because they are judicial guarantees essential for the protection of the rights and freedoms whose suspension Article 27(2) prohibits.

The reasoning in this Advisory Opinion by the IACtHR has been followed by, for instance, Costa Rica's Constitutional Chamber in 1992. The Chamber establishes strict parameters for the justification of a declaration of national emergency, in states of necessity and national urgency, in order to safeguard essential legal interests. The Chamber defines a state of emergency as 'internal

53 Art 7(6): Anyone who is deprived of his liberty shall be entitled to recourse to a competent court, in order that the court may decide without delay on the lawfulness of his arrest or detention and order his release if the arrest or detention is unlawful. In States Parties whose laws provide that anyone who believes himself to be threatened with deprivation of his liberty is entitled to recourse to a competent court in order that it may decide on the lawfulness of such threat, this remedy may not be restricted or abolished. The interested party or another person in his behalf is entitled to seek these remedies.

54 Art 25(1): Everyone has the right to simple and prompt recourse, or any other effective recourse, to a competent court or tribunal for protection against acts that violate his fundamental rights recognized by the constitution or laws of the State concerned or by this Convention, even though such violation may have been committed by persons acting in the course of their official duties.

commotion, disturbances, external aggression, epidemics, famine and other public calamities, as manifestations of what is known in the doctrine of Public Law as a state of necessity and urgency' when, by virtue of the principle '*salus populi suprema ex est*', the weakest legal right (i.e., the preservation of the normal order of legislative powers) must yield to the strongest legal right (i.e., the preservation of the legal and social order, which, on occasions, does not allow waiting for that a law be processed and approved). Such a declaration must be absolutely necessary to address the dangers caused by the exceptional situation, and should be extended only for the time strictly necessary.[55]

For its part, the Inter-American Commission on Human Rights (IACHR), a principal and autonomous organ of the OAS set up under the American Convention to promote respect for and defence of human rights in the Americas, has affirmed that no de facto government coming into power by unconstitutional means has legitimacy *ab initio* to declare a state of emergency. On 30 December 2009, the IACHR issued an exhaustive opinion on human rights and the *coup d'état* in Honduras that took place on 28 June 2009,[56] the last *coup* in the Americas as of this writing.[57] Its reasoning is especially illustrative of how domestic judges must uphold fundamental rights and freedoms during the declared state of emergency post-*coups*.

Stressing the interrelationship between democracy, the rule of law and the observance of human rights, the IACHR confirms that the *coup d'état* that deposed the constitutionally elected President of Honduras had and still has an immediate adverse impact on the rule of law and human rights. Under the American Convention, a series of requirements must be met for suspension of guarantees, the first of which is that the suspension must be ordered by a government that exercises public power legitimately, within the context of a democratic society.[58] The IACHR quotes the aforesaid IACtHR's Advisory Opinion that the suspension of guarantees lacks all legitimacy whenever it is resorted to for the purpose of undermining the democratic system.[59]

Of special interest is the IACHR's on-site visit to Honduras where a meeting was held with the judges of the Constitutional Chamber of the Supreme Court. The judges said there was no state of emergency; instead, there were curfews for certain hours and, during the curfew hours, constitutional guarantees were not suspended; instead, the suspension mainly had to do with 'freedom of movement and of association, in order to prevent uprisings'. As for the curfew formalities, the judges said curfews were ordered by the executive branch and confirmed by the National Congress and the confirmation was broadcast daily by a national network.[60] The IACHR concludes, however, that the state of emergency was in

55 Judgment No 1992–341 O (10 November 1992).
56 OEA/Ser.L/V/II. Doc 55 (30 December 2009).
57 Assuming that Bolivia's constitutional crisis in November 2019 was a not *coup*. See Chapter 2 n 155.
58 OEA/Ser.L/V/II. Doc 55 (30 December 2009) paras 208–12.
59 Ibid para 212.
60 Ibid para 216.

fact established by a decree issued by a de facto government, and was decreed for a period shorter than it actually lasted, without ever being published in the Official Gazette, and that Congress' subsequent ratification of the executive decree and its subsequent publication did not correct the original defects. Irrespective of the Constitutional Chamber's interpretation, the curfews were 'states of exception' during which guarantees were restricted—and some restriction even exceeded what was allowed under Honduran domestic law governing a state of emergency—all this without taking the precautions required under Honduran law and Article 27 of the American Convention. The IACHR considers the curfews in the context of the *coup d'état* in Honduras to have been ordered without any explanation of their reasons or their relevance to the situation that prompted the state of emergency. Even in a legitimate state of emergency, each measure taken must be reasonable, strictly appropriate to the cause and to the scope of the state of emergency and without any type of discrimination.[61]

The IACHR also scrutinized the de facto government's subsequent executive decree suspending the following guarantees for 45 days (the maximum allowed under the Constitution): the right to personal liberty, freedom of expression without prior censorship, freedom of association and assembly, freedom of movement and the right to be brought before a competent authority within 24 hours if arrested or detained. The decree additionally prohibited public meetings or assemblies unless authorized by the police or military authorities. Four different petitions of *amparo* were filed challenging that decree, but none was taken up by the Constitutional Chamber. About a month later, the decree was revoked by the very authorities who had issued it. As the state of emergency declared by those who unlawfully seized power had adverse consequences for the rights of individuals and for the administration of justice in Honduras, it was essential to have judicial oversight of government measures.[62] The IACHR finds the difficulties and obstacles that judges executing writs of *habeas corpus* encountered, both when the police refused to release persons being held and when the judges themselves were assaulted or otherwise attacked.[63] Furthermore, the authorities in the judicial branch denounced the steps taken by the de facto government to transfer, remove and replace judges without following proper procedure; hence, a breach of the independence of judiciary and possible violations of the guarantee of the impartiality of judges.[64]

The IACHR considers the requirement for a police permit for any public event, assembly, election, conference, parade, congress or sports related, cultural, artistic or family event to be disproportionately restrictive. Although the Honduran Constitution provides for the possibility that special permits may be required for demonstrations held in the open air or those of political nature, the de facto government

61 Ibid paras 218–23.
62 Ibid para 227.
63 Ibid 230.
64 Ibid 232.

apparently had been demanding permits as a way of restricting, controlling and criminalizing demonstrations against the *coup*.[65]

The IACHR finds thousands of unlawful and arbitrary detentions were made since the *coup*, both in enforcing the curfew and during the demonstrations in support of Honduras' ousted President Zelaya. Specifically, the IACHR received information regarding detentions in which the requirements stipulated in domestic and international law were not observed. This pattern also revealed how the de facto government resorted to practices intended to criminalize public protests, all in order to control and deter the opposition to the *coup*.[66]

In the IACHR's conclusion, serious violations of the human rights, including no fewer than seven deaths, occurred in Honduras since the *coup*. Apart from the ones mentioned earlier, there were serious violations of political rights, such as the right to participate in political life and the right to serve in public office enshrined in Article 23 of the American Convention and Article 3 of the 2001 Inter-American Democratic Charter[67] binding on all OAS Member States. Ministers, governors, members of Congress and mayors were targets of reprisals, threats, acts of violence, budgetary cuts and military occupation of their offices. Also, de facto and de jure restrictions were imposed on the activities of the political parties, groups and leaders of the opposition to the de facto government. Besides, the de facto government took measures that were egregious, arbitrary, unnecessary and disproportionate restrictions on the mass media, in violation in international law of the right of every Honduran to express himself or herself freely and to receive information from a plurality and diversity of sources. The IACHR states categorically that that no de facto government has legitimacy *ab initio* to declare a state of emergency. In the case of Honduras, it was used as a justification for the control mechanisms introduced by the de facto authorities and implemented by the security forces in violation of Article 27 of the American Convention. Although Honduras had an international obligation under the American Convention to prevent violations of human rights and, should they occur, to investigate, try and punish those responsible, the judicial remedies were ineffective and the internal investigations had not made any significant headway in identifying and punishing those responsible. The de facto authorities and the Supreme Court of Honduras consistently denied the existence of these human rights violations, thereby enabling their repetition with impunity. Since the organs of the Inter-American system for the protection of human rights have repeatedly held that the democratic system of government is the best guarantee of the exercise and enjoyment of human rights, the IACHR considers the restoration of democratic institutions in Honduras to be a condition *sine qua non* for effective protection and observance of the human rights of all inhabitants of Honduras.[68]

65 Ibid para 306.
66 Ibid paras 340–82.
67 (2001) 40 ILM 1289.
68 OEA/Ser.L/V/II. Doc 55 (30 December 2009) paras 386–406, 551–60.

Indeed, two months after the *coup*, the OAS suspended Honduras' membership in August 2009 before readmitting it two years later, after democratic elections were held in that country.

With respect to Africa, the 1981 African Charter on Human and Peoples' Rights[69] does not contain any derogation or suspension clause. It neither explicitly prohibits nor allows its States Parties to derogate from their human rights obligations under the Charter. In individual complaints, the African Commission on Human and Peoples' Rights rejected the defence of derogation in a series of cases on the grounds that the African Charter does not allow derogation and States Parties cannot invoke the right to derogate from the human and peoples' rights in times of war or other circumstances where the life of the nation is at risk.[70] However, when examining States' reports, the African Commission took a completely different approach on the issues of derogation. The African Commission omitted to reiterate its position as expressed in individual communications but focused instead on regulating the behaviour of States Parties during a declared state of emergency.[71]

A domestic court in Africa may sometimes step in to protect rights and freedoms in time of the declaration of the state of emergency. For example, after the Sudanese military *coup* on 25 October 2021 the junta declared a state of emergency and shut down the Internet as of the early hours of that day. On 9 November 2021, ruling on the complaint on behalf of the Sudanese Consumer Protection Society, the Khartoum North Court ordered Sudan's main telecommunication companies to immediately restore Internet services.[72] The Internet service was eventually restored on 18 November 2021.

Military tribunals

The military usurper of power often uses specially established or permanent military tribunals to sustain its rule.[73]

69 (1982) 21 ILM 58, in force 21 October 1986.

70 *Commission Nationale des Droits de l'Homme et des Liberties v Chad*, Communication 74/92, (2000) AHRLR 66, (ACHPR 1995), ACHPR 9th Annual Activity Report; *Media Rights Agenda and Others v Nigeria*, Communications 105/93, 128/94, 130/94 and 152/96, (2000) AHRLR 227, (ACHPR 1998), ACHPR 12th Annual Activity Report; *Constitutional Rights Project, Civil Liberties, and Media Rights Agenda v Nigeria*, Communications 140/94, 141/94 and 145/95, (2000) AHRLR 227, (ACHPR 1999), ACHPR 13th Annual Activity Report; *Amnesty International and Others v Sudan*, Communications 48/90, 50/91, 52/91 and 89/93, (2000) AHRLR 297, (ACHPR 1999), ACHPR 13th Annual Activity Report; and *Article 19 v Eritrea*, Communication 275/2003, (2007) AHRLR 73 (ACHPR 2007), ACHPR 22nd Annual Activity Report. These cases are discussed in Melkamu Tolera, 'Absence of a Derogation Clause Under the African Charter and the Position of the African Commission' (2013–14) 4 Bahir Dar U J Law 229, 244–56.

71 Tolera, 'Absence of a Derogation Clause Under the African Charter and the Position of the African Commission' 258–61.

72 'Sudanese court rules in favor of immediately restoring internet service' *Xinhua* (9 November 2021), http://www.news.cn/english/2021-11/09/c_1310301109.htm.

73 See also Brett Kyle and Andrew Reiter, *Military Courts, Civil-Military Relations, and the Legal Battle for Democracy: The Politics of Military Justice* (Routledge 2021) 5–11, 48–123, 159–95, 224–34. Military

For instance, a special military court was set up after the military takeover of the Turkish Government in 1960[74] to try leading members of the ousted civilian regime. On 15 September 1961, the court rendered its judgment acquitting 123 of the 587 defendants, sentencing 15 other defendants to death and 31 others to life imprisonment, and imposing various prison sentences on the remaining 418 defendants. Among those sentenced to death were Adnan Menderes, the civilian Prime Minister toppled by the *coup*, his foreign minister and finance minister who were each convicted of corruption, violation of the constitution and treason.[75] In June 2020 the Turkish Parliament ratified the bill declaring the legal grounds for their trial and execution null and void, having the criminal and archive records of the *coup* trial victims expunged by the Ministry of Justice, and paving the way for compensatory damages for the *coup* trial victims.[76]

According to *Radio Free Asia*, as of 27 January 2022, 101 persons opposed to the 1 February 2021 military *coup* in Myanmar had been sentenced to death, 50 of whom by secretive military tribunals without access to legal representation, with the rest being sentenced *in absentia*. Most of them came from regions where martial law had been declared amid resistance to military rule. Two of the better known prisoners facing the death penalty were Phyo Zeyar Thaw, a former Member of Parliament from the National League for Democracy Party that had won the largest number of seats in the November 2020 general elections, and Ko Jimmy, a leader of a pro-democracy movement. Both were convicted of violating the Anti-Terrorism Law, and their photographs released by the junta showed signs of their having been severely tortured during interrogation.[77] They and two other political prisoners opposed to the military regime were executed in July 2022, drawing widespread international condemnation, including from the UN Security Council.

In Thailand, Section 38 of the Statute of Military Courts Act, B.E. 2498 (1955), as amended, provides, inter alia, that when martial law is declared, the authority with the power to declare martial law may issue an order for military courts to assume jurisdiction over criminal offences not normally within their jurisdiction, and that

---

tribunals in some countries with democratic government have very broad jurisdiction over civilians. In Lebanon, for example, the military court system falls under the jurisdiction of the Ministry of Defence and it has jurisdiction over civilians for offences such as espionage; treason; military draft evasion; unlawful contact with the enemy (Israel); weapons possession; crimes endangering the interest of the military, the internal security forces or the general security; and any conflict between civilians and military or security personnel or the civilian employees of the Ministry of Defence, army, security services or military courts (International Commission of Jurists, *The Jurisdiction and Independence of the Military Courts System in Lebanon in Light of International Standards: A Briefing Paper* (May 2018)).

74 For a relatively favourable, but controversial, analysis of this military takeover, see Ozan Varol, 'The Diplomatic Coups d'État' (2012) 53 Harvard ILJ 291, 323–33.

75 Reuben Silverman, 'Show (and Tell) Trials: Competing Narratives of Turkey's Democrat Party Era' (2022) 23 Turkish Studies 147.

76 'Turkish Parliament Quashes Results of 1960 Coup Trials' *Hurriyet Daily News* (24 June 2020), https://www.hurriyetdailynews.com/turkish-parliament-oks-bill-nullifying-1960-coup-trial-155955.

77 'More Than 100 Sentenced to Death in Yangon Since Myanmar Coup' *Radio Free Asia* (27 January 2022), https://www.rfa.org/english/news/myanmar/deaths-01272022181610.html.

after the end of martial law military courts shall continue to exercise jurisdiction over criminal cases pending before them or cases already in their docket whose trial has yet to commence. As a result of the Thai Army's declaration of martial law on 20 May 2014 and National Council for Peace and Order (NCPO) Orders 37/2014 and 38/2014, issued three days after the 22 May 2014 military *coup*, military courts assumed jurisdiction over several categories of offences, including *lèse-majesté* (Section 112 of the Criminal Code) and sedition (Section 116 of the Criminal Code), committed from 25 May 2014. Despite the revocation of martial law on 1 April 2015, the NCPO continued to use military courts for the same categories of offences until 12 September 2016, when the NCPO issued Order 55/2016 to terminate the practice of trying civilians in military courts for offences allegedly committed from 12 September 2016. From 25 May 2014 to 30 November 2016, military courts across Thailand tried 2,177 civilians in 1,716 cases and, as of 30 November 2016, it was estimated that 416 cases involving civilians remained under the jurisdiction of military tribunals.[78] Most of those detained were human rights defenders, student activists, academics, writers, journalists, advocates for the reform of *lèse-majesté* law, former members of the House of Representatives, former Cabinet ministers of the Government deposed by the NCPO, and leaders and supporters of the United Front for Democracy Against Dictatorship. The systematic practice of detaining critics was explained as 'attitude adjustments', with harsh conditions imposed on those released from 'attitude adjustment' detention, such as a punishment of two years' imprisonment and/or a fine of 40,000 baht (about US$1,200) if those freed subsequently failed to fulfil the conditions of their release by leaving Thailand without the NCPO's prior permission and/or by carrying out any political activities.[79]

In Tunisia, on 25 July 2021 President Kais Saied cited emergency clauses under the Tunisian Constitution to dismiss the Government, suspend Parliament until the general elections to be held on 17 December 2022 elected new MPs after a national referendum on a new constitution on 25 July 2022, waive the parliamentary immunity of the incumbent MPs, and make himself head of the Judiciary and the public prosecution.[80] His reasons were to save Tunisia from corruption and political paralysis. Several of his critics were put on trial by military tribunals. This was the case of, for example, Seif Eddine Makhlouf, an opposition MP, who was accused of having insulted security staff at the airport months earlier. On 21 September 2021, two MPs—Nidal Saudi and Saif Eddine Makhlouf, from the Karama Party opposed to President Saied—were imprisoned by a Tunisian military judge, the latter, after being refused permission to represent the former as a lawyer,

78 International Federation for Human Rights, Union for Civil Liberties, and Internet Law Reform Dialogue, *Joint Shadow Report (Thailand)*, submitted to the Human Rights Committee, 119th Session (6–29 March 2017) 11 and 12, citing the Judge Advocate General Department, *Statistics of Civilians Being Tried in Military Courts*, 13 January 2017.

79 The International Federation for Human Rights *et al.*, *Joint Shadow Report (Thailand)* 6.

80 However, he has been accused of exceeding the authority given to the President under Art 80 of the 2014 Tunisian Constitution (www.constituteproject.org/constitution/Tunisia_2014.pdf).

for making a threat to a military judge and for accusing military judges of being involved in President Saied's '*coup*'.[81]

These are just four of the examples of resorting to military tribunals after a military *coup* or a self-*coup*.

An authoritative analysis of the legitimacy of military tribunals can be found in the report by Emmanuel Decaux, Special Rapporteur of the Sub-Commission on the Promotion and Protection of Human Rights of the UN Commission on Human Rights, the predecessor of the UN Human Rights Council. This report on the issue of administration of justice through military tribunals was submitted in January 2006 to the Commission under the agenda item 'Civil and political rights, including the question of independence of the judiciary, administration of justice, impunity'.[82] The report proceeds on the basis that military justice must be an integral part of the general judicial system, and that the 20 draft principles identified in the report, which rely extensively on the CCPR's interpretation of the ICCPR, constitute a minimum system of universally applicable rules, leaving scope for stricter standards to be defined under domestic law. The following draft principles, developed in consultation with human rights experts, jurists and military personnel from throughout the world, are relevant to the discussion in this chapter.

Under Principle No 1, military tribunals, when they exist, may be established only by the constitution or the law, respecting the principle of the separation of powers, and they must be an integral part of the general judicial system. This is to ensure the independence of judiciary and that the existence of military tribunals in a number of countries should not place them outside the scope of ordinary law or above the law but, on the contrary, should include them in the principles of the rule of law within the overall unity of justice.

According to Principle No 2, military tribunals must in all circumstances apply standards and procedures internationally recognized as guarantees of a fair trial, including the rules of international humanitarian law even in times of crisis, particularly as regards Article 4 of the ICCPR. This Principle is reinforced by Principle No 3, propounding that, in times of crisis, recourse to martial law or special regimes should not compromise the guarantees of a fair trial, and derogations 'strictly required by the exigencies of the situation' should be consistent with the principles of the proper administration of justice. Consequently, all the principles relating to the administration of justice by military tribunals should continue to apply in full. In particular, military tribunals should not be substituted for ordinary courts, in derogation from ordinary law, by being given jurisdiction to try civilians.

81 'Tunisia Military Judge Jails Two Members of Parliament' *Al Jazeera* (22 September 2021), https://www.aljazeera.com/news/2021/9/22/tunisia-military-judge-jails-two-members-of-parliament. On 30 March 2022, the President dissolved Parliament after the latter had held a plenary session online and voted through a bill to revoke all emergency measures imposed by the President including the suspension of Parliament. In addition, Tunisia's Minister of Justice instructed the Attorney General to open an investigation against MPs on charges of conspiring against State security.

82 E/CN.4/2006/58 (13 January 2006).

Principle No 5 states in a sweeping manner that military courts should, in principle, have no jurisdiction to try civilians, and that, in all circumstances, the State shall ensure civilians accused of a criminal offence of any nature are tried by civilian courts. While the ICCPR does not prohibit military courts, the conditions it lays down clearly indicate that the trying of civilians by such courts should be very exceptional and take place under conditions which genuinely afford the full guarantees stipulated in Article 14 (rights to equality before courts and tribunals and to fair trial) of the ICCPR. According to Principle No 8, the jurisdiction of military courts should be limited to offences of a strictly military nature committed by military personnel and persons treated as military personnel for the latter's infractions strictly related to their military status. Nonetheless, such jurisdiction should not constitute a derogation in principle from ordinary law, corresponding to a jurisdictional privilege or a form of justice by one's peers. Such jurisdiction should remain exceptional and apply only to the requirements of military service, particularly as regards field operations, when the territorial court cannot exercise its jurisdiction. Only such a functional necessity can justify the limited but irreducible existence of military justice. This is because the national court is prevented from exercising its jurisdiction for practical reasons arising from the remoteness of the action, while the local court that would be territorially competent is confronted with jurisdictional immunities.

Pursuant to Principle No 9, in all circumstances, the jurisdiction of military courts should be set aside in favour of the jurisdiction of the ordinary courts to conduct inquiries into serious human rights violations such as extrajudicial executions, enforced disappearances and torture, and to prosecute and try persons accused of such crimes. Nowadays, there is a growing tendency to consider that persons accused of serious human rights violations cannot be tried by military tribunals insofar as such acts would, by their very nature, not fall within the scope of the duties performed by such persons. Moreover, the military authorities might be tempted to cover up such cases by questioning the appropriateness of prosecutions, tending to file cases with no action taken or manipulating 'guilty pleas' to the detriment of victims. Civilian courts must therefore be able, from the outset, to conduct inquiries and prosecute and try those charged with such violations so as to avoid all forms of impunity. The authority of the civilian judge should also enable the rights of the victims to be taken fully into account at all stages of the proceedings. The doctrine and jurisprudence of the CCPR and other human rights treaty monitoring bodies such as CAT and the Committee on the Rights of the Child, the African Commission on Human and Peoples' Rights, the IACtHR and the IACHR and the country-specific and thematic procedures of the then UN Commission on Human Rights are unanimous: military tribunals are not competent to try military personnel responsible for serious human rights violations against civilians.

Principle No 10 limits the invocation of military secrecy. The rules that make it possible to invoke the secrecy of military information should not be diverted from their original purpose so as to obstruct the course of justice or to violate human rights. Military secrecy may be invoked, under the supervision of independent monitoring bodies, when it is strictly necessary to protect information concerning national defence. Military secrecy may not be invoked: (a) where measures involving deprivation of liberty are concerned, which should not, under any circumstances, be kept secret, whether this involves the identity or the whereabouts of persons deprived of their liberty; (b) to obstruct the initiation or conduct of inquiries, proceedings or trials, whether they are of a criminal or a disciplinary nature, or to ignore them; (c) to deny judges and authorities delegated by law to exercise judicial activities access to documents and areas classified or restricted for reasons of national security; (d) to obstruct the publication of court sentences; or (e) to obstruct the effective exercise of *habeas corpus* and other similar judicial remedies. Also, the invocation of military secrecy should not lead to the holding incommunicado of a person who is the subject of judicial proceedings, or who has already been sentenced or subjected to any degree of deprivation of liberty.

Principle No 11 requires military prisons to comply with international standards, including the United Nations Standard Minimum Rules for the Treatment of Prisoners (or the Nelson Mandela Rule),[83] the Basic Principles for the Treatment of Prisoners[84] and the Body of Principles for the Protection of All Persons under Any Form of Detention or Imprisonment,[85] and military prisons must be accessible to domestic and international inspection bodies. In this regard, States should be encouraged to ratify the Optional Protocol to the Convention against Torture as soon as possible.

Under Principle No 12, anyone who is deprived of his or her liberty shall, in all circumstances, be entitled to take proceedings, such as *habeas corpus* proceedings, before a court, so that the court may decide without delay on the lawfulness of his or her detention and order his or her release if the detention is not lawful. The right to petition for a writ of *habeas corpus* or other remedy should be considered as a personal right, the guarantee of which should, in all circumstances, fall within the exclusive jurisdiction of the ordinary courts. In all circumstances, the judge must be able to have access to any place where the detainee may be held.

Principle No 13 stipulates that the organization and operation of military courts should fully ensure the right of everyone to a competent, independent and impartial tribunal at every stage of legal proceedings from initial investigation to trial. The persons selected to perform the functions of judges in military courts must display integrity and competence and show proof of the necessary legal training and qualifications. Military judges should have a status guaranteeing their independence and impartiality, in particular vis-à-vis the military hierarchy. In no circumstances should military courts be allowed to resort to procedures involving anonymous or 'faceless' judges and prosecutors. The statutory independence of judges vis-à-vis the military hierarchy must be strictly protected, avoiding any direct or indirect

83 https://www.unodc.org/documents/justice-and-prison-reform/Nelson_Mandela_Rules-E-ebook.pdf.
84 A/RES/45/111 (14 December 1990).
85 A/RES/43/173 (9 December 1988).

subordination, whether in the organization and operation of the system of justice itself or in terms of career development for military judges.

According to Principle No 14, as in matters of ordinary law, public hearings must be the rule, and the holding of sessions in camera should be altogether exceptional and be authorized by a specific, well-grounded decision the lawfulness of which is subject to review. The only restrictions on this Principle are those laid down in ordinary law, in keeping with Article 14(1) of the ICCPR. All these grounds must be strictly interpreted, particularly when 'national security' is invoked, and must be applied only where necessary in 'a democratic society'.

Principle No 15 has a long list of guarantees of the rights of the defence and the right to a just and fair trial in all judicial proceedings in military courts and in all circumstances. Everyone charged with a criminal offence shall be presumed innocent until proved guilty according to law. Every accused person must be informed promptly of the details of the offence with which he or she is charged and, before and during the trial, must be guaranteed all the rights and facilities necessary for his or her defence. No one shall be punished for an offence except on the basis of individual criminal responsibility. Everyone charged with a criminal offence shall have the right to be tried without undue delay and in his or her presence. Everyone charged with a criminal offence shall have the right to defend himself or herself in person or through legal assistance of his or her own choosing;[86] to be informed, if he or she does not have legal assistance, of this right; and to have legal assistance assigned to him or her, in any case where the interests of justice so require, and without payment by him or her in any such case if he or she does not have sufficient means to pay for it. No one may be compelled to testify against himself or herself or to confess guilt. Everyone charged with a criminal offence shall have the right to examine, or have examined, the witnesses against him or her and to obtain the attendance and examination of witnesses on his or her behalf under the same conditions as witnesses against him or her. No statement or item of evidence which is established to have been obtained through torture, cruel, inhuman or degrading treatment or other serious violations of human rights or by illicit means may be invoked as evidence in the proceedings. No one may be convicted of a crime on the strength of anonymous testimony or secret evidence. Everyone convicted of a crime shall have the right to have his or her conviction and sentence reviewed by a higher tribunal according to law. Every person found guilty shall be informed, at the time of conviction, of his or her rights to judicial and other remedies and of the time limits for the exercise of those rights.

Without prejudice to the principles relating to the jurisdiction of military courts, Principle No 16 requires military courts not to exclude the victims of crimes or

86 The reports notes that provision of legal assistance by military lawyers, particularly when they are officially appointed, has been challenged as inconsistent with respect for the rights of the defence. However, it considers that military lawyers may provide accused persons with an effective defence, provided that the principle of free choice of defence counsel by the accused is safeguarded, and that the strict independence of the military lawyer is guaranteed.

their successors from judicial proceedings, including inquiries. The judicial proceedings of military courts should ensure the rights of the victims of crimes, or their successors, are effectively respected, by guaranteeing they: (a) have the right to report criminal acts and bring an action in the military courts so that judicial proceedings can be initiated; (b) have a broad right to intervene in judicial proceedings and are able to participate in such proceedings as a party to the case (e.g., a claimant for criminal indemnification, an *amicus curiae* or a party bringing a private action); (c) have access to judicial remedies to challenge decisions and rulings by military courts against their rights and interests; and (d) are protected against any ill treatment and any act of intimidation or reprisal that might arise from the complaint or from their participation in the judicial proceedings.

Under Principle No 17, military tribunals' authority should be limited to ruling in first instance, and recourse procedures, particularly appeals, should be brought before the civil courts. In all situations, conflicts of authority and jurisdiction between military tribunals and ordinary courts must be resolved by a higher judicial body, such as a supreme court or constitutional court, that forms part of the system of ordinary courts and is composed of independent, impartial and competent judges.

Principle No 18 provides that due obedience may not be invoked to relieve a member of the military of the individual criminal responsibility incurred by him or her as a result of the commission of serious violations of human rights, such as extrajudicial executions, enforced disappearances and torture, war crimes or crimes against humanity. The fact that such a serious violation of human rights has been committed by a subordinate does not relieve his or her superiors of criminal responsibility if they failed to exercise the powers vested in them to prevent or halt their commission, if they were in possession of information that enabled them to know that the crime was being or was about to be committed.[87]

According to Principle No 19, codes of military justice should reflect the international trend towards the gradual abolition of the death penalty, in both peacetime and wartime. In no circumstances shall the death penalty be imposed or carried out for offences committed by persons aged under 18, on pregnant women or mothers with young children and on persons suffering from any mental or intellectual disabilities.[88]

Principle No 20 states that codes of military justice should be subject to periodic systematic review, conducted in an independent and transparent manner, so as

87 This Principle surprisingly omits to mention that the superiors may also be criminally liable if they failed to take the necessary and reasonable measures to punish, or to submit the matter to the competent authorities for investigation and prosecution of, the subordinate who had committed such a violation. See Art 7(3) of the ICTY Statute (S/RES/808 (1993), Art 6(3) of the ICTR Statute (S/RES/995 (1994) Annex) and Art 28(a)(ii) of the Rome Statute of the ICC.

88 This extends the scope of protection against death penalty stipulated in Art 6(5) of the ICCPR, which provides: 'Sentence of death shall not be imposed for crimes committed by persons below eighteen years of age and shall not be carried out on pregnant women'. The report cites the trend against the death penalty and the UN Commission on Human Rights' resolution 2005/59 on the question of the death penalty (para 7(a), (b) and (c)) in support of this extension of the scope of protection.

to ensure the authority of military tribunals correspond to strict functional necessity, without encroaching on the jurisdiction that can and should belong to ordinary civil courts. More generally, this periodic review should ensure that military justice is appropriate and effective in relation to its practical justification. It would also embody the fully democratic nature of an institution that must be accountable for its operations to the authorities and all citizens in a completely transparent manner in a democratic society.

In her report titled 'Independence of judges and lawyers' submitted to the UN General Assembly in August 2013,[89] the Special Rapporteur on the independence of judges and lawyers (Gabriela Knaul) focuses on the administration of justice through military tribunals which, in many countries, raises serious concerns in terms of access to justice, impunity for past human rights abuses perpetrated by military regimes, the independence and impartiality of judiciary and respect for fair trial guarantees for the defendant. The report focuses on four issues of concern: (a) the independence and impartiality of military tribunals; (b) the personal jurisdiction of military tribunals, including the question of investigation and prosecution of civilians; (c) the subject-matter jurisdiction of military tribunals, including the question of investigation and prosecution of serious human rights violations allegedly perpetrated by military personnel and (d) fair trial guarantees in proceedings before military tribunals. Using military or emergency courts to try civilians in the name of national security, a state of emergency or counterterrorism is a regrettably common practice that runs counter to all international and regional standards and established case law. The Special Rapporteur proposes a number of solutions, premised on the view that the jurisdiction of military tribunals should be restricted to offences of a military nature committed by military personnel. States with military justice systems should aim to guarantee the independence and impartiality of military tribunals, as well as the exercise and enjoyment of a number of human rights, including the right to a fair trial[90] and the right to an effective remedy.

The Special Rapporteur refers to *Palamara Iribarne v Chile*,[91] in which the IACtHR held that military tribunals in Chile lacked independence and impartiality. The organic structure and composition of military tribunals in Chile implied they were made up of active-duty military members hierarchically subordinate to higher-ranked officers through the chain of command, their designation did not depend on their professional skills and qualifications to exercise judicial functions, they did not have sufficient guarantees against being removed and they had not received the legal education required to sit as judges or serve as prosecutors. In *Castillo Petruzzi v Peru*,[92] the fact that members of the Supreme Court of Military Justice, the highest body in the military judiciary in Peru, were appointed by the minister of the

89 A/68/285 (7 August 2013).

90 See further Amal Clooney and Philippa Webb, *The Right to a Fair Trial in International Law* (OUP 2021).

91 Judgment of 22 November 2005, Ser C No 135.

92 Judgment of 30 May 1999, Ser C No 52.

pertinent sector was enough for the IACtHR to call the independence of the military judges into serious question. In *Ergin v Turkey (No 6)*,[93] in which a newspaper editor was tried by a military tribunal for inciting the evasion of military service, the European Court of Human Rights (ECtHR) held that situations in which a military tribunal has jurisdiction to try a civilian for acts against the armed forces may give rise to reasonable doubts about such court's objective impartiality. A judicial system in which a military tribunal is empowered to try a person who is not a member of the armed forces may easily be perceived as reducing to nothing the distance that should exist between the court and the parties to criminal proceedings, even if there are sufficient safeguards to guarantee that court's independence.

The Special Rapporteur also alludes to the CCPR's General Comment No 32 (Article 14: Rights to equality before courts and tribunals and to fair trial)[94]—while the ICCPR does not prohibit the trial of civilians in military or special courts, it nonetheless requires such trials to be in full conformity with the requirements of Article 14 of the ICCPR and its guarantees not to be limited or modified because of the military or special character of the court concerned. Furthermore, trials of civilians by military or special courts should be exceptional, in the sense of being limited to cases where the ICCPR State Party can show resorting to such trials is necessary and justified by objective and serious reasons and where, with regard to the specific class of individuals and offences at issue, the regular civilian courts are unable to undertake the trials. It is therefore incumbent on the said State Party to demonstrate, with regard to a specific class of individuals, that: (a) the regular civilian courts are unable to undertake the trials; (b) other, alternative, forms of special or high-security civilian courts are inadequate for the task and (c) recourse to military tribunals ensures the full protection of the rights of the accused pursuant to Article 14. In its concluding observations on reports submitted by States Parties as required by Article 40 of the ICCPR, the CCPR has gone further by calling on governments in several countries to prohibit the trial of civilians before military tribunals altogether.[95] Also, the mere invocation of domestic legal provisions for the trial by military tribunals of certain categories of serious offences does not constitute a valid argument under the ICCPR to justify recourse to such tribunals. In the absence of a specific justification as to the necessity of trying a specific class of civilians in military tribunals, the CCPR has invariably found such trials to be inconsistent with the guarantees set out in Article 14.[96]

93 App no 47533/99, Judgment of 4 May 2006.

94 CCPR/C/GC/32 (2007).

95 A/68/285 (7 August 2013) para 51, citing the concluding observations on the reports submitted by Slovakia (CCPR/C/79/Add.79 para 20), Lebanon (CCPR/C/79/Add.78 para. 14), Chile (CCPR/C/CHL/CO/5 para 12), Tajikistan (CCPR/CO/84/TJK para 18) and Ecuador (CCPR/C/ECU/CO/5 para 5).

96 A/68/285 (7 August 2013) para 52, citing *Ebenezer Derek Mbongo Akwanga v Cameroon*, CCPR/C/101/D/1813/2008, 19 May 2011; *Abdelhamid Benhadj v Algeria*, CCPR/C/90/D/1173/2003, 26 September 2007; *Salim Abbassi v Algeria*, CCPR/C/89/D/1172/2003, 28 March 2007; and *Kurbanova v Tajikistan*, CCPR/C/79/D/1096/2002, 6 November 2003.

The Special Rapporteur affirms the tendency in State practice towards limiting the personal jurisdiction of military tribunals to criminal offences and breaches of discipline allegedly committed by active members of the armed forces, with any exception with regard to civilians who are assimilated to military personnel being crafted and interpreted narrowly.[97] In this respect, the widespread human rights abuses committed by military juntas in Latin American countries have led many countries in the region to curtail the competence of military tribunals to try military personnel who have committed human rights violations. In Colombia, Article 221 of the Constitution was amended to exclude serious human rights violations such as genocide, forced disappearance, extrajudicial execution, sexual violence, torture and forced displacement from military jurisdiction. In August 2012 the Mexican Supreme Court limited the use of the military justice system for trying cases involving alleged human rights abuses after finding Article 57, section II (a), of the Code of Military Justice to be inconsistent with Articles 2 and 8(1) of the American Convention on Human Rights as interpreted by the IACtHR.[98]

Law enforcement measures

Law enforcement measures taken by government authorities to maintain law and order during and after a *coup* must not escalate into atrocious abuses of human rights or crimes normally punishable under domestic law and/or international criminal law.

The 1990 UN Basic Principles on the Use of Force and Firearms by Law Enforcement Officials[99] is the leading international instrument dedicated to regulating the use of force for law enforcement purposes. There are 26 Basic Principles founded upon the principle of legality, the principle of necessity, the principle of proportionality, the duty of precaution and the principle of accountability.[100]

With respect to the principle of legality, Basic Principle 1 provides that governments and law enforcement agencies shall adopt and implement rules and regulations on the use of force and firearms against persons by law enforcement officials and shall keep the ethical issues associated with the use of force and firearms constantly under review. This is because the police power to use force needs to be sufficiently based in domestic legislation, serve a legitimate objective as established by law in the sense that force is used for a lawful law enforcement purpose and in line

97 A/68/285 (7 August 2013) paras 53–62.

98 Ibid para 71.

99 Adopted by the 8th UN Congress on the Prevention of Crimes and the Treatment of Offenders, Havana, Cuba, 27 August–7 September 1990. In its Resolution 45/166, adopted without a vote on 18 December 1990, the UN General Assembly welcomed the Basic Principles and invited governments to respect them.

100 Amnesty International, *Use of Force: Guidelines for the Implementation of the UN Basic Principles on the Use of Force and Firearms by Law Enforcement Officials* (Amnesty International, Dutch Section 2015); Geneva Academy of International Humanitarian Law and Human Rights, *Use of Force in Law Enforcement and the Right to Life: The Role of the Human Rights Council*, Academy In-Brief no 6 (November 2016) 6–10.

with international human rights law and standards. When the use of force is not aimed at achieving a legitimate objective as established in domestic legislation (e.g., punishment or use of physical means to obtain a confession), it is unlawful *per se*.[101]

Necessity[102] is reflected in Basic Principle 4, according to which law enforcement officials, in carrying out their duty, shall, as far as possible, apply non-violent means before resorting to the use of force and firearms as the last resort and only if other means remain ineffective or without any promise of achieving the intended result. The principle of necessity serves to determine whether force should be used at all and, if so, how much force. The principle has three components: qualitative (Is force necessary at all or is it possible to achieve the legitimate objective without resorting to force?); quantitative (How much force is needed to achieve the objective, bearing in mind that the level of force used should be the minimum that can still be considered effective?); and temporary (The use of force must stop once the objective has been achieved or is no longer achievable).[103] The principle of necessity is affirmed by the IACtHR, the CCPR and the ECtHR,[104] among others.

Proportionality is encapsulated in Basic Principle 5(a): Whenever the lawful use of force and firearms is unavoidable, law enforcement officials shall exercise restraint in such use and act in proportion to the seriousness of the offence and the legitimate objective to be achieved. Proportionality serves to determine whether there is a balance between the benefits of the use of force and the possible consequences and harm caused by its use. This principle prohibits the use of such force where the harm inflicted outweighs the benefits of the use of force (i.e., the achievement of a legitimate objective). As such, it requires law enforcement officials to refrain from using such force and, ultimately, to accept that the legitimate objective may not be achieved because the end does not justify all means, particularly when it comes to the right to life. This means law enforcement officials are only allowed to put life at risk if it is for the purpose of saving or protecting another life.[105] The closely related 'protect life' principle appears in Basic Principle 5(b): Whenever the lawful use of force and firearms is unavoidable, law enforcement officials shall minimize damage and injury, and respect and preserve human life. Lethal force is to be understood as a type of force that involves either the high likelihood of causing death (potentially lethal force), or is used with the clear knowledge it will lead to the loss of life (i.e. intentional lethal use of force).[106]

101 Amnesty International, *Use of Force* 17.

102 Not to be confused with the principle of necessity in unconstitutional usurpation of power discussed in Chapter 2.

103 Amnesty International, *Use of Force* 18.

104 Geneva Academy of International Humanitarian Law and Human Rights, *Use of Force in Law Enforcement and the Right to Life* 7–8, citing IACtHR, *Nadege Dorzema et al. v Dominican Republic*, Judgment (Merits, Reparations and Costs), 24 October 2012 para 85(iii); CCPR, *Suarez de Guerrero v Colombia*, Views, Communication no R.11/45, 9 April 1981, Supp no 40 (A/37/40) at 137 (1982); and ECtHR, *Bouyid v Belgium*, Grand Chamber, Judgment, App no 23380/09, 28 September 2015 paras 88 and 100, respectively.

105 Amnesty International, *Use of Force* 18.

106 Ibid 53.

According to Basic Principle 9, law enforcement officials shall not use firearms against persons except in self-defence or defence of others against the imminent threat of death or serious injury, to prevent the perpetration of a particularly serious crime involving grave threat to life, to arrest a person presenting such a danger and resisting their authority or to prevent his or her escape, and only when less extreme means are insufficient to achieve these objectives. In any event, intentional lethal use of firearms may only be made when strictly unavoidable in order to protect life. Basic Principle 10 adds that, in the circumstances provided for under Basic Principle 9, law enforcement officials shall identify themselves as such and give a clear warning of their intent to use firearms, with sufficient time for the warning to be observed, unless to do so would unduly place the law enforcement officials at risk or would create a risk of death or serious harm to other persons, or would be clearly inappropriate or pointless in the circumstances of the incident. An example of disproportionate use of force would be to use a firearm to stop an unarmed person from escaping. As the ECtHR held in *Nachova and Others v Bulgaria*, an escaping suspect who does not pose a threat to life may not be shot 'even if a failure to use lethal force may result in the opportunity to arrest the fugitive being lost'.[107]

The duty of precaution serves as a precursor to the principles of necessity and proportionality by requiring the law enforcement authorities to plan law enforcement operations in such a manner as to minimize the risk that its law enforcement agencies and officials may kill or injure a member of the public or another law enforcement official. There are cases decided by the EctHR and the IACtHR in support of this duty.[108]

Basic Principles 6, 7, 11 and 18 through 26 of the 1990 UN Basic Principles explain how full accountability is expected of individual law enforcement personnel at all relevant levels (i.e., acting law enforcement officials, witnessing colleagues and superior officers) in discharging their duties. Accountability can only be ensured if appropriate measures are implemented at various levels and stages. These measures include a supervision and control set-up, adequate training and operational reviews to prevent repetition of mistakes or otherwise undesirable results of law enforcement actions; the existence of a clear chain of command; and a system of checks and balances allowing for the evaluation of any law enforcement action with regard to its compliance with the law, including human rights, as well as with internal regulations and operational procedures. Accountability therefore requires a range of mechanisms, involving the Judiciary, the Legislature, the Executive and the public to hold accountable those responsible for violations of the law, including violations of human rights, and to provide for redress and compensation

107 Grand Chamber, Judgment, App nos 43577/98 and 43579/98, 6 July 2005 para 95, cited in Geneva Academy of International Humanitarian Law and Human Rights, *Use of Force in Law Enforcement and the Right to Life* 9.

108 Geneva Academy of International Humanitarian Law and Human Rights, *Use of Force in Law Enforcement and the Right to Life* 9–10, citing *McCann et al. v UK*, ECtHR, Grand Chamber, App no 18984/91, Judgment, 27 September 1995 para 194; and IACtHR, *Nadege Dorzema et al. v Dominican Republic* para 87.

for victims of such violations; to prevent future violations; and to improve the work of the law enforcement agency as a whole through an effective lessons learned process leading to corrective measures. Effective accountability mechanisms should encompass criminal and disciplinary proceedings, independent external oversight and an institutional lessons learned process.[109]

Basic Principle 8 makes clear that exceptional circumstances such as internal political instability or any other public emergency may not be invoked to justify any departure from these basic principles. Pursuant to Basic Principle 12, as everyone is allowed to participate in lawful and peaceful assemblies, in accordance with the principles embodied in the 1948 Universal Declaration of Human Rights[110] and the ICCPR, governments and law enforcement agencies and officials shall recognize that force and firearms may be used only in accordance with Basic Principles 13 and 14. Pursuant to Basic Principle 13, in dispersing assemblies which are unlawful but non-violent, law enforcement officials shall avoid the use of force or, where that is not practicable, shall restrict such force to the minimum extent necessary. According to Basic Principle 14, in dispersing violent assemblies, law enforcement officials may use firearms only when less dangerous means are not practicable and only to the minimum extent necessary. Law enforcement officials shall not use firearms in such cases, except under the conditions stipulated in Basic Principle 9.

Basic Principles 15 and 16 deal with policing persons in custody or detention and prohibit the use force, except when strictly necessary for the maintenance of security and order within the institution, or when personal safety is threatened, and law enforcement officials shall not use firearms except in self-defence or in the defence of others as set out in Basic Principle 9.

According to the Inter-American Commission on Human Rights, the use of force is a last resort that is to be limited both qualitatively and quantitatively, employed solely to prevent a more serious occurrence than the one that prompted the State to intervene. Law enforcement officials may not, under any circumstances, resort to illegal practices to obtain the objectives entrusted to them, and the means the State may employ to protect its security or that of its citizens are not without limits.[111] The legitimate use of public force implies, inter alia, that it must be both necessary and proportional to the situation, with moderation and in proportion to the legitimate end being sought, while at the same time endeavouring to keep personal injury and loss of human life to an absolute minimum. The degree of force exercised by State agents must not exceed what is absolutely necessary. While in states of emergency the armed forces can be called upon to participate in crowd control at demonstrations, this practice must be limited to the maximum, being the exception rather than the rule, because soldiers are trained to defeat an enemy; they do not receive the training the police receive for their job, which is to protect

109 Amnesty International, *Use of Force* 19–20, 85, 188.

110 UNGA res 217A (III), UN Doc A/810 (1948) 71.

111 Opinion of the IACHR on the human rights situation and the 28 June 2009 *coup d'état* in Honduras (OEA/Ser.L/V/II. Doc 55 (30 December 2009) para 310.

and control civilians. Force or other means of coercion should only be used when all other means have been exhausted and failed.[112]

A 46-page *Guidance on Less-Lethal Weapons in Law Enforcement*[113] was formally launched in Geneva on 25 October 2019 during the 127th session of the CCPR. The *Guidance* is the result of a two-year process of research, drafting and consultation led by the Office of the UN High Commissioner for Human Rights in collaboration with an international group of experts. The 1990 UN Basic Principles on the Use of Force and Firearms by Law Enforcement Officials refers to less-lethal weapons in two of its provisions. Basic Principle 2 calls on governments and law enforcement agencies to develop 'a range of means as broad as possible', which 'should include the development of non-lethal incapacitating weapons for use in appropriate situations'. Basic Principle 3 calls for the development and deployment of less-lethal weapons to be 'carefully evaluated in order to minimize the risk of endangering uninvolved persons', and stipulates that their use 'should be carefully controlled'. These Basic Principles remain valid and applicable to law enforcement operations, and the *Guidance* is adopted to provide direction on the lawful and responsible design, production, transfer, procurement, testing, training, deployment and use of less-lethal weapons and related equipment, as well as to promote accountability for failure in this regard. The *Guidance* is addressed to States, law enforcement agencies, manufacturers, human rights bodies and mechanisms, private security companies, police oversight bodies and human rights defenders, and to individuals seeking to assert their right to a remedy for human rights violations. It is not intended to serve as a set of standing operating procedures for individual officers, but may assist States and their law enforcement agencies in fulfilling their duty to put such procedures in place. The *Guidance* is based on international law, in particular international human rights law and law enforcement rules, as well as good law enforcement practice, especially those pertaining to the rights to life; freedom from torture or other forms of cruel, inhuman or degrading treatment or punishment; security of person; and the right of peaceful assembly.[114]

One frequently overlooked aspect of such law enforcement, which was highlighted in the annual report issued by Thailand's National Human Rights Commission on 24 December 2021, is that children who join protests against the government should be accorded due protection in accordance with the 1989 Convention on the Rights of the Child, binding upon its States Parties, in particular Article 37(b) through (d) thereof. By virtue of these provisions, no child shall be deprived of his or her liberty unlawfully or arbitrarily. The arrest, detention or imprisonment of a child shall be in conformity with the law and shall be used only as a measure of last resort and for the shortest appropriate period of time. Every child deprived of liberty shall be treated with humanity and respect for the inherent dignity of the human person, and in a manner which takes into account the needs

112 Ibid paras 311–4.

113 www.geneva-academy.ch/joomlatools-files/docman-files/LLW_Guidance.pdf.

114 Ibid paras 1.3 and 1.4.

of persons of his or her age. In particular, every child deprived of liberty shall be separated from adults unless it is considered in the child's best interest not to do so[115] and shall have the right to maintain contact with his or her family through correspondence and visits, save in exceptional circumstances. Every child deprived of his or her liberty shall have the right to prompt access to legal and other appropriate assistance, as well as the right to challenge the legality of the deprivation of his or her liberty before a court or other competent, independent and impartial authority, and to a prompt decision on any such action. Article 1 of the Convention defines a child as 'every human being below the age of eighteen years unless under the law applicable to the child, majority is attained earlier'.

Refusal to render judgments on 'political questions'

In the leading case of *Tañada v Cuenco*, decided by the Philippine Supreme Court in 1957, Chief Justice Roberto Concepcion defines the term 'political question' as a question of policy which under the Constitution is to be decided by the people in their sovereign capacity or in regard to which full discretionary authority has been delegated to the Legislature or the Executive—it is concerned with issues dependent upon the wisdom, not legality, of a particular measure.[116]

The Philippine Supreme Court's judgment in *Garcia v The Executive Secretary, The Secretary of the Department of Energy and Others*,[117] decided in 2009, reiterates that the power of judicial review to test the validity of executive and legislative acts for their conformity with the Constitution does not extend to questions of policy or wisdom, otherwise referred to as 'political questions' as explained in *Tañada v Cuenco.* Thus, 'if an issue is clearly identified by the text of the Constitution as matters for discretionary action by a particular branch of government or to [*sic*] the people themselves then it is held to be a political question'. The Court then quotes the opinion of US Supreme Court Justice Brennan, delivering the opinion of the Court, in *Baker v Carr*[118] to the effect that prominent on the surface of any case held to involve a political question is found a textually demonstrable constitutional commitment of the issue to a coordinate political department, or a lack of judicially discoverable and manageable standards for resolving it, or the impossibility of deciding without an initial policy determination of a kind clearly for non-judicial discretion, or the impossibility of a court's undertaking independent resolution

115 Cf. Art 10(2)(b) of the ICCPR: 'Accused juvenile persons shall be separated from adults and brought as speedily as possible for adjudication'.

116 *Tañada v Cuenco*, 103 Phil 1051, 1067 (1957).

117 G.R. No 157584 (2 April 2009).

118 *Baker v Carr*, 369 U.S. 186, 217 (1962). For a legal history of the political question doctrine in US courts, see Fritz Scharpf, 'Judicial Review and the Political Question: A Functional Analysis' (1966) 75 Yale LJ 517; Louis Henkin, 'Is There a "Political Question" Doctrine?' (1976) 85 Yale LJ 597. See also Nada Mourtada-Sabbah and Bruce Cain (eds), *The Political Question Doctrine and the Supreme Court of the United States* (Lexington Books 2007); John Harrison, 'The Political Question Doctrines' (2018) 67 American U L Rev 457.

without expressing lack of the respect due coordinate branches of government, or an unusual need for unquestioning adherence to a political decision already made, or the potentiality of embarrassment from multifarious pronouncements by various departments on the one question.

Nonetheless, it has been deplored that during martial law under President Ferdinand E. Marcos, whose dictatorship was terminated in February 1986, the role of the Philippine Judiciary was impeded considerably by the circumstance that, in a number of cases against the Government, the Solicitor General set up the defence of political questions and got away with it. As a consequence, certain principles concerning particularly the writ of *habeas corpus*, that is, the authority of courts to order the release of political detainees, and other matters related to the operation and effect of martial law failed because of the Supreme Court's ruling that since it was political, the Court had no authority to pass judgment upon it.[119]

There are a few US cases involving the application of the political question doctrine in the context of a military *coup*.

The US case of *Schneider v Kissinger* concerns the United States' alleged involvement in covert activities, including a military *coup*, in Chile during the 1970s, and, in particular, in the death of General René Schneider, Commander-in-Chief of the Chilean Army. The plaintiffs were General Schneider's surviving sons and the personal representative of General Schneider's estate. The respondents were the United States and Dr Henry Kissinger, who served as National Security Advisor to President Nixon during the events at issue. The plaintiffs filed suit against the respondents in the US District Court for the District of Columbia alleging various tort claims arising from General Schneider's death. The District Court dismissed the plaintiffs' claims. The US Court of Appeals affirmed the lower court's decision holding the claims to be non-justiciable against the United States and Dr Kissinger for measures allegedly taken in the 1970s to implement the US foreign policy with respect to Chile. In particular, the Court of Appeals dismissed the case on the basis of the political question doctrine, ruling it could not determine the plaintiffs' claims without passing judgments on the decision of the executive branch to participate in the alleged covert operations against the newly elected Chilean leftist leader Salvador Allende. However, the Court of Appeals also added that 'the lack of judicial authority to oversee the conduct of the executive branch in political matters does not leave the executive power unbounded . . . the nation has recompense, and the checks and balances of the Constitution have not failed [since t]he political branches effectively exercise such checks and balances on each other in the area of political questions'.[120] The US Supreme Court denied a writ of *certiorari* in this case.[121]

119 *Francisco v House of Representatives*, G.R. No 160261, Supreme Court, Judgment (10 November 2003) *per* Carpio Morales J. The Court in that case held that Philippine courts are to determine whether there are constitutionally imposed limits on powers or functions conferred upon political bodies, and that if there are, Philippine courts are duty-bound to examine whether the branch or instrumentality of the government properly acted within such limits.

120 412 F3d 190, 200 (D.C. Cir 2005).

121 *Schneider v Kissinger* 547 US 1069 (2006).

In another US case, *Gonzales-Vera v Kissinger*,[122] the plaintiff, a victim and survivor of human rights abuses carried out by the Chilean Government of General Pinochet, brought an action against the United States and Dr Henry Kissinger, seeking damages for actions including torture allegedly taken in support of the Pinochet regime. The District Court found the plaintiffs' claims justiciable but dismissed the action because the United States had not waived its sovereign immunity and the plaintiffs had failed to state a claim upon which relief could be granted against Dr Kissinger. The US Court of Appeals, citing as controlling its earlier and related decision in *Schneider v Kissinger*, affirmed the plaintiffs' claims were non-justiciable under the political question doctrine. The US Supreme Court also denied a writ of *certiorari* in this case.[123]

As can be seen, these US judgments invoke the political question doctrine so as not to adjudicate on the conduct of US foreign affairs abroad, and not otherwise.[124]

In the view of one learned author, granted that the political question doctrine exists (albeit with the uncertainty over its actual scope), it is doubtful if the doctrine can justifiably be amplified to cover questions of legitimacy of a *coup d'état* and its subsequent acts. In its original sense, the political question doctrine covers cases in which the political branches have exercised their discretion on matters unequivocally assigned to them by the constitution and the issue before a court is for one of the political branches, not the Judiciary, to decide. However, since a *coup d'état* typically dissolves the executive and legislative branches, the question arises as to which political branch is left to decide the issue of the status of the usurper regime. Should the usurpers themselves decide the issue? In any case, the status of a usurper regime is not an issue committed by the constitution to any of the political branches. In that learned author's opinion, with which the present author fully concurs, the political doctrine is 'a mere theoretical expedient serving only as a means of escape for fearful judges unwilling to address challenges to unconstitutional usurpation of power'.[125]

Any court invoking the political question doctrine to evade rendering judgments on acts resulting from unconstitutional usurpation of power would be at odds with an overwhelming number of decisions in several jurisdictions, discussed in Chapters 2, 4 and 5, in which courts insist on subjecting acts of the usurper's regime to judicial scrutiny and without treating such acts as giving rise to non-justiciable political questions. It may be recalled also that the US Court of Appeals in *Schneider v Kissinger* finds some comfort in avoiding adjudicating on 'political questions' because the lack of judicial authority of US courts to oversee the

122 449 F3d 1260 (D.C. Cir 2006).

123 *Gonzales-Vera v Kissinger* 127 S Ct 1356 (2007).

124 For a view that the US Supreme Court and federal Judiciary have the power and duty to play a robust judicial role in the conduct of US foreign policy without deference to the other branches of government, see Martin Flaherty, *Restoring the Global Judiciary: Why the Supreme Court Should Rule in U.S. Foreign Affairs* (Princeton U Press 2019).

125 Ambrose Ekpu, 'Judicial Response to Coup D'État: A Reply to Tayyab Mahmud (From a Nigerian Perspective)' (1996) 13 Arizona J Int'l & Comp L 1, 8–9.

conduct of the executive branch in political matters does not leave the executive power unbounded since the acts of the executive branch are still subject to other mechanisms of checks and balance under the US Constitution. Therefore, invoking the political question doctrine to keep acts of the usurper completely beyond the reach of all checks-and-balances mechanisms would not be justifiable whatsoever.

Concluding remarks

A usurper of power of government may rebut that most of the principles and judicial decisions discussed earlier in this chapter are 'soft law' or judicial rulings not legally binding on his or her country. Such argument can be disposed of as follows.

First, the international community of nations does use the aforesaid principles and judicial decisions to assess the legitimacy and credibility of the regime installed by the usurper, the reasoning used by judges of domestic courts in that country in relation to the regime's conduct and the judges' roles in this regard. Soft law can reflect either 'best practice' guidelines or (re)statements of applicable law that are frequently positioned as authoritative statements of what the law *is* and are sometimes incorporated into binding legal instruments.[126] For instance, the ECtHR and the IACtHR are among those which have cited the 1990 UN Basic Principles as authoritative statements of international rules governing use of force in law enforcement.[127]

Second, an analysis of a large number of domestic court decisions on matters of customary international law between 2000 and 2014 demonstrates that domestic courts do not normally identify norms of customary international law on the basis of the textbook method of ascertaining a general practice accepted as law. Rather, they tend to outsource the determination of custom to treaties, non-binding documents, doctrines or international judicial practice. Sometimes, domestic courts simply assert, without citing persuasive practice authority, the existence of a customary norm and only in rare cases do domestic courts engage in extensive analysis.[128]

126 Emily Crawford, *Non-Binding Norms in International Humanitarian Law: Efficacy, Legitimacy, and Legality* (OUP 2021) 2–39, 174–218. See also Dinah Shelton, *Routledge Handbook of International Law* (Routledge 2008) ch 3 ('Hard' and 'Soft' Law in International Relations); Christine Chinkin, 'The Challenge of Soft Law: Development and Change in International Law' (1989) 38 ICLQ 850; Kenneth Abbott and Duncan Snidal, 'Hard and Soft Law in International Governance' (2003) 54 Int'l Organization 421; Andrew Guzman and Timothy Meyer, 'International Soft Law' (2010) 2 J Legal Analysis 171; Riccardo Pisillo Mazzeschi, *International Human Rights Law: Theory and Practice* (Springer 2021) 119–22; Barbara Boschetti and Maria Daniela Poli, 'A Comparative Study on Soft Law: Lessons from the COVID-19 Pandemic' (2021) 23 Cambridge YB European Legal Studies 20; Rossana Deplano, *Empirical and Theoretical Perspectives on International Law: How States Use the UN General Assembly to Create International Obligations* (CUP 2022).

127 See, e.g., ECtHR's Judgment in *Benzer v Turkey*, Former Second Section, App no 23502/06, 12 November 2013 (as rendered final on 24 March 2014) para 90; and IACtHR's Judgment in *Cruz Sánchez et al. v Peru*, Judgment (Preliminary Objections, Merits, Reparation, and Costs) 17 April 2015 para 264, cited in Geneva Academy of International Humanitarian Law and Human Rights, *Use of Force in Law Enforcement and the Right to Life* 6–7.

128 Cedric Ryngaert and Duco Hora Siccama, 'Ascertaining Customary International Law: An Inquiry into the Methods Used by Domestic Courts' (2018) 65 Netherlands Int'l L Rev 1.

Third, the law of law enforcement is a body of international law derived from a combination of customary rules, international human rights treaties and the best practices common to the various legal systems of the world as enunciated in the various 'soft law' documents discussed in this chapter.[129]

Some judges may argue there is no authority to enforce international law in the domestic sphere, and the UN Security Council can exercise its enforcement power under Chapter VII (Action with respect to threats to the peace, breaches of the peace and acts of aggression) of the UN Chapter in very rare occasions. Others take a fundamentally 'dualist view' of international law, seeing domestic and international law as operating on different planes. The latter group may assert that rules of international law, including the obligations under the treaties to which their country is party, may become enforceable as part of the domestic law only after their incorporation by means of the enactment into law by their country's Legislature or, after the suspension or dissolution of the Legislature by a *coup*, by a person or body authorized to legislate.

With regard to the first group of judges of domestic courts, they must be fully conscious of the international sanctions, condemnation and other negative measures directed at the usurpation of power, as explained in Chapter 2. Should judges play a role in sustaining the usurpation of power, they may fall into the category of members of the Judiciary held criminally liable for their respective judicial roles in a repressive regime, as elucidated in the judgment of the post–Second World War US Military Tribunal in the *Justice* case,[130] discussed in Chapter 4. Judges, like other individuals, can be punished after their country's return to democracy or, as will be explained in Chapter 6, face prosecution in the International Criminal Court, an ad hoc tribunal, a hybrid court or a foreign criminal court exercising universal jurisdiction, if all the requisite conditions are met. It has also been pointed out that the interplay of domestic and international pressures can bring about prosecution of the usurper of power in the country where he staged a *coup*, as in the case of the prosecution of Pinochet in Chile after Spain had sought his extradition from the United Kingdom to stand trial in Spain, which did not recognize Chile's 1978 Amnesty Act that had been blocking prosecution of Pinochet in Chile.[131] In addition, '[j]udges and prosecutors within the International Criminal Court and regional human rights systems participate in interpretive dialogues with domestic

129 Geneva Academy of International Humanitarian Law and Human Rights, *Use of Force in Law Enforcement and the Right to Life* 5 and 21. See also Stuart Casey-Maslen, *The Right to Life under International Law: An Interpretative Manual* (CUP 2021) 141–79.

130 *In re Josef Altstoetter and Others*, Military Tribunal III Case 3, Report of the Trials of War Criminals before the Nuremberg Military Tribunals under Control Council Law No 10, October 1946–April 1949, vol III.

131 Hugo Rojas and Miriam Shaftoe, *Human Rights and Transitional Justice in Chile* (Palgrave Macmillan 2021) 137–54; Naomi Roht-Arriaza, 'After Amnesties Are Gone: Latin American National Courts and the New Contours of the Fight Against Impunity' (2015) 37 Human Rts Quarterly 341, 349; Ezequiel Gonzále-Ocantos, *Shifting Legal Visions: Judicial Change and Human Rights Trials in Latin America* (CUP 2016) 1–26.

judicial and political actors implementing international norms attributing responsibility to perpetrators of grave human rights violations'.[132] Indeed, decisions of regional human rights courts, such as the IACtHR, have been influential, leading, for example, to prosecution in and punishment by Peru's domestic courts of Peruvian soldiers, police officers, intelligence agents and ultimately even former President Alberto Fujimori himself.[133]

The second group of judges of domestic courts should find informative the judgments of their peers in some other countries who take into consideration rules of international law and treaty obligations not yet incorporated into domestic law by legislative acts, as discussed in this chapter and Chapter 5. Bear in mind also the tendency among usurpers of power to deviate sharply from their countries' obligations under international human rights treaties in the aftermath of *coups*. Even in a country with the 'dualist' approach to international law, there is a strong presumption that domestic law can and should be read consistently with international law,[134] especially treaty obligations to which the country has already expressed its consent to be bound.[135]

132 Ely Aaronson and Gregory Shaffer, 'The Transnational Ordering of Criminal Justice' in id (eds), *Transnational Legal Ordering of Criminal Justice* (CUP 2020) 3, 4–5.

133 Rebecca Root, *Transitional Justice in Peru* (Palgrave Macmillan 2021) 101–27. See also Carlo Osmo, 'Mobilization and Judicial Recognition of the Right to the Truth: The Inter-American Human Rights System and Brazil' in Cristiano Paixão and Massimo Meccarelli (eds), *Comparing Transitions to Democracy. Law and Justice in South America and Europe* (Springer 2021) 137–61; Laura Clérico and Celeste Novelli, 'Argentina: Strong Linkage between IHRL and Domestic Law' in Grote, Antoniazzi, and Paris (eds), *Research Handbook on Compliance in International Human Rights Law* 248–71; Nuno Garoupa and Tom Ginsburg, *Judicial Reputation: A Comparative Theory* (U Chicago Press 2015) 167–98; Tom Ginsburg, *Democracies and International Law* (CUP 2021) 1–30, 103–85, 288–305; Ezequiel Gonzales-Ocantos and Wayne Sandholtz, 'Constructing a Regional Human Rights Legal Order: The Inter-American Court, National Courts, and Judicial Dialogue, 1988–2014' (2021) 19 Int'l J Constitutional L 1559.

134 Lord Mance, 'International Law in the UK Supreme Court', Speech delivered at King's College, London, 13 February 2017, esp para 8, www.supremecourt.uk/docs/speech-170213.pdf.

135 As the IACtHR has repeatedly reiterated, the obligation of a State to comply with international obligations voluntarily contracted corresponds to a basic principle of law of international responsibility of States, backed by international and national jurisprudence, according to which States must comply with their conventional international obligations in good faith (*pacta sunt servanda*), and that States cannot, due to domestic order reasons, decline to assume their already established international obligations. Treaty obligations thus bind all the powers and organs of the State Party, which must guarantee compliance with such obligations and their effects (*effet utile*) in the design of that State's domestic law (*Gomes Lund et al. ('Guerrilha Do Araguaia') v Brazil*, Judgment of 24 November 2010, Ser C No 219 para 177 and *Moiwana Community v Suriname*, Judgment of 15 June 2005, Ser C no 125 para 167). See also Ñusta Carranza Ko, *Truth, Justice, and Reparations in Peru, Uruguay, and South Korea: The Clash of Advocacy and Politics* (Palgrave Macmillan 2021) 265–91.

4

AVAILABILITY OR NON-AVAILABILITY OF DEFENCES FOR JUDGES IN RELATION TO JUDICIAL RESPONSIBILITY POST-*COUPS*

Like any repressive regime, the unconstitutional usurper of power of government may attempt to control the Judiciary by various means.

For example, after President Alberto Fujimori staged a self-*coup* in Peru in 1992 he 'reorganized' the Judiciary in such a way that the Peruvian Judiciary became under his control, stripped of judicial independence. Several judges who were members of the National Council of Magistrates overseeing judicial conduct resigned in protest. The political intervention in the Judiciary that made the interests of the Judiciary dependent upon the re-election of President Fujimori and the judicial impunity of the Peruvian armed forces led to the suppression of fundamental rights.[1]

Another example was the Greek Judiciary during the military dictatorship from 1967 to 1974. There were practically no cases brought by persons or entities against the junta before Greek courts. Such challenges were made virtually impossible due to the issuance of a series of 'Constitutional Acts'[2] by the dictatorial government providing, inter alia, that anything done by it as authorized by these Constitutional Acts could not be challenged in court. At the same time, judges were controlled by special councils to ensure their abidance by the 'law' (or, in reality, the government's

1 César Landa, *The Scales of Justice in Peru: Judicial Reform and Fundamental Rights* (Institute of American Studies, U London, Occasional Paper 2001). For other actions by repressive regimes in Latin American to have in courts those judges who will assist the regimes' iron grip on power, see Gretchen Helmke, *Courts under Constraints: Judges, General and Presidents in Argentina* (CUP 2004) 1–19; José Miguel Vivanco, 'The Rule of Law Is Disintegrating in Central America' *Human Rights Watch* (28 October 2021), https://www.hrw.org/news/2021/10/28/rule-law-disintegrating-central-america. See also Sergio Verdugo, 'How Judges Can Challenge Dictators and Get Away with It: Advancing Democracy while Preserving Judicial Independence' (2021) 59 Columbia J Transn'l L 554, 561–70.

2 Among the first and most important was the Constitutional Act of 2 July 1967, Official Journal no 125 (1967).

DOI: 10.4324/9781003358428-4

instructions). The clampdown on and the persecution of resisting judges, including prosecutions against them, made it impossible to have meaningful court cases on such matters. Many judges who resisted the junta were dismissed from their office.[3] The Supreme Administrative Court (*Conseil d'État*) took action in connection with the dismissal of judges by refusing to accept the legality of such dismissals, as the judges concerned 'had been deprived of their right of prior hearing'.[4] Although these judgments of the *Conseil d'État* were overruled by the regime, the right of prior hearing found its place in the democratic Constitution of 1975 after the fall of the junta.

In some countries, judges are required to take a new oath of allegiance after a *coup*, as in the case of Pakistan which will be explained in more detail in what follows.

In numerous cases of transition from repressive regimes to democracy, the Judiciary is severely compromised and was very much a part of the previous regimes, implementing the regimes' repression and wrapping it in the mantle of law.[5]

A crucial question of general principle is whether judges may be held accountable under domestic law in their own country after a regime change or in a foreign country exercising universal jurisdiction and, where applicable, international criminal law applied by a competent international criminal court, an ad hoc international criminal tribunal or a hybrid court.

There is some evidence that the answer to this question is in the affirmative.

For instance, the US Government imposed sanctions on 31 January 2022, the first anniversary of the 1 February 2021 military *coup* in Myanmar, on seven individuals and two entities connected to Myanmar military regime. The three government officials under sanctions were Attorney General Thida Oo, whose Office crafted the military regime's destruction of the rule of law and Myanmar's democratic institutions; Tun Tun Oo, Chief Justice of the Supreme Court under whose leadership had been involved in the regime's prosecution of Aung San Suu Kyi and other pro-democracy leaders, undermining the rule of law and Myanmar's democratic institutions; and Tin Oo, Chairman of the Anti-Corruption Commission under whose leadership had brought spurious corruption charges against Aung San Suu Kyi and other former civilian government officials to remove them and the National League for Democracy, which had won the November 2020 general election, as a political force. These three Myanmar officials were also subjected to sanctions by the Canadian Government, whereas the UK Government imposed sanctions against the Attorney-General, the Chairman of the Anti-Corruption Commission and the Chairman of Myanmar's Union Election Commission

3 Georgios Stavropoulos, 'Justice and the Dictatorship of 21.4.1967: Court cases against judges of the *Conseil d'État*', January 2019, www.constitutionalism.gr (in Greek).

4 Conseil d'État, Judgment s. 1811–1831/1969. See Spyros Vlahopoulos, 'When the Junta Was Firing Judges', *Kathimerini* newspaper (in Greek), 26 February 2018.

5 Neil Kritz, 'The Dilemma of Transitional Justice' in Neil Kritz (ed.), *Transitional Justice* (United States Institute of Peace Press 1995) xix, xxv.

appointed by the junta after the *coup*. The UK Government did not explain why it did not impose sanctions on the Chief Justice. According to the reasons expounded in this book, the US and Canadian Governments' inclusion of the Chief Justice in their respective sanctions is more justifiable than the UK Government's omission to include him. Even if none of these officials might have assets in or dealings with nationals of the sanctioning countries, their stigmatization of being criminally accountable for their respective roles after the *coup* does matter and could eventually lead to their future prosecution when an opportunity arises.

Ironically, a regime change that lead to prosecution of judges may be brought about by a military *coup*. For instance, on 4 May 2022 the military regime in Guinea that came to power by a *coup* in September 2021 commenced prosecution of the President ousted by the *coup* and his allies including a former President of the Constitutional Court on charges ranging from murder, assault, destruction of property, detention, torture, kidnapping, forced disappearances, rape and other sexual abuses.

The rest of this chapter will commence by analyzing the individual criminal responsibility arising from the roles of judges of domestic courts in sustaining oppressive regimes. This will be followed by the examination of the principle of independence of judiciary, particularly when judges are required to take a new oath of allegiance to the new 'constitutional' order after a *coup*. The chapter will then consider whether the judges have valid defences (i.e., superior orders, duress and judicial immunity) against any potential prosecution at home and abroad.

Individual criminal responsibility arising from judges' roles in an oppressive regime

One study finds that in discharging their judicial function judges are motivated by personal, group or institutional interest; sudden or impulsive passions, be they temporary or permanent ones; and/or a genuine, altruistic and impartial concern for the public good or for individual rights and freedoms.[6]

In countries which have experienced unconstitutional usurpation of power, judges are not always replaced by the usurper after the *coup*. This was the case with Chile under General Augusto Pinochet's dictatorship from September 1973 to March 1990. Chilean judges during that time quickly recognized the dictatorship regime and the Chilean Supreme Court tended to avoid reviewing the regime's decrees. Chile's Supreme Court and lower appellate courts frequently declined the thousands of *habeas corpus* petitions presented to them by Chileans subjected to arbitrary prosecution and detention by the regime and other systematic violations of human rights and neutralization of the political opposition.[7] Surprisingly, it was the Chilean Constitutional Court set up under the 1980 Chilean Constitution drafted by those appointed by the military regime that constantly upheld the

6 Jon Elster, 'Forces and Mechanisms in Constitution-Making Process' (1995) 45 Duke LJ 364, 376–86.
7 Verdugo, 'How Judges Can Challenge Dictators and Get Away with It' 585–6.

principles of democratic government despite the fact that the Constitution limited the Constitutional Court's independence by controlling the appointment of all the judges and providing for renewable judicial terms that lasted eight years. The Constitutional Court played an essential and unexpected role in the design of the electoral rules for the 1988 plebiscite that resulted in the victory of those casting the 'No' vote—in essence, a vote to remove General Pinochet from the Presidency and force Pinochet and the junta to return to the barracks. It managed to achieve this outcome by means of creative interpretation of the Constitution and challenging the regime, holding that electoral principles in the Constitution required the creation of the Electoral Court as an essential requirement of the electoral process, without which the plebiscite could not be legitimate. The decision helped create fairer electoral conditions, which reduced the regime's options to influence the electoral process, thereby building up a decisive step towards the transition to democracy. In 1987 the Chilean Constitutional Court prevented the junta from promulgating a set of provisions included in the bill establishing the regulations for the creation and internal organization of political parties. In a subsequent decision in 1987 the Constitutional Court declared to be unconstitutional six provisions included in the junta's draft law to regulate Chile's electoral system and construed two other provisions narrowly. The Chilean military regime had to comply with the Constitutional Court's decisions because the expected costs of disobeying them were higher than the costs of compliance since the Court was a cornerstone institution of the constitutional order Pinochet himself intended to use to perpetuate the iron grip of the regime and the military.[8]

Like judges of the Chilean Constitutional Court just mentioned, judges in some other countries have tried their best to uphold the rule of law after unconstitutional usurpation of power. For instance, on 20 January 2022, in a rare public statement 55 Sudanese judges, including four from the Supreme Court, accused the Sudanese military leaders of extra-judicial killings and 'heinous violations against unarmed demonstrators' since the 25 October 2021 *coup*. The judges promised to take the necessary measures to protect Sudanese citizens. These judges were supported by more than 220 prosecutors, who also called for an end to the state of emergency imposed by the *coup*.[9]

Fijian judges have provided another example. In December 2006, Commodore Frank Bainimarama, Commander of the Fijian Armed Forces since 1999, staged

8 Ibid 591–605. Cf. Lisa Hilbink, *Judges beyond Politics in Democracy and Dictatorship: Lessons from Chile* (CUP 2007), who argues that only a minority of Chile's high court judges (Supreme Court and top regional courts) were loyal supporters of Pinochet, and that another sizable group had democratic inclinations, but the latter group either feared losing their jobs or facing other forms of punishment by the regime and therefore considered remaining 'apolitical' to be appropriate. Another study, focusing on Argentina, finds the phenomenon of 'strategic defection' by judges in which judges rule against the incumbent dictatorial or democratic regime once it begins to lose power because they fear being punished by the regime's incoming successors (Helmke, *Courts under Constraints* 20 ff).

9 Gwennaëlle Lenoir, 'Sudan: A Coup against Justice' *JusticeInfo.Net* (28 January 2022), https://www.justiceinfo.net/en/87063-sudan-coup-against-justice.html.

his second *coup*, this time on the grounds that the Government of Fijian Prime Minister Laisenia Qarase was corrupt and ineffective and discriminated against Indian-Fijians. On 5 January 2007, Bainimarama was appointed interim Prime Minister by Fiji's President. Fifteen days later, Qarase brought proceedings to challenge the constitutionality of the President's actions. In *Qarase v Bainimarama*, the Fijian High Court validated the Presidential actions.[10] The Fijian Court of Appeal overturned the High Court's judgment,[11] ruling that under Fiji's Constitution it was not intended for the President, in the exercise of discretion, to dismiss a Prime Minister in circumstances other than those expressly stipulated in the Constitution and in effect establish an interim government. The Court of Appeal refused leave by the Interim Government to appeal to the Supreme Court. As a response, on the very next day Fiji's President abrogated the Constitution, revoked the commission of all judges and appointed another Interim Government with Bainimarama as Acting Prime Minister 'for the sake of national stability'. Bainimarama occupied that position until 2014 when his political party won the general election as a result of which he officially became Fiji's Prime Minister.[12]

Many domestic court judges are not as conscientious in safeguarding the constitution and rights and freedoms enshrined therein as the Chilean, Sudanese and Fijian judges just mentioned. In this regard, the judgment of the post–Second World War US Military Tribunal[13] in the *Justice* case[14] is illustrative of how judges could be held criminally liable for their respective judicial roles in a repressive regime.

There were 16 defendants in the *Justice* case,[15] all of whom held high judicial office, and all but one of whom were trained lawyers. They were judges, public prosecutors or high-level officials in the Reich Ministry of Justice. They were

10 [2008] FJHC 241.

11 [2009] FJCA 9. See a detailed account of this case in Anita Jowitt, 'The Qarase v Bainimarama Appeal Case' (2009) 13 J South Pacific L 24.

12 See also Venkat Iyer, 'The Judiciary in Fiji: A Broken Reed?' in H.P. Lee and Marilyn Pittard (eds), *Asia-Pacific Judiciaries: Independence, Impartiality and Integrity* (CUP 2017) 109–30.

13 Not to be confused with the International Military Tribunal (IMT) set up in Nuremberg, Germany, to try major war criminals from November 1945 through 1946. The Four Powers (USA, UK, France and USSR) then occupying vanquished Germany after the Second World War passed Control Council Law No 10 on 20 December 1945 ((1946) 3 Official Gazette Control Council for Germany 50–55)) to authorize each of them to use its own legal system to try, independently of the IMT and in their respective sectors in occupied Germany, those war criminals not prosecuted at the IMT. There were 12 proceedings under Control Council Law No 10. See also Matthew Lippman, 'The Prosecution of Josef Altstoetter *et al.*: Law, Lawyers and Justice in the Third Reich' (1997–8) 16 Dickinson JIL 343.

14 *In re Josef Altstoetter and Others*, Military Tribunal III Case 3, Report of the Trials of War Criminals before the Nuremberg Military Tribunals under Control Council Law No 10, October 1946–April 1949, vol III.

15 However, the defendant Carl Westphal died before the commencement of the trial. On 22 August 1947, the Tribunal entered an order declaring a mistrial as to the defendant Karl Engert, who had been able to attend court for only two days since 5 March 1947 (ibid 954). Without elaboration, the Tribunal acquitted the defendants Paul Barnickel, Hans Petersen and Guenther Nebelung of all charges since their guilt was not proven beyond any reasonable doubt (ibid 1156–7).

charged with enacting and enforcing statutes, decrees and orders of an essentially criminal nature and with working with German Security Police organizations for essentially criminal purposes, in the course of which, by distortion and denial of judicial process, they committed crimes against civilian inhabitants of occupied territories, prisoners of war and German nationals. The Prosecution pointed out that this case was unusual in that the defendants were charged with *crimes committed in the name of the law and in the guise of legal process.* These men, leaders of the German judicial system, were accused of having *consciously and deliberately* suppressed the law, engaged in an unholy masquerade of brutish tyranny disguised as justice, and converted the German judicial system to an engine of despotism, conquest, pillage and slaughter. The defendants and their colleagues allegedly distorted, perverted and finally accomplished the complete overthrow of justice and law in Germany by *making the system of courts an integral part of dictatorship.* They allegedly established and operated special tribunals obedient only to the political dictates of the Hitler regime, thereby abolishing all semblance of judicial independence. The defendants were not called to account for violating constitutional guarantees or withholding due process of law. On the contrary, they were accused of participation in and responsibility for the killings, tortures and other atrocities which resulted from, and which the defendants *knew* were *an inevitable consequence* of, the conduct of their offices as judges, prosecutors and Ministry of Justice officials. They could no more escape that responsibility by virtue of their judicial robes than the general by his uniform. That is to say, the defendants were charged with *judicial murder* and other atrocities which they committed by destroying law and justice in Germany, and by then utilizing the emptied forms of legal process for persecution, enslavement and extermination on a vast scale with all its methods of terror and its cynical and open denial of the rule of law.[16] In their defence, all the defendants claimed that what they had done was legal under German domestic law at that time.[17] The prosecution and the judges of the US Military Tribunal proceeded on the premises that the Nazi legal regime was so evil that its 'law' was deemed 'non-law' since it propelled Germany's descent into barbarism in violation of rules of international law and moral standards of the civilized world.[18]

The Prosecution's indictment contained four counts: (1) conspiracy to commit war crimes and crimes against humanity between January 1933 and April 1945; (2) war crimes of violations of the laws and customs of war, alleged to have been committed between September 1939 and April 1945; (3) crimes against humanity committed between September 1939 and April 1945; and (4) membership of

16 *In re Josef Altstoetter and Others* 31–3.

17 For an analysis of the legal principles and constitutional developments of the Third Reich, see Ernst Fraenkel, *The Dual State: A Contribution to the Theory of Dictatorship* (OUP 1940); Ingo Müller, *Hitler's Justice: The Courts of the Third Reich* (trans. Deborah Lucas Schneider, Harvard U Press 1991) chs 1–21; Hans Petter Graver, *Judges Against Justice: On Judges When the Rule of Law is Under Attack* (Springer 2015) 143–50.

18 Christiane Wilke, 'Reconsecrating the Temple of Justice: Invocations of Civilization and Humanity in the Nuremberg Justice Case' (2009) 24 Canadian J Law & Society 181.

certain defendants in organizations declared to be criminal by the International Military Tribunal (IMT) set up in Nuremberg, Germany, to try major war criminals from November 1945 through 1946. The defendants were not charged with specific overt acts against named victims. They were charged with *criminal participation in government-organized atrocities and persecutions.* During the course of the trial, the Tribunal ruled with respect to count one that it had no jurisdiction to try any defendant upon a charge of conspiracy as a separate substantive offence.[19]

The Tribunal's judgment was based upon a consideration of all of the evidence upon the part which the respective defendants played and, in pronouncing sentences, the Tribunal gave due consideration to circumstances of mitigation and to the proven character and motives of the respective defendants.[20]

The function of the Nazi courts was judicial only in a limited sense. They more closely resembled administrative tribunals *acting under directives from above* in a quasi-judicial manner. In reality, the Nazi system forced the judges into one of two categories. In the first were the judges who still retained ideals of *judicial independence* and who administered justice with a measure of impartiality and moderation. Judgments which they rendered were set aside by the employment of the nullity plea and the extraordinary objection. The defendants they sentenced were frequently transferred to the Gestapo on completion of prison terms and were then shot or sent to concentration camps. The judges themselves were threatened and criticized and sometimes removed from office. In the other category were the judges who, with fanatical zeal, enforced the will of the Nazi Party with such severity that they experienced no difficulties and little interference from party officials.[21]

The defendant Oswald Rothaug was, from April 1937 to May 1943, director of the district court in Nuremberg. During that time he was chairman of the Court of Assizes, of a penal chamber and of the Special Court. From May 1943 to April 1945 he was public prosecutor of the public prosecution at the People's Court in Berlin, where, as head of Department I, he handled for a time cases of high treason in the southern Reich territory, and, from January 1944, cases concerning the undermining of public morale in the Reich territory. As to counts two and four of the indictment, the Tribunal found the defendant not guilty. As regards count three of the indictment, the Tribunal found that he *took a consenting part* in the plan for the persecution, oppression and extermination of Poles and Jews. From the evidence, the trials by the defendant clearly lacked the essential elements of legality. In these cases the defendant's court, in spite of the legal sophistries which he employed, was merely an instrument in the programme of the leaders of the Nazi State of persecution and extermination. That the number the defendant could wipe out within his competency was smaller than the number involved in the mass persecutions and exterminations by the leaders whom he served did not mitigate

19 This was because neither the Charter of the IMT nor Control Council Law No 10 had defined conspiracy to commit a war crime or crime against humanity as a separate substantive crime.

20 *In re Josef Altstoetter and Others* 955 and 1177. See also Graver, *Judges Against Justice* 125–33.

21 *In re Josef Altstoetter and Others* 1024–5.

his contribution to the programme of those leaders. *His acts were more terrible in that those who might have hoped for a last refuge in the institutions of justice found these institutions turned against them and constituted a part of the programme of terror and oppression.* Rothaug participated in the national programme of racial persecution. He identified himself with this national programme and gave himself utterly to its accomplishment. He participated in the crime of genocide. In determining the degree of guilt, the Tribunal considered the entire record of the defendant's activities, not alone under the head of racial persecution but in other respects also. Despite protestations that his judgments were based solely upon evidence introduced in court, the Tribunal was firmly convinced that in numberless cases Rothaug's opinions were formed and decisions made, and in many instances publicly or privately announced, before the trial had even commenced and certainly before it was concluded. He was in constant contact with his confidential assistant Elkar, a member of the criminal SD (a Nazi Party intelligence service), who sat with him in weekly conferences in the chambers of the court. He formed his opinions from dubious records submitted to him before trial. By his manner and methods he made his court an instrumentality of terror and won the fear and hatred of the population. *Under any civilized judicial system he could have been impeached and removed from office or convicted of malfeasance in office on account of the scheming malevolence with which he administered injustice.* The Tribunal therefore found Rothaug guilty under count three of the indictment, with no mitigating circumstances; no extenuation.[22] He was sentenced to life imprisonment.

The defendant Rudolf Oeschey joined the Nazi Party on 1 December 1931. He was appointed on 1 January 1939 to the office of senior judge of the district court at Nuremberg, which office he held until 1 April 1941. He was then appointed district court director at the same court. He was a presiding judge of the Special Court in Nuremberg. He was drafted into the army in February 1945, and remained in the army until the end of the Second World War; however, he was released for the period from 4 April until 14 April 1945, during which time he functioned as chairman of the civilian court martial at Nuremberg. The record disclosed that he and the defendant Rothaug were the guiding, if not controlling, spirits of the Special Court at Nuremberg, which was known as the most brutal of the special courts in Germany, where German *laws were in many instances applied in an arbitrary and brutal manner shocking to the conscience of mankind* and punishable before the Tribunal. The Tribunal found Oeschey guilty under counts three and four of the indictment. In view of the sadistic attitude and conduct of the defendant, there was no mitigation of punishment.[23] He was sentenced to life imprisonment.

The defendant Franz Schlegelberger was appointed, on 10 October 1931, Secretary of State in the Reich Ministry of Justice under Minister of Justice Guertner, which position he held until Guertner's death on 29 January 1941, when he was

22 Ibid 1143–56.
23 Ibid 1159–70.

put in charge of the Reich Ministry of Justice as Administrative Secretary of State or acting Minister of Justice. When Thierack became the new Minister of Justice on 20 August 1942, Schlegelberger resigned from the Ministry. Schlegelberger was 'a tragic character' who 'loathed the evil that he did, but he sold that intellect and that scholarship to Hitler for a mess of political pottage and for the vain hope of personal security'. He was found guilty under counts two and three of the indictment for his primary responsibility for his support of Hitler's assumption of power to deal with life and death in disregard of even the pretence of judicial process. By his exhortations and directives, Schlegelberger contributed to the *destruction of judicial independence* by signing the decree of 7 February 1942 which imposed upon the Ministry of Justice and the courts the burden of the prosecution, trial and disposal of the victims of Hitler's Night and Fog decree, a secret order issued by Hitler in December 1941 to arrest and then shoot or spirit away persons endangering German security in the German-occupied territories of Western Europe. He was found guilty of instituting and supporting procedures for the wholesale persecution of Jews and Poles. Concerning Jews, his ideas were less brutal than those of his associates, but they could scarcely be called humane. Schlegelberger's defence, which was also claimed in some measure by most of the defendants, was that the administration of justice was under persistent assault by Heinrich Himmler, chief of the SS (the elite Nazi Party paramilitary organization), and other advocates of the police State, and that if he were to resign, a worse man would take his place. As the event proved, there was much truth in this also. Under Minister of Justice Thierack the police did usurp the functions of the administration of justice and murdered untold thousands of Jews and political prisoners. However, upon analysis, the Tribunal found this plausible claim of the defence square neither with the truth, logic or the circumstances. The evidence conclusively showed that in order to maintain the Ministry of Justice in the good graces of Hitler and to prevent its utter defeat by Himmler's police, Schlegelberger and the other defendants who joined in this claim of justification took over the dirty work which the leaders of the State demanded, and employed the Ministry of Justice as a means for exterminating the Jewish and Polish populations, terrorizing the inhabitants of occupied countries and wiping out political opposition at home. That their programme of racial extermination under the guise of law failed to attain the proportions which were reached by the pogroms, deportations and mass murders by the police was cold comfort to the survivors of the 'judicial' process and constituted a poor excuse before this Tribunal. In the view of the Tribunal: 'The prostitution of a judicial system for the accomplishment of criminal ends involves an element of evil to the State which is not found in frank atrocities which do not sully judicial robes'.[24] Schlegelberger resigned after feeling the cruelties of the system which he had helped to develop were too much for him, but he resigned too late. The damage was already done. He was sentenced to life imprisonment.

24 Ibid 1086.

The defendant Herbert Klemm was found guilty of counts two and three of the indictment. During the time Klemm was State Secretary of the Ministry of Justice, the plan of the leaders of the Nazi State to inspire the lynching of Allied fliers by the people of Germany was inaugurated, and during this period the matter of execution of approximately 800 political prisoners, prior to evacuation of the penitentiary at Sonnenburg, took place. Klemm's career under the Third Reich moved smoothly from comparative insignificance to the position of State Secretary because he was close to some significant figures in the Nazi leadership. Under the circumstances it was *not credible that he was ignorant of the policies and methods of these ruthless figures*. The defendant emphasized an order of Hitler as to secrecy and argued that in connection with this order he adhered strictly to it; and that he did not attempt to hear anything outside of his official duties. Such orders as to secrecy were not confined to Germany during the war; they were standard procedures in other countries and by no means excluded knowledge of secret matters derived from normal human contacts, particularly friends and acquaintances in the higher levels of state affairs. Further, the confidential position held by the defendant gave him a wide scope as to secret matters within the sphere of his official duties. As State Secretary of the Ministry of Justice and deputy of the minister in his absence, the defendant's official duties required knowledge of the higher spheres of State policy. More specifically, Klemm *knew of abuses* in concentration camps, the practice of severe interrogations, and the persecution and oppression of the Jews, Poles and gypsies. As State Secretary in the Ministry of Justice, he necessarily exercised supervision over the enforcement of the decree against Poles and Jews and dealt with clemency matters pertaining to cases tried under that decree. When Rothenberger was ousted as State Secretary because he was not brutal enough, it was Klemm who was chosen to replace him and work in closest cooperation with the heads of the Nazi conspiracy. Klemm was *in the inner circle of the Nazi war criminals*. He must have shared with his now dead friend, Justice Minister Thierack (with whom he had lived), and his now missing friend, Nazi Party Chancellery chief Martin Bormann, the responsibility, at a high policy level, for the crimes committed in the name of justice.[25] He was sentenced to life imprisonment.

The defendant Curt Rothenberger was, from 1935 to 1942, president of the district court of appeals in Hamburg. In 1942 he was appointed Under Secretary in the Ministry of Justice under Justice Minister Thierack. He remained in that office until he left the Ministry in December 1943, after which he served as a notary in Hamburg. Rothenberger not only participated in securing the enactment of a discriminatory law against Jews, but he also enforced it when enacted and, in the meantime, before its enactment, upon his own initiative he acted without authority of any law in denying to Jewish paupers the aid of the courts as a part of the government-organized plan for the persecution of the Jews, not only by murder and imprisonment but also by depriving them of the means of livelihood and of equal

25 Ibid 1093–1107.

rights in the courts of law. Rothenberger must have known that the inmates of the Mauthausen concentration camp were there either without trial, or after acquittal or after the expiration of their term of imprisonment. His inspection of the Mauthausen concentration camp, an institution which would go down in history as a human slaughterhouse, was made in company with the man who became the chief butcher. Although he was kind to many half-Jews, and occasionally publicly aided them, he was instrumental in denying them the rights to which every litigant was entitled. The Tribunal was convinced that Rothenberger was deceived and abused by his superiors, that evidence was 'framed' against him, and that he was ultimately removed, in part at least, because he was not sufficiently brutal to satisfy the demands of the hour. He was retired to the apparently quiet life of a notary in Hamburg, but even then he was receiving some pay as an Under Secretary and was assisting a regional leader of the Nazi Party in political matters in that city. Rothenberger was guilty of taking a *minor but consenting part* in the Night and Fog decree. He *aided and abetted* in the programme of racial persecution, and notwithstanding his many protestations to the contrary he *materially contributed toward the prostitution of the Ministry of Justice and the courts and their subordination to the arbitrary will* of Hitler, the Nazi Party minions and the police. He participated in the *corruption and perversion of the judicial system*. The defendant Rothenberger was found guilty under counts two and three of the indictment.[26] He was sentenced to seven years in prison.

The defendant Ernst Lautz was, from 20 September 1939 until the end of the Second World War, Chief Public Prosecutor at the People's Court in Berlin. His duty was to sign all indictments, all suspensions of proceedings and all reports to the Minister of Justice. This work assumed such proportions that it became necessary to delegate parts thereof to his subordinates, but Lautz required important matters to be reported directly to him. Lautz was criminally implicated in enforcing the law against Poles and Jews as a part of the established governmental plan for the extermination of those races. He was *an accessory to, and took a consenting part in*, the crime of genocide. He was likewise guilty of a violation of the laws and customs of war in connection with prosecutions under the Night and Fog decree, and he *participated in the perversion of the laws* relating to treason and high treason under which Poles guilty of petty offences were executed. There was much to be said in mitigation of punishment. Lautz was not active in Nazi Party matters. He resisted all efforts of Nazi Party officials to influence his conduct but yielded to influence and guidance from Hitler through the Reich Ministry of Justice, *believing that to be required under German law*. He was a stern man and a relentless prosecutor, but it might be said in his favour that *if German law were a defence, which it was not*, many of his acts would be excusable. It should be re-emphasized in this connection that the Tribunal categorically rejected the defence of 'mistake of law'. The Tribunal found the defendant Lautz guilty as charged upon counts two and three of the indictment.[27] He was sentenced to ten years' imprisonment.

26 Ibid 1113–8.
27 Ibid 1118–34.

The defendant Wolfgang Mettgenberg held the position of head of section in Divisions III and IV of the Reich Ministry of Justice. In Division III, for penal legislation, he dealt with questions of international law, formulating secret, general and circular directives. He exercised wide discretion and had extensive authority over the entire plan from the time a Night and Fog prisoner was arrested in an occupied territory and continuously after his transfer to Germany, his trial and execution or imprisonment. Mettgenberg assumed the burden of defending the illegality of the Night and Fog proceedings under the Ministry of Justice not only for himself but for all defendants connected therewith. The Tribunal thus found Mettgenberg guilty under counts two and three of the indictment. He *acted as a principal, aided, abetted and was connected with* the execution and carrying out of Hitler's Night and Fog decree in violation of numerous principles of international law.[28] He was sentenced to ten years' imprisonment.

The defendant Wilhelm Von Ammon joined the paramilitary wing of the Nazi Party in December 1933 and his career progressed ever since. After the German annexation of Austria, he was employed as liaison officer of Department III (penal matters) in connection with Department VIII (Austria) in the Reich Ministry of Justice. He was consultant in the Department for the administration of penal law before his transfer to the Munich Court of Appeals as Counsellor where he served until June 1940, at which time he was recalled to the Reich Ministry of Justice. As of 1 March 1943 he was appointed Ministerial Counsellor in the Ministry of Justice. The Tribunal convicted von Ammon of war crimes and crimes against humanity under counts two and three of the indictment.[29] He was sentenced to ten years' imprisonment.

The defendant Guenther Joel worked in many capacities, including as chief of the Reich Ministry of Justice's Central Public Prosecution, 'Referent' (Adviser) for special cases in the Ministry's Penal Department and a liaison officer between the Ministry and the SS, where he climbed to high positions including as leader in the Main Office of the SD. On 17 August 1943 Joel became chief prosecutor of the court of appeals in Hamm, covering all of Westphalia and the district of Essen, which office he continued to hold until the end of the Second World War. In this position he was in charge of the Night and Fog programme for the Special Courts in Hamm and Essen until 15 March 1944 when these courts were transferred farther east to Oppeln in the Katowice district. He attended conferences both in Hamm and in Belgium on Night and Fog matters. The district of which he was the highest, and therefore the most responsible, prosecuting authority was, in area and population, one of the largest in Germany. He had under his supervision the senior public prosecutors and their staffs at the Special Courts at Hamm and in Essen. It was his task to supervise the work of all prosecutors assigned to his office. The Special Courts in Hamm and Essen tried more Night and Fog cases than the

28 Ibid 1129–32.
29 Ibid 1133–4.

combined total of all other Special Courts and the People's Court. In law, Joel had to be held to have had the responsibility of these cases and the record further showed that Joel assumed this responsibility. As 'Referent' in the department of justice and as liaison officer between the department and the SS, Joel obtained extensive information and exercised far-reaching power in the execution of the law against Jews and Poles. He therefore *took an active part in the execution of the plan or scheme* for the persecution and extermination of Jews and Poles. Concerning Joel's membership in the SS and SD, he *retained such membership with full knowledge of the criminal character of those organizations.* The Tribunal found Joel guilty under counts two, three and four.[30] He was sentenced to ten years' imprisonment.

In 1943 the defendant Josef Altstoetter was assigned to the Reich Ministry of Justice where he was made Chief of the Civil Law and Procedure Division, with the title of head of section, and served in that capacity until Nazi Germany's surrender. The Tribunal acquitted the defendant Altstoetter of the charges under counts two and three of the indictment. The question which remained to be determined as to the defendant Altstoetter was whether, *knowing of its criminal activities, he joined or retained membership in the SS*, an organization defined as criminal by the IMT. The evidence clearly established that he joined and retained his membership in the SS on a voluntary basis, and with considerable interest in his SS rank and honours. The activities of the SS and the crimes which it committed were of so wide a scope that no person of the defendant's intelligence, and one who had achieved the rank of senior leader in the SS, could have been unaware of its illegal activities, particularly a member of the organization from 1937 until Nazi Germany's surrender. According to his own statement, he joined the SS with misgivings, not only on religious grounds but also because of practices of the police as to protective custody in concentration camps. Upon the evidence in this case, the Tribunal found Altstoetter guilty under count four of the indictment.[31] He was sentenced to five years' imprisonment.

The defendant Hermann Cuhorst was Chief Justice of the Special Court in Stuttgart, Chief Justice of the First Criminal Senate of the District Court in Stuttgart, an executive member of the Leadership Corps of the Nazi Party in a regional district and a sponsoring member of the SS. He was charged under counts two, three and four of the indictment. There was no evidence to substantiate the charge under counts two and four. As to count three, it could not be proven beyond a reasonable doubt that the defendant was guilty of inflicting the punishments which he imposed on racial grounds or that he used the discriminatory provisions of the decree against Poles and Jews to the prejudice of the Poles whom he tried. Certain things could be said in his favour. He was severely criticized for his leniency by the defendant Klemm in a number of cases which he tried. He was tried by a Nazi Party court for statements considered to reflect upon the Party, which he made

30 Ibid 1136–42.
31 Ibid 1170–7.

in a trial involving Nazi Party officials. Subsequently he was relieved as a judge in Stuttgart because he apparently did not conform to what the State and Nazi Party demanded of a judge. He was acquitted of all the charges against him.[32]

The issue of the validity of Nazi law enforced by the defendants in the *Justice* case and the legal system in which they operated has been subject to extensive discussion among Western legal philosophers after the end of the Second World War. For some of these jurists, written law as it is must be distinguished from law as it ought to be, the latter being 'moral' judgments, morality or moral principles rather than law and a decision not to obey Nazi laws presented not only a question of prudence or courage, but also a genuine moral dilemma in which the ideal of fidelity to the written law had to be sacrificed in favour of a more fundamental goal.[33] An opposite view is that written law also contains its own implicit morality of order and the authority to make law must be supported by moral attitudes which accord to it the competency it claims; hence, if a law is the product of a system so oblivious to the morality of law it is not entitled to be recognized as a law.[34] Yet, morality may be arbitrarily and subjectively asserted, as in the case of the Nazi legal theorists' unification of law and 'morality' conforming to the substantive concept of justice as reflected in the values of National Socialism propagated by the Nazi Party to realize its political goals.[35] International law, which encompasses international human rights law and international criminal law, has developed in great depth and scope since the post–Second World War era. Whatever the genesis of the US Military Tribunal in the *Justice* case,[36] crimes committed by the defendants who were convicted by the Tribunal can never be lawful nowadays. By no stretch of imagination can anyone justify heinous atrocities and violation of fundamental human rights on the ground that the written law passed by the regime in power says so. On the whole, each modern-day judge discharging his or her duty after unconstitutional usurpation of government will need to consider carefully which description of the defendants in the *Justice* case would fit him or her. It seems that

32 Ibid 1157–9.

33 H.L.A. Hart, 'Positivism and the Separation of Law and Morals' (1958) 71 Harvard L Rev 593, as interpreted by Lon Fuller, 'Positivism and Fidelity to Law: A Reply to Professor Hart' (1958) 71 Harvard L Rev 630, 633.

34 Fuller, 'Positivism and Fidelity to Law' 645, 661. See also Gustav Radbruch, *Statutory Lawlessness and Supra-Statutory Laws* (1946), trans Bonnie Litschewski Paulson and Stanley Paulson (2006) 26 Oxford J Legal Studies 1–11.

35 As explained by Herlinde Pauer-Studer, 'Law and Morality under Evil Conditions: The SS Judge Konrad Morgen' (2012) 3 Jurisprudence 367 and Oren Gross, 'What Both Hart and Fuller Got Wrong' (2021) 11 Wake Forest L Rev Online 54.

36 For a harsh criticism of the *Justice* case itself, see David Fraser, 'Evil Law, Evil Lawyers? From the *Justice Case* to the Torture Memos' (2012) 3 Jurisprudence 391. In short, Fraser contends that ultimately the only incontrovertible claim for the legitimacy of the US Military Tribunal's proceedings against the defendants in the *Justice* case rested in the simple and obvious reality of military conquest of Germany and the annihilation of both domestic institutions like courts and the underlying normative structure (i.e., Nazi ideology and German sovereignty) on which these institutional norms were based (ibid 408).

any judge like Cuhorst would be impervious to individual criminal responsibility either domestically after a regime change or outside his own country.

Under a regime that is inherently heinous, such as the then apartheid regime in South Africa, there could still be some room for judges to manoeuvre and advance the cause of justice by interpreting the law to serve the oppressed as much as they could. This in itself may outweigh any veneer of legitimacy the judges may be perceived to provide to the repressive regime when they discharge their judicial function thereunder.[37]

Independence of judiciary and allegiance to the new 'constitutional' order

The Judiciary needs a positive perception of independence to gain the trust of society, which, in turn, bolsters the legitimacy of the Judiciary, including the perception of impartiality of the court and the judge towards the issues and parties in a case.[38]

According to the Basic Principles of the Independence of the Judiciary, endorsed by the UN General Assembly in 1985,[39] the independence of judiciary shall be guaranteed by the State and enshrined in its constitution or its law, to be respected and observed by all governmental and other institutions. The Judiciary shall decide matters before it impartially, on the basis of facts and in accordance with the law, without any restrictions, improper influences, inducements, pressures, threats or interferences, direct or indirect, from any quarter or for any reason. The Judiciary shall have jurisdiction over all issues of a judicial nature and shall have exclusive authority to decide whether an issue submitted for its decision is within its competence as defined by law. There shall not be any inappropriate or unwarranted interference with the judicial process. Judicial decisions by the courts shall not be subject to revision, except for judicial review or mitigation or commutation by competent authorities of sentences imposed by the Judiciary, in

37 John Dugard, 'Should Judges Resign?—A Reply to Professor Wacks' (1984) 101 South Africa LJ 286, 292–4; Stephen Ellmann, 'To Resign or not to Resign' (1997) 19 Cardozo L Rev 1047; David Dyzenhaus, *Judging the Judges: Judging Ourselves: Truth, Reconciliation and the Apartheid Legal Order* (Hart 1998) 75–6; id, *Hard Cases in Wicked Legal Systems: Pathologies of Legality* (2nd end, OUP 2010) chs 1, 8–10. See also Jeffrey Brand-Ballard, *Limits of Legality: The Ethics of Lawless Judging* (OUP 2010), essentially arguing that judges are not always morally obligated to apply the law correctly, provided that such departure from strict interpretation of the law in fact upholds the rule of law and avoids results that are otherwise objectionable on moral or policy grounds.

38 Frans van Dijk, *Perceptions of the Independence of Judges in Europe: Congruence of Society and Judiciary* (Palgrave Macmillan 2021) 7–28. See also Shimon Shetreet and Christopher Forsyth (eds), *The Culture of Judicial Independence: Conceptual Foundations and Practical Challenges* (Brill 2012); Theodore Meron, *Standing Up for Justice: The Challenges of Trying Atrocity Crimes* (OUP 2021) 116–32; Kossi Dedry, *Le courage de juger: Protection des droits de l'hommes, indépendance et impartialité du tribunal dans les méchanismes régionaux (CEDH, CIDH, CADHP)* (L'Harmattan 2021); Stephen Breyer, *The Authority of the Court and the Peril of Politics* (Harvard U Press 2021).

39 UNGA res 40/32 (29 November 1985) and UNGA res 40/146 (13 December 1985).

accordance with the law. Everyone shall have the right to be tried by ordinary courts or tribunals using established legal procedures. Tribunals that do not use the duly established procedures of the legal process shall not be created to displace the jurisdiction belonging to the ordinary courts or judicial tribunals. The Judiciary is entitled and required to ensure judicial proceedings are conducted fairly and the rights of the parties are respected. It is the duty of each UN Member State to provide adequate resources to enable the Judiciary to properly perform its functions. Persons selected for judicial office shall be individuals of integrity and ability with appropriate training or qualifications in law. Any method of judicial selection shall safeguard against judicial appointments for improper motives. In the selection of judges, there shall be no discrimination against a person on the grounds of race, colour, sex, religion, political or other opinion, national or social origin, property, birth or status. However, a requirement that a candidate for judicial office must be a national of the country concerned shall not be considered discriminatory. The term of office of judges, their independence, security, adequate remuneration, conditions of service, pensions and the age of retirement shall be adequately secured by law. Judges, whether appointed or elected, shall have guaranteed tenure until a mandatory retirement age or the expiry of their term of office, where such exists. Promotion of judges, wherever such a system exists, should be based on objective factors, in particular ability, integrity and experience. The assignment of cases to judges within the court to which they belong is an internal matter of judicial administration. Judges shall be bound by professional secrecy with regard to their deliberations and to confidential information acquired in the course of their duties other than in public proceedings, and shall not be compelled to testify on such matters.

The Basic Principles touch upon possible actions against judges as follows. Without prejudice to any disciplinary procedure or to any right of appeal or to compensation from the State, in accordance with national law, judges should enjoy *personal immunity from civil suits* for monetary damages for improper acts or omissions in the exercise of their judicial functions. A charge or complaint made against a judge in his or her judicial and professional capacity shall be processed expeditiously and fairly under an appropriate procedure. The judge shall have the right to a fair hearing. The examination of the matter at its initial stage shall be kept confidential, unless otherwise requested by the judge. Judges shall be subject to suspension or removal *only* for reasons of incapacity or behaviour that renders them unfit to discharge their duties. All disciplinary, suspension or removal proceedings shall be determined in accordance with established standards of judicial conduct. Decisions in disciplinary, suspension or removal proceedings should be subject to an independent review, but this may not apply to the decisions of the highest court and those of the Legislature in impeachment or similar proceedings.[40]

40 Cf. Richard Devlin and Sheila Wildeman (eds), *Disciplining Judges: Contemporary Challenges and Controversies* (Edward Elgar Publishing 2021).

Subsequently, chief justices and senior justices from several Common Law and Civil Law jurisdictions jointly drafted principles of judicial conduct, culminating in the 'Bangalore Principles of Judicial Conduct', which was unanimously adopted by the UN Commission on Human Rights, the predecessor of the UN Human Rights Council, on 29 April 2003. The Bangalore Principles reiterate the authoritative value of the UN Basic Principles of the Independence of the Judiciary.[41] According to Value 1 of the Bangalore Principles, judicial independence is a prerequisite to the rule of law and a fundamental guarantee of a fair trial; a judge shall therefore uphold and exemplify judicial independence in both its individual and institutional aspects. Towards this end, a judge shall, first of all, exercise the judicial function independently on the basis of the judge's assessment of the facts and in accordance with a conscientious understanding of the law, free of any extraneous influences, inducements, pressures, threats or interference, direct or indirect, from any quarter or for any reason. Second, a judge shall be independent in relation to society in general and in relation to the particular parties to a dispute which the judge has to adjudicate. Third, a judge shall not only be free from inappropriate connections with, and influence by, the executive and legislative branches of government, but must also appear to a reasonable observer to be free therefrom. Fourth, in performing judicial duties, a judge shall be independent of judicial colleagues in respect of decisions which the judge is obliged to make independently. Fifth, a judge shall encourage and uphold safeguards for the discharge of judicial duties so as to maintain and enhance the institutional and operational independence of the Judiciary. Last, a judge shall exhibit and promote high standards of judicial conduct in order to reinforce public confidence in the Judiciary, which is fundamental to maintain judicial independence.[42]

Since 1994, the UN Special Rapporteur on the Independence of Judges and Lawyers discharges his or her mandate to, among other things, identify and record not only attacks on the independence of the Judiciary, lawyers and court officials but also progress achieved in protecting and enhancing their independence, and make concrete recommendations, including the provision of advisory services or technical assistance when they are requested by the State concerned. Additionally, the Special Rapporteur is to identify ways and means to improve the judicial system, and make concrete recommendations thereon; to study, for the purpose of making proposals, important and topical questions of principle with a view to protecting and enhancing the independence of the Judiciary, lawyers and court officials. In discharging these functions, the Special Rapporteur acts on information submitted to his or her attention concerning alleged violations relating to the independence and impartiality of the Judiciary and the independence of the legal profession by sending allegation letters and urgent appeals to concerned governments to clarify

41 UN Office on Drugs and Crime, *Commentary on the Bangalore Principles of Judicial Conduct* (UNODC 2007) para 17.

42 Ibid paras 22–50.

and/or bring these cases to their attention. The Special Rapporteur may conduct country visits when invited by the relevant government and submits a report on the visit to the Human Rights Council, presenting his or her findings, conclusions and recommendations. The Special Rapporteur presents annual thematic reports to the Human Rights Council (June session) and the UN General Assembly highlighting important issues or areas of concern related to the mandate. This process serves to name and shame those countries that do not uphold the independence of judiciary and, at the same time, to make constructive recommendations to them in this regard. Not all the countries approached by the Special Rapporteur accept his or her requests to visit. For example, Myanmar did not accept the request made in 2009 and repeated in 2012. Neither did Bangladesh in 2007 (after the January 2007 *coup*) and the follow-up request in 2012.

In the case of Myanmar, despite its rejection of the Special Rapporteur's request to visit the country the lack of independence of Myanmar's Judiciary is reported by the United Nations Independent International Fact-Finding Mission on Myanmar, set up by the UN Human Rights Council in March 2017 to establish the facts and circumstances of the alleged recent human rights violations and abuses by military and security forces in Myanmar, in particular in Rakhine state, with a view to ensuring full accountability for perpetrators and justice for victims. According to the Fact-Finding Mission, State structures, in particular civilian oversight of the military and an independent Judiciary, are weak.[43] Given the gross and systematic nature of human rights violations in Myanmar over a period of many years, and the lack of accountability, there is an indication that those human rights violations are the result of a State policy that involves authorities in the Executive, military and *Judiciary* at all levels.[44] The Judiciary has been systematically undermined, weakened and neglected during the long period of military dictatorship. Despite some progress reported since 2011, it is consistently assessed as lacking independence, poorly trained and resourced, inefficient and prone to corrupt practices—all these factors impact on its ability to guarantee fair trial rights. Since the President of the Union of Myanmar appoints judges to the Supreme Court and the Chief Justices of the High Courts, with a very limited role for review by the Union Parliament, and a law degree or legal practice is not required for these judicial appointments and since most judges on the Supreme Court are military appointees and several have military backgrounds, there is undue influence from State authorities, in particular the Executive and the military, particularly in politically sensitive cases, including those regarding human rights violations. Other challenges include insufficient legal expertise and judicial experience. A general lack of adequate resources results in low remuneration, under-staffing and limited training options. Many experts, observers and practitioners consider corruption widespread. Even the then State Counsellor and Myanmar's

43 Detailed findings of the Independent International Fact-Finding Mission on Myanmar, A/HRC/42/CRP.5 (16 September 2019) para 241.

44 Report of the detailed findings of the Independent International Fact-Finding Mission on Myanmar, A/HRC/42/CRP.2 (17 September 2018) para 97.

de facto leader Aung San Suu Kyi herself admitted at the Conference on the Justice Sector Coordinating for Rule of Law held in Naypyidaw in March 2018 that 'the public trust in people who are working in the justice sector has eroded . . . because of corruption, exercising the law for their own interests, failing the principle of upholding justice without favour and not performing their work efficiently and lacking expertise'.[45] The Fact-Finding Mission, therefore, recommends a judicial reform, including measures to strengthen the independence of judiciary and build judges' legal and judicial expertise. No civilian justice personnel should be under the control or influence of the military or the other branches of government. All judges in superior and appellate courts should be legally qualified. Additionally, programmes are required to build capacity to adequately investigate, prosecute and bring to trial cases of serious human rights violations. Such cases, in particular where they amount to crimes under international law, require specialized knowledge and expertise.[46]

In the Americas, the Inter-American Court of Human Rights (IACtHR) has reiterated that the guarantee of impartiality is applicable in disciplinary proceedings conducted against judges. This guarantee requires the judge who intervenes in a particular dispute to approach the facts of the case free of any subjective prejudice and also offer sufficient objective guarantees to exclude any doubt that the Judiciary or the general public may entertain as to his or her lack of impartiality. In order to inspire the necessary confidence in the parties to the case as well as in the citizens in a democratic society, the members of the court should not have a direct interest, preconceived position or preference for any of the parties, nor are they involved in the dispute.[47] In the IACtHR's case law, tenure of judges are protected under the following provisions of the 1969 American Convention on Human Rights:[48] Article 8 (right to a fair trial), Article 25 (right to judicial protection against acts that violate fundamental rights recognized by the constitution or laws of the State concerned or by this Convention) and Article 23 (right to participate in government).[49] The IACtHR has ordered States Parties to the American Convention that have interfered with judicial independence to rectify its misconduct, including by restoring due process rights and the right to an effective legal recourse, in cases involving the arbitrary dismissal of judges.[50]

45 Ibid paras 1586–8.

46 Ibid para 1636. See also Melissa Crouch, 'Judicial Power in Myanmar and the Challenge of Judicial Independence' in H.P. Lee and Marilyn Pittard (eds), *Asia-Pacific Judiciaries: Independence, Impartiality and Integrity* (CUP 2017) 264–83; id, 'Dictators, Democrats, and Constitutional Dialogue: Myanmar's Constitutional Tribunal' (2018) 16 Int'l J Constitutional L 426.

47 *Urrutia Laubreaux v Chile*, Judgment of 27 August 2020, Ser C no 409 para 118.

48 OAS Treaty Series No 36, in force 18 July 1978.

49 See, e.g., *Constitutional Court v Peru*, Judgment of 31 January 2001, Ser C no 55; *Supreme Court of Justice (Quintana Coello et al.) v Ecuador*, Judgment of 23 August 2013, Ser C no 266; *Constitutional Tribunal (Camba Campos et al.) v Ecuador*, Judgment of 28 August 2013, Ser C no 68. These cases are discussed in Tom Ginsburg, 'International Courts and Democratic Backsliding' (2019) 37 Berkeley JIL 265, 281–5.

50 See, e.g., *Apitz Barbera and others v Venezuela*, Judgment of 5 August 2008, Ser C no 182; *Reverón Trujillo v Venezuela*, Judgment of 20 June 2009, Ser C no 197; *Chocrón Chocrón v Venezuela*, Judgment of 1 July 2011, Ser C no 227.

In *Chocrón Chocrón v Venezuela*, the IACtHR emphasizes that although it is not competent to decide specifically the best institutional framework for guaranteeing judicial independence, it can exercise contentious jurisdiction to analyze whether the 1969 American Convention has been violated in a particular case in which a specific institutional framework has been applied and, when appropriate, to determine the pertinent reparations. The scope of judicial guarantees and effective judicial protection for judges must be analyzed in relation to the standards for judicial independence under the system of separation of public powers. In the case law of both the IACtHR and the European Court of Human Rights,[51] as well as according to the UN Basic Principles on the Independence of the Judiciary, the following guarantees are derived from judicial independence: an adequate appointment process, tenure in the post and guarantees against external pressure. When States establish procedures for the appointment of their judges, they must take into account that not just any procedure satisfies the conditions required by the 1969 American Convention for the adequate implementation of a truly independent regime. If basic parameters of objectivity and reasonableness are not respected, it would be possible to design a regime that permitted a high degree of discretionary authority in the selection of career judicial personnel, owing to which the individuals selected would not necessarily be the most suitable.

In *Cuya Lavy et al. v Peru*, decided in September 2021, the IACtHR reiterates that judges and prosecutors' guarantee of security of tenure and irremovability in their position implies: the removal from their positions must exclusively follow grounds that are allowed, whether through a process that fulfils judicial guarantees or because they have reached the full term of their mandate; they may only be dismissed for serious disciplinary misconduct or incompetence; and all proceedings must be resolved in accordance with established standards of judicial conduct and through appropriate procedures to ensure objectivity and impartiality in accordance with the constitution or the law. In the case at bar, the IACtHR finds Peru internationally responsible for a series of violations committed, in the framework of the process for evaluation and ratification of the appointment of two judges and two prosecutors by Peru's National Council of the Judiciary between 2001 and 2002. These prosecutors and judges faced proceedings determined by the aforesaid Council resulting in decisions not to ratify their appointments. They were not allowed to know in advance and in detail the accusation made, nor did they have the appropriate time and means for their defence. No reason was given for the decisions for the non-ratification and their appeals were declared inadmissible on the ground that the Council's decisions could not be reviewed in court. Therefore, rules the IACtHR, Peru has violated, inter alia, the rights protected under Articles 8, 23 and 25 of the American Convention as well as the right to privacy in the sense of having one's honour respected and dignity recognized under Article 11(1)

51 *Campbell and Fell v the United Kingdom*, Judgment of 28 June 1984, Ser A no 80 para 78; *Langborger v Sweden*, Judgment of 22 January 1989, Ser A no 155 para 32.

of that Convention, to the detriment of the four petitioners. Consequently, Peru is ordered to publish this judgment of the IACtHR and its summary; adapt, within a reasonable time, its domestic legal system to comply with the judgment; and pay the amounts established in the judgment for restitution, damages, tangible and intangible, and the reimbursement of costs and expenses.[52]

In the European Union (EU), it is settled jurisprudence of the European Court of Justice that the guarantees of independence and impartiality of the Judiciary required under EU law presuppose rules, particularly as regards the composition of the judicial body and the appointment, length of service and grounds for abstention, rejection and dismissal of its members, that are such as to dispel any reasonable doubt in the minds of individuals as to the imperviousness of that body to external factors and its neutrality with respect to the interests before it. In that regard, it is necessary to protect judges from external intervention or pressure that might jeopardize their independence. The rules applicable to the status of judges and the performance of their duties must, in particular, be such as to preclude not only any direct influence, in the form of instructions, but also types of influence which are more indirect and which are prone to have an effect on the decisions of the judges concerned, and thus preclude a lack of appearance of independence or impartiality on their part likely to prejudice the trust which justice in a democratic society governed by the rule of law must inspire in individuals. As regards specifically the rules governing the disciplinary regime applicable to judges, the regime in power must provide the necessary guarantees to prevent any risk of its being used as a system of political control of the content of judicial decisions. Rules which define, in particular, both forms of conduct amounting to disciplinary offences and the penalties actually applicable provide for the involvement of an independent body in accordance with a procedure which fully safeguards the rights enshrined in Articles 47 (right to an effective remedy and to a fair trial) and 48 (presumption of innocence and right of defence) of the Charter of the Fundamental Rights of the European Union.[53] These rules, which also lay down the possibility of bringing legal proceedings challenging the disciplinary bodies' decisions, constitute a set of guarantees essential for safeguarding the independence of judiciary.[54] The EU has made it a precondition for any country aspiring to join the EU to prove that the candidate country safeguards the independence of judiciary.

With respect to Africa, in *XYZ v Republic of Benin* before the African Court on Human and Peoples' Rights the Applicant argued that the lack of independence of Benin's Constitutional Court was evidenced by the fact that the terms of office of the judges were renewable and the Court did not enjoy financial autonomy. He also alluded to the close relationship between the President of the Constitutional

52 Judgment of 28 September 2021, www.corteidh.or.cr/docs/casos/articulos/seriec_438_esp.pdf.
53 OJ C 326/391.
54 *Commission v Poland*, C-791/19, European Court of Justice (Grand Chamber), Judgment of 15 July 2021 paras 59–61.

Court and the President of the Republic, and the fact that the former had, in his capacity as Minister of Justice and Legislation, participated in the approval of previous attempts to amend the Constitution, thereby having an impact on the impartiality of the Constitutional Court. The African Court considered that although Benin's Organic Law No 91–009 of 4 March 1991 on the Constitutional Court contained provisions guaranteeing the administrative and financial autonomy of the said Constitutional Court, the renewable nature of the judges' terms in office was likely to weaken their independence, particularly when judges were seeking a renewal of their terms. Benin was thus held by the African Court to have violated Article 26 of the African Charter on Human and Peoples' Rights[55] which guarantees independence of judiciary. On the other hand, with regard to the alleged violation of the obligation to guarantee the impartiality of the Constitutional Court, the Applicant had not proved that the President of the Constitutional Court acted in a biased manner, prejudged or in any way imposed his opinions on other judges of the Constitutional Court; hence, Benin did not violate the obligation to safeguard the impartiality of tribunals prescribed under Article 7(1)(d) of the Charter. The African Court ordered Benin to take all legislative and regulatory measures to guarantee the independence of the Constitutional Court, particularly with regard to the process of renewing the term of its judges.[56]

In Tunisia, after President Kais Saied staged a self-*coup* on 25 July 2021 by dismissing the Government and suspending Parliament, on 6 February 2022 he dissolved the Supreme Judicial Council set up in 2016 to ensure the independence of judiciary, discipline judges and grant them professional promotions. This came after the President had condemned senior officials in the Judiciary and accused them of being linked to 'criminal gangs' and accused Council members of taking 'billions' in bribes and delaying politically sensitive investigations. In January 2022, he revoked all financial privileges for Council members, alleging that, in this Council, positions and appointments were sold according to loyalties.[57] Article 80 of the Tunisian Constitution invoked by Saied to rule by decree did not empower the President to dissolve the Council, however. His act was criticized by the UN High Commissioner for Human Rights as a clear violation of Tunisia's obligations under international human rights law and a step back for the rule of law, separation of powers and independence of judiciary in Tunisia. It was also denounced by the ambassadors of France, Germany, Italy, Japan, the United States, the United Kingdom, Canada and the EU. On 13 February 2022, Saied officially issued a decree establishing a new provisional Supreme Judiciary Council whose members were to be appointed by the President. The Supreme Judicial Council, for its part, immediately insisted it would maintain its current composition, rejecting the presidential decree as unlawful and an attack on the independence of judiciary in violation of

55 (1982) 21 ILM 58, in force 21 October 1986.

56 *XYZ v Republic of Benin*, Application no 010/2020, Judgment of 27 November 2020.

57 'Tunisia's President Dissolves Top Judicial Watchdog' *Al Jazeera* (6 February 2022), https://www.aljazeera.com/news/2022/2/6/tunisias-president-dissolves-top-judicial-watchdog.

the fundamental rights of magistrates. The Union of Administrative Magistrates of Tunisia called on Tunisian judges not to recognize the provisional Council set up by the President and to boycott its work as well as to engage in all forms of struggle to defend the Judiciary's independence and confront any attacks against the judicial authority. The Union said it would challenge the decree in national courts and international bodies. The Union also took the matter to the UN Special Rapporteur on the Independence of Judges and Lawyers as well as to the International Association of Judges. On 1 June 2022 the President issued a decree dismissing 57 judges, including the former head of the Supreme Juridical Council, who were accused of corruption and protecting 'terrorists'. Tunisia is one of the African Union Member States that have made a declaration recognizing the competence of the African Court on Human and Peoples' Rights to receive complaints from non-government organizations and individuals. As of this writing, there is no publicly available information about any complaint by the aggrieved individuals to challenge this action by President Saied before the African Court.

The Supreme Court of Pakistan's success in confronting the junta's attempts to undermine the principle of independence of judiciary post-*coups* should be emulated by judges in other countries.

Article 209 of the Constitution of Pakistan[58] ensures that, through the Supreme Judicial Council, the security of tenure and independence of Pakistan's Judiciary are adequately safeguarded. The Council consists of the Chief Justice of Pakistan, the two next most senior judges of the Supreme Court and the two most senior Chief Justices of High Courts. If, on information from any source, the Council or the President of Pakistan is of the opinion that a judge of the Supreme Court or of a High Court may be incapable of properly performing the duties of his office by reason of physical or mental incapacity or may have been guilty of misconduct, the President shall direct the Council to, or the Council may, on its own motion, inquire into the matter. If, after inquiring into the matter, the Council reports to the President that the judge is incapable of performing the duties of his office or has been guilty of misconduct, and that he should be removed from office, the President may remove the judge from office. A judge of the Supreme Court or of a High Court shall not be removed from office except as provided by this Article. In addition, the Council shall issue a code of conduct to be observed by judges of the Supreme Court and of the High Courts.[59]

On 9 March 2007, Chief Justice of Pakistan Iftikhar Muhammad Chaudhry was made a 'non-functional Chief Justice' by General Pervez Musharraf who had staged a military *coup* to oust the Government in October 1999 and assumed the Presidency of Pakistan on 20 June 2001. The Chief Justice was accused of misconduct and abuses of his position for personal gains.[60]

58 http://www.pakistani.org/pakistan/constitution/part7.ch4.html.

59 On a critical analysis of the roles of judicial councils, see Nuno Garoupa and Tom Ginsburg, *Judicial Reputation: A Comparative Theory* (U Chicago Press 2015) 98–140.

60 https://archive.md/20071106095513/http://proud-pakistani.com/2007/03/21/text-of-reference-filed-against-the-cjp/.

Interestingly, after that *coup* Chaudhry was among Musharraf's handpicked judges appointed to the Supreme Court, replacing the six judges who refused to take an oath under Provisional Constitution Order promulgated by the junta after the 1999 *coup*. Chaudhry was promoted to Chief Justice in June 2005. It was the exercise of judicial independence to uphold the rights of citizens against abuses by the military regime that enraged Musharraf. The Supreme Court did its jobs well in regulating construction safety, enforcement of urban planning regulations, oil and sugar price controls and, along the way, exposed the military regime and targeted both low- and high-level corruption.[61]

Pakistan supported the US-led invasion of Afghanistan following the 11 September 2001 terrorist attacks on US soil. Pakistani authorities implemented a policy of arbitrarily rounding up suspected members of al Qaeda and the Taliban and handed them over to US authorities without any due process of law. Beginning in December 2005, the Supreme Court of Pakistan began to seek explanations from the Musharraf Government about the fate and whereabouts of 'disappeared' persons. Over the course of 2006 and 2007, Pakistan's Judiciary made a concerted attempt to address serious human rights abuses including enforced disappearances. In March 2007, the Human Rights Commission of Pakistan supplied a list of 148 missing persons to the Supreme Court, alleging the intelligence agencies were detaining these people. Chaudhry was suspended by Musharraf the day after a bench headed by him accepted the petition and sent notices to provincial and federal governments.[62]

On 18 and 24 April 2007, Chief Justice Chaudhry petitioned the Supreme Court seeking the setting up of a full court comprising all judges on the Supreme Court to hear his petition as well as other petitions related to the same issues, on the ground that some members of the Supreme Judicial Council harboured bias against him. There were widespread nationwide protests, spearheaded by members of the legal profession, against General Musharraf's action, and, as of 12 May 2007, no fewer than 42 people had been reportedly killed, 140 injured in riots erupting across the city of Karachi, the most populous city in Pakistan, and more than 800 members of labour and student organizations arrested. On 20 July 2007, the 13-judge panel of the Supreme Court hearing the case unanimously reinstated the Chief Justice. By the vote of 10 to 3, it quashed the charges against him as filed by Musharraf. Also by the vote of 10 to 3, it quashed the law that could send a judge on forced leave. Chief Justice Chaudhry resumed his judicial duty on 23 July 2007. The Chief Justice's cause and defiance which gained widespread national support created the greatest challenge to Musharraf since he came to power in the *coup* eight years previously. When Musharraf stood for re-election as President in October 2007, the Supreme Court blocked the election result in order to review the fact

61 Shoaib Ghias, 'Miscarriage of *Chief* Justice: Judicial Power and Legal Complex in Pakistan under Musharraf' (2010) 35 L & Social Inquiry 985, 991–5.

62 Ibid. See also Moeen Cheema, 'Two Steps Forward One Step Back: The Non-linear Expansion of Judicial Power in Pakistan' (2018) 16 Int'l J Constitutional L 503, 515–23.

that he was a presidential candidate while still in the army. On 3 November 2007, before the Supreme Court could announce its decision in this matter, Musharraf declared the state of emergency across Pakistan, suspended the Constitution and dismissed the Chief Justice of the Supreme Court once again. The emergency was proclaimed on the grounds of 'increasing interference by some members of the Judiciary in government policy, adversely affecting economic growth' and the Judiciary's 'constant interference in executive functions, including but not limited to the control of terrorist activity, economic policy, price controls, downsizing of corporations and urban planning', which had weakened the Government. Troops entered the Supreme Court building, arrested the judges and kept them detained in their homes. A Provisional Constitutional Order was issued prescribing a special oath for judges of the Superior Courts as a requirement for continuing to hold office. Thirteen out of the 18 judges of the Supreme Court and 61 out of 93 judges of the various High Courts did not take the oath and were dismissed.[63] Justice Abdul Hameed Dogar who took a new oath of office was made Chief Justice of the Supreme Court. With him, four other judges of the Supreme Court who took the new oath of office were allowed to stay on their job at the Supreme Court.

The relationship between the independence of judiciary and taking such a new oath has been exhaustively examined in the 12 May 2000 judgment of the Supreme Court of Pakistan in *Zafar Ali Shah v General Pervez Musharraf*[64] concerning the Oath of Judges Order No 1 of 2000 promulgated by General Musharraf, which allows all the courts to continue to function and exercise powers. This Oath was a reiteration of what had been earlier stated by the Oath of Office (Judges) Order No 10 of 1999. Pursuant to paragraph 3 of Order No 1 of 2000, it shall apply to newly appointed judges, the Oath shall be made before the constitutional authority and it would be in accordance with the appropriate form set out in the Third Schedule to the 1973 Constitution.

The Supreme Court rules that Pakistan's superior courts continue to function under the 1973 Constitution despite the fact that the judges of the superior courts have taken 'a new bath' under that Order No l of 2000. This is because the courts were originally established under the 1973 Constitution, and have continued in their functions in spite of the Proclamation of Emergency of 1999 and other legislative instruments issued by the *coup* leader, officially titled 'the Chief Executive of Pakistan', from time to time. The Oath of Judges Order No 1 of 2000 requires the newly appointed judges to take oath before the constitutionally designated authority and according to the procedure prescribed by the Constitution, and not by Order No 1 of 2000 itself. Moreover, no form of oath taken by or administered to the judges of superior courts can restrict the judicial power and derogate from the legal position that the courts, as final arbiters in any constitutional controversy, retain their power and jurisdiction to say what a particular provision of the

63 See also Tariq Hassan, 'Supreme Court of Pakistan: The Case of Missing Persons' (2009) 10 Asia Pacific J Hum Rts & L 23.
64 [2000] PLD SC 869.

Constitution or the law means or does not mean even if that particular provision is one seeking to oust such jurisdiction of the courts.[65] There is an oft-repeated argument that any court making a finding adverse to 'a revolutionary regime' is certain to be disbanded, so that in reality a Judiciary will be allowed to function only if it is subservient to the new regime. The Supreme Court counters this argument by alluding to the very submission by the 'revolutionaries' to litigation before the Supreme Court concerning their own legitimacy as a proof of the Supreme Court's inherent authority arising from the submission of both parties, rulers and ruled, to its jurisdiction.

According to the Pakistani Supreme Court, the Judiciary is the only forum recognized by both the rulers and the ruled where questions of validity and legitimacy are capable of being resolved finally with a view to controlling the recklessness of the government in power, and where declining to resolve it would be tantamount to self-condemnation, self-destruction and betrayal of the trust of the people of Pakistan. Any attempt to control or circumscribe the judicial power of the superior courts, with a view to denying them the right to decide the validity and the quantum of legislative power of the usurper's regime, would be an exercise in futility. Changing the form of oath will neither take away power of judicial review nor the jurisdiction of the Supreme Court. Notwithstanding the new oath or its language, Pakistan's courts shall continue to have jurisdiction to decide the controversy involved as if the new oath and the 'new constitutional documents' under which the oath is administered do not adversely affect the jurisdiction and power of the courts. Superior courts follow the Code of Conduct prescribed for the judges and inherently owe allegiance to the State of Pakistan, which requires the Supreme Court to decide the issue of validity of the usurper's regime under which the judges are being asked to take a new oath inasmuch as such allegiance cannot be taken away.[66] The oath administered under the Constitution has to be respected because the Constitution draws its authority from the people of Pakistan and the oath under the Constitution to defend the same has a different meaning from an oath administered under another document (i.e., Order No 1 of 2000), the validity whereof is yet to be determined and thus the two are incomparable.

The Objectives Resolution contained in the Preamble to the Constitution of Pakistan, which now forms a substantive part thereof, envisages the independence of judiciary. The Objectives Resolution recognizes the 'Islamic doctrine of sovereignty' as expounded in the Holy Book (Qur'an)—sovereignty belongs neither to the ruler nor the ruled but Almighty Allah alone which is to be exercised by the

65 The Pakistani Supreme Court in this case closely follows the reasoning of the Pakistani Supreme Court in *Bhutto v Chief of Army Staff* ([1977] PLD SC 657) concerning a new oath of office for judges as ordered by the junta after the *coup* by General Zia Ul Haq in July 1977.

66 As Mark Stavsky, ('The Doctrine of State Necessity in Pakistan' (1983) 16 Cornell ILJ 341, 386) has rightly observed, had the Pakistani Supreme Court willingly accepted the military regime's limits upon its powers of judicial review, 'the judges would appear to be silent partners to any and all forms of political terror promulgated by the regime'.

people of Pakistan through their chosen representatives. A fundamental principle of jurisprudence requires courts to always endeavour to expand their jurisdiction to guard the rights of the people against arbitrary violations by the Executive. The orders of the Chief Executive of Pakistan are subject to the jurisdiction of the Constitutional Courts of the land. By including such provisions in the Provisional Constitution Order, 1999, promulgated by the Chief Executive, it has been recognized that the superior courts, which are respected by the people as being an embodiment of the ideals of justice and guardian of the rights of the people, are not merely entitled to continue to discharge their judicial functions but have, in fact, done so in the past as well.

Any provision purporting to restrain the power of judicial review of the superior courts is to be ignored altogether. *A judge acting in his conscience and in good faith may decide to resign or he may decide that in the higher public interest he would retain office* as has been done by the judges of Supreme Court and other judges of the Superior Judiciary. The contention that after having taken oaths of their offices under the Provisional Constitution Order, 1999 as amended, the judges of the superior courts are bound to defend the Proclamation of Emergency and the Provisional Constitution Order, 1999 as amended, in that the old Constitution has been replaced by a new revolutionary order is totally misconceived. The old constitutional order has not been replaced by a new unconstitutional order—the latter being merely a case of constitutional deviation for a temporary period.

The Pakistani Supreme Court reiterates several times the independence of judiciary as a basic principle of the constitutional system of governance, as evident from the Preamble and Article 2A of the Constitution stipulating: 'The independence of the Judiciary shall be fully secured', and, with a view to achieving this objective, Article 175 thereof provides that 'the Judiciary shall be separated progressively from the Executive'. The Constitution makes it the exclusive power and responsibility of the Judiciary to ensure the sustenance of system of 'separation of powers' based on checks and balances. This requires the Judiciary to decide matters before it in accordance with its impartial assessment of the facts and its understanding of the law *without improper influences, direct or indirect, from any source.*

A requirement of the Code of Conduct issued by the Supreme Judicial Council is that the oath of a judge implies complete submission to the Constitution, and under the Constitution to the law. Subject to these governing obligations, the judge's function of interpretation and application of the Constitution and the law is to be discharged for the maintenance of the *rule of law* over the whole range of human activities within the nation. Thus, the new oath merely indicates that the Superior Judiciary, like the rest of the country, accepted the fact that, on 12 October 1999, a radical transformation took place by means of a military *coup*. The fresh oath taken under Order No 1 of 2000 does not in any way preclude the judges of the Supreme Court from examining the questions raised in the constitutional petitions which have to be decided *in accordance with their conscience and law* so as to resolve the grave crises and avoid disaster by preventing imposition of martial law for which the Constitution does not provide any remedy. The new oath of office was taken by the judges of the Supreme Court with 'a view to reiterating the well-established principle that the first and the foremost duty of the judges of the superior courts is to save the judicial organ of the State'.

For its part, Pakistan's Supreme Court, while performing its role as 'the beneficial expression of a laudable political realism', had three options open to it in relation to the situation arising out of the military takeover on 12 October 1999. First, it could tender resignation *en bloc*, which most certainly could be equated with sanctifying chaos or anarchy and denial of access to justice to every citizen of Pakistan wherever he may be. Second, it could completely surrender to the military regime by dismissing constitutional petitions for lack of jurisdiction in view of the purported ouster of its jurisdiction by the military regime. Third, it could accept of the situation as it is, in an attempt to save what 'institutional values remained to be saved'. The Supreme Court—after conscious deliberations and in an endeavour to defend and preserve the national independence, the security and stability of Pakistan, the sovereignty and honour of the country, and to safeguard the interest of the community as a whole—decided to maintain and uphold the independence of the Judiciary, which, in its turn, would protect the State fabric and guarantee human rights and fundamental rights. It took the new oath so as to secure the enforcement of law, extending help to the law enforcing agencies for maintenance of public order and, with a view to restoring democratic institutions, achieving their stability and guaranteeing constitutional rights to the people of Pakistan. A duty is cast upon the Superior Judiciary to offer some recompense for those rights purportedly violated by the military regime. *This could be achieved only by taking the oath and not by declining to do so and thereby becoming a party to the closure of the Courts, which would not have solved any problem whatsoever but would have resulted in chaos, anarchy and disruption of peaceful life.* Indeed, the latter course would have been the most detestable thing to happen.

Clearly, the judges of the Superior Judiciary enjoy constitutional guarantees against arbitrary removal. Judges of the Supreme Court and High Courts cannot be removed without resorting to the procedure prescribed in Article 209 of the Constitution by filing an appropriate reference before the Supreme Judicial Council, and not otherwise. Yet, the cases of judges who were removed after refusing to take a new oath of allegiance were hit by the doctrine of past and closed transaction and could not be reopened. Although the validity of the action of the Chief Executive of Pakistan was open to question, none of the removed judges took any remedial steps and accepted pension as also the right to practise law and thereby acquiesced in the action by the Chief Executive. Furthermore, the appropriate course of action for the Supreme Court in these proceedings would be to declare the law to avoid the recurrence in future, but not to upset earlier actions or decisions taken in this behalf by the Chief Executive, these being past and closed transactions and neither the relevant authorities nor Supreme Court might reopen the cases of the above judges which had become final.

Although Musharraf won the general elections held in February 2008, he resigned as President on 18 August 2008 to avoid impeachment for alleged corruption and went to live in exile abroad.[67] Chief Justice Chaudhry was restored to his post by a Presidential executive order on 16 March 2009. In *Sindh High Court Bar Association v Federation of Pakistan* decided on 31 July 2009,[68] Pakistan's Supreme Court ruled that former President Musharraf violated the constitution by declaring emergency rule in November 2007 including by promulgating Provisional Constitutional Order 2007 and the Oath of Office (Judges) Order 2007. It reasoned that the Constitution could not be suspended even for a single moment in a manner not authorized by the Constitution itself, and that all the amendments to the Constitution and other statutes were unconstitutional, bearing in mind also that Musharraf's unconstitutional acts were not validated by Parliament through a constitutional amendment. The appointments of all those judges by Musharraf as well as those in consultation with Justice Dogar were declared unconstitutional and void *ab initio*,[69] with those appointed from the Bar being declared to have ceased to hold office and those taken from the Judiciary being reverted to their respective courts. Citing *Zafar Ali Shah*, the Court set aside as being *per incuriam* those judgments of the Supreme Court under Justice Dogar[70] that validated on the basis of the doctrine of necessity and the principle of *salus populi suprema est lex* Musharraf's aforesaid impugned acts. However, in the interest of justice, the Supreme Court in *Sindh High Court Bar Association* gave protection to the judgments and orders rendered by Justice Dogar and by such other judges in the cases of the ordinary litigants. It also ruled that Parliament should decide which laws passed under emergency rule would stand.

In the view of this present author, the reasoning of the Pakistani Supreme Court in protecting the independence of judiciary is of practical importance, setting an excellent example for judges in other countries facing a similar situation to follow.

Superior orders

A question may be asked whether owing to the principle of independence of judiciary, judges can have recourse to the defence of superior orders, particularly in the case of judges of military courts or tribunals.[71]

The defence of superior orders is stipulated in Article 33 of the 1998 Rome Statute of the International Criminal Court (ICC).[72] By virtue of this provision, the fact that a crime within the ICC's jurisdiction has been committed by a person pursuant to an order of a government or of a superior, whether military or civilian, shall

67 Ghias, 'Miscarriage of *Chief* Justice' 985–7, 1002–10, 1013–18.

68 [2009] PLD SC 879.

69 This was affirmed by the Supreme Court of Pakistan in *Justice Khurshid Anwar Bhindar v Federation of Pakistan* [2010] PLD SC 483.

70 *Tikka Iqbal Muhammad Khan* [2008] PLD SC 6 and [2008] PLD SC 178 and *Review Petition* [2008] PLD SC 615.

71 See also Graver, *Judges Against Justice* 171–8, 215–25, 237–52.

72 2187 UNTS 3, in force 1 July 2002.

not relieve that person of criminal responsibility *unless* the person was under a legal obligation to obey orders of the government or the superior in question, the person did not know the order was unlawful and the order was not manifestly unlawful. However, orders to commit genocide or crimes against humanity are deemed to be manifestly unlawful.[73] In comparison, Article 6(4) of the Statute of the Special Court for Sierra Leone,[74] concluded in 2002, does not follow the provision of Article 33 of the Rome Statute, which seems to depart from the established case law and which was a compromise reached at the time of drafting the Rome Statute to accommodate the US position to protect US servicemen on the battlefield from international criminal responsibility in the event that they obey orders, the legality of which they are not in a position to appraise, to carry out combat operations. However, the US Government considers genocide and crimes against humanity to be always part of a widespread or systematic practice involving higher political and military authorities in non-democratic States and, therefore, the absolute liability approach regarding these crimes would not affect US servicemen serving overseas.[75]

Under Article 6(4) of the Statute of the Special Court for Sierra Leone, the fact that an accused person acted pursuant to an order of a government or of a superior shall not relieve him or her of criminal responsibility, but may be considered in *mitigation of punishment* if the Special Court determines that justice so requires. This provision follows Article 7(4) of the Statute of the International Criminal Tribunal for the former Yugoslavia[76] and Article 6(4) of the International Criminal Tribunal for Rwanda.[77]

Closely related to the defence of superior order is the defences of mistake of fact and mistake of law. By virtue of Article 32(1) of the Rome Statute, a mistake of fact shall be a ground for excluding criminal responsibility only if it negates the mental element required by the crime. Article 32(2) of the Rome Statute provides that a mistake of law as to whether a particular type of conduct is a crime within the ICC's jurisdiction shall not be a ground for excluding criminal responsibility, except where it negates the mental element required by such a crime, or as provided for in Article 33.[78] Awareness or knowledge of the illegality of the act charged is the test based on evidence, and presumption in the case of genocide and crimes against humanity, to determine whether the defence of superior order can be upheld as valid.[79]

73 See also Otto Triffterer, *Commentary on the Rome Statute of the International Criminal Court* (2nd edn, Hart 2008) 915–29; Emmanuel Sarpong Owasu, '"Guilty of Having Been Obedient": A Fresh Dissection of the Superior Orders Controversy' (2021) 12 J Int'l Humanitarian Legal Studies 279.

74 UN Doc S/2002/246 p 32.

75 Paola Gaeta, 'The Defence of Superior Orders: The Statute of the International Criminal Court *versus* Customary International Law' (1999) 10 EJIL 172, 189.

76 S/RES/827 (1993) of 25 May 1993.

77 S/RES/955 (1994) of 8 November 1994.

78 For a drafting history of this provision, see Mark Klamberg (ed.), *Commentary on the Law of the International Criminal Court* (Torkel Opsahl Academic EPublisher 2017) 327–35.

79 Yoram Dinstein, *The Defence of 'Obedience to Superior Orders' in International Law* (OUP 2012) xviii–xxv. Cf. Jessica Liang, 'Defending the Emergence of the Superior Orders Defense in the Contemporary Context' (2010) 2 Goettingen JIL 871, 885–9. See also Rebecca Jonassen, 'The Defence of Superior Orders in New Zealand Law: A Soldier's Dilemma?' (2002) 9 Auckland U L Rev

The independence of judiciary as elucidated here negates any justification to invoke the defence of superior orders. How can a judge who discharges his or her function independently of any person or authority claim that he or she decides a case on an order of his or her superior? There can be no mistake of fact or mistake of law concerning the independence of judiciary which would negate the *mens rea* of the judge in question. This is made clear by the US Military Tribunal in the *Justice* case in relation to the defendant Ernst Lautz, who resisted all efforts of Nazi Party officials to influence his conduct but yielded to influence and guidance from Hitler through the Reich Ministry of Justice, *believing that to be required under German law*. The Tribunal found Lautz guilty as charged even after holding that *if German law were a defence, which it was not*, many of his acts would be excusable.[80]

According to the Inter-American Court of Human Rights, prohibiting judges from criticizing the functioning of the power of the State of which they form part, which necessarily involves the criticism of the conduct of other judges, or requiring that they request authorization from the President of the highest court to do this and, moreover, that they must act in the same way when they wish to defend their own judicial actions, signifies opting for 'a hierarchized model of the Judiciary' in the form of a corporation in which judges lack internal independence, with a propensity towards unconditional subordination to the authority of their own collegiate organs. Although, formally, the intention may be to limit this to the disciplinary sphere, in practice, owing to an inherent fear of this power, it results in subjugation to so-called superior jurisprudence and paralyzes the interpretive dynamic in the application of the law.[81]

Moreover, the standard of manifest illegality under Article 33 of the Rome Statute should inform every single judge deciding cases after the unconstitutional usurpation of power in his or her country that there are limits how far the judge can toe the line with the usurper. For instance, the judge must not decide cases in such a way as to condone the usurper's conducts amounting to genocide or crimes against humanity (such as torture as part of the military regime's widespread or systematic attack on those opposed to it). If one follows the rule in Article 6(4) of the Statute of the Special Court for Sierra Leone, one may question how judges toeing the line with the usurper deserve mitigation of their punishment.

Duress

In a repressive regime, judges can be put under duress in the forms of threats to their person or liberty or threats to remove them from their judicial positions, as in the case of the mass dismissals of Pakistani and Tunisian judges mentioned earlier.

643; Christopher Penny, 'Obeying Restraints: Applying the Plea of Superior Orders to Military Defendants before the International Criminal Court' (2011) 48 Canadian YBIL 3; Ziv Bohrer, 'The Superior Order Defense: A Principal-Agent Analysis' (2012) 41 Georgia J Int'l & Comp L 1; Elies van Sliedregt, *Individual Responsibility in International Law* (OUP 2012) 287–306.

80 *In re Josef Altstoetter and Others* 1118–34.

81 *Urrutia Laubreaux v Chile* para 137.

The defence of duress appears in Article 31(1)(d) of the Rome Statute, stipulating that a person shall not be criminally responsible if, at the time of that person's conduct, the conduct which is alleged to constitute a crime within the ICC's jurisdiction has been caused by *duress* resulting from a threat of imminent death or of continuing or imminent serious bodily harm against that person or another person, and the person acts necessarily and reasonably to avoid this threat, provided that the person does not intend to cause a greater harm than the one sought to be avoided. Such a threat may either be made by other persons or constituted by other circumstances beyond that person's control.[82]

The Statute of the International Criminal Tribunal for the former Yugoslavia (ICTY) does not include any defence which the defendant may raise. In *Prosecutor v Erdemovic*,[83] the ICTY Appeals Chamber held, by a majority of 3 to 2, that duress does not afford a complete defence to a soldier charged with a crime against humanity and/or a war crime involving the killing of innocent human beings. It is the ICTY Appeals Chamber's detailed survey of the defence of duress in several jurisdictions that is of relevance to our analysis here.

Superior orders and duress are conceptually distinct and separate issues and often the same factual circumstances engage both notions, particularly in armed conflict situations.[84] Obedience to superior orders is merely a factual circumstance to be considered when determining whether the defence of duress is made out on the merits.[85]

Although duress is commonly raised in conjunction with superior orders, superior orders may be issued without being accompanied by any threats to life or limb. Equally, duress may be raised entirely independently of superior orders, for example, where the threat is from a fellow serviceman.[86]

The surveys of the criminal codes and legislation of the following Civil Law jurisdictions reveal that duress is prescribed as a general exculpatory principle applying to all crimes: Belgium, Chile, France, Italy, Finland, Mexico, the Netherlands, Nicaragua, Germany, Norway, Panama, Sweden, Venezuela and the former Yugoslavia. In contrast, the various countries throughout the world applying the Common Law categorically reject duress as a defence to murder, with the sole exception of the United States, where a few federal states have accepted section 2.09 of the US Penal Code which provides that duress is a general defence to all crimes.[87] After surveying criminal law of other States (namely, Japan, China, Morocco, Somalia and Ethiopia), the majority of the ICTY Appeals Chamber concludes there is

82 See also Dinstein, *The Defence of 'Obedience to Superior Orders' in International Law* xxvi–xxviii; Klamberg (ed.), *Commentary on the Law of the International Criminal Court* 367; Windell Nortje and Noëlle Quénivet, *Child Soldiers and the Defence of Duress under International Criminal Law* (Palgrave Macmillan 2020) 21–47, 109–44, 145–53. Cf. Graver, *Judges Against Justice* 166–9.

83 Case No IT-96–22-A (7 October 1997).

84 Joint Separate Opinion of Judges McDonald and Vorah, with whom Judge Li concurs, para 34.

85 Ibid para 36.

86 Separate and dissenting opinion of Judge Cassese, para 15.

87 Joint Separate Opinion of Judges McDonald and Vorah, with which Judge Li concurs, paras 49, 59–60.

no consistent concrete rule which answers the question whether or not duress is a defence to the killing of innocent persons. It is not possible to reconcile the opposing positions and this problem of inconsistency should be settled by bearing in mind the specific context in which the ICTY was established, the types of crimes over which it has jurisdiction, and the ICTY's mandate to prosecute persons responsible for 'serious violations of international humanitarian law'.[88]

Yet, the majority of the ICTY Appeals Chamber notes that 'practical policy considerations' compel the Legislatures of most Common Law jurisdictions to withhold the defence of duress not only from murder but from a vast array of offences without engaging in a complex and tortuous investigation into the relationship between law and morality. The Common Law in England denies recognition of duress as a defence not only for murder but also for certain serious forms of treason. In Malaysia, duress is not available as a defence in respect not only of murder but also of a multitude of offences against the State which are punishable by death. In the federal states of Australia which have criminal codes, the statutory provisions contain a list of excepted offences, with the Criminal Code of Tasmania having the longest, making the defence of duress unavailable to persons charged with murder, attempted murder, treason, piracy, offences deemed to be piracy, causing grievous bodily harm, rape, forcible abduction, robbery with violence and robbery and arson. Legislatures which have denied duress as a defence to specific crimes are therefore content to leave the interest of justice to be satisfied by mitigation of sentence.[89]

The notion of proportionality is raised with great frequency in the limited jurisprudence on duress. Proportionality is merely another way of referring to the utilitarian approach of weighing the balance of harms; it adds nothing to the debate when it comes to human lives having to be weighed and when the law must determine, because a certain legal consequence will follow, that one life or a set of lives is more valuable than another.[90] In the particular case at bar, the majority of the ICTY Appeals Chamber rejects duress as a complete defence to the killing of innocent human not because they apply the test as to what the reasonable person is expected to do, but on 'an absolute moral postulate which is clear and unmistakable for the implementation of international humanitarian law'.[91] This is because soldiers or combatants are expected to exercise fortitude and a greater degree of resistance to a threat than civilians, at least when it is their own lives which are being threatened. Soldiers, by the very nature of their occupation, must have envisaged the possibility of violent death in pursuance of the cause for which they fight. What is to be expected of such an ordinary soldier is not analyzed in terms of a utilitarian approach involving the weighing up of harms. Rather, it is based on the proposition that it is unacceptable to allow a trained fighter, whose job necessarily

88 Ibid paras 61, 72.

89 Ibid para 77.

90 Ibid para 81.

91 Ibid para 83.

entails the occupational hazard of dying, to avail himself of a complete defence to a crime in which he killed one or more innocent persons although duress may be taken into account in mitigation of punishment.[92]

Applying the aforesaid contextual approach to the defence of duress in relation to domestic judges under a repressive regime, the judges cannot invoke duress as a complete defence for their failure to uphold fundamental rights and freedoms of citizens. Compared to the soldiers referred to by the majority of the ICTY Appeals Chamber in *Erdemovic*, judges must be assessed in light of the independence of judiciary and what is expected of judges as enunciated in the 1985 UN Basic Principles of the Independence of the Judiciary. As the US Military Tribunal has ruled in the *Justice* case in relation to the defendant Rothaug, his acts were more terrible in that those who might have hoped for a last refuge in the institutions of justice found these institutions turned against them and constituted a part of the programme of terror and oppression.

Judicial immunity

The defendants in the *Justice* case were tried by the US Military Tribunal despite the fact that the Ministry of Justice under Hitler's regime had granted *immunity* to and *amnesty* following prosecutions and convictions of Nazi Party members for major crimes committed against civilians of occupied territories, and that *pardons* had been granted by the Ministry to members of the Nazi Party who had been sentenced for proved offences. The Tribunal held that although in Nazi Germany's legal theory Hitler's law under the Third Reich was a shield to those who acted under it, but before a tribunal authorized to enforce international law, Hitler's decrees were a protection neither to the Fuehrer himself nor to his subordinates, if in violation of the law of the community of nations.[93] The Tribunal thus saw no merit in the suggestion that Nazi judges were entitled to the benefit of the Anglo-American doctrine of *judicial immunity* since the doctrine that judges are not personally liable for their judicial actions is based on the concept of an independent judiciary administering impartial justice. Furthermore, it has never prevented the prosecution of a judge for malfeasance in office.[94]

The 1985 UN Basic Principles of the Independence of the Judiciary merely state in relation to judicial immunity that, without prejudice to any disciplinary procedure or to any right of appeal or to compensation from the State, in accordance with national law, judges should enjoy personal immunity from *civil* suits for monetary damages for improper acts or omissions in the exercise of their judicial functions. For its part, the European Commission for Democracy through Law (Venice Commission), an advisory body of the Council of Europe, is in favour of a limited functional immunity of judges: although, according to general standards,

92 Ibid paras 84, 85.
93 *In re Josef Altstoetter and Others* 1011.
94 Ibid 1024–5.

judges need protection from *civil* suits for actions done in good faith in the course of their functions, they should *not* benefit from a general immunity which protects them against *prosecution for criminal acts* committed by them for which they should be answerable before the courts. The functional immunity to be accorded to judges is immunity from prosecution for acts performed in the exercise of their functions, with the exception of intentional crimes.[95]

The argument that *all* judges who apply the law passed by a repressive regime, however oppressive or reprehensible that law may be, should not, without any exception, be held criminally responsible is unconvincing for the reasons explained earlier in this chapter. Judges must uphold the rule of law, not rule by law for the sake of keeping the repressive regime in power.[96] Where the judge is under instruction by the repressive regime, collaborates with the regime in the breakdown of the rule of law or is engaged in a systematic undermining of the rule of law, the resulting acts fulfil the condition of illegality. *A fortiori*, the judge cannot escape individual criminal responsibility if his or her conduct constitutes crimes of international concern such as crimes against humanity when their conduct fits the requisite elements of these crimes.[97]

Concluding remarks

Although a successfully executed *coup* might present a political system with a *fait accompli* and it would be hard to expect every segment of society not to collaborate through passivity, judges are 'accomplices to unconstitutional usurpations and the evidence of their guilt is furnished by the very decisions they gave' and '[t]o rely now on the unsafe jurisprudence they spawned is to perpetuate the cycle of *coups*'.[98]

The aforesaid vicious circle can be averted.

When the usurper is still in power, domestic judges in that country should emulate the reasoning of the Supreme Court of Pakistan in *Zafar Ali Shah* which shields them from any personal accountability, provided that they discharge their judicial functions independently and impartially. The advice given by that Supreme Court is for judges to proceed on a pragmatic basis, or 'a political realism', in light of the *fait accompli*, but they must protect the independence of judiciary as well as negate any semblance of being subservient to the regime. Furthermore, while an idealist judge acting in his conscience and in good faith may decide to resign, a more pragmatic one should decide that in the higher public interest he or she will retain office and vigilantly guard against violations by the regime so that all acts

95 Report on the Independence of the Judicial System Part 1: The Independence of Judges, adopted by the Venice Commission at its 82nd Plenary Session on 12–13 March 2010 (CDL-AD(2010)004 paras 60, 61 and 82(10)).

96 Hans Petter Graver, 'Judging without Impunity: On the Criminal Responsibility of Authoritarian Judges' (2016) Bergen J Crim L & Crim Justice 125, 133–4.

97 Ibid 140–8.

98 John Hatchard and Tunde Ogowewo, *Tackling the Unconstitutional Overthrow of Democracies: Emerging Trends in the Commonwealth* (Commonwealth Secretariat 2003) 17.

and actions leading to infringement of fundamental rights and freedoms are nullified and the rule of law upheld. As Judge Fieldsend of the Appellate Division of the Rhodesian High Court cogently opines in *Madzimbamuto v Lardner-Burke and another*, 'It may be a vain hope that the judgment of court will deter a usurper, or have the effect of restoring legality, but for a court to be deterred by fear of failure is merely to acquiesce in illegality'.[99]

During or even after the transition from a repressive regime or dictatorship to full-fledged democracy, the democratic regime may encounter the dilemma of having judges appointed by the previous regime whose tenure is guaranteed under the constitution.[100] These judges must be held accountable for their past wrongs, if any, and whenever they fail to maintain their judicial independence and uphold the fundamental rights and freedoms under the democratic regime.

99 (1968) 2 SALR 284, 430. The three-judge Appellate Division of the High Court, Judge Fieldsend dissenting, held that the Government of Ian Smith which had unilaterally declared the independence of Rhodesia in 1965 was the de facto government of Rhodesia by virtue of its effective control over the State's territory and could lawfully do anything which its predecessor could lawfully have done. The decision of the Privy Council, on appeal from the said High Court, is discussed in Chapter 2.

100 See, e.g., the situations in Argentina and Chile after the end of dictatorship (Owen Fiss, 'The Limits of Judicial Independence' (1993) 25 Inter-American L Rev 57, 70–6).

5

AMNESTIES, PARDONS, IMMUNITIES AND OTHER RESTRICTIONS ON THE PROSECUTION OF USURPERS OF POWER AND THEIR ACCOMPLICES OR COLLABORATORS

The preceding chapters discuss the types of judicial behaviour after *coups d'état* that merit investigation and punishment in accordance with international standards and best practices among domestic judicial decisions. This chapter looks closely at amnesties, pardons, immunities and other restrictions on the prosecution of usurpers of power and their accomplices or collaborators, including statutes of limitations prescribing a certain time after which rights cannot be enforced by legal action or offences cannot be punished. Judges of domestic courts have two roles in this respect. First, they have to consider whether they are required by domestic law and/or applicable rules of international law to uphold these restrictions. Second, the judges themselves may benefit from such restrictions on the prosecution of crimes under the usurper's regime in which they are co-perpetrators or accomplices. The chapter then analyzes the role of transitional justice after the country's return to democracy that may have some impact on judicial responsibility arising from repression post-*coups*. There are different approaches to transitional justice, and the chapter seeks to strike a delicate balance in this respect.

Amnesties, pardons and immunities

Overview

When *coup* leaders succeed in running the country for only a brief period, as in the case of Grenada's Bernard Coard, who took power for three days on 14–19 October 1983, and that of Hudson Austin, who toppled Coard and ruled for six days on 19–25 October 1983, they are quickly apprehended and brought to justice to serve severe punishment.[1] The same may be said of the eight-hour bloodless

1 Coard and Austin's death sentences were declared invalid by the Judicial Committee of the Privy Council which remitted their cases to Grenada's Supreme Court for re-sentencing (*Coard & Ors v*

DOI: 10.4324/9781003358428-5

coup in Ecuador in 22 January 2000 that ended the Presidency of Jamil Mahuad and installed the junta composed of Ecuador's most influential ethnic group and a group of junior military officers led by Colonel Lucio Gutiérrez. The junta was quickly dissolved by the high command of the Armed Forces of Ecuador which proceeded to arrest all the military officers who participated in the junta. The then Ecuadorian Vice President Gustavo Noboa assumed the Presidency.[2] Such cases can be considered 'failed' *coups*.

Usurpers who are able to hold onto power for a relatively longer period and not killed during that time usually take steps to shield themselves as well as their accomplices and collaborators from liability when they are in power and thereafter. The law for this purpose may be in the form of a specific decree, a statutory law or a provision in the new constitution promulgated after the *coup*.

An amnesty is given to a group of Individuals who have not been prosecuted and convicted or before the rendering of the final judgment of the court trying them. A pardon is granted individually to convicted persons although their criminal records are not erased after the pardon. There are two main types of immunity from criminal prosecution: personal immunity based on the official status of a person and functional immunity for acts performed by a person in an official capacity.

One positive aspect of such measures is that they provide a strong incentive for usurpers to cede power peacefully, or else they will fight to the death by all means for fear that they would be subsequently punished for what they have done. Because of this consideration, some amnesties have been internationally mediated so as to end the *coup* and return the country to democracy as quickly as possible. This was the case of São Tomé and Príncipe in July 2003 when the military junta that overthrew the President signed an agreement with a team of 30 international mediators from Portugal, Brazil, the United States, South Africa and several other African countries for the junta to cede power a week after the *coup* in return for an amnesty for the *coup* leaders and their civilian collaborators, and the formation of a new government.[3] The first military *coup* in São Tomé and Príncipe, staged in August 1995, had also ended in the same manner and with the junta staying in power only after six days.[4] As for immunity, the agreement of 23 November 2011 brokered by the Gulf Cooperation Council to end the political crisis in Yemen has led to Yemen's Law No 1 of 21 January 2012 concerning the Granting of Immunity from Legal and Judicial Prosecution. In exchange for the transfer of his Presidency and its power to another person, the then Yemeni President Ali

---

The Attorney General (Grenada) [2007] UKPC 7). The Grenadian Supreme Court subsequently sentenced each of them to 30 years' imprisonment.

2 John Samuel Fitch, 'Post-Transition Coups: Ecuador 2000—An Essay in Honor of Martin Needler' (2005) 33 J Political & Military Sociology 39.

3 'Coup Leaders Hand Power Back to Civilian President' *New Humanitarian* (23 July 2003), https://www.thenewhumanitarian.org/report/45122/sao-tome-and-principe-coup-leaders-hand-power-back-civilian-president.

4 Gerhard Seibert, 'São Tomé e Príncipe: Military Coup As a Lesson?' (1996) 3 Lusotopie 71.

Abdullah Saleh was accorded complete immunity by the Law from prosecution, whereas his associates were given immunity from criminal prosecution for 'politically motivated acts' carried out during the course of their official duties. Proponents of such measures also argue that these measures might help facilitate national reconciliation after years of widespread national conflicts between the oppressors and the oppressed.[5] In general, peace agreements to end an internal armed conflict or civil war adopt three main mechanisms: amnesty (particularly general amnesty provisions), prisoner release and combatant reintegration measures.[6]

However, from the United Nations' perspective, the removal of restrictions on the prosecution of State officials and other individuals responsible for atrocities can help strengthen national legal frameworks for accountability. In addition, addressing past violations helps to restore the dignity of victims, facilitate redress of violations and enable national reconciliation. Above all, States must ensure those responsible for atrocities such as genocide, war crimes or crimes against humanity in their territory are prosecuted, and, if they fail to do so, the international community should consider all legal options available to secure justice for victims and to prevent recurrence.[7]

Due to these diverging opinions, a possibility of including a provision on amnesty was too controversial for the negotiations for both the 1998 Rome Statute of the International Criminal Court[8] and the 2006 International Convention for the Protection of All Persons from Enforced Disappearance[9] that the final Statute and Convention omit any such provision.[10]

Whatever may be the case, States are bound by the treaties to which they are parties. For example, in its General Comment No 31 (The Nature of the General Legal Obligation Imposed on States Parties to the Covenant), the Human Rights

5 See, e.g., Louise Mallinder, *Amnesty, Human Rights and Political Transitions: Bridging the Peace and Justice Divide* (Hart 2008). Mallinder suggests, however, that international actors should work to limit the scope of amnesty by encouraging States to make them conditional and to introduce complementary programmes to repair the harm and prevent a repetition of the crimes. Cf. Mark Osiel, *Making Sense of Mass Atrocity* (CUP 2009) 218–40; Renée Jeffery, *Amnesties, Accountability, and Human Rights* (U Pennsylvania Press 2014).

6 Leslie Vinjamuri and Aaron Boesenecker, *Accountability and Peace Agreements, Mapping Trends from 1980 to 2006* (Centre for Humanitarian Dialogue 2007) 16.

7 Report of the UN Secretary-General on Implementing the Responsibility to Protect: Accountability for Prevention, A/71/1016–S/2017/556 (10 August 2017). Cf. Francesca Lessa and Leigh Payne (eds), *Amnesty in the Age of Human Rights Accountability: Comparative and International Perspectives* (CUP 2012).

8 2187 UNTS 3, in force 1 July 2002.

9 2716 UNTS 3, in force 23 December 2010.

10 This was despite the fact that according to the legally non-binding Declaration on the Protection of All Persons from Enforced Disappearance adopted by the UN General Assembly in 1992, persons who have or are alleged to have committed offences of enforced disappearance shall not benefit from any special amnesty law or similar measures which might have the effect of exempting them from any criminal proceedings or sanction, and that in the exercise of the right of pardon, the extreme seriousness of acts of enforced disappearance shall be taken into account (A/RES/47/133 of 18 December 1992, Art 18).

Committee (CCPR) authoritatively posits that States Parties to the 1966 International Covenant on Civil and Political Rights (ICCPR)[11] must investigate and ensure that those responsible for violations of the ICCPR are brought to justice, and that the States Parties concerned may not relieve perpetrators from personal responsibility, as has occurred with certain amnesties and prior legal immunities and indemnities.[12] In the case of the 1984 Convention against Torture and Other Cruel, Inhuman or Degrading Treatment or Punishment,[13] the Committee against Torture has declared categorically that amnesties preventing the investigation of acts of torture, the judgment and eventual punishment of those responsible are in violation of this Convention.[14]

In one case, the Grand Chamber of the European Court of Human Rights (ECtHR) has extensively analyzed the case law and international development regarding amnesties. Croatia's General Amnesty Act of 1996 gives a general amnesty in respect of all criminal offences committed in connection with the war in Croatia between 17 August 1990 and 23 August 1996, save in respect of those acts which amounted to the gravest breaches of humanitarian law or to war crimes, including the crime of genocide. The ECtHR held that the killing and serious wounding of civilians violate their right to life, which ranks as the most fundamental human right, the violation of which requires the State to secure the effective implementation of the domestic laws which protect the right to life and to ensure the accountability of the perpetrators. The ECtHR also reaffirms its case law that where a State agent has been charged with crimes involving torture or ill treatment, it is of the utmost importance that criminal proceedings and sentencing are not time-barred and that the granting of an amnesty or pardon should not be permissible. In that particular case before the ECtHR, the Applicant was granted amnesty for acts which amounted to grave breaches of fundamental human rights such as the intentional killing of civilians and inflicting grave bodily injury on a child. *A growing tendency in international law, as of 2014, is to see such amnesties as unacceptable because they are incompatible with the unanimously recognized obligation of States to prosecute and punish grave breaches of fundamental human rights.* Even if it were to be accepted that amnesties are possible where there are some particular circumstances, such as a reconciliation process and/or a form of compensation to the victims, the amnesty granted to the Applicant would still not be acceptable since there was nothing to indicate the existence of any such circumstances.[15]

11 999 UNTS 171, in force 23 March 1976.

12 CCPR/C/21/Rev.1/Add.13 (26 May 2004) para 18.

13 1465 UNTS 85, in force 26 June 1987.

14 *General Comment 2: Implementation of Article 2 by States Parties*, UN Doc CAT/C/GC/2 of 24 January 2008 para 5; *Final observations regarding the test of the reports presented by the State Parties regarding Article 19 of the Convention*, in relation to: Benin, UN Doc CAT/C/BEN/CO/2 of 19 February 2008 para 9, and the former Republic of Yugoslavia of Macedonia, UN Doc CAT/C/MKD/CO/2 of 21 May 2008 para 5.

15 *Marguš v Croatia* [GC], App no 4455/10, Judgment of 27 May 2014 paras 124–39.

If, as of 2014, there was already a 'growing tendency in international law' against amnesties and other restrictions on the prosecution of human rights abusers, the developments in international law since then may have already consecrated the prohibition of such restrictions, subject to 'some particular circumstances' on a case-by-case basis, as narrowly interpreted, bearing in mind also treaty obligations and other rules of international law binding on the State concerned. In any case, as will be explained later, there cannot be any restriction on the prosecution of perpetrators of crimes of international concern which are proscribed by peremptory norms of international law (*jus cogens*).

Permissible scope

There are two related crucial questions confronting governments during the transition from a repressive regime to a non-repressive one. First, who are to be prosecuted—only the leaders of the ousted regime and their henchmen high up in the chain of command or every person playing a role in that regime's repression? Second, how far back in time should their crimes be subject to prosecution after a regime change—even beyond the duration prescribed in statutes of limitations and irrespective of whether their conducts were not criminalized under the domestic law at the time when they took place?[16] The latter question will be dealt with when this chapter discusses statutes of limitations.

The judgment in 1996 of the South African Constitutional Court in *Azanian Peoples Organization (AZAPO) and Others v President of the Republic of South Africa and Others* can be helpful in answering the first question. The case involves a challenge to amnesties after the end of the apartheid regime in South Africa for criminal and civil liabilities granted to perpetrators having disclosed the truth about past atrocities. The epilogue, titled 'National Unity and Reconciliation', of the 1993 Interim Constitution states that this Constitution provides a historic bridge between the past of a deeply divided society characterized by strife, conflict, untold suffering and injustice, and a future founded on the recognition of human rights, democracy, peaceful co-existence and development opportunities for all South Africans, irrespective of colour, race, class, belief or sex. The pursuit of national unity, the well-being of all South African citizens and peace requires reconciliation between South Africans and the reconstruction of society. The adoption of this Constitution lays the secure foundation for the people of South Africa to transcend the divisions and strife of the past, which generated gross violations of human rights, the transgression of humanitarian principles in violent conflicts and a legacy of hatred, fear, guilt and revenge. These can now be addressed on the basis that there is a need for understanding but not for vengeance, a need for reparation but not for retaliation,

16 Neil Kritz, 'The Dilemma of Transitional Justice' in Neil Kritz (ed.), *Transitional Justice: How Emerging Democracies Reckon with Former Regimes*, vol I (United States Institute of Peace Press 1995) xix, xx–xxiv.

and a need for *ubuntu* (humanity towards others) but not for victimization. In order to advance such reconciliation and reconstruction, *amnesty shall be granted in respect of acts, omissions and offences associated with political objectives and committed in the course of the conflicts of the past.* Pursuant to the provisions of the epilogue, the South African Parliament enacted the Promotion of National Unity and Reconciliation Act 34 of 1995 that, among other things, determines a firm cut-off date, which shall be a date after 8 October 1990 and before 6 December 1993, and provides for the mechanisms, criteria and procedures, including tribunals, if any, through which such amnesty shall be dealt with.

The South African Constitutional Court upheld the granting of amnesties, while acknowledging this involved 'a difficult, sensitive, perhaps even agonizing, balancing act between the need for justice to victims of past abuse and the need for reconciliation and rapid transition to a new future' and that it was 'an act calling for a judgment falling substantially within the domain of those entrusted with law-making in the era preceding and during the transition period'.[17] The Court found South Africa was not alone in being confronted with a historical situation which required amnesty for criminal acts to be accorded for the purposes of facilitating the transition to, and consolidation of, an overtaking democratic order. Chile, Argentina and El Salvador are among the countries which have in modern times been confronted with a similar need. Although the mechanisms adopted to facilitate that process have differed from country to country and from time to time, the principle that amnesty should, in appropriate circumstances, be accorded to violators of human rights in order to facilitate the consolidation of new democracies has been accepted and truth commissions established in all these countries. What emerges from the experience of these and other countries that have ended periods of authoritarian and abusive rule is that there is no single or uniform international practice in relation to amnesty. Of significance is the South African Constitutional Court's statement that

> *[d]ecisions of States in transition, taken with a view to assisting such transition, are quite different from acts of a State covering up its own crimes by granting itself immunity*. In the former case, it is not a question of the governmental agents responsible for the violations indemnifying themselves, but rather, one of a constitutional compact being entered into by all sides, with former victims being well-represented, as part of an ongoing process to develop constitutional democracy and prevent a repetition of the abuses.[18]

Specifically, the Court held that amnesty for criminal and civil liabilities is permitted by the epilogue because without it there would be no incentive for offenders

17 1996 (4) SA 672 (CC), 25 July 1996, para 21 (*per* Mahomed D.P., with whom all the other eight judges concur).

18 Ibid paras 22–4 (emphasis added).

to disclose the truth about past atrocities.[19] The truth might unfold with such an amnesty, assisting in the process of reconciliation and reconstruction. Furthermore, such an amnesty is a crucial component of the negotiated settlement itself, without which the Constitution would not have come into being. It found the amnesty provisions neither inconsistent with international norms nor in violation of South Africa's obligations under international agreements.[20]

Beyond the very unique post-apartheid regime in South Africa which gave rise to the legal solution just discussed, the African Commission on Human and Peoples' Rights[21] consistently ruled after the aforesaid 1996 judgment of the South African Constitutional Court that amnesty laws cannot protect the African State which adopts them from complying with their international treaty obligations, and that, in prohibiting the prosecution of perpetrators of serious human rights violations by granting amnesty, the amnesty-granting African State not only promotes impunity, but also shuts down the possibility of the said violations being investigated and their victims having an effective remedy.[22]

In the case of Liberia, the blanket amnesty for acts and crimes committed during the Liberian civil wars, approved by the then Liberian President Charles Taylor on 7 August 2003 shortly before his resignation, was not mentioned in the peace agreement concluded one week after Taylor's resignation and the transitional government set up under the agreement evidently decided not to introduce a blanket amnesty.[23] However, in *Williams v Tah*, decided in January 2011, the Liberian Supreme Court rules as unconstitutional the Liberian Truth and Reconciliation Commission's recommendation that 50 named people be specifically barred from holding public offices, elected or appointed, for a period of 30 years for their association with former warring factions in the Liberian Civil War. Prince Yormie Johnson, who staged the *coup* to overthrow the then Liberian President Samuel Doe in September 1990, was one of the 50 named individuals. The Supreme Court reasons that banning several individuals without their right to due process

19 The epilogue is held to have no lesser constitutional status than any other part of the Constitution (ibid paras 12–14).

20 See also D.M. Davis, 'The South African Truth Commission and the *AZAPO* Case: A Reflection Almost Two Decades Later' in Karen Engle, Zinaida Miller and D.M. Davis (eds), *Anti-Impunity and the Human Rights Agenda* (CUP 2016) 125–48.

21 The African Commission on Human and Peoples' Rights, set up in 1987, promotes and protects human and peoples' rights under the 1981 African (Banjul) Charter on Human and Peoples' Right ((1982) 21 ILM 58, in force 21 October 1986) as well as interprets the Charter. It is composed of 11 human rights experts, elected by secret ballot at the Assembly of Heads of State and Government of the African Union for six-year renewable terms.

22 *Malawi African Association and Others v Mauritania*, Communication nos 54/91, 61/91, 98/93, 164/97 to 196/97 and 210/98, Decision of 11 May 2000 para 83; *Zimbabwe Human Rights NGO Forum v. Zimbabwe*, Communication no 245/2002, Decision of 21 May 2006 paras 211 and 215.

23 This fact was alluded to, *obiter*, by the Dutch Supreme Court in *Public Prosecutor v Guus Kouwenhoven* (HR 18 December 2018, Case 17/02109, *NJB* 2019, 25, rejecting the defence's appeal that there was a blanket amnesty which prevented prosecution of the defendant, a Dutch national, in the Netherlands for grave international crimes.

in keeping with law is a clear violation of the Liberian Constitution.[24] The right protected by the Liberian Supreme Court in that case should not be equated with amnesties to the persons in question, however.

Criminal justice has been actually meted out against *coup* leaders in certain African countries. For example, in October 1998 the restored Government of Sierra Leone convicted and executed 24 junta leaders for their treasonous acts in the *coup* of 25 May 1997. Among those executed were two former chiefs of defence staff and Colonel F. Y. Koroma, brother of ex-junta leader Lt Col Johnny Paul Koroma, who went into hiding with the remnants of his forces. Thirty-four officers had been sentenced to death by a military court a week earlier, but the death sentences of the remaining ten officers were commuted to prison terms. Sixteen more civilians were convicted by a High Court on treason, murder and arson charges linked to the *coup* while many others remained on trial and hundreds were put in prison without being charged.[25]

In Asia, the issue of amnesties by unconstitutional usurpers of power has been dealt with by the Supreme Court of Bangladesh.

The Indemnity Ordinance of 1975[26] was promulgated on 26 September 1975 by Bangladeshi President Khondaker Mostaq Ahmad who had come to power by the *coup* of 15 August 1975. It shielded the persons involved in the assassination of President Sheikh Mujibur Rahman along with most of his family members during that *coup*. On 6 April 1979, the Bangladeshi Government under General Ziaur Rahman, a member of the instigators of the August 1975 *coup* who later became President, incorporated the Ordinance into the Constitution by means of the Constitution (Fifth Amendment) Act, 1979 to legitimize all constitutional and unconstitutional changes between 15 August 1975 and 9 April 1979. General Hussain Mohammed Ershad, who staged a *coup* on 24 March 1982, had the Constitution (Seventh Amendment) Act enacted on 11 November 1986, validating all his constitutional and extra-constitutional actions, including past military *coups*, martial law decrees and orders. In particular, it provided that no lawsuit, prosecution or other legal proceedings could lie in any court or tribunal against any person or authority for or on account of or in respect of any order made, act or thing done or action or proceedings taken whether in the exercise or purported exercise of the powers of the President or the junta leader or in execution of or in

24 *Archie Williams of the City of Monrovia v Christiana Tah in her capacity as minister of justice and attorney general*, cited in Gawuga Thompson Baala and Otokpom Charles Asuk, 'Post-Conflict Peace Building and Transitional Justice in Liberia' (2020) 7 Int'l J Research & Scientific Innovation 1, 4.

25 Clarence Roy-Macaulay, 'Sierra Leone Firing Squad Kills 24' *AP* (20 October 1998), https://apnews.com/article/f5d3c7cc97a30716cfee4b7094f36cf3. In *Lance Corporal Daniel Sandy and 10 Others v the State* (Cases CR APPS 4 through 14/2005, 14 November 2008), the Court of Appeals of Sierra Leone allowed the appeals of the 11 Appellants against their respective convictions and sentences to ten years' imprisonment for the offences of treason and misprision of treason by the High Court in December 2004 for their alleged roles in a *coup*. The Court of Appeals, after finding the verdicts unreasonable and could not be supported by evidence, set aside all the convictions and sentences.

26 Ordinance no 50 of 1975.

compliance with orders made or sentences passed in exercise or purported exercise of such powers. After Bangladesh's transition to democracy, three persons suspected of assassinating Sheikh Mujibur Rahman were arrested in August 1996 and criminal investigation was launched into the case. By then, Khondaker Mostaq Ahmad who became President after the 1975 *coup* had died. On 14 November 1996, the Indemnity Ordinance of 1975 was repealed by Parliament at the time when Sheikh Hasina, Sheikh Mujibur Rahman's daughter, was Prime Minister of Bangladesh. Nineteen persons were put on trial for the 15 August 1975 massacre. This repeal was upheld by the Appellate Division of the Supreme Court, leading to prosecution and punishment of 12 of the ex-army officers.[27]

As for the Constitution (Fifth Amendment) Act 1979, it was declared unconstitutional in 2005 by the High Court Division of the Supreme Court of Bangladesh in *Bangladesh Italian Marble Works Ltd v Bangladesh*.[28] The ruling was upheld on 1 February 2010 by the Appellate Division of the Supreme Court in *Khondker Delwar Hossain and others v Bangladesh Italian Marble Works Ltd, Dhaka and others*.[29] The Appellate Division put on record its total disapproval of martial law and the suspension of the Constitution or any part thereof in any form. In its opinion, the perpetrators of such illegalities were to be suitably punished and condemned so that in future no adventurist, no usurper, would dare to defy the people, their Constitution, their Government, established by them with their consent.

The Constitution (Seventh Amendment) Act 1986 was held to be void *ab initio* in *Siddique Ahmed v Bangladesh*,[30] decided by the Supreme Court of Bangladesh (High Court Division) on 26 August 2010. Since the usurpation of power by General Ershad was void *ab initio*, as was the authoritarian rule before Ershad, all martial law instruments including the impugned Act were also held to be void *ab initio* as they were purportedly made/issued by the person who, in total disregard of the Constitution, illegally assumed the State power, de facto, as a usurper and illegally suspended the Constitution. As all the instruments purportedly validated and ratified by Parliament through the impugned Act were illegal, being bereft of lawful authority, it was beyond Parliament's competence to ratify and validate them and then infuse them into the Constitution for the usurpers to illegally use them. The Court then opined that not only General Ershad but also all his accomplices as well as such perpetrators of 1975 martial law who were still alive had to face the wrath of ultimate justice. The question as to how General Ershad was to be dealt with was best left with the Government. The Court subscribed to 'the overriding view' that punishing the perpetrators would act as a deterrent against future adventurers; hence, all the 'martial law perpetrators' and those who were equally culpable for the wrongs committed (i.e., '*par delictum*') with them, were to be thrown to the long arms of justice in order to protect the Constitution from 'future vultures'. The

27 Ashutosh Sarkar, 'Long road to justice' *Daily Star* (29 January 2010).
28 (2006) BLT (Special) (HCD) 1.
29 (2010) 62 Dhaka L Rep (AD) 298.
30 http://supremecourt.gov.bd/resources/documents/270095_WritPetitionNo7thAmendment.pdf.

Government might also explore whether there was sufficient evidence to indict the perpetrators under any existing provision of the Penal Code or under any provision of any other special law.

In the Americas, *coups* were once a common phenomenon and amnesty laws were enacted in several countries under dictatorship. Many of the usurpers, their accomplices and collaborators have been brought to justice without any impunity.

As will be seen in what follows, it has become well-established jurisprudence of the Inter-American Court of Human Rights (IACtHR) that amnesties and other devices to circumvent prosecution of grave human rights violations cannot override the State's duty under international obligations as stipulated in the relevant human rights treaties to investigate, prosecute and punish those responsible, and to provide reparation to victims—any laws to the contrary must be repealed or amended accordingly.[31]

In 1986, the army general who staged the *coup d'état* to overthrow President José Efrain Ríos Montt in 1983 granted an amnesty to the latter, who himself had come to power by the *coup* in 1982. As part of Guatemala's 1996 Peace Agreement to end internal armed conflicts, Guatemala's 1996 National Reconciliation Law grants amnesty for conflict-related offences but excludes from the scope of the amnesty genocide, forced disappearances, torture and other crimes with no statutes of limitations under national or international law that must be prosecuted under Guatemala's treaty obligations.[32] Ríos Montt also enjoyed immunity from prosecution while he served as a Guatemalan congressman for 15 years until he lost his re-election bid late in 2011 and was put under house arrest. On 1 March 2012 a Guatemalan court ruled the 1986 amnesty could not be applied in violation of the provisions of the 1948 Convention on the Prevention and Punishment of the Crime of Genocide,[33] to which Guatemala had become party in 1950 and which was implemented in Guatemala's domestic law in 1973. Ríos Montt was therefore not entitled to amnesty or immunity from the charges, brought in January 2012, of ordering 1,771 murders, 1,400 human rights violations, including rapes and tortures and displacement of 29,000 indigenous Guatemalans in a 'scorched earth' campaign to eliminate the support for a left-wing guerrilla movement during his regime in 1982–3. On 10 May 2013 he was found guilty of genocide for the

31 Naomi Roht-Arriaza, 'After Amnesties Are Gone: Latin American National Courts and the New Contours of the Fight Against Impunity' (2015) 37 Human Rts Quarterly 341, 346–8, citing *Barrios Altos v Peru*, Judgment of 30 November 2001, Ser C no 87 para 3; *Almonacid-Arellano et al. v Chile*, Judgment of 26 September 2006, Ser C no 154 para 22; *Gomes Lund et al. ('Guerrilha do Araguaia') v Brazil*, Judgment of 26 September 2006, Ser C no 219; *Gelman v Uruguay*, Judgment of 24 February 2011, Ser C no 221; and *Massacres of El Mozote and Neighboring Locations v El Salvador*, Judgment of 25 October 2012, Ser C no 252. See also Louise Mallinder, 'The End of Amnesty or Regional Overreach? Interpreting the Erosion of South America's Amnesty Laws' (2016) 65 ICLQ 645, 660–8.

32 Decreto No 145–1996 [Law of National Reconciliation] 27 December 1996 (Guatemala), cited in Roht-Arriaza, 'After Amnesties are Gone' 351 (n 20).

33 78 UNTS 277, in force 12 January 1951.

slaughter of 1,771 members of the Mayan Ixil indigenous group and was sentenced to 80 years' imprisonment. This was the first time for a former Head of State to have been convicted of genocide within his or her own country. However, ten days later, Guatemala's Constitutional Court annulled his sentence and ordered a retrial from the middle on the ground that the trial court did not properly carry out earlier procedural instructions.[34] A three-judge panel in 2015 ordered a retrial, which commenced in 2017, this time for the genocide by the killing of some 200 persons during a massacre in 1982. On 1 April 2018, Ríos Montt died of a heart attack at the age of 91. Since the signing of the peace accords in December 1996 to end the Guatemalan civil war lasting from November 1960, Guatemalan courts have handed down 26 convictions and sentences in 21 cases of civil war-era human rights violations, including genocide, massacres, forced disappearance, extrajudicial executions, sexual violence and other crimes against humanity. Nearly 70 military personnel, soldiers, policemen and members of the civil defence patrols have been convicted for serious human rights violations. Among those convicted are senior military officials who designed and implemented counter-insurgency policies that resulted in serious atrocities against the non-combatant civilian population. In addition, the IACtHR has rendered 14 judgments against Guatemala for human rights violations during the armed conflicts in that country.[35]

In the case of Chile, its 1978 Amnesty Act provided amnesty to 'all individuals who performed illegal acts . . . during the state of siege'.[36] This blanket amnesty protected the junta leaders and their security forces from prosecution for atrocities, except theft or rape, committed between 1973 and 1978. In 2004, the Chilean Supreme Court ruled that the proscription of murder and cruel treatment as war crimes under common Article 3 of the four Geneva Conventions of 1949[37] as well

34 See also Roht-Arriaza, 'After Amnesties are Gone' 364–8.

35 Jo-Marie Burt and Paulo Estrada, 'Hope amidst the darkness: Victims continue to press for justice for wartime atrocities in Guatemala' (Washington Office on Latin America), www.wola.org/wp-content/uploads/2021/12/TJ-in-Guate-WOLA-COMMENTARY-12.2021.pdf. The most recent decision as of this writing was *Los Josefinos Village Massacre v Guatemala*, IACtHR, Judgment of 3 November 2021 (www.corteidh.or.cr/docs/casos/articulos/seriec_442_esp.pdf), in which the IACtHR found the State of Guatemala internationally responsible for the human rights violations related to the Los Josefinos Village massacre that took place on 29 and 30 April 1982, in the context of the internal armed conflict in Guatemala. The IACtHR ordered various measures of reparation, including removing all obstacles, de facto and de jure, that maintain impunity in this case, and initiate, continue, promote and/or reopen the investigations necessary to identify, judge and, where appropriate, punish those responsible for the human rights violations in present case; and pay pecuniary and non-pecuniary damages as determined by the IACtHR.

36 Decree Law No 2.191 of 18 April 1978. See also Naomi Roht-Arriaza, *The Pinochet Effect: Transitional Justice in the Age of Human Rights* (U Pennsylvania Press 2005).

37 Convention for the Amelioration of the Condition of the Wounded and Sick in Armed Forces in the Field (75 UNTS 31); Convention for the Amelioration of the Condition of the Wounded, Sick, and Shipwrecked Members of Armed Forces at Sea (75 UNTS 85); Convention Relative to the Treatment of Prisoners of War (75 UNTS 135); and Convention Relative to the Protection of Civilian Persons in Time of War (75 UNTS 287). They came into force on the same day, on 21 October 1950.

as the need to prosecute crimes against humanity meant the amnesty law then in force could not be construed to exclude perpetrators of these crimes from criminal liability.[38] In a subsequent case, the Chilean Supreme Court annulled a verdict of not guilty and invalidated the application of the Chilean amnesty law. It reasoned that the crime of kidnapping had the character of a crime against humanity and the amnesty law enacted by the de facto authority which took on the 'Supreme Command of the Nation' had to be interpreted in such a way to conform with the protective covenants of fundamental rights of persons and to sanction the serious violations committed against them by the Supreme Command of the Nation. The self-amnesty was ruled null and void by the Court because it also implicated a suspension of the effectiveness of pre-existing criminal justice institutions designed to operate in a state of social peace in which they were called to serve.[39] Even so, in *Almonacid Arellano et al. v Chile*, decided in 2006, the IACtHR notes that crimes against humanity such as murder, forced disappearance and torture as well as genocide are among those not excluded from the amnesty under the 1978 law. Leaving victims defenceless and perpetuating impunity for such crimes are clearly incompatible with the wording and the spirit of the 1969 American Convention, which Chile ratified on 21 August 1990, and undoubtedly affect rights embodied therein. Insofar as Chile's Amnesty Law of 1978 is incompatible with the American Convention, it has no legal effects.[40] This is reiterated by the IACtHR in 2013 in *Garcia Lucero et al. v Chile*.[41]

In the case of Peru, the IACtHR has held in *Barrios Altos v Peru*[42] that Peru's two amnesty laws enacted in 1995[43] under President Alberto Fujimori, granting amnesty to State agents who had killed some 15 persons in 1991, violated the constitutional guarantees as well as the 1969 American Convention's guarantee of the right to life, which is non-derogable. The IACtHR sternly condemns such self-amnesty provisions as violations of the rights of access to justice and to remedies for violations thereof. It emphasizes that in view of the general obligations established in Articles 1(1) and 2 of the American Convention, the States Parties are bound to take all measures to ensure no one is deprived of judicial protection and the exercise of the right to a simple and effective recourse under Articles 8 and 25 of the Convention. By precluding the identification of the individuals responsible for human rights violations, because it obstructs the investigation and access to justice and prevents the victims and their next of kin from knowing the truth and receiving

38 *Miguel Angel Sandoval*, Rol No 517–2004, Case 2477, Chilean Supreme Court Judgment of 17 November 2004, Revista Gaceta Jurídica No 272 at 109, cited in Roht-Arriaza, 'After Amnesties Are Gone' 352.

39 *Claudio Abdón Lecaros Carrasco followed for the crime of aggravated kidnapping*, Rol No 47.205, Recurso No 3302/2009, Order 16698, Judgment of Appeals, and Order 16699, Judgment of Replacement, 18 May 2010. See also Hugo Rojas and Miriam Shaftoe, *Human Rights and Transitional Justice in Chile* (Palgrave Macmillan 2022) 137–54.

40 IACtHR, Judgment of 26 September 2006, Ser C no 154 paras 116–22, 171(3).

41 IACtHR, Judgment of 28 August 2013, Ser C no 267 paras 150–4, 223.

42 *Barrios Altos v Peru*, Merits, IACtHR, Judgment of 14 March 2001, Ser C no 75.

43 Law No 26.479 (1995) and Law No 26.492 (1995).

the corresponding reparation, this type of law is manifestly incompatible with the aims and spirit of the Convention and is without legal effect. Subsequently, the Peruvian Constitutional Court, in its decision of 2 March 2007, rules that Peru's aforesaid self-amnesty laws violate Peru's human rights treaty obligations, and that the amnesty laws must be subject to the presumption that Peru's Legislature intended to carry out within the scope of the Constitution and respect for fundamental rights. Such presumption does not apply when it is proven that during the exercise of the competence to enact amnesty laws, the Legislature intended to also cover up the commission of crimes against humanity or to 'guarantee' impunity for serious violations of human rights. On the merits, the Peruvian Constitutional Court held the amnesty laws in question to be null and void and lack legal effect *ab initio*. Therefore, the orders enacted so as to guarantee impunity of the violation of human rights by State agents are also null and void.[44]

Furthermore, on 30 May 2018 the IACtHR ruled in *Barrios Altos and La Cantuta v Peru*[45] that Peruvian courts had to review whether the 'pardon on humanitarian [health] reasons' granted by Peru's then President Pablo Kuczynski on 24 December 2017 to Fujimori, then aged 79, constituted an unnecessary and disproportionate impact on the right of access to justice of the victims of serious human rights violations which constituted crimes against humanity, as determined and confirmed by Peru's own highest courts. According to the IACtHR, a measure designed to protect the physical integrity or life of the person convicted of these crimes should only be applied in very extreme cases and should not necessarily result in Fujimori's release, much less extinguish his criminal liability. On 3 October 2018, the Peruvian Supreme Court complied with IACtHR's decision in that case and, after examining the merits of the presidential pardon through a special procedure set up to assess the pardon's conformity with international human rights law, annulled the presidential pardon. On 17 March 2022, Peru's Constitutional Court reinstated the presidential pardon, but on 8 April 2022, the IACtHR ruled that Peru had to refrain from releasing Fujimori from prison since the aforesaid decision of Peru's Constitutional Court did not comply with 'certain conditions', particularly the right to justice of Fujimori's victims. Regarding the permissibility of pardons, the IACtHR reiterated its ruling of May 2018 but without prejudice to adopting other alternative measures to safeguard Fujimori's health.[46] Fujimori, therefore, had to serve out his sentence of 25 years' imprisonment, passed in 2009, for ordering, when he was President, the killings of 25 people by a government-backed death squad.[47]

44 *Santiago Martín Rivas,* Constitutional Tort Action, Case No 679–2005-PA/TC, Constitutional Court, Judgment of 2 March 2007 paras 30, 52–3, 60, 63.

45 (2019) 113 AJIL 568–74.

46 https://cejil.org/en/press-releases/inter-american-court-orders-peru-to-refrain-from-releasing-alberto-fujimori-in-compliance-with-its-treaty-obligations/.

47 See further, Javier de Balaunde de Cardenas, 'Holding the Line on Human Rights Accountability: Explaining the Unlikely Judicial Overturn of the Pardon and Immunity Granted to Human Rights Violator Alberto Fujimori' (2020) 85 Derecho PUCP 413, 435–6; Maria Rodriguez, 'The Never-Ending Fight for Justice: A Review of the Year after the Humanitarian Pardon Was Granted

In Uruguay, the Expiry Law was enacted in December 1986[48] to prevent prosecution of crimes committed by the military before 1 March 1985. In its Communication addressed to Uruguay in August 1994, the CCPR refuses to accept that, due to an amnesty law, a State Party to the ICCPR (in this case Uruguay) is not obligated to investigate human rights violations committed during a prior regime. In the CCPR's opinion, amnesty for serious human rights violations are incompatible with the ICCPR since the amnesty would contribute to the creation of an atmosphere of impunity that can undermine the democratic order and bring about other serious human rights violations.[49] Several years later, Juan María Bordaberry, who headed the civic-military dictatorship in Uruguay from 1973 to 1976,[50] was arrested in November 2006 together with his then foreign minister in connection with the assassination of two Uruguay opposition politicians in Buenos Aires, Argentina, and the disappearance of nine other persons, allegedly as part of the Operation Condor in which the regimes in Argentina and Uruguay joined forces to exterminate their dissidents. In December 2007, Gregorio Alvarez, the last leader of the civic-military dictatorship set up by Bordaberry, was put on trial. On 22 October 2009, Alvarez was convicted of 37 murders during his time as head of the army in the 1970s and later as President in 1981–5 and sentenced to 25 years in jail.[51] Subsequently, in February 2010, Bordaberry was convicted and sentenced to the maximum sentence of 30 years' imprisonment without the right to pardon.[52]

---

to Fujimori' *Lawyers without Borders* (8 February 2019), https://www.asfcanada.ca/en/blogue/the-never-ending-fight-for-justice-a-review-of-the-year-after-the-humanitarian-pardon-was-granted-to-fujimori/; Ñusta Carranza Ko, *Truth, Justice, and Reparations in Peru, Uruguay, and South Korea: The Clash of Advocacy and Politics* (Palgrave Macmillan 2021) 57–124.

48 Ley de Caducidad de la Pretensión Punitiva del Estado, No 15848 (31 December 1986). Although Art 4 of the law requires the Executive to investigate cases of enforced disappearances, which are by nature 'ongoing crimes', this provision was not effectively implemented at first due to the lack of political will, until ordered by Uruguay's courts to do so (Mallinder, 'The End of Amnesty or Regional Overreach?' 652).

49 *Hugo Rodríguez v Uruguay*, Communication no 322/1988, UN Doc CCPR/C/51/D/322/1988, Report of 9 August 1994 paras 12.3 and 12.4. See also the CCRP's *Consideration of reports submitted by States Parties under Article 40 of the Covenant,* regarding: Peru, UN Doc CCPR/C/79/Add.67 of 25 July 1996 para 9; Yemen, UN Doc CCPR/C/79/Add.51 of 3 October 1995 numeral 4 para 3; Paraguay, UN Doc CCPR/C/79/Add.48 of 3 October 1995 numeral 3 para 5; and Haiti, UN Doc CCPR/C/79/Add.49 of 3 October 1995 numeral 4 para 2; Anja Seibert-Fohr and Christine Weniger, 'Compliance Monitoring under the International Covenant on Civil and Political Rights' in Rainer Grote, Mariela Morales Antoniazzi and Davide Paris (eds), *Research Handbook on Compliance in International Human Rights Law* (Edward Elgar Publishing 2021) 425–47.

50 In June 1973, President Bordaberry, citing as the main reason the need to crush a Marxist urban guerrilla movement, dissolved the bicameral Parliament and established the civic-military dictatorship under the Council of State to exercise both the legislative and executive powers. Although Bordaberry was forced to resign by the military in 1976, the dictatorship continued until 1985 under three consecutive Presidents who succeeded him.

51 'Uruguay Ex-military Ruler Gregorio Alvarez Dies Aged 91' *BBC* (28 December 2016), https://www.bbc.com/news/world-latin-america-38453193.

52 'Uruguay's Ex-ruler Bordaberry Jailed for 30 Years' *BBC* (11 February 2010), http://news.bbc.co.uk/2/hi/americas/8511204.stm.

Their convictions were made possible by the Uruguayan Supreme Court's judgment of 19 October 2009, which has since been affirmed in its judgment of 29 October 2010, that the provisions of the 1986 Expiry Law were unconstitutional because they violated Uruguay's international obligations as well as the principle of separation of powers.[53] In October 2011, the Uruguayan Parliament enacted an 'Interpretative Law'[54] to exclude crimes against humanity from the scope of the 1986 Expiry Law. The Prosecutor's Office for Crimes against Humanity was set up in 2018, leading to the start of 13 prosecutions in 2020 for forced disappearance, homicide, genocide, torture and other crimes committed during the 1973–85 dictatorship rule in Uruguay.

As for El Salvador, the 15 October 1979 military *coup* established the Revolutionary Government Junta of El Salvador and triggered the civil war that lasted until 1992. El Salvador's General Amnesty Law for the Consolidation of Peace enacted in 1993 grants amnesty to anyone involved in a political crime[55] or a common crime with 20 or more participants before 1 January 1992, irrespective of whether they were the direct or intermediate perpetrators of, or accomplices in, the aforesaid offences.[56]

In *Massacres of El Mozote and Neighboring Locations v El Salvador*,[57] decided in October 2012, the IACtHR condemned El Salvador's Amnesty Law of 1993. Unlike the cases examined previously by the IACtHR, the instant case deals with a general amnesty law that relates to acts committed in the context of an internal armed conflict, or a civil war. More than 1,000 civilian villagers in the village of El Mozote and nearby places were killed by El Salvador's Armed Forces in December 1981 as part of an alleged counterinsurgency operation during the Salvadorian Civil War. The IACtHR held that, according to the international humanitarian law applicable to these situations, the enactment of amnesty laws on the conclusion of hostilities in non-international armed conflicts are sometimes justified to

53 *Nibia Sabalsagaray*, Sentencia No 365/2009, Supreme Court of Justice, Judgment of 19 October 2009, and *Organización de los Derechos Humanos*, Sentencia No 1525, Supreme Court of Justice, Judgment of 29 October 2010, cited in Roht-Arriaza, 'After Amnesties Are Gone' 354–5.

54 Law No 18831 of 27 October 2011.

55 A layman may consider a political crime as a crime associated with a particular ideological perspective committed by and against the State, but there is no generally accepted legal definition of political crime. See the evolution in the discussion on the legal meaning of 'political crime' in Theodore Schroeder, 'Political Crimes Defined' (1919) 18 Michigan L Rev 30; Robert Ferrari, 'Political Crimes' (1920) 20 Columbia L Rev 308; Stephen Schafer, 'The Concept of the Political Criminal' (1971) 62 J Crim L, Criminology & Police Science 380; Dennis Szabo, 'Political Crimes: A Historical Perspective' (1972) 2 Denver JIL & Policy 7; Francis Allen, *The Crimes of Politics: Political Dimensions of Criminal Justice* (Harvard U Press 1974); Frank Hagan, *Political Crimes: Ideology & Criminality* (Allyn & Bacon 1997); and Jeffrey Ian Ross, *An Introduction to Political Crime* (Policy Press 2012).

56 Art 1 of the Law. Art 2 provides that offences committed by reason or in consequence of the armed conflict shall likewise be deemed to be political offences, irrespective of political status, membership of a political party, political affiliation or ideology. Art 4(e) adds that amnesty granted under this law shall in all cases extinguish civil liability.

57 Judgment of 25 October 2012, Ser C no 252.

pave the way to a return to peace. However, this norm is not absolute, because, under international humanitarian law, States also have an obligation to investigate and prosecute war crimes. Consequently, persons suspected or accused of having committed war crimes, or who have been convicted of this cannot be covered by an amnesty. Therefore, the IACtHR declared El Salvador to be responsible for the violation of Articles 8(1) (judicial guarantees) and 25(1) (judicial protection) of the American Convention on Human Rights, in relation to Articles 1(1) and 2 (duty to adopt domestic legal effects) of the aforesaid Convention, and for the violation of the obligations established in Articles 1, 6 and 8 of the 1985 Inter-American Convention to Prevent and Punish Torture[58] and 7(b) of the 1994 Inter-American Convention for the Prevention, Punishment and Eradication of Violence against Women,[59] to the detriment of the surviving victims and the next of kin of the victims who were executed in this case, in their respective circumstances.

In 2016, the Constitutional Chamber of the Supreme Court of El Salvador, in a 4 to 1 decision, ruled that the broad provision of the 1993 Amnesty Law violates international law and El Salvador's Constitution, and the Government of El Salvador had an obligation to investigate, identify and sanction the material and intellectual authors of human rights crimes and grave war crimes as well as to provide reparations to victims. Specifically, the Amnesty Law may not be interpreted unconditionally or in a manner incompatible with the Constitution—especially the provision recognizing the right to life and personal safety and the right to their preservation and defence (Article 2) and the provision which prohibits the granting of amnesty for violations, infringements or breaches of the Constitution (Article 244). The Constitutional Chamber noted that amnesty is expressly recognized in Article 6(5) of the Additional Protocol II to the Geneva Conventions Relating to the Protection of Victims of Non-International Armed Conflicts,[60] to which El Salvador is party. The said Article 6(5) stipulates that

> [a]t the end of hostilities, the authorities in power shall endeavour to grant the broadest possible amnesty to persons who have participated in the armed conflict, or those deprived of their liberty for reasons related to the armed conflict, whether they are interned or detained.

Nevertheless, this provision must be interpreted restrictively and confined to acts of war of the parties to the conflict and must not encompass grave and systematic violations of constitutional rules and international law, such as crimes against humanity and war crimes constituting serious violations of international humanitarian law. Consequently, this expansive extension of amnesty is contrary to the right to judicial and non-judicial protection (Article 2(1) and Article 144(2) of the Constitution, read with Articles 1(1) and (2) of the American Convention on

58 OAS Treaty Series No 67, in force 28 February 1987.

59 (1994) 33 ILM 1534, in force 5 March 1995.

60 1225 UNTS 609, in force 7 December 1978.

Human Rights, Article 2(2) of the ICCPR and Article 4 of Additional Protocol II), because it prevents compliance with the State's obligations to prevent, investigate, prosecute, punish and redress serious breaches of fundamental rights. In the Constitutional Chamber's conclusion, the 1993 Amnesty Law will continue to apply to and must continue to protect only those persons who have not participated in acts constituting crimes against humanity and/or war crimes constituting serious violations of international humanitarian law.[61]

As mentioned before, another impediment to bringing unconstitutional usurpers of power to account is the *immunity* accorded to them.

Some usurpers and their accomplices/collaborators try to get parliamentary immunity to shield them from prosecution, as in the case of General Augusto Pinochet of Chile, who became a senator for life. Guatemala's Ríos Montt also enjoyed immunity from prosecution while he served as a Guatemalan congressman for 15 years until he lost his re-election bid late in 2011. *Barbosa de Souza et al. v Brazil*, decided on 7 September 2021, is the first judgment in which the IACtHR analyzes parliamentary immunity within the framework of the right of access to justice. In the view of the IACtHR, parliamentary immunity has been designed as a guarantee of the independence of the legislative body as a whole and of its members, and it cannot be considered as a parliamentarian's personal privilege. Under no circumstances could it become a mechanism of impunity, otherwise it would erode the rule of law and be contrary to equality before the law, making access to justice unattainable for the victims. The case concerns Márcia Barbosa de Souza, a 20-year-old student living in poverty, who was last seen meeting with the then Paraíba state Representative, Aércio Pereira de Lima, at a motel before her body was dumped from a car onto a vacant lot on the following day. Due to the parliamentary immunity enjoyed by the main suspect, authorizations were requested from the Paraíba Legislative Assembly on two different occasions to initiate criminal proceedings against him, but these were rejected. With the adoption of Constitutional Amendment No 35/2001 on 20 December 2001, criminal actions against legislators could proceed irrespective of whether these were authorized by the Legislative Assembly. Pereira was eventually sentenced on 26 September 2007 to 16 years' imprisonment for the crimes of homicide and concealment of Barbosa de Souza's body. Pereira appealed the sentence, but he died before his appeal was examined. The IACtHR concluded that the legislative body's refusal to lift his parliamentary immunity was arbitrary, transforming this refusal into the mechanism which led to impunity for the murder of the victim, making effective access to justice for her family unrealistic. On the evidence, the IACtHR found that Brazil violated the rights to judicial guarantees, equality before the law, judicial protection and personal integrity, to the detriment of the victim's mother and father. The

61 Judgment on Constitutionality 44/2013–45/2013, www.jurisprudencia.gob.sv/VisorMLX/PDF/44-2013AC.PDF, as translated and summarized by Silvia Scozia, *El Salvador, Supreme Court Judgment on the Unconstitutionality of the Amnesty Law*, https://casebook.icrc.org/case-study/el-salvador-supreme-court-judgment-unconstitutionality-amnesty-law.

IACtHR ordered Brazil to adopt various measures of reparation.[62] The reasoning in this judgment is equally applicable to any parliamentary immunity given to usurpers of power and their accomplices/collaborators under their country's constitution or domestic law.

This seems to be the case in relation to Pierre Buyoya, who staged two *coups* in Burundi, in September 1987 and July 1996, to topple the then Governments and became President from 1987 to 1992 and from 1996 to 2003. In March 2003, a two-day mini-summit on Burundi held in Tanzania reaffirmed the need to give immunity to all affected political players in Burundi as part of the transition to democracy and ceasefire during the civil war that started in 1993. Buyoya in his capacity of President of Burundi and chairman of the Great Lakes Regional Peace Initiative on Burundi, President Benjamin Mkapa of Tanzania, Deputy President Jacob Zuma of South Africa who was also facilitator in the Burundi ceasefire negotiations, and the Secretary General of the National Council for the Defence of Democracy, which was the most important rebel group in the civil war, attended the summit. Pursuant to the 2005 Constitution, Buyoya became senator for life as a former President and enjoyed immunity from prosecution. Nonetheless, on 19 October 2020 Burundi's Supreme Court convicted Buyoya *in absentia* of perpetrating attack against the Head of State, attack against the authority of the State and attack tending to bring about massacre and devastation in the murder in October 1993 of Melchior Ndadaye, who had defeated Buyoya to become Burundi's first freely elected President. The murder of Burundi's first ethnic Hutu President triggered a ten-year civil war between the army, dominated by the Tutsi minority, and Hutu rebel groups in which about 300,000 people were killed. Buyoya was sentenced to life imprisonment. Eighteen senior military and civilian officials close to Buyoya were sentenced to the same sentence, three others to 20 years' imprisonment for complicity in the same crimes, and only one, the former transitional Prime Minister, Antoine Nduwayo, was acquitted. Only five defendants—four retired Tutsi high-ranking officers, and a serving police general, Ildephonse Mushwabure—were present at the trial. Buyoya denounced the trial and judgment as contrary to the agreement to end the civil war and was neither 'fair' nor 'equitable' as the rights of the accused were allegedly violated.[63] At the time of his conviction and sentencing, Buyoya was High Representative of the African Union for Mali and the Sahel. In December 2020 Buyoya contracted COVID-19 in Mali and died of the pandemic after being transferred to France for medical treatment.

A court in Athens, Greece, has gone one step further, ruling that the unconstitutional usurper can never be entitled to immunity from criminal prosecution. During his trial for the bloody suppression of student demonstrators at the Athens Polytechnic in November 1973, Colonel Georgios Papadopoulos, head of the Greek junta, asserted Presidential immunity because he was President of Greece

62 https://www.corteidh.or.cr/docs/casos/articulos/seriec_435_esp.pdf.

63 Jerry Fisayo-Bambi, 'Ex Burundian president Pierre Buyoya rejects his conviction for murder', *Africa News* (21 October 2020).

during the time of the event. The judges in that case unanimously rejected his immunity defence. The court held that the military *coup* by a group of Greek military officers on 21 April 1967 usurped the authority and the sovereign rights of the Greek people, thereby making the consequent governments installed by the junta 'governments of violence' and anyone who exercised duties of governmental authority under any office, including that of the Head of State, did not in reality exercise legal authority and consequently they had no immunity for their actions during the exercise of such authority. Papadopoulos was held not to be the legitimate President of the Republic and therefore he had no Presidential immunity.[64]

On the whole, the case law of domestic courts discussed before has been overwhelmingly opposed to amnesties, pardons and immunities for *former* usurpers, their accomplices and their collaborators.

Judicial considerations when the usurper's regime is still in power

The preceding analysis informs readers that amnesties, pardons and immunities are denied to those involved in unconstitutional usurpation of power *who are no longer in power*.

What if coup leaders are still in control of the country? This is the case of Fiji, for example. Fiji's Limitation of Liability for Prescribed Political Events Decree 2010[65] 'irrevocably' grants 'absolute and unconditional immunity' from any criminal prosecution and from civil and other liability to all persons involved in the *coup* by taking of the then Prime Minister and his Cabinet Ministers hostage for 56 days in 2000 and to those staging a successful counter-*coup* apparently to solve the hostage crisis who have been staying in power ever since. Subsequently, Chapter 10 of the 2013 Constitution of Fiji provides, among other things, that the 2010 Decree shall, in its entirety, continue in existence and shall not be reviewed, amended, altered, repealed or revoked by Parliament. In addition, it 'irrevocably' grants 'absolute and unconditional immunity' to any person (whether in their official or personal or individual capacity) holding the office of, or holding the office in, as the case may be: (a) the President; (b) the Prime Minister and Cabinet Ministers; (c) the Republic of Fiji Military Forces; (d) the Fiji Police Force; (e) the Fiji Corrections Service; (f) *the Judiciary*; (g) public service; and (h) any public office. Such immunity protects the aforesaid persons from any criminal prosecution as well as any civil or other liability in any court, tribunal or commission, in any proceeding including any legal, military, disciplinary or professional proceedings and from any order or judgment of any court, tribunal or commission, as a result of any direct or indirect participation, appointment or involvement in the Government from 5 December 2006, the date of the last *coup d'état* in Fiji, to the date of the first sitting of the first Parliament elected after the commencement of this Constitution. Any

64 https://www.primidi.com/greek_junta_trials/the_polytechnic/trial_of_the_polytechnic.
65 Fijian Govt Gazette, vol 11 no 36 (29 March 2010) at 405.

such immunity shall not apply to any act or omission that constitutes an offence of corruption and abuse of office, offence against property, fraudulent conduct, traffic in obscene publication, criminal trespass and other offences unrelated to the governance of the country. Such immunity has not been challenged in any Fijian court as of this writing.

Another example is that of Myanmar. The 2008 Constitution of Myanmar[66] was drafted by the then military regime.[67] Pursuant to its Section 204(b), Myanmar's President has the power to grant amnesty in accordance with the recommendation of the National Defence and Security Council. Section 445, in the 'Transitory Provisions' Chapter of the Constitution, stipulates that no proceeding shall be instituted against the former junta which seized power in September 1988 or any member thereof *or any member of the Government in respect of any act done in the execution of their respective duties*. When the military seized power on 1 February 2021, it invoked various provisions of the 2008 Constitution to justify the nationwide state of emergency and to authorize the commander-in-chief of the armed forces to assume the authority of the nation's law making, governance and jurisdiction. Therefore, the junta has not abrogated the 2008 Constitution in its entirety and clearly intends to benefit from the amnesty provisions thereunder as well. There is no reported challenge of this amnesty in Myanmar courts.

Following the end of Thailand's absolute monarchy on 24 June 1932, there have been 12 military *coups* which succeeded in usurping the power of government of the country. Impunity for the usurpers and their collaborators/accomplices has been secured in eight military *coups* by stand-alone laws, in two military *coups* by provisions in post-*coup* constitutions, in one military *coup* by both a constitutional provision and a stand-alone law, and in only one case with no special legal measure promulgated. Each amnesty provision or law has retroactively legalized the *coups* and protected the usurpers from possible prosecution or other sanction. In each instance, the amnesty has turned the illegal act of rebellion into a lawful one.[68]

The Thai Supreme Court has upheld such amnesty in *Punsak Sritape and 14 Others v General Prayuth Chan-o-cha and four others*.[69] The 15 plaintiffs in that case alleged that by staging the military *coup* on 22 May 2014 the five defendants who were members of the junta committed the offences under the Criminal Code, punishable by three years' to life imprisonment. The head of the junta assumed the position of Prime Minister after the *coup* and was still Prime Minister at the time of the plaintiffs' complaint and the Supreme Court's judgment in this case. In the Court's opinion, after the junta fully seized power, abrogated the 2007 Thai Constitution as well as dissolved the Cabinet and the Senate, Thailand had no agency to

66 www.constituteproject.org/constitution/Myanmar2008.pdf?lang=en. See also Melissa Crouch, *The Constitution of Myanmar: A Contextual Analysis* (Hart 2019) chs 1–3 and 11.

67 See further, Melissa Crouch, 'Pre-emptive Constitution-Making: Authoritarian Constitutionalism and the Military in Myanmar' (2020) 54 L & Society Rev 487.

68 Tyrell Haberkorn, 'Without Account: Coups, Amnesty and Justice in Thailand' in Andrew Harding and Munin Pongsapan (eds), *Thai Legal History: From Tradition to Modern Law* (CUP 2021) 265.

69 Supreme Court Case no 1688/2561 (27 March 2018).

act as a Legislature other than the National Council for Peace and Order (NCPO), set up by the junta, which exercised the 'sovereign power'. Although usurping the power of government was unconstitutional and its legitimacy might be questioned in other ways, the NCPO had de facto authority to exercise the executive and legislative powers over Thailand's State apparatuses and agencies. Therefore, the (Interim) Constitution of the Kingdom of Thailand of 2014 promulgated by the NCPO had the force of law. The legal question to be considered by the Supreme Court, as raised by the plaintiffs, was whether the provision of Section 48 of the 2014 Interim Constitution granting the blanket amnesty to those involved in the *coup* and all acts pursuant to the NCPO's orders and announcements could be upheld. The plaintiffs submitted, inter alia, that they were not, since the 2014 (Interim) Constitution was enacted to support the exercise of power in flagrant violation of the principles of democracy, the existing law of the land, morality and fundamental justice for all humankind. The Court disagreed, ruling that the aforesaid provisions completely absolved from all criminal offences and liabilities all those acts performed in connection with the *coup* by the NCPO head and the other members of the NCPO, including all acts incidental thereto by any person and all acts of any person entrusted or ordered by the NCPO head or the NCPO, for the benefit of the *coup*. This was irrespective of whether such acts were performed to have constitutional, legislative, executive or judicial force, including punishments and other official administrative acts, and irrespective of whether the persons performed such acts as a principal, an accomplice, an instigator or an agent and whenever those acts took place. When the new Constitution was promulgated on 6 April 2017, its Section 279 expressly makes constitutional, lawful and effective under this 2017 Constitution all announcements, orders and acts of the NCPO or of the NCPO head in force on the day prior to the date of promulgation of this Constitution or which will be issued thereafter as well as the performance of acts in compliance therewith. Any repeal of or amendment to such announcements or orders shall be by an Act of Parliament, except in the case of announcements or orders in the exercise of executive power which shall be repealed or amended by an order of the Prime Minister or a Cabinet resolution, as the case may be. Therefore, the Supreme Court held that the acts of the five defendants mentioned in the plaintiffs' petition were not unlawful and did not incur their liability in anyway whatsoever, as provided in the (Interim) Constitution of 2014.

In some respects, the amnesty granted by the 2014 Thai Constitution to those involved in a *coup* is much narrower, less sweeping in scope, than that granted by some other countries such as Fiji to such individuals. It does not cover those organizing and participating in mass demonstrations to paralyze the democratically elected government which led to the political crisis and culminated in the military *coup* of 22 May 2014.[70]

70 *Prosecutor v Suthep Thaaugsuban and Others*, Criminal Case (Red) No Or 317/2564 (24 February 2021). See also *Election Commission v Chumpol Julsai and Others*, Constitutional Court Judgment of 8 December 2021.

On 17 November 2021, the 723-member Thai Parliament[71] rejected by the votes of 473 against, 206 in favour, and 6 abstentions the amendments to the Constitution of 2017 proposed by 135,247 eligible Thai voters.[72] One of the proposed amendments would repeal Section 279 of the 2017 Constitution as well as Section 48 of the 2014 (Interim) Constitution. These provisions were to be replaced by two provisions. One of them would make it a right and a duty on every Thai citizen to oppose military *coups*. It would also require government officials not to obey orders of their military commanders or civilian superiors that are unlawful and in flagrant violation of human rights as well as not to obey the military junta or any group of persons that usurps the power of government. Another proposed provision would stipulate that the provisions in this Part of the Constitution shall have the status of an entrenched customary and fundamental law of the Constitution of the Kingdom of Thailand and shall be *in force in perpetuity* even after the termination of this Constitution.[73] One of the reasons cited by those voting against this proposed amendment was that its retroactive application would subject the junta members as well as their accomplices and collaborators to prosecution under the Criminal Code, and that it would annul all the orders, decrees and other announcements by the junta in force since 2014 thereby voiding rights already acquired thereunder.

In any event, it is doubtful whether such a formal 'eternity clause' can survive a *coup* that annuls or at least suspends the constitution. For example, the Thai Constitution of 1974 which prohibited any amnesty for unconstitutional usurpers of power was abrogated by the *coup* of October 1976, with the junta members of that *coup* and subsequent ones continuing to benefit from the amnesties as explained earlier.[74]

71 Under the 2017 Constitution, there are 500 Members of the House of Representatives, 350 of whom are elected on a constituency basis and 150 of whom are elected from party lists of political parties, and 250 non-elected members of the Senate. By 17 November 2021, several of the members of this bicameral Parliament had been either disqualified or suspended from office by court orders or resigned.

72 Section 256(1) of the 2017 Constitution provides, inter alia, that amendment to the Constitution may be made by a motion for amendment proposed by no fewer than 50,000 persons who have the right to vote according to the law on the public submission of a bill.

73 On perpetuity, entrenched or eternity clauses, see Silvia Suteu, *Eternity Clauses in Democratic Constitutionalism* (OUP 2021) 1. For a legislative history of constitutional entrenchment clauses from the beginning of modern constitutionalism until today, see Michael Hein, 'Entrenchment Clauses in the History of Modern Constitutionalism' (2018) 86 Legal History Rev 434; id, 'Impeding Constitutional Amendments: Why Are Entrenchment Clauses Codified in Contemporary Constitutions?' (2018) 54 Acta Politica 1.

74 Andrew Friedman, ('Dead Hand Constitutionalism: The Danger of Eternity Clauses in New Democracies' (2011) 4 Mexican L Rev 77, 94–5) argues that an entrenched, eternity clause should not be used in countries with a clear history of *coups* or other extra-constitutional regime changes. This is because once an eternity clause creates a gridlock or conflict, the temptation to alter the constitution is immense and, in States where *coups* have historically been a viable option for constitutional change, this temptation can foment a desire to use extra-constitutional means for unconstitutional modification or regime change. This is especially so in a country that has recently experienced a *coup*, where the current politicians most involved with the current constitutional gridlock will often have been part of the last *coup* and therefore consider a *coup* as a possibility or be adept at staging

Instead of formal eternity clauses, the Judiciary may create eternity of a constitutional clause through the doctrine of 'implicit unamendability' as the embodiment of the constitution's basic structure or minimum core.[75] This is achieved, for example, by the Bolivian Supreme Court in the *Meza* case where the Court proceeds, inter alia, on the basis that sovereignty residing in the people—who delegate its exercise to the Legislature, Executive and Judiciary—is inalienable, not subject to limitation, imprescriptible and indivisible according to the Constitution.[76] As another example, the Supreme Court of Pakistan in *Zafar Ali Shah* resorts to implicit unamendability plus the Pakistani Constitution's minimum core, by deeming the welfare of the people to be the supreme law (*salus populi est suprema lex*) for the Court to uphold as well as by invoking the 'Islamic doctrine of sovereignty' as expounded in the Holy Book (Qur'an) according to which sovereignty belongs neither to the ruler nor the ruled but Almighty Allah alone which is to be exercised by the people of Pakistan through their chosen representatives.

It may be recalled that the legal question before the Thai Supreme Court in *Punsak Sritape and 14 Others*, as raised by the plaintiffs, was whether the blanket amnesty granted to those involved in the *coup* and all acts pursuant to the junta's orders and announcements could be upheld. Unlike Member States of the Organization of American States or the African Union, there is no international treaty binding on Thailand, a Member State of the Association of Southeast Asian Nations, which punishes the act of unconstitutional usurpation of power in and of itself, as explained in Chapter 2. Had the legal question been that of the validity of the amnesty granted to these individuals for their violations of fundamental rights and freedoms of Thai citizens, the Court would have been bound to follow the CCPR's General Comment No 31 that States Parties to the ICCPR, of which Thailand is one, must investigate and ensure those responsible for violations of the ICCPR are brought to justice, and that they may not be relieved from personal responsibility by means of amnesties, prior legal immunities and indemnities.

In conclusion, *irrespective of whether the usurper's regime is still or no longer in power*, judges of domestic courts must implement the obligations under the relevant international treaties and applicable rules of customary international law binding on their respective countries. Rulings by competent regional courts with jurisdiction over their countries must also be complied with. The judges should likewise find authoritative rulings from international treaty bodies, such as the CCPR, when rendering their judgments on this issue. Otherwise, the judges may be held accountable in a domestic court after a regime change, or before a competent international/hybrid court or a foreign court exercising universal jurisdiction, for sustaining or having a consensual role in the repressive regime.

---

another *coup*. Friedman sites as an example the constitutional crisis in Honduras in 2009 in which incumbent President Manuel Zelaya was captured from the Presidential Palace and flown to Costa Rica at night (ibid 82–3). See also Silvia Suteu, 'Eternity Clauses in Post-Conflict and Post-Authoritarian Constitution-Making: Promise and Limits' (2017) 6 Global Constitutionalism 63, 89–90.

75 Suteu, *Eternity Clauses in Democratic Constitutionalism* 125–66.

76 https://www.derechos.org/nizkor/bolivia/doc/meza.html.

Statutes of limitations

The Uruguayan Supreme Court treats as a de facto amnesty the statute of limitations in the 1986 Expiry Law, which prevents the government from bringing cases involving crimes committed by the military before 1 March 1985. In one of these cases, *Nibia Sabalsagaray*, decided in 2009, the Court proceeds as follows. By virtue of a law enacted by a special majority and in extraordinary cases, the State may decide to waive punishment for criminal acts. However, the impugned law is unconstitutional because the legislative power exceeds the constitutional scope for granting amnesties by declaring the expiry of criminal prosecutions which encroaches on a function constitutionally assigned to judges. Moreover, the current regulation of human rights is not based on the position of sovereign States, but in the individual person as holder, given his or her status as such, of essential rights that cannot be ignored. In this framework, the 'amnesty law under consideration' affects the rights of many people (notably, the victims, the next of kin or those harmed by the human rights violations whose right to a remedy as well as an impartial and exhaustive investigation to ascertain the facts, to identify those responsible and to impose the appropriate penalties has been frustrated) to the extent that the legal consequences of the law regarding the right to judicial guarantees are incompatible with the 1969 American Convention on Human Rights. Indeed, the unlawfulness of an amnesty law enacted for the benefit of military and police officials who committed serious violations of human rights, who enjoyed impunity during de facto regimes of dictatorship, has been declared by both the international community and the States that went through similar processes experienced by Uruguay during the same period in time. Such rulings, given the similarity with the issue under analysis and the relevance they have had, cannot be ignored in the examination of the constitutionality of Uruguay's impugned amnesty law.[77]

Uruguay has been a State Party to the 1968 Convention on the Non-Applicability of the Statute of Limitations to War Crimes and Crimes Against Humanity[78] since 2001. Yet, the 2009 judgment did not base its reasoning squarely on the 1968 Convention, but on the American Convention and the practice by both the international community and the States sharing the same experience as Uruguay. By contrast, the Gambian Supreme Court in *The State v Yankuba Touray*[79] alludes to the fact that The Gambia, as one the 56 States Parties to the 1968 Convention,[80] is

77 *Nibia Sabalsagaray*, Sentencia No 365/2009, quoted by the IACtHR in *Gomes Lund et al.* para 167. Cf. Mallinder, 'The End of Amnesty or Regional Overreach?' 656–7. See also Lessa, *Memory and Transitional Justice in Argentina and Uruguay* 131–213; Carranza Ko, *Truth, Justice, and Reparations in Peru, Uruguay, and South Korea* 125–97.

78 754 UNTS 73, in force 11 November 1970.

79 Case no SC Co CR/001/2020, Supreme Court's Judgment, 19 March 2021.

80 The 56 parties as of this writing are Afghanistan, Albania, Argentina, Armenia, Azerbaijan, Belarus, Bolivia, Bosnia and Herzegovina, Bulgaria, Cameroon, Costa Rica, Croatia, Cuba, Czech Rep, DR Korea, Ecuador, Estonia, The Gambia, Georgia, Ghana, Guinea, Honduras, Hungary, India, Kenya, Kuwait, Lao PDR, Latvia, Liberia, Libya, Lithuania, Mexico, Mongolia, Montenegro, Nicaragua, Nigeria, North Macedonia, Panama, Paraguay, Peru, the Philippines, Poland, Rep of

bound not to apply statutory limitations to war crimes and crimes against humanity, irrespective of the date of their commission.

The issue of the statute of limitations arose in the trial of General Luis García Meza Tejada, who staged a violent *coup* on 17 July 1980 and became de facto President of Bolivia from that date up to 4 August 1981. He and members of the junta, members of his 1980 Ministerial Cabinet, members of the Armed Forces and the National Police and civilian personnel who were his collaborators/accomplices were accused of committing crimes against the Constitution, including sedition, armed uprising, organization of irregular armed groups, undermining the rights of the people, enacting resolutions contrary to the Constitution and the laws, deprivation of liberties, attacks against the freedom of the press, obtaining advantages for the importation of vehicles and violation of university autonomy. Meza, his minister of interior, certain members of the Ministry of the Interior, a special security group and another irregular armed group were also accused of perpetrating genocide and the bloody massacre in La Paz, Bolivia's capital city, on 15 January 1981. Although Bolivia signed the 1948 Convention on the Prevention and Punishment of the Crime of Genocide[81] on 11 December 1948, it did not ratify this Convention until 14 June 2005. Nonetheless, the Bolivian Penal Code, which has been in force since 2 April 1973, proscribes the crime of genocide in Article 138, punishable by imprisonment from 10 to 20 years and, if the culprits are government officials, the penalty shall be increased by a fine of from 100 to 500 days' pay. In its judgment of 21 April 1993, the Bolivian Supreme Court dealt with the preliminary question of the statute of limitations as follows. On 6 October 1983 Bolivia became party to the 1968 Convention, pursuant to which there is no statute of limitations for crimes committed in time of war and in time of peace 'according to the definitions of crimes contained in the Charter of the [post–Second World War] International Military Tribunal at Nuremberg,[82] as confirmed by resolutions of the UN General Assembly, particularly as regards the crime of genocide as defined in the 1948 Genocide even if these acts did not constitute a violation of the domestic law of the country where they were committed'. The Court also referred to the UN Economic and Social Council's resolution dated 2 March 1993,[83] on the protection of freedom, security and recognition of the legal personality of human rights, stating that 'no State should commit, authorize or tolerate enforced disappearances' and condemning such crimes against humanity as attacks against international law and a denial of the objectives of the1948 American Declaration on the Rights and Duties of Man.[84] Meza was convicted and sentenced to 30 years' imprisonment, without the right to pardon. He died of cardiac arrest and respiratory failure in 2018, aged

Moldova, Romania, Russia, Rwanda, Serbia, Slovakia, Slovenia, St Vincent and the Grenadines, State of Palestine, Tunisia, Ukraine, Uruguay, Vietnam and Yemen.

81 78 UNTS 277, in force 12 January 1951.

82 8 UNTS 279.

83 The present author has not been able to locate this resolution, however.

84 (1949) 43(S3) AJIL 133.

88, at a military hospital where he was serving his prison sentence. Several other members of the junta were convicted and received long-term imprisonments. All the penalties imposed also entailed the obligation of the convicted persons to compensate the civil damage mentioned in each case.

The statute of limitations became a controversial issue in South Korea, which is not party to the 1968 Convention, during its transition to full democracy after a military *coup*. Chun Doo Wan became South Korea's President on 1 September 1980 following the dissolution of the National Assembly and revision of the Constitution under martial law imposed by him after the military *coup* he led on 12 December 1979. He was succeeded by Roh Tae Woo, who was elected President from 25 February 1988 to 24 February 1993. After South Korea returned to full democracy and by popular demand, the Special Act Concerning the May 18 Democratization Movement was enacted in December 1995[85] to suspend the statute of limitations for crimes against constitutional order committed on or around 12 December 1979, the date of the *coup*, and 18 May 1980, the start of the popular uprising in the city of Kwangju against the martial law government which tragically ended with hundreds, or even more than 2,000, of those participating in the uprising killed, raped or injured by government forces. The cut-off date apparently prevented potential prosecution of those involved in the uprising against the regime. This Act enabled the criminal prosecutions of Chun, Roh and 23 other former high-ranking officers for mutiny and treason for their roles in the 1979 *coup*. The Act was challenged by the defendants on the grounds that it violated equal protection principles, as it was directed only to punish a specific group of individuals, and that it constituted retrospective punishment in violation of the principle of legality. In 1996 the Constitutional Court of the Republic of Korea upheld the constitutionality of the Act since the Act was founded upon a national demand to rectify past wrongs and establish legitimate constitutionalism in South Korea.[86] Chun was subsequently sentenced by the Supreme Court to death, later commuted to life imprisonment, while Roh was sentenced to 22 and a half years in jail, which was reduced to 17 years on appeal. Both were stripped of their national honours and ordered to pay large sums of fines.

The South Korean Supreme Court, affirming the defendants' convictions for treason and killing for the purpose of treason, stated:

> The defendants grasped political power after they stopped the exercise of the authority of constitutional State institutions by mutiny and rebellion. Even if they had arguably ruled the State based on the Constitution, which was revised *by popular referendum*, it should not be overlooked that a new legal order was established by mutiny and rebellion. It cannot be tolerated under

85 Special Act Concerning May 18 Democratization Movement, Act no 5029, 21 December 1995.

86 Constitutional Court, 96 HunKa 2, 16 February 1996, (8–1 KCCR, 51), cited in Paul Hanley, 'Transitional Justice in South Korea: One Country's Restless Search for Truth and Reconciliation' (2014) 9 East Asia L Rev 139, 150.

> any circumstances under our constitutional order to stop the exercise of the authority of constitutional State institutions and grasp political power by violence, not following democratic procedure. Therefore, the mutiny and rebellion can be punishable.[87]

For parties to the 1998 Rome Statute of the International Criminal Court, Article 29 of the Statute excludes the crimes within the ICC's jurisdiction from being subject to a statute of limitations. In addition, according to Rule 160 of the International Committee of the Red Cross's authoritative *Customary International Law*, updated in December 2019, the principle that statutes of limitations do not apply to war crime committed in both international and non-international armed conflicts is a norm of customary international law binding on all States.

A closely related issue is the classification of crimes excluded from a statute of limitations.

Although Uruguay's Interpretative Law of October 2011 excludes crimes against humanity from the scope of the 1986 Expiry Law, there have been some problems arising from the Uruguayan Supreme Court's interpretation of the principle of legality in relation to crimes against humanity. For example, in May 2011 the Court ruled that two former military officers could not be charged with enforced disappearance, a crime against humanity, because the crime was not incorporated into Uruguayan law until 2006; they were only convicted of aggravated murder, an 'ordinary crime' under Uruguayan law, in connection with the deaths of 28 persons and sentenced to 25 years in prison.[88] One study finds that in its judgments in 2013, 2014, 2015 and 2017 the Uruguayan Supreme Court shifts back and forth between recognizing atrocious acts under the repressive regime as crimes against humanity excluded from the Expiry Law and not recognizing them as such at the time they were committed during the 1973–85 period. The Uruguayan judges who consider that crimes against humanity existed under Uruguayan law during the aforesaid period of dictatorship contend that these crimes have been proscribed under peremptory norms of international law (*jus cogens*) binding on all States since their prosecution at the post–Second World War Nuremberg Tribunal and their inclusion in the 1968 Convention on the Non-Applicability of Statutory Limitations to War Crimes and Crimes Against Humanity.[89]

Without entering into a debate which interpretation in the judgments of the Uruguay Supreme Court is correct, as a State Party to the 1969 American

87 Decision of 17 April 1997, 96 Do 3376 (Korean Supreme Court) at chapter 1(1), translated by and quoted in Kuk Cho, 'Transitional Justice in Korea: Legally Coping with Past Wrongs after Democratization' (2007) 16 Pacific Rim L & Policy J 579, 584 (emphasis added).

88 *Gavazzo Pereira, José Nino y Arab Fernández, José Ricardo for 28 crimes of homicide*. Case 98/247/2006, 6 May 2011.

89 Francesca Lessa and Jo-Marie Burt, 'New Ruling by Uruguay's Supreme Court of Justice Once Again Jeopardizes the Search for Truth and Justice for Dictatorship-Era Crimes' *WOLA* (7 November 2017), https://www.wola.org/analysis/new-ruling-uruguays-supreme-court-justice-jeopardizes-search-truth-justice-dictatorship-era-crimes/.

Convention Uruguay has to follow the IACtHR's oft-cited established jurisprudence that amnesties and other devices to circumvent prosecution of grave human rights violations cannot override the State's duty under international obligations stipulated in the relevant human rights treaties to investigate, prosecute and punish those responsible, and to provide reparation to victims—any laws to the contrary must be repealed or amended accordingly. *Nibia Sabalsagaray*, decided by the Uruguayan Supreme Court in 2009, stands as an exemplary judgment in this regard. To solve the aforesaid problem of classification where this arises, heinous crimes which shall not benefit from a statute of limitations should be discretely enumerated, with their elements of crime clearly elaborated, in the relevant law.

Transitional justice

Overview

There are several types of justice. Retributive justice demands proportionate punishment as a morally justifiable response to crime so that the victim of the crime can find satisfaction and society can be saved by the deterrence of further commission of crime. Restorative justice, also known as reparative justice, emphasizes the needs of victims and perpetrators of crimes, whereby the latter are to acknowledge and take responsibility for their conduct by giving reparation to their victims after having dialogue with them.[90] Restorative justice overlaps conceptually with transitional justice and can be a catalyst for the latter in societies emerging from civil wars and systematic or widespread human rights abuses.

Transitional justice in post-conflict situations in a nation State usually involves balancing prosecution of large-scale serious violations of human rights, on the one hand, and the need to achieve national reconciliation, on the other hand.[91] According to the United Nations, 'transitional justice is the full range of processes and mechanisms associated with a society's attempt to come to terms with a legacy of

90 Kathleen Daly, 'Restorative Justice Versus Retributive Justice' (2005) 60 Crim Justice Matters 28; Wesley Cragg, *The Practice of Punishment: Towards a Theory of Restorative Justice* (Routledge 1992) 15. See also Rosario Figari Layus, *The Reparative Effects of Human Rights Trials: Lessons from Argentina* (Routledge 2019).

91 Nicola Palmer, Phil Clark and Danielle Granville (eds), *Critical Perspectives in Transitional Justice* (Intersentia 2012); Moses Chrispus Okello, Chris Dolan, Undine Whande, Nokukhanya Mncwabe, Lewis Onegi and Stephen Oola (eds), *Where Law Meets Reality: Forging African Transitional Justice* (Pambazuka Press 2012); Ruti Teitel, *Globalizing Transitional Justice* (OUP 2014); Susanne Buckley-Zistel, Teresa Koloma Beck, Christian Braun and Friederike Mieth (eds), *Transitional Justice Theories* (Routledge 2015); Noha Aboueldahab, *Transitional Justice and the Prosecution of Political Leaders in the Arab Region: A Comparative Study of Egypt, Libya, Tunisia and Yemen* (Hart 2017); Cheryl Lawther and Luke Moffett (eds), *Research Handbook on Transitional Justice* (Edward Elgar Publishing 2019); Iosif Kovras, 'The Future of Transitional Justice: Mercy or Impunity?' in Michael Stohl and Alison Brysk (eds), *A Research Agenda for Human Rights* (Edward Elgar Publishing 2020) 75–88; Natasha Stamenkovikj, *The Right to Know the Truth in Transitional Justice Processes: Perspectives from International Law and European Governance* (Brill 2021) 17–52, 77–172; Rojas and Shaftoe, *Human Rights and Transitional Justice in Chile* 1–28.

large-scale past abuses, in order to ensure accountability, serve justice and achieve reconciliation'. It consists of both judicial and non-judicial processes and mechanisms, including prosecution initiatives, truth-seeking, reparations programmes, institutional reform or an appropriate combination thereof, in conformity with international legal standards and obligations. Transitional justice should further seek to take account of the root causes of conflicts and the related violations of all rights so as to contribute to achieving the broader objectives of prevention of further conflict, peace-building and reconciliation.[92]

A truth and reconciliation commission set up after the end of the apartheid regime in South Africa is an example of both restorative justice and transitional justice resorted to in lieu of prosecuting hundreds of thousands of individuals accused of implementing apartheid, which would be costly, time-consuming and disruptive to national reconciliation and harmony.

Domestic politics and options chosen by democratic means

The role of domestic politics in shaping the course of transitional justice is of utmost importance. A government elected after transition to democracy needs to weigh all the options and feasibility in pursuing prosecution or non-prosecution of past atrocities committed during the previous repressive regime.

Afghanistan's failure to end impunity of and amnesty for human rights violators over 23 years of war from the Soviet-backed *coup* of 30 April 1978 to the fall of the Taliban Government in 2001 is illustrative. This is despite the recommendations in the 'Peace, Reconciliation and Justice in Afghanistan: Action Plan of the Government of the Islamic Republic of Afghanistan',[93] drafted by the Government of Afghanistan in cooperation with the Afghan Independent Human Rights Commission and the UN Assistance Mission in Afghanistan. It was presented and agreed upon at the Hague Conference on Peace, Reconciliation and Justice in Afghanistan in June 2005, with the participation of the Dutch Minister of Foreign Affairs; the senior advisors to President Karzai of Afghanistan; a representative of the Afghan Supreme Court; and representatives of the European Commission and the Governments of Canada, Finland, France, Germany, Italy, the Netherlands, Sweden, the United Kingdom and the United States, as well as experts from the International Centre on Transitional Justice and the Afghanistan Justice Project, among others.

Key Action 4 (Promotion of reconciliation and national unity) of the Action Plan aims to explore ways to promote reconciliation, strengthen national unity and enhance solidarity and trust among people. In this respect, it states categorically that in the case of systematic violation of human rights, war crimes and crimes against humanity, criminal justice can be established based on the legal norms. Considering the realities of the country, the findings of the Afghan Independent Human

92 United Nations, *Guidance Note of the Secretary General: United Nations Approach to Transitional Justice* (United Nations, March 2010) 3.

93 www.aihrc.org.af/media/files/Reports/Thematic%20reports/Action_Pln_Gov_Af.pdf.

Rights Commission through the National Consultation and bitter experience of human rights violation, the Afghan Government will submit a scheme to Parliament to make the necessary decisions and end impunity in Afghanistan. In making such a decision, attention should be paid to this reality that, 'considering the clear Koranic verses and international law', no amnesty should be provided for war crimes, crimes against humanity and other gross violations of human rights. Key Action 5 (Establishment of effective and reasonable accountability mechanisms) aims at ending impunity in Afghanistan and ensuring that there will be no amnesty for war crimes, crimes against humanity and other gross human rights violations, and that the conditions for fair and effective justice procedures are established in accordance with the principles of the sacred religion of Islam, international law and transitional justice. Besides, considering the lofty values of the sacred religion of Islam and in accordance with internationally recognized standards, the perpetrators of war crimes, crimes against humanity and other serious human rights violations will not be ignored. The Afghan President Office is entrusted with 'clarification on non-amnesty as soon as possible'. Nevertheless, in March 2007 the Afghan Parliament passed the National Reconciliation, General Amnesty and National Stability Law[94] to give blanket amnesty to all perpetrators of human rights abuses of the past regimes from 1970 to 2001.

According to the Preamble of the Law, 'the realization of national reconciliation policy and ending of war and bloodshed, strengthening of national unity and building of trust among all segments of society is crucial in this juncture of time'. Article 1 explains the purposes of this law as strengthening the reconciliation and national stability, ensuring the supreme interests of the country, ending rivalries and building confidence among the belligerent parties, based on their *immunity* in case of adherence to the Constitution and other enforced laws of the country. By virtue of Article 3(1), all political factions and hostile parties who were involved in one way or another in hostilities before the setting up of the Interim Administration after the fall of the Taliban Government in 2001 shall be included in the reconciliation and a *general amnesty* programme for the purpose of reconciliation among different segments of society, strengthening of peace and stability and starting of new life in the contemporary political history of Afghanistan, and shall enjoy all their legal rights and not be legally and judicially prosecuted. Article 3(2) stipulates that this Law benefits those individuals and groups who are still in opposition to the Islamic Republic of Afghanistan but who cease enmity after the enforcement of this Law, join the process of national reconciliation as well as respect the Constitution and other laws and abide by them. Under Article 3(3), the provisions set forth in Article 3(1) and (2) shall not affect the claims of individuals against other individuals based up on *Haqullabd* (rights of people) and criminal offences in respect of individual crimes. Pursuant to Article 4(1), those people who are 'under prosecution' due to crimes against internal and external security of the country shall not enjoy the

94 Official Gazette, 13 Qaus 1387 Serial No 965.

benefits of this Law. However, Article 4(2) stipulates that those people who are sentenced after their conviction of crimes against internal and external security of the country shall be forgiven or their punishment mitigated by separate decrees, according to the situation and based on recommendations and guarantee of the Commission for Consolidation of Peace, provided that they make a commitment not to resume their activities against the Islamic Republic of Afghanistan.

Afghanistan experienced international wars as well as civil wars within its territory for decades. The transitional justice model utilized under the 2007 Law might be the best possible one to ensure the survival of the fragile democratic regime coming to power after the fall of the Taliban Government in 2001. The choice finally made by the Afghan Parliament is not unique. For instance, after the end of the Francoist dictatorship in Spain, lasting from 1939 to General Francisco Franco's death in 1975, Spain resorted to a blanket amnesty rather than purges, mechanisms to bring the dictatorship to trial for crimes against humanity or truth commissions and so forth—and this was due to a relative weakness of democracy and a society characterized by the fear of a return to political violence.[95] A blanket amnesty approved by Parliament was also resorted to by, for example, those staging the military *coup* in Niger on 18 February 2010 to oust the incumbent President who was trying to remain in office after the expiry of his term. The junta drafted a constitution and submitted it to a national referendum on 31 October 2010, which approved it by 90.19 per cent in favour and in a 52.02 per cent turnout. Article 185 of the 2010 Constitution grants an amnesty to the authors, co-authors and accomplices of the February 2010 *coup* and provides that '[a] law will be voted, to this effect, during the first session of the National Assembly'. As proof of its good faith, the junta ceded power to a civilian government after a general election 14 months after the *coup*.

Where a *coup* is quickly quelled without much damage to the nation or deleterious effects on the fundamental rights and freedoms of the populace, for the sake of transitional justice the country may take a softer approach than criminal prosecution of those behind the *coup*. This happened to the bloodless eight-hour military *coup* in Ecuador in January 2000 that deposed the incumbent President. The *coup* was too brief for the junta to have opportunities to abuse human rights or perpetrate crimes of international concern. On 31 May 2000, in an effort to achieve national reconciliation at a politically sensitive time the Ecuadoran Congress decreed a general amnesty for the civilians and members of the armed forces as well as other authors and participants in the *coup*. This amnesty was given exclusively for the political crimes and for the criminal processes that have been initiated or could be initiated. The congressional pardon, which lifted criminal charges but left open possible military discipline, was approved by 90 of the 115 deputies present in the 123-seat unicameral Congress. Ecuador's President Gustavo Noboa, who had served as Vice President at the time of the *coup* and became President

95 Roldan Jimeno, *Amnesties, Pardons and Transitional Justice: Spain's Pact of Forgetting* (Routledge 2018).

right after the junta was dissolved by the high command of the Armed Forces, explained that the amnesty would reduce tensions between government authorities and the social movements that had made amnesty a rallying cry. On 2 June 2000, after the amnesty was approved, the President of the Military Tribunal ordered the case against the military officers involved in the insurrection closed. On 5 June 2000, the military officers who received amnesty were informed they no longer had the trust of the armed forces of Ecuador and would be 'placed under the Defence Ministry' for 90 days, after which they would be unposted for six months, a step preceding their eventual discharge from military service.[96]

Following the popular uprising lasting several months, known as the Jasmine Revolution, Tunisia's President Zine El Abidine Ben Ali, who had come to power by the bloodless *coup* on 7 November 1987 and stayed in office through successive elections, was deposed on 14 January 2011. Tunisia's Constituent Assembly elected on 23 October 2011 promulgated a new Constitution in January 2014, Article 148(9) of which provides that the State 'undertakes to apply the transitional justice system in all its domains and according to the deadlines prescribed by the relevant legislation', and that, in this context, 'the invocation of the non-retroactivity of laws, the existence of previous amnesties, the force of *res judicata*, and the prescription of a crime or a punishment are considered inadmissible'. Whatever the meaning of Article 148(9), Ben Ali did not benefit from it. On 20 June 2011 Ben Ali together with his wife had been convicted *in absentia* of theft and unlawful possession of cash and jewellery, sentenced to 35 years in prison and fined approximately US$64 million. In September 2019, Ben Ali died while living in exile in Saudi Arabia, which had refused to extradite him and his wife to Tunisia.

A true democracy occasionally manages to reverse a flagrant effort by the preceding repressive regime to shield the usurper and his collaborators/accomplices from responsibility, as in the case of Türkiye in 2010. The military *coup* led by General Kenan Evren on 12 September 1980 was the bloodiest military intervention in Turkish history. Mostly for political reasons, hundreds of thousands of people were detained or put on trial, 50 were executed and another 299 died from torture and unhealthy prison conditions. The new Turkish Constitution drafted by the military junta received 98 per cent of votes of approval at a referendum held in 1982, with many questioning the reliability of the results as the military junta was in full charge of all organizations of the referendum. Provisional Article 15 was inserted in the 1982 Constitution to grant the junta members immunity from prosecution. In 2004, the ECtHR held in *Abdülsamet Yaman v Turkey* that where a State agent has been charged with crimes involving torture or ill treatment, it is of the utmost importance for the purposes of an 'effective remedy' that criminal proceedings and sentencing are not time-barred, and that the granting of an amnesty or pardon should not be permissible. The ECtHR also underlines the importance of the suspension from duty of the agent under investigation or on

96 Latin America Digital Beat, U New Mexico Digital Repository, *Ecuadoran Officers Who Led Coup Granted Amnesty* (2000), https://digitalrepository.unm.edu/notisur/12786.

trial as well as his dismissal if he is convicted.[97] After Türkiye's return to democracy, a new referendum on September 2010 removed the Article, paving the way for prosecution of the junta members in civilian courts. Evren, who became Türkiye's seventh President, and former Air Force General Tahsin Sahinkaya were put on trial in April 2012, marking the first time in Turkish history that *coup* leaders were tried although neither of them appeared in court due to ill health. On 18 June 2014, a Turkish court sentenced them to life imprisonment and demoted their military rank down to private, for leading the 1980 military *coup*, obstructing democracy by deposing the then Prime Minister, abolishing Parliament and the Senate and annulling the Constitution. Their sentences were on appeal at the time of Evren's death in May 2015 at the age of 97 and Sahinkaya's death in July 2015, aged 90.

Not every decision resulting from national elections or referenda should always be accepted as beyond reproach. It is not unusual for the usurper who wields considerable power and influence as well as controls the country's financial resources to return to power by election ballots[98] or organize a referendum in such a way as to ensure the constitution drafted by those appointed by the junta will be approved, at the time when dissent and opposition against the usurper's regime are largely suppressed. A referendum may be boycotted by the overwhelming majority of those eligible to vote, as in the case of the low turnout of 31.4 per cent at the 25 July 2022 referendum which approved the new Constitution of Tunisia by 92 per cent. Concededly, disillusionment with democracy over the lack of economic and social progresses under democratically elected leaders sometimes makes voters turn to autocrats with promises to lead the nation to greater economic prosperity and social harmony. It is of importance to heed the ruling of the IACtHR in *Gelman v Uruguay*, refusing to recognize Uruguay's amnesty law, which has already been confirmed in a plebiscite. According to the IACtHR, the fact that a law has been approved in a democratic regime and ratified or supported by the public does not automatically or by itself grant legitimacy under international law. The IACtHR reasons that the democratic legitimacy of specific facts in a society is limited by the norms of protection of human rights recognized in international treaties, such as the 1969 American Convention on Human Rights, in such a form that the existence of one true democratic regime is determined by both its formal and substantial characteristics and therefore, particularly in cases of serious violations of non-revocable norms of international law, the protection of human rights constitutes 'an impassable limit to the rule of the majority'.[99]

Judges should recognize the decision of representatives of the people who are duly elected to govern the country, be they members of the Executive or the

97 App no 32446/96, Judgment of 2 November 2004 para 55.

98 Apart from Ben Ali, the following are some of the *coup* leaders who were subsequently elected Presidents of their respective countries: Jerry John Rawlings of Ghana, Lansana Conté of Guinea, François Bozizé of the Central African Republic and Gnassingbé Eyadéma of Togo.

99 *Gelman v Uruguay* (Merits and Reparations), IACtHR (24 February 2011) Ser C no 110 paras 238–9.

Legislature, provided that their transitional justice choice is made in good faith as the 'lesser evil' in the prevailing circumstances. Nonetheless, the transitional justice measures chosen must be subject to treaty obligations and/or customary international law binding on the country. Judges of domestic courts caught up in the nation's transitional justice process must, therefore, ensure that conducts amounting to crimes of international concern be punished.

An example of bad faith efforts to give impunity to usurpers may be that of a bill[100] granting house arrest to all convicted persons aged over 65 submitted to Uruguay's Senate by three senators from the far-right Cabildo Abierto Party, a member of the governing coalition, which had a large military membership. If passed, this law would immediately benefit the 26 former military and civilians in prison either convicted or accused of crimes against humanity committed during the dictatorship. The other 14 convicted of such crimes in Uruguay were already under house arrest. This law would also immediately benefit the dozens of former perpetrators of atrocities during the dictatorship whose trials, long stalled or greatly slowed down, were still, almost 50 years after the events, at the stage of preliminary investigations, assuring them of almost total and definitive impunity. This would also benefit the majority of such perpetrators who had managed to escape justice completely.[101] In a jointly signed letter of 16 November 2021, five UN Special Rapporteurs petitioned the President of Uruguay not to sign this bill into law.[102]

A similar amnesty bill, titled Legislative Proposal 5377, was submitted to the Guatemalan Congress in 2017. It was approved in two of three required readings in Congress, but legislators opposing the bill walked out on several different occasions, preventing a quorum, so that the bill could not be approved in a third reading. On 12 March 2019, the IACtHR ordered Guatemala to cease discussion, and the immediate shelving, of Legislative Proposal 5377.[103] On 18 July 2019 the Guatemalan Constitutional Court, by the majority of 3 to 2, granted a provisional injunction to victims of human rights violations, who sought to block the approval of a blanket amnesty law, and ordered the immediate suspension of consideration of Legislative Proposal 5377. Yet, a similar bill was submitted to Congress on 22 September 2021 by nine legislators from the ultra-conservative Valor Party that

100 A bill to add to Law No 19.293, of 19 December 2014 (Criminal Procedure Code) the following article: 'Article 235 *bis* (Home detention regime)'.

101 Elena Salgueiro, 'Uruguay: A Law to Benefit Perpetrators of Crimes against Humanity?' *JusticeInfo.Net* (30 November 2021), https://www.justiceinfo.net/en/84967-uruguay-law-benefit-perpetrators-crimes-against-humanity.html.

102 Note No OL URY 2/2021 of 12 November 2021 from the Special Rapporteur on the promotion of truth, justice, reparation and guarantees of non-recurrence; Chair-Rapporteur of the Working Group on Enforced or Involuntary Disappearances; Special Rapporteur on extrajudicial, summary or arbitrary executions; Special Rapporteur on the right of everyone to the enjoyment of the highest attainable standard of physical and mental health; and Special Rapporteur on Torture and Other Cruel, Inhuman or Degrading Treatment or Punishment.

103 *Case of the Members of the Village of Chichupac and neighboring communities of the Municipality of Rabinal, Case of Molina Theissen and 12 other Guatemalan's Cases v Guatemala*, Provisional Measures and Monitoring Compliance with Judgment, IACtHR, Order of 12 March 2019.

would free all former military personnel and paramilitary patrolmen convicted or accused of crimes during the armed conflict in Guatemala. This came after the arrest in May 2021 of 11 former military officers during Ríos Montt's regime for enforced disappearance, extrajudicial execution, torture, sexual violence and other crimes committed against 195 victims between 1983 and 1985 as documented in the 'Diario Militar', a death squad diary. The preamble to the proposed 'Law of Consolidation of Peace and Reconciliation' stipulates, inter alia, that there was no genocide in Guatemala and that enforced disappearance, torture and other crimes against humanity should not have been excluded from amnesty provisions in the National Reconciliation Law of 1996.[104]

What if the national political climate is not conducive to large-scale or high-profile prosecution?

The IACtHR in *Moiwana Community v Suriname* deals with the *argument that the political climate in a State Party to the American Convention is not conducive to prosecution of members of a former repressive regime* under Dési Bouterse, who led the military *coups* in 1980 and 1990 which resulted in the military dictatorship from 1980 to 1991. Bouterse ruled as Suriname's de facto leader from 25 February 1980 to 27 November 1987 and became Suriname's President by elections from 12 August 2010 to 16 July 2020. The military regime under Bouterse has been accused of carrying out the massacre in November 1986 of no fewer than 40 women and children of the Moiwana village and razing the village to the ground. On 19 August 1992, Suriname's President Ronald Venetiaan, who had earlier been deposed by the 1980 *coup*, officially promulgated the Amnesty Act,[105] granting amnesty to those who committed certain criminal acts, with the exception of crimes against humanity, as classified as such according to international law, during the period from 1 January 1985 through 19 August 1992. In its judgment of June 2005 the IACtHR notes that the event in November 1986 took place one year prior to Suriname's accession to the American Convention and its recognition of the IACtHR's jurisdiction, effective as of 12 November 1987. The IACtHR distinguishes between alleged violations of the American Convention that are of a continuing nature, and those that occurred after 12 November 1987. With respect to the former, as the perpetration of a massacre in 1986 has been alleged, Suriname is obligated to investigate, prosecute and punish the responsible parties. In that regard, Suriname initiated very limited investigative steps starting in 1989, and this investigation can be assessed by the IACtHR starting from the date when Suriname recognized the IACtHR's competence. Furthermore, the alleged victims were

104 See also Jo-Marie Burt, *Strategic Litigation in Cases of Gross Human Rights Violations in Guatemala: Impact and Lessons Learned* (Impunity Watch, May 2021); Elin Skaar, Jemima Garcia-Godos and Cath Collins (eds), *Transitional Justice in Latin America: The Uneven Road from Impunity towards Accountability* (Routledge 2016).

105 Statutes of the Republic of Suriname No 68 (19 August 1992).

forcefully displaced from their ancestral lands in 1986 and their inability to return to those territories has allegedly continued.[106] The IACtHR rejects Suriname's explanation that the *political climate in Suriname* after the November 1986 attack prevented an independent and impartial investigation since the position of power held by the former military leaders had not yet ended and democracy was still not stable. While acknowledging the difficult circumstances endured by Suriname in its struggle for democracy, the IACtHR states categorically that *country conditions, however difficult, generally may not release a State Party to the American Convention from the obligations arising therefrom.*[107] The IACtHR reaffirms its well-established jurisprudence that no domestic law or regulation—including amnesty laws and statutes of limitation—may impede the State's compliance with the IACtHR's orders to investigate and punish perpetrators of human rights violations. If this were not the case, the rights found in the American Convention would be deprived of effective protection. This conclusion is consistent with the letter and spirit of the American Convention as well as general principles of international law, prominent among which is *pacta sunt servanda*, requiring that a treaty's provisions be given meaningful effect within a State Party's internal legal order.[108] The IACtHR therefore orders Suriname to, among other things, pay US$3 million in compensation to 130 survivors of the massacre, and to establish a US$1.2 million fund for the development of the village of Moiwana as well as prosecute and punish the persons responsible for the atrocities in question.[109] This ruling by the IACtHR in favour of the victims in that case has not been implemented by Suriname as of this writing. Nonetheless, Bouterse has been subject to prosecution and punishment in another case, proving that *the political climate in the country is not a justification not to prosecute members of a former repressive regime.*

In December 1982, 15 leading opposition figures in Suriname—lawyers, journalists, soldiers, businessmen, academics and a trade union leader—were tortured and then summarily executed. In November 2007, Bouterse and 24 other persons were tried for their murder. However, Suriname's Parliament passed the Amnesty (Amendment) Act on 4 April 2012 granting amnesty to any offence that took place between 1 April 1980 and 19 August 1992 'in the context of the defence of the State', thereby effectively shielding the 25 defendants, two months before the expected verdict in the case. The Surinamese Government then under Bouterse explained the Act was necessitated by socio-political concerns, and the Act needed to be implemented together with finding truth and bringing national reconciliation, taking into consideration sentiments of the society as a whole, in particular of all the groups and individuals immediately involved and impacted. The objective of the Act was said to open avenues for achieving complete and lasting reconciliation, harmony and peace in Suriname, as guided by experiences and results of other

106 *Moiwana Community v Suriname*, Judgment of 15 June 2005, Ser C no 125 para 43.
107 Ibid para 153.
108 Ibid para 167.
109 Ibid para 233.

countries that had followed the path of truth finding and reconciliation.[110] The Act was subsequently declared invalid by a Surinamese court and in November 2019 a Surinamese military court convicted and sentenced Bouterse to 20 years' imprisonment for the murders.[111] Bouterse submitted his appeal in January 2020. The appeal is still pending as of this writing.

Yet, in several countries the 'political climate' has hindered full-scale prosecutions of all those accused of atrocities during repressive regimes although the usurpers are no longer in power. In pursuing transitional justice in good faith, Argentina and Brazil are among those facing political difficulties in undertaking such full-scale prosecutions.

In Argentina, after the National Commission on the Disappeared, established by the democratically elected government following the collapse of dictatorship, issued its report, the Argentine military was compelled by legislation to try, in military courts and by a specified time frame, the senior officers who had presided over atrocities during the dictatorship, failing which the jurisdiction would shift automatically to civilian courts. After the Supreme Council of the Armed Forces refused to punish members of the Armed Forces, the Attorney General initiated prosecution of nine members of the military juntas which had successively governed Argentina from March 1976 until the restoration of civilian rule in 1983. Ultimately, in December 1985, after ruling that the amnesty the last junta had generously granted to all members of the Armed Forces before Argentina's return to civilian rule was unconstitutional, the National Appeals Court (Criminal Division) convicted six of the nine defendants, including General Jorge Videla who staged the *coup* on 24 March 1976 and became President from 29 March 1976 to 29 March 1981, of several crimes long established by Argentine law, including aggravated homicide, torture, unlawful arrest, robbery, violence and threats thereof.[112] This judgment was upheld by the Supreme Court on 30 December 1986. This was the first time in Latin American history that military leaders were held criminally responsible for actions committed by their governments following *coups*. Faced with a series of open or threatened mutinies by units of the Armed Forces against prosecution of less senior military figures, the civilian President Raúl Alfonsin ushered through the Argentine Congress a law known as 'Punto Final', meaning 'full stop',[113] which set a 60-day statute of limitations for new prosecutions. Even with this, hundreds of new cases still beat the deadline, making it necessary to pacify

110 Statement by the Government of the Republic of Suriname with Regard to the Amendment of the Amnesty Law of 1992, adopted on 4 April 2012, www.derechos.org/intlaw/doc/sur8.html.

111 Ank Kuipers, 'Suriname President Bouterse Convicted of Murder for 1982 Executions' *Reuters* (29 November 2019) https://www.reuters.com/article/us-suriname-court-idUSKBN1Y327O; International Commission of Jurists, *Suriname: The Rule of Law Must Be Respected by All Concerned* (6 December 2019), https://www.icj.org/suriname-the-rule-of-law-must-be-respected-by-all-concerned/.

112 (1987) 26 ILM 317–72. Life imprisonment was imposed on General Videla, Admiral Emilio Massera and General Leopoldo Galtieri. General Roberto Viola, who succeeded Videla as President, was sentenced to 17 years' imprisonment, Air Force General Orlando Ramón Agosti four and a half years, and Admiral Armando Lambruschini eight years.

113 Law 23.492 of 24 December 1986.

the military even further by supporting the enactment of the 'Due Obedience' law,[114] which allowed defendants to invoke orders from their superiors as a defence for their crimes (although they could still be prosecuted for exceeding orders).[115] In effect, the law created a conclusive presumption that anyone under the rank of commander was following orders and therefore not liable, although theft of babies or property was not covered by that presumption.

Subsequent Argentine Governments had to cope with the task of balancing the need to make leading junta members criminally accountable for their heinous crimes, on the one hand, and national healing during the transitional justice phase as influenced by domestic politics, on the other.[116]

In 1990, Argentine President Carlos Menem pardoned Videla and many other former members of the junta who were being imprisoned. In 2003, after the election of President Néstor Kirchner, Congress enacted a law to declare amnesties null and void.[117] In 2005, the 2003 law was upheld by the Supreme Court, ruling that the amnesty law had been unconstitutional all along, thereby permitting renewed efforts to prosecute those complicit in atrocities during the junta's rule.[118] In 2006 and 2007 Argentine courts ruled that the pardons granted by President Menem were unconstitutional and restored the junta members' convictions. In 2010, Videla himself also faced new criminal charges relating to the deaths of 31 prisoners who died under his rule, and he was sentenced to life imprisonment.[119] General Reynaldo Benito Antonio Bignone, who served as Argentina's President from 1 July 1982 to 10 December 1983, also faced a series of charges. In April 2010, Bignone was sentenced to 25 years' imprisonment for the kidnapping, torture and murder of 56 persons suspected of opposing the government during the dictatorship. In April 2011, Bignone was convicted and sentenced to life imprisonment for the torture and murder of political opponents more than three decades earlier.[120] On 5 July 2012, Videla and Bignone were convicted and sentenced to 50 and 15 years' imprisonment, respectively, for their participation in a systematic theft,

114 Law 23.521 of 4 June 1987. See also Kathryn Lee Crawford, 'Due Obedience and the Rights of Victims: Argentina's Transition to Democracy' (1990) 12 Hum Rts Quarterly 17.

115 Tom Farer, 'I Cried for You, Argentina' (2016) 38 Hum Rts Quarterly 851, 906–10; Human Rights Watch's 2001 Report on Argentina, www.hrw.org/reports/2001/argentina/argen1201-02.htm.

116 Thomas Wright, *State Terrorism in Latin America: Chile, Argentina, and International Human Rights* (Rowman & Littlefield 2007) ch 5 (Argentina: The Sinuous Path of Transitional Justice).

117 Law No 25.779 of 2 September 2003.

118 *Simón, Julio Héctor et al. s/illegal deprivation of liberty, etc*, Case 17.768, Order of 14 June 2005.

119 Alexei Barrionuevo, 'Argentina: Ex-Dictator Sentenced in Murders' *New York Times* (23 December 2010), https://www.nytimes.com/2010/12/23/world/americas/23briefs-EXDICTATORSE_BRF.html.

120 Also sentenced to life in prison were former General Santiago Riveros, former army intelligence officer Martin Rodriguez and the former mayor of Escobar, Luis Patti, who was a policeman at the time of the killings, whereas another former policeman, Juan Fernando Meneghini, was sentenced to six years in prison ('Argentina Former Military Ruler Bignone Gets Life' *BBC* (14 April 2011), https://www.bbc.com/news/world-latin-america-13088782).

retention and concealment of babies from political prisoners under the military regime and giving them to military families for illegal adoption under new identities. Several lower-ranking Argentine officials involved in the junta's repression have likewise received heavy sentences for their crimes.[121] However, there is no record that members of the Judiciary during the dictatorship were put on trial for their respective roles during the dictatorship regimes. One probable explanation is that the regimes did not normally resort to courts to validate their repression.

In Brazil, the military staged the bloodless *coup* in 1964 which led to a dictatorship lasting 21 years, with a brutal and repressive regime that ended with a negotiated transition of power.[122] The complicated process of political transition was not initiated until the 1979 self-amnesty was in place, ensuring to this day the impunity for State agents accused of virtually all crimes of political nature or carried out for political reasons. Specifically, Article 1 of the amnesty law[123] grants amnesty to all persons who, in the period between 2 September 1961 and 15 August 1979, committed 'political crimes or derived crimes to these or electoral crimes'; had their political rights suspended; were direct or indirect public servants of the administration or of foundations that belonged to the public power, public servants of the legislative and *judicial* powers, members of the military, leaders and union representatives, who were punished on the basis of their 'institutional and complementary acts'. 'Derived crimes' are those crimes of any nature related to political crimes or carried out with political motivation. Excluded from the benefit of this amnesty are persons convicted of terrorism, assault, kidnapping and personal attacks.

Brazil's 1985 indirect presidential election resulted in members of Congress electing the first civilian President since 1964, ending military rule in Brazil. In November 2002, Congress enacted a law to grant amnesty to and compensate those compelled to withdraw from their professional or educational activities due to punishment or a well-founded threat of punishment imposed by the military junta for exclusively political reasons. It grants the reintegration of civil servants and public employees punished by the military regime for joining the strike in public services and in essential activities in the interest of national security for political reasons.[124] After 2005, many Brazilians who stood against the military regime in their

121 'Former Dictators Found Guilty in Argentine Baby-Stealing Trial' *CNN* (10 July 2010), https://edition.cnn.com/2012/07/05/world/americas/argentina-baby-theft-trial/index.html#:~:text=Reynaldo%20Benito%20Bignone%2C%20who%20ruled,and%20giving%20them%20new%20identities. See also Francesca Lessa, *Memory and Transitional Justice in Argentina and Uruguay: Against Impunity* (Palgrave Macmillan 2013) 49–129; Ezequiel Gonzále-Ocantos, *Shifting Legal Visions: Judicial Change and Human Rights Trials in Latin America* (CUP 2016) 71–140; Juan Grigera and Luciana Zorzoli (eds), *The Argentinian Dictatorship and its Legacy: Rethinking the Proceso* (Palgrave Macmillan 2020).

122 For a concise background information, see Eduardo Monteiro Burkle, *When Forgetting Is Dangerous: Transitional Justice, Collective Remembrance and Brazil's Shift to Far-Right Populism*, European Master's Degree in Human Rights and Democratization thesis (Global Campus of Human Rights 2020) 4–12.

123 Law No 6.683 of 28 August 1979.

124 Law No 10.559 of 13 November 2002.

youth and later pursued political careers became Brazilian leaders in the Executive and Legislature and launched projects to further rectify the past wrongs committed by the junta. In this process, the State took responsibility for the crimes committed by the armed forces, offered moral and financial compensation to victims and sought to establish a new understanding of the dark days of dictatorship. Yet, the projects, making up Brazil's large but uncoordinated reparations programme, have so far excluded the criminal prosecution of perpetrators, focusing instead on financial and moral reparations alongside truth initiatives. Beyond compensation to individual victims, their activities include documentation-gathering projects, the publication of history books, the construction of new memorial sites and a national truth commission.[125]

In April 2010, the Brazilian Supreme Court, in a 7 to 2 decision, upheld the impugned 1979 amnesty law on the grounds that it was enacted on a demand of civil society and had eased the transition from past authoritarianism to democracy. In its view, even if the amnesty violated the Constitution, it could only be annulled through legislation. The Supreme Court also reasoned that the international norm prohibiting amnesties for crimes against humanity merely emerged after 1979, and, as such, could not be applied retroactively to the amnesty law.[126] Nonetheless, in November 2010 the IACtHR ruled in *Gomes Lund et al. v Brazil*[127] that Brazil's amnesty law was not compatible with the 1969 American Convention on Human Rights legally binding on Brazil, lacked legal effect and could not continue as obstacles for the investigation of the facts of the case at bar, neither for the identification and punishment of those responsible, nor could they have equal or similar impact regarding other serious violations of human rights enshrined in the American Convention which occurred in Brazil.

The IACtHR in *Gomes Lund et al.* considers the obligation to investigate, and where applicable, punish the serious violations of human rights to have been affirmed by all of the international systems for the protection of human rights, as interpreted by the previous judgments and decisions of the IACtHR itself as well as the Inter-American Commission on Human Rights, the various human rights treaty monitoring bodies, the United Nations system, the European system and the African system.[128] When a State is party to an international treaty such as the American Convention, all of its organs, *including its judges*, are also subject to

125 Gisele Iecker de Almeida, 'Undoing Brazil's Dictatorial Past' in Natasha Mueller-Hirth and Sandra Rios Oyola (eds), *Time and Temporality in Transitional and Post-Conflict Societies* (Routledge 2018) ch 9; Janaína de Almeida Teles, 'Democratic Transition and Reconciliation: Human Rights and the Legacy of the Brazilian Dictatorship' in Nina Schneider (ed.), *The Brazilian Truth Commission: Local, National and Global Perspectives* (Berghahn Book 2019) 86–109.

126 *Ordem dos Advogados do Brasil por meio de Arguição de Descumprimento de Preceito Fundamental*, Federal Supreme Court, Case no 153/2008 (29 April 2010) para 5, cited in Roht-Arriaza, 'After Amnesties Are Gone' 354. For a background of the amnesty law, see Monteiro Burkle, *When Forgetting Is Dangerous* 12–16, 48–52.

127 *Gomes Lund et al.* paras 134–80, 325.

128 Ibid paras 141–62, and the authorities cited therein.

it—they are to ensure the legal effects of the American Convention's provisions are not reduced by the application of norms contrary to the Convention's object and purpose. The Judiciary, in this sense, is internationally required to analyze the compatibility of national acts or omissions in light of international standards (i.e., to exercise 'control of conventionality' *ex officio* between the domestic norms and the American Convention). In this task, the domestic Judiciary must take into account not only the American Convention, but also the interpretation that the IACtHR, as the final interpreter of the American Convention, has given it.[129] In the case at bar, the control of conventionality was not exercised by Brazil's competent authorities, but rather, the decision of the Brazilian Federal Supreme Court confirmed the validity of the interpretation of the amnesty law without considering Brazil's international obligations deriving from international law, particularly those established in the relevant provisions of the American Convention.[130] The IACtHR recalls, once again, a basic principle of international law, backed by international and national jurisprudence, according to which every State must comply with its treaty obligations in good faith (*pacta sunt servanda*) and a State may not invoke the provisions of its internal law as justification for its failure to fulfil obligations under a treaty to which it has voluntarily become a party. Hence, treaty obligations bind all the powers and organs of the State Party, which must guarantee compliance with such obligations and their effects (*effet utile*) within that State's domestic law.[131] The IACtHR refers to examples of Argentina, Chile, Colombia, Peru and Uruguay whose laws granting self-amnesties to dictators and their accomplices or collaborators were subsequently amended, taking into account in good faith the international obligations binding upon each of these countries.[132]

As of this writing, Brazil has failed to comply with the judgments of the IACtHR and most of its recommendations in this matter, except for the setting up of a national truth commission. However, the Brazilian National Truth Commission itself is criticized for its limitations caused by the long passage of time and the long-standing amnesty guaranteed by the amnesty, although its archival project to collect and preserve information arguably provides the best avenue through which to acknowledge serious human rights violations and their victims in a meaningful way.[133] According to one learned author, the Brazilian National Truth Commission has achieved three main goals: improving historical accountability, promoting

129 Ibid para 176.
130 Ibid para 177.
131 Ibid.
132 See also André de Carvalho Ramos, 'Control of Conventionality and the Struggle to Achieve a Definitive Interpretation of Human Rights: The Brazilian Experience' (2016) 64 Revista IIDH 11.
133 Ann Schneider, 'Truth Commissions and Their Archives in El Salvador, Peru and Brazil' in Nina Schneider (ed.), *The Brazilian Truth Commission* 266, 277–9. See also Monteiro Burkle, *When Forgetting Is Dangerous* 42–8, 52–60, 66–71; Eric Wiebelhaus-Brahm and Dylan Wright, 'Temporal Patterns in Latin American Truth Commission Recommendation Formulation and Implementation' (2021) 21 Int'l Crim L Rev 990.

international human rights norms and challenging the veto power that the Brazilian military still wields.[134]

One possible reason why Brazil has not implemented the IACtHR's aforesaid rulings is that Dilma Rousseff, a victim of the Brazilian dictatorship who became President from 1 January 2011 to 31 August 2016, was awaiting the report of the Brazilian National Truth Commission on the ways and means for the nation to proceed further. When the report was finally issued on 10 December 2014, Roussel was already fighting for her political survival and prosecuting former junta members and their accomplices/collaborators would further undermine her political support.[135] Michel Temer took over the Presidency for the remainder of Rousseff's second four-year term, from 31 August 2016 until 31 December 2018, after Rousseff's impeachment and removal from office. As a lame duck President, Temer could not embark upon such politically controversial endeavours as repealing the 1979 amnesty law. With the pro-military Jair Bolsonaro, a retired military officer, as Brazil's President as of 1 January 2019, annulling the 1979 amnesty law in order to prosecute the junta members and their accomplices/collaborators was simply not politically feasible.

Indeed, political will at the highest level of leadership is a must for transitional justice to take hold, especially when, like in Brazil, the military still wields considerable power in the country in transition from decades of dictatorship. This has been the case with Nigeria. Since its independence from Britain in October 1960, Nigeria have experienced six *coups* (in January 1966, July 1966, July 1975, December 1983, August 1985 and November 1993) and two attempted *coups* (in February 1976 and April 1990). General Sani Abacha, the leader of the last *coup*, was Nigeria's President from 17 November 1993 until he died in a mysterious circumstance in June 1998, and was immediately succeeded as President by General Abdulsalami Abubakar up to 29 May 1999, when he handed over power to the newly elected civilian President Olusegun Obasanjo and retired from the Nigerian army. President Obasanjo set up the Human Rights Violations Investigation Commission to investigate gross human rights violations from 15 January 1966 to 28 May 1999. Due to budgetary constraints and the 90 days allocated for accomplishing the task, the Commission was forced to round off its work with only over 200 petitions heard out of the 10,000 petitions received. According to the Commission's report, the data and evidence it had gathered very indisputably showed the military was primarily responsible for the persistence of human rights violations in the country. It recommended institutional reforms as well as investigation and prosecution of 150 criminal cases. The Commission also condemned the last military government of Abubakar alongside several high-ranking military officers

134 Marcelo Torelly, 'Assessing a Late Truth Commission: Challenges and Achievements of the Brazilian National Truth Commission' (2018) 12 Int'l J Transitional Justice 194.

135 Gisele Iecker de Almeida, 'Dealing with the Authoritarian Past in Brazil: From Cardoso to Rousseff', book discussion organized by the Oxford Transitional Justice Research, Oxford University (1 November 2021).

for the systematic institutionalization of human rights violations in Nigeria. The Commission resolved a number of issues, for example, by forging reconciliation among the warring communities of Maroko Village in Lagos and by facilitating the resolution of the communal conflict between Ife and Modakeke communities in the state of Osun as well the conclusion of a peace accord among the warring factions in Ogoniland of Rivers state. Nevertheless, its recommendations for the prosecution of those who had violated human rights and committed crimes during the military regimes were not implemented, arguably because of opposition from the still powerful Nigerian military establishment.[136]

Sometimes, it is best for a toppled dictator not to return to face punishment in his country, at least for the time being. For example, in the case of the Philippines' Ferdinand E. Marcos, US President Ronald Reagan granted him and his close associates asylum in Hawaii thereby eliminating any chance of their extradition back to stand trial in the Philippines whose legal system does not allow trials *in absentia.*[137] Yet, it was President Corazon Aquino, Marcos' successor, who barred Marcos and his family members from returning to the Philippines. In its Judgment of 15 September 1989, the Philippine Supreme Court, by a vote of 8 to 7, found that President Aquino did not act arbitrarily or with grave abuse of discretion in determining that the return of former President Marcos and his family 'in the present time and under present circumstances' posed a threat to national interest and welfare and in prohibiting their return to the Philippines.[138] While President Aquino recognized the need to assert civilian supremacy and redefine the role of the military in society, the military still had powerful influence in Philippine society and politics and there were at least eight attempted *coups* during the years 1986–90, soon after Marcos' ouster, as well as one failed mutiny in October 1990.[139]

136 Emmanuel Zwanbin, 'The Challenge of Transitional Justice in Nigeria: Echoes from the Oputa Panel, 1999' (2017) 8 J Language, Technology & Entrepreneurship in Africa 73. Indonesia has a similar experience after the country's transition to full democracy in May 1998 following 32 years of authoritarian rule by President Soeharto. See International Center for Transitional Justice and Kontras, *Derailed: Transitional Justice in Indonesia Since the Fall of Soeharto* (2011); Patrick Burgess, 'De Facto Amnesty? The Example of Post-Soeharto Indonesia' in Lessa and Payne (eds), *Amnesty in the Age of Human Rights Accountability* 263–90; Sri Lestari Wahyuningroem, *Transitional Justice from State to Civil Society: Democratization in Indonesia* (Routledge 2021); Jiwon Suh, *The Politics of Post-Suharto Transitional Justice in Indonesia*, PhD thesis (Ohio State U 2012) 64–270.

137 Spencer Roush, 'Justice in the Philippines: A Checkered Past with Implications for the Future' (2019) 11 Pepperdine Policy Rev Article 7.

138 *Marcos v Manglapus*, G.R. No 88211 (S.C., 15 September 1989) (Phil). Marcos passed away in Hawaii less than two weeks later, on 28 September 1989. See also *Marcos et al. v Manglapus*, G.R. No 88211 (S.C., 27 October 1989) (Phil), where the Philippine Supreme Court denied a motion challenging President Aquino's decision, taken 'in the interest of the safety of those who [would] take the death of Mr Marcos in widely and passionately conflicting ways and for the tranquility of the State and the order of society, that the remains of Ferdinand E. Marcos [would] not be brought to our country until such time as the Government, be it under this administration or the succeeding one, shall otherwise decide'.

139 See also Robert Francis Garcia, *Disrupting Cycles of Discontent: Transitional Justice and Prevention in the Philippines* (Int'l Center for Transitional Justice 2021) 15–16.

In effect, the Philippines cannot pursue criminal prosecution of usurpers, having to be content instead with forfeiture of the vast, and allegedly ill-gotten, fortunes of the ousted usurper, former President Ferdinand E. Marcos, for distribution to the victims.[140] For example, the court in *Republic v Sandiganbayan* declared Swiss deposits held in escrow as ill-gotten and forfeited the same in favour of the Republic of the Philippines.[141] In *Marcos, Jr v Republic,*[142] the court made a similar finding as to the assets, properties and funds of Arelma, S.A. (an entity created by the late Ferdinand E. Marcos to maintain an account and a portfolio in Merrill Lynch) and likewise forfeited the same in favour of the Republic of the Philippines. The court in *Marcos Estate v Republic*[143] upheld the finding that pieces of jewellery known as the 'Malacañang Collection' are also ill-gotten wealth and therefore forfeited in favour of the Republic of the Philippines. In tandem with the aforesaid, the Commission on Human Rights established by the 1987 Constitution of the Philippines is entrusted with the guarantee of non-recurrence of the repression during the Marcos regime's rule by martial law. In 2013 the Philippine Parliament enacted the Human Rights Reparation and Recognition Act,[144] pursuant to which the Philippine State acknowledges its legal and moral obligation for the gross human rights violations committed by the Marcos regime during martial law from 21 September 1972 to 25 February 1986 and one month before and after the period. The Act provides reparation to the victims and/or their families for the deaths, injuries, sufferings, deprivations and damage they suffered under the Marcos regime during which civil, political and economic rights were violated. The Act allocates 10 billion pesos plus accrued interests for the reparation and for the establishment of a memorial museum and library. The funds came from Marcos' Swiss deposits which were transferred to the Philippine Government by virtue of the 10 December 1997 Order of the Swiss Federal Supreme Court, adjudged by the Supreme Court of the Philippines as final and executory in *Republic v Sandiganbayan*. The Act also sets up the Human Rights Victims' Claims Board and the Human Rights Violations Victims' Memorial Commission. The former has evaluated and assessed more than 75,000 applications and has recognized 11,103 victims eligible for reparations, from among 2,326 killings and enforced disappearances, approximately 2,000 cases of torture, no fewer than 3,000 instances of arbitrary detention and more than 3,000 cases of involuntary exile.[145] A Wall of Remembrance has been set up in the Bantayog ng Mga Bayani (Monument of Heroes), where the names of 320 Filipinos who stood up against the Marcos dictatorship are etched. Nevertheless,

140 Ibid 47–9.

141 *Republic of the Philippines v Sandiganbayan, Ferdinand E. Marcos and Imelda Romualdez Marcos*, G.R. No 152154, 15 July 2003. Yet, in 2019, the Philippine corruption court dismissed three cases for the recovery of the allegedly ill-gotten wealth against Marcos, his widow and associates due to insufficient evidence.

142 G.R. No 189434, 25 April 2012.

143 G.R. No 213027, 18 January 2017.

144 Republic Act no 10368, in force 25 February 2013.

145 https://hrvvmemcom.gov.ph/hrvvmc_post/human-rights-victims-claims-board-hrvcb/.

the transitional justice in the Philippines post-Marcos lacks the elements of apologies by those accused of atrocities during the Marcos regime.[146] The Philippine Supreme Court even ruled in 2016 that there was no clear legal basis to justify a judicial check on the President's decision to allow the burial of Ferdinand E. Marcos in a cemetery reserved for heroes, which was Marcos' rightful place at the cemetery.[147]

Transitional justice in South Korea did not sacrifice other types of justice altogether although the democratic government was established with support from many politicians with military backgrounds. This was due mainly to the need for the government to consider the people's power that overthrew the old regime. The trials and convictions of those with leading roles in the *coup* served the purpose of stigmatizing their blatant unconstitutional usurpation of power, whereas the subsequent commutation of their sentences and pardons served to bridge the differences for the sake of national reconciliation between the political forces supporting the old regime and those opposed to undemocratic, authoritarian military rule. While former Presidents Chun Doo Wan and Roh Tae Woo together with other former military leaders were punished, a number of governmental officials or agents who tortured citizens, distorted substantial facts to convict citizens and even murdered citizens remain unpunishable. Although the Presidential Truth Commission on Suspicious Deaths, set up in 2001, recognized the crimes of the latter group of persons, they were not prosecuted because their crimes did not fall within the scope of the 1995 Special Act Concerning the May 18 Democratization Movement and the given period in the statute of limitations had expired. According to the Criminal Procedure Code, crimes such as murder are subject to statutory limitations of only 15 years.[148] The South Korean way of dealing with past usurpation of power means retroactive criminal sanction is limited to the core perpetrators who acted under the authoritarian regime, retroactive civil sanction is given broadly to the victims of the authoritarian rule and the contribution by past activists for democratization of Korea is officially recognized and counter-violence by them is leniently examined.[149]

Chun and Roh were released from prison in December 1997 after being pardoned by President Kim Young-sam. Both were deprived of their liberty only briefly, from the time of their arrest in late 1995 and conviction by the Seoul High

146 Ruby Rosselle Tugade, 'Beyond Legal Transformation: Assessing the Impact of Transitional Justice Mechanism in the Philippines' (2019) 93 Philippine LJ 77.

147 *Ocampo v Enriquez*, G.R. Nos 225973, 225984, 226097, 226116, 226117, 226120, & 226294 (S.C., 8 November 2016) (Phil) esp at 34–5. For criticisms of this judgment, see Dante Gatmaytan, 'Judicial Historical Revisionism in the Philippines: Judicial Review and the Rehabilitation of Ferdinand Marcos' (2020) 15 U Penn Asian L Rev 339. See also Garcia, *Disrupting Cycles of Discontent* 65–8.

148 Cho, 'Transitional justice in Korea' 585–6.

149 Ibid 586–611. See also Carranza Ko, *Truth, Justice, and Reparations in Peru, Uruguay, and South Korea* 199–264; Kuk Cho, 'Transitional Justice in Korea: Legally Coping with Past Wrongs after Democratization' in Hyunah Yang (ed.), *Law and Society in Korea* (Edward Elgar Publishing 2013) 189–224; Hun Joon Kim, 'Transitional Justice in South Korea' in Renée Jeffery and Hun Joon Kim (eds), *Transitional Justice in the Asia-Pacific* (CUP 2013) 229–58.

Court in August 1996 which was upheld by the Supreme Court in April 1997. Roh passed away on 26 October 2021 at the age of 88, and Chun died almost one month later, on 23 November 2021, aged 90. The leniency both received might be characteristic of the Korean society, which has been divided for generations into North and South Koreas, to bridge differences among the various political fractions. This impression is confirmed when, on 24 December 2021, the South Korean Government granted a special pardon to the former first female President of South Korea, Park Geun-hye, aged 69, who was sentenced by the Seoul Central District Court in 2018 to 24 years' imprisonment plus a fine of almost US$17 million for bribery and abuse of power, which sentence was eventually reduced by the Supreme Court in January 2021 to 20 years plus two additional years for violating election law. According to the South Korean Justice Ministry, the special pardon was granted due to Park's deteriorating health and, hopefully, in order to overcome unfortunate past history and promote national unity. Park's predecessor Lee Myung-bak, aged 80, who was serving a 17-year prison sentence over embezzlement and bribery convictions, was not pardoned, however. The special pardon decision came as many supporters and politicians of the main opposition conservative People Power Party had been calling for Park's pardon ahead of the March 2022 presidential election in which the People Power Party and the governing Democratic Party were in a tight race. Incidentally, the People Power Party's Presidential candidate Yoon Suk-yeol was Prosecutor-General who investigated the Park scandal which eventually brought down Park. This special pardon might also be seen as an election tactic by the Democratic Party to win votes from Park's supporters.[150] South Korea also seems confident in the strength of its current democracy to withstand the threat of any future *coup*. The South Korean approach to transitional justice and to pardons may therefore be considered by its critics as too lenient to represent a best practice to be emulated by other countries freshly emerging from years of repressive dictatorships and where future *coups* cannot be ruled out or where the incumbent governments emphasize eliminating corruption as a top priority. Indeed, a drafted law to grant amnesty to any person charged with offences committed during the political turmoil following the September 2006 *coup* in Thailand led to widespread nationwide demonstrations by those fearing the amnesty would allow a former Thai Prime Minister convicted *in absentia* of abuse of power for personal gains to return to Thailand a free man, thereby leading to one political crisis after another, culminating in the 22 May 2014 *coup*.

It should be borne in mind also that the 2003 UN Convention against Corruption[151] has 189 parties. The nine nation States which are not party to the 2003 Convention are Andorra, Barbados, Eritrea, Monaco, North Korea, St Kitts and Nevis, St Vincent and the Grenadines, San Marino and Syria. Articles 17 through

150 On 9 March 2022, Yoon was elected President for a single five-year term effective as of May 2022, beating his rival from the Democratic Party, Lee Jae-myung, by less than 1 per cent.

151 2349 UNTS 41, in force 14 December 2005.

20 of the Convention obligate its States Parties to criminalize acts of corruption by 'public officials'. Its Article 30(5) requires each State Party to take into account the gravity of the offences concerned when considering the eventuality of early release or parole of persons convicted of such offences. These offences are often committed by members of repressive regimes who think they are beyond the long arm of the law and some of them have been punished therefor after a regime change, as in the case of General Ershad, leader of the military *coup* to oust the then Bangladeshi President in March 1982 who stayed in power until forced to step down on 6 December 1990 by widespread student protests although he continued to be active in national politics thereafter. Ershad was found guilty of abuse of power leading to the corruption in the *Janata Tower* case[152] and was sentenced by the trial court in November 2000 to seven years in prison, which was subsequently reduced by the High Court Division in August 2004 to five years' imprisonment. Owing to his conviction, Ershad was not eligible to stand for election in the 2001 elections. Separately, in 1995 Bangladesh's Bureau of Anti-Corruption accused Ershad of misappropriating 330 million taka (approximately US$8.25 million) in buying 520 Japanese-made boats and ten water purification machines for relief operation in 1989. In December 2006, Bangladesh's High Court upheld Ershad's conviction by a lower court over the 1989 purchase, but reduced his sentence to two years from the original three-year term imposed by the lower court. In January 2017, after Ershad had already served out six years on a variety of several corruption charges, a Bangladeshi court freed him on bail pending his trial on other corruption charges. Ershad passed away in July 2019, aged 89.

To recapitulate, a country's national political climate is *not* a valid legal excuse for it not to undertake, as part of transitional justice, large-scale or high-profile prosecutions of violators of fundamental rights and freedoms. Where the country is bound by an international treaty, such as the American Convention on Human Rights or the ICCPR, it must proceed with the prosecution, or else it is in breach of its treaty obligations.

The oft-cited 'national reconciliation' excuse is susceptible of abuses, as in the case of Burkina Faso. On 11 October 2021, the trial of 14 men, including former President Blaise Compaoré, started in Burkina Faso for their roles in the assassination the country's revered revolutionary leader Thomas Sankara and 12 other persons in the military *coup* in October 1987 that brought Compaoré to the Presidency. On 6 April 2022, the military court sentenced Compaoré, his right-hand man and the leader of his hit squad to life imprisonment, whereas eight other defendants received sentences ranging from three to 20 years in prison and the three other defendants were acquitted. The trial had continued even after the military *coup* in Burkina Faso on 24 January 2022. However, in July 2022 the leader

152 The tower was a building in a business district of Dhaka, Bangladesh's capital city. Ershad was charged with abuse of power or collusion with a politician in allotting the land for the project and possessing unaccounted money.

of the January 2022 *coup* invited Compaoré to return from exile in neighbouring Côte d'Ivoire to participate in the junta's 'reconciliation summits' for several days with former Presidents of Burkina Faso in an effort to project social and political unity amidst widespread national discontent over spiralling armed attacks by terrorists armed groups linked to al-Qaeda and ISIL, which the junta cited as the main reason for its usurpation of power, with the military regime losing control of more than a third of the country's territory and, according to the UN High Commission for Refugees, more than 1.9 million people out of the 21.5 million population displaced from their home as of June 2022.[153] The *coup* leader's invitation of Compaoré back to the country with safe passage and impunity was a travesty of justice and did not serve any objectively justifiable transitional justice goal. In any event, the junta that came to power by the January 2022 *coup* was toppled by another military *coup* on 30 September 2022, allegedly due to the former's inability to effectively tackle the ongoing terrorist attacks.

As a matter of *realpolitik*, certain countries have not been able to bring usurpers and their ilk to account for the time being, but when an opportune moment arrives they must revisit this matter, bearing in mind also the inapplicability of statutes of limitations discussed earlier in this chapter. Since crimes of international concern are proscribed by peremptory norms (*jus cogens*) binding on all nation States, every one of them must prosecute the perpetrators of these crimes without fail; otherwise, the International Criminal Court, an ad hoc or hybrid court, or a foreign criminal court exercising universal jurisdiction may step in, as explained in Chapter 6.

A right balance

A right balance between criminal punishment and transitional justice must be maintained.

In March 2021, the five judges of the Gambian Supreme Court in *The State v Yankuba Touray* unanimously rules that the immunity provided by the 1997 Gambian Constitution to members of the junta under Yahya Jammeh who overthrew the Government in a military *coup* in July 1994 did not shield junta member Yankuba Touray, a former Local Government Minister, from prosecution for the murder of Finance Minister Ousman Koro Ceesay, who was found beaten to death in a partially burnt vehicle in July 1995. The military regime under Jammeh, who ruled The Gambia until January 2017, was implicated in the murder but it did nothing to solve the case until The Gambia's Truth, Reconciliation and Reparations Commission took up the case and paved the way for Touray's prosecution.

The Gambian Supreme Court's detailed reasoning in this case should serve as a benchmark for courts in other jurisdictions in balancing between meting out a full-scale punishment of unconstitutional usurpers of power and their accomplices/collaborators, on the one hand, and narrowing the scope of or even doing

153 https://reporting.unhcr.org/document/2735.

away with such punishment for the sake of transitional justice, on the other hand. The exemplary sophistry of this reasoning is largely attributable to the presiding Chief Justice, Hassan Bubacar Jallow, who has served as Prosecutor of the International Criminal Tribunal for Rwanda from 2013 to 2015 and, from 2012 to 2016, Prosecutor of the International Residual Mechanism for International Criminal Tribunals set up by the UN Security Council in 2010 to perform the remaining functions of the International Criminal Tribunal for the former Yugoslavia and that for Rwanda following the completion of these Tribunals' respective mandates. The Chief Justice, who was The Gambia's Minister of Justice and Attorney General from 1984 to 1994, is thus well versed in Gambian law, international criminal law, international human rights law and *realpolitik*.

The main point at issue in *Touray* is paragraph 13 of the Second Schedule to the 1997 Gambian Constitution, which reads:

> (1) No member of the Armed Forces Provisional Ruling Council [AFPRC], any person appointed Minister by the [AFPRC] or other appointees of the [AFPRC] shall be held liable or answerable before a court or authority or under this Constitution or any other law, either jointly or severally, for an act or omission in the performance of his or her official duties.
>
> (2) After the coming into force of this Constitution, it shall not be lawful for any court or tribunal to entertain any action or take any decision or make any order or grant any remedy or relief in any proceedings instituted against the Government of The Gambia or any person acting under the authority of the Government of the Gambia, or against any person or persons acting in concert or individually to assist or bring about the change in government which took place on [22] July 1994, in respect of any act or omission relating to, or consequent upon:
>
> (a) the overthrow of the government in power before the formation of the [AFPRC]; or
> (b) the suspension or abrogation of the Constitution of The Gambia 1970; or
> (c) the establishment of the [AFPRC]; or
> (d) the establishment of this Constitution.
>
> (3) For the avoidance of doubt, it is declared that no action taken or purported to have been taken in the exercise of the executive, legislative or judicial power by the [AFPRC] or a member thereof, or by any person appointed by the [AFPRC] in the name of the [AFPRC] except judges of the Supreme Court or the Court of Appeal, shall be questioned in any proceedings whatsoever and, accordingly, it shall not be lawful for any court or tribunal to make any order or grant any remedy or relief in respect of any such act.
>
> (4) The provisions of subparagraph 3 shall have effect notwithstanding that any such action as is referred to in that subparagraph was not taken in accordance with any procedure prescribed by law.

> (5) It shall not be lawful for any court or tribunal to entertain an action instituted in respect of an act or omission against a person acting or omitting to act on the instructions or authority of the [AFPRC], or a member thereof, and alleged to be in contravention of any law whether substantive or procedural, in existence before or during the administration of the [AFPRC].

The Gambian Supreme Court finds these provisions irrelevant to the facts and the circumstances of this case as the actions or omissions of the AFPRC are not in question nor is it alleged that the defendant's alleged conduct which is the subject of the charge was carried out on the AFPRC's instructions. Nor are the military overthrow of the Government in 1994, the abrogation of the 1970 Constitution and the promulgation of the 1997 Constitution relevant to this case. Paragraph 13(1) is *stricto sensu* what purports to grant immunity to members of the AFPRC, persons appointed as Ministers by the AFPRC or other appointees of the AFPRC from liability or being accountable before a court of law 'for an act or omission in the performance of his or her official duties'.

Apart from the issue of statutory interpretation, what makes this judgment a role model for domestic courts in other jurisdictions to emulate is the sound reasoning that cites various systems, sources of law and treaties to reach the final judgment.

The Gambian Supreme Court notes that, generally speaking, *international law* does not form part of the body of Gambian law whose sources are clearly enumerated under Section 7 of the Constitution. There is a distinction in the rules relating to application of international law within The Gambia's jurisdiction between, first, customary international law; second, treaties; and third, judicial decisions of international courts, tribunals and other institutions. Customary international law is part and parcel of the Common Law, insofar as it is not inconsistent therewith or with local statute law. Treaties, whether bilateral or multilateral, are generally not applicable in The Gambia unless their provisions have been domesticated by their legislative incorporation into the laws of The Gambia. Unincorporated treaties may not however be totally irrelevant to the domestic legal order. They may, particularly those relating to human rights, be referred to as aids to the interpretation of the local law, to fill in gaps and also clear ambiguities in such law. Unincorporated treaties may also create a legitimate expectation on the part of the beneficiaries or even pass into the realm of customary international law. In this connection, the Gambian Supreme Court recognizes the special place of the *1981 African (Banjul) Charter on Human and Peoples' Rights* within this body of *international human rights law*. Whilst unincorporated treaties cannot change the law of the land or have any effect on citizen's rights and duties in Common Law or statute law, they might have an indirect effect upon the construction of statutes or might give rise to a legitimate expectation by citizens that the government, in its acts affecting them, would observe the terms of the treaty.[154] Also, some international instruments on

154 Citing the Judicial Committee of the Privy Council in *Higgs and Anor v Minister National Security and others* (*Times*, 23 December 1999) and the Nigerian Supreme Court in *General Sanni Abacha and others v Chief Gani Fawehinimi* (S/C 45/1997, 28 April 2000).

human rights such as the Universal Declaration of Human Rights,[155] whilst initially not legally binding, have, by the universal recognition of States over an extended period passed into the realm of customary international law and thus become binding on States. This Universal Declaration is regarded by many as part of the body of the English Common Law which is applicable to The Gambia. In the view of the present author, this part of the Court's reasoning should serve as a useful guide to courts in other jurisdictions with a similar 'dualist' system treating international law and domestic law as separate from and independent of one another unless the former is incorporated, or 'domesticated', through the legislative process into the domestic legal system.

The Gambian Supreme Court then considers that the *Gambian Constitution* should be read as a whole and each provision given effect as far as possible. Against the immunity provisions of paragraph 13 of the Second Schedule should be read the provisions of the Constitution promoting respect for human rights, guaranteeing the observance of specific rights and requiring accountability for violations of rights.

Whilst a Preamble in any instrument or enactment is not an operative part of that instrument or enactment, it provides the context in which the operative part is to be interpreted and understood and applied. What stands out clearly from the Preamble to the Constitution is the national commitment to justice and to accountability which should guide all actions and be taken into account in interpreting the provisions of paragraph 13 of the Second Schedule. Chapter IV of the Constitution provides for the protection of fundamental rights and freedoms including civil rights, political rights as well as economic, social and cultural rights. Section 17(1) of the Constitution obliges all organs of the Executive and its agencies, the Legislature as well as all natural and legal persons to respect and uphold the rights guaranteed by the Constitution without any distinction. Section 37 of the Constitution vests original jurisdiction in the High Court to enforce the observance of the fundamental rights and freedoms and to provide relief and remedies in case of violations. The general provision of immunity under paragraph 13 must be made subject to the specific Constitutional commitments to accountability, to justice and to the enforcement of the human rights provisions and to providing relief, remedy and accountability for the violations. To do otherwise would be to give a free reign to impunity, rather than immunity, contrary to the national commitment to justice and accountability which is enshrined in the Constitution.

By their nature, provisions granting immunity—particularly of the general kind in paragraph 13(1), because they also affect the rights of others such as access to justice by victims and the accountability of perpetrators—must be narrowly construed as against the promotion of respect for human rights and accountability for crimes or violations of human rights. Provisions guaranteeing human rights and their enforcement should on the other hand be given a more generous and expansive interpretation and, where necessary, limit the extent of any general provisions of immunity in order to promote accountability and suppress impunity.

155 A/RES/217(III).

The Court rules that the defendant's general immunity under paragraph 13(1) cannot override the specific right to life of individuals and the constitutional duty of the State and others to enforce the observance of the right to life and accountability of perpetrators where it is unlawfully violated. If there is a hierarchy of rights, the right to life must rank as the primary and topmost right, together with those associated with it such as the protection from torture and inhuman or degrading treatment or punishment guaranteed by Section 21 of the Constitution and of the right to security guaranteed by Section 19(1) of the same.

The Constitution provides, in Section 18(4), defences in a trial for an otherwise unlawful deprivation of life. In the absence of such defences the State has a duty pursuant to Section 17(1) of the Constitution to 'uphold' the right to life in the form of prosecution to ensure the accountability of the alleged perpetrator. Others too have the right to ensure such accountability.

Furthermore, Section 34 of the Gambian Constitution authorizes the declaration of a state of emergency by the President, with the approval of the National Assembly, and pursuant to such declaration, the enactment of an Act and regulations thereunder which authorize the taking of reasonably justifiable measures for dealing with the grave situation (Section 35(1)). It is important and of relevance to this case that pursuant to Section 35(2) of the Constitution no derogation from the right to life and to freedom from torture is permitted by the Constitution, whereas all other rights can be abridged during a state of emergency.

In sum, the Court finds the broad provisions of paragraph 13(1) on immunity to be necessarily limited and qualified by the more specific provisions of the constitutional guarantees of fundamental rights and freedoms, their enforcement and the obligation of accountability of perpetrators of crimes, particularly of those rights which are non-derogable at any time. The African (Banjul) Charter obligates all State Parties to it, including The Gambia, to 'recognize the rights, duties and freedom enshrined in this Charter and [to] undertake to adopt legislative or other measures to give effect to them' (Article I). Such a duty of recognition clearly includes taking such measures as investigations and prosecutions. The Charter, like the Gambian Constitution, places emphasis on accountability, not immunity and impunity. Besides, Article 8 of the Universal Declaration of Human Rights provides: 'Everyone has the right to an effective remedy by the competent national tribunals for acts violating the fundamental rights granted him by the Constitution or law'. Like the Constitution of The Gambia, both instruments also permit no derogation from the right to life, the right to security and freedom from torture, cruel and inhuman treatment or punishment. The same may be said of the *1950 European Convention for the Protection of Human Rights and Fundamental Freedoms*[156] as well as the *1969 American Convention on Human Rights.*

The Court refers to the case of *Zimbabwe Human Rights Forum v Zimbabwe*[157] where the African Commission on Human and Peoples' Rights held that the

156 ETS 5, in force 3 September 1953.
157 Communication no 245 of 2002.

primary responsibility for the protection of human rights in a country lies with the Government of that country, and that the State cannot abdicate that duty. The nature and extent of this obligation was further elaborated by the African Committee on the Rights and Welfare of the Child in 2018, in its decision on the *Communication submitted by the Institute of Human Rights and Development in Africa and Finders Group Initiative on behalf of TCA (A minor) against the Government of the Republic of Cameroon*. The Committee declares that the obligation to protect requires States to protect rights holders against other subjects by legislation and provision of significant remedies, and that this obligation requires the States to prevent, investigate, and prosecute human rights violations and ensure the punishment of their perpetrators. According to the ECtHR in *Nachova and others v Bulgaria*,[158] States should be guided in this respect by, inter alia, the UN Principles on the Effective Prevention and Investigation of Extra-legal, Arbitrary and Summary Executions[159] which require a thorough, prompt and impartial investigation of all suspected cases of extra-legal arbitrary and summary executions. The Gambian Supreme Court then refers to the IACtHR's judgment in *Barrios Altos v Peru* that Peru's amnesty laws violated the constitutional guarantees as well as the provisions of the American Convention on Human Rights.

The Gambian Supreme Court adds that The Gambia, as a State Party to the 1968 Convention on the Non-Applicability of Statutory Limitations to War Crimes and Crimes Against Humanity, is bound not to apply statutory limitations to war crimes and crimes against humanity, irrespective of the date of their commission.

In conclusion, the Gambian Supreme Court finds and holds that on a true construction of paragraph 13 of the Second Schedule to the Gambian Constitution and other provisions of the said Constitution and having regard to the persuasive international law and jurisprudence on the subject, the immunity stipulated in that paragraph 13 does not extend to violations of non-derogable rights such as the right to life or to security and freedom from torture, cruel or other inhuman or degrading treatment or punishment which are guaranteed by the Gambian Constitution.

A question may be asked whether this landmark reasoning can also be applied to violations of derogable rights, as opposed to non-derogable ones. One research on amnesties concludes, among other things, that during the transition from dictatorship to democracy judges need to adopt a flexible approach in assessing measures taken by States to balance their obligation to prevent further violations by bringing a conflict to an end, on the one hand, with their obligations to victims of past violations, on the other hand, and that limiting the effects of amnesty is likely to require a multi-pronged and nuanced approach addressing the full range of obstacles to accountability in transitional societies.[160] Although there may be some leeway, in light of prevailing circumstances, as regards violation of derogable human rights,

158 App nos 43577/98 and 43579/98, Judgment of 6 July 2005 [GC].
159 E/CN.4/RES/1991/71 (6 March 1991).
160 Mallinder, 'The End of Amnesty or Regional Overreach?' 677–80.

judges, when performing the judicial balancing act, must always bear in mind that violation of derogable rights may eventually culminate in violation of non-derogable ones, and that non-punishment of such violation may be misinterpreted as condoning the policy or culture of impunity for human rights abuses however serious they are.[161]

In any event, such flexibility and judicial balancing act must not shield from prosecution perpetrators of crimes of international concern which are proscribed by peremptory norms of international law (*jus cogens*) such as genocide, crimes against humanity, war crimes and torture or, as the Gambian Supreme Court has held in *Touray*, violators of non-derogable human rights.

The UN Security Council Resolution 1325 of 31 October 2000

> [e]mphasizes the responsibility of all States to put an end to impunity and to prosecute those responsible for genocide, crimes against humanity and war crimes including those relating to sexual and other violence against women and girls, and in this regard stresses the need to exclude these crimes, where feasible from amnesty provisions.[162]

The word 'where feasible' was inserted because amnesty clauses were usually included in peace agreements as an incentive for parties to come to the negotiating table and cease hostilities as part of transitional justice. Peace agreements with amnesty provisions are difficult to reconcile with the goal of ending the culture of impunity, which has inspired the setting up of ad hoc international criminal tribunals, hybrid courts and the International Criminal Court. Even before the UN Security Council's adoption of Resolution 1325, in the Lomé Peace Agreement of 7 July 1999[163] to end the civil war in Sierra Leone that commenced in May 1991, the United Nations did not recognize the blanket amnesty negotiated because it contradicted the internationally recognized imperative to prosecute crimes of genocide, crimes against humanity, war crimes and other serious violations of international humanitarian law.[164]

Subsequent practice concerning peace agreements have rejected amnesties for crimes of international concern.

In November 2016, the Final Peace Agreement was concluded between the Colombian Government and the insurgent or 'rebel' group under the name 'the Revolutionary Armed Forces of Colombia' to terminate the internal armed conflict lasting more than half a century. The Agreement recognizes that, on termination of the hostilities, in accordance with international humanitarian law, the

161 United Nations, *Framework Analysis for Atrocity Crimes: A Tool for Prevention* (2014) 11.

162 S/RES/1325 (2000) para 11.

163 S/1999/777 (12 July 1999) Annex.

164 UN Development Fund for Women, *Security Council Resolution 1325 Annotated and Explained* (2000) 11. See also Alexander Orakhelashvili, *Peremptory Norms in International Law* (OUP 2006) 223–38.

Colombian State will be able to grant 'the broadest possible' amnesty to rebels belonging to organizations that have signed a final peace agreement along with those accused or convicted of politically motivated crimes (Item 23). In this connection, the Colombian Constitution allows amnesties or pardons to be granted for the crime of rebellion and other politically motivated crimes (Item 24). Nonetheless, some crimes will be ineligible for an amnesty or a pardon, in accordance with Items 40 and 41 of this document, and neither crimes against humanity nor other crimes set out in the Rome Statute of the ICC are eligible for an amnesty (Item 25). Item 39 elaborates the two criteria for determining acts related to a political crime, one inclusive and the other restrictive by nature. The first criterion consists of including as politically motivated crimes: those crimes specifically linked to the development of the crime of rebellion committed due to the armed conflict, such as apprehending combatants during military operations; crimes in which the passive subject of the action is the State and its current constitutional system; and conduct aimed at facilitating, supporting, financing or concealing the development of the rebellion, for which the content of each of the previous types of action will need to be defined. Any crimes which have not resulted in the personal enrichment of the rebels and are not deemed to be crimes against humanity, serious war crimes or genocide shall be regarded as conduct intended to finance the rebellion. The Judicial Panel for Amnesty and Pardon shall determine the connection with political crime on a case-by-case basis. The second criterion, of a restrictive nature, excludes international crimes, in accordance with the provisions of Items 40 and 41, as established in international law in accordance with the Rome Statute. According to Item 40, crimes against humanity, genocide, serious war crimes (i.e., any violation of international humanitarian law committed as part of a systematic attack), hostage taking or other serious deprivations of freedom, torture, extrajudicial executions, forced disappearances, rape and other forms of sexual violence, child abduction, forced displacement and the recruitment of minors will all be ineligible for an amnesty or pardon, in every case as established in the Rome Statute. The Amnesty Law will specify the scope and reach of these acts in accordance with the provisions of the Rome Statute, international human rights law and international humanitarian law. Item 41 adds that common crimes unrelated to the rebellion shall also be ineligible for an amnesty or pardon.[165]

Pursuant to the Revitalized Agreement on the Resolution of the Conflict in the Republic of South Sudan,[166] dated 12 September 2018, the African Union Commission of Inquiry on South Sudan establishes the Hybrid Court for South Sudan (HCSS) to investigate and where necessary prosecute individuals bearing responsibility for violations of international law and/or applicable South Sudanese law, committed from 15 December 2013 through the end of the Transitional

165 Final Agreement to End the Armed Conflict and Build Stable and Lasting Peace, dated 24 November 2016, Doc S/2017/272 (21 April 1017) Annex II. See also César Rojas-Orozco, *International Law and Transition to Peace in Colombia: Assessing Jus Post Bellum in Practice* (Brill 2021) ch 2.

166 https://docs.pca-cpa.org/2016/02/South-Sudan-Peace-Agreement-September-2018.pdf.

Period. The HCSS is independent of and distinct from the national Judiciary in its operations, and shall carry out its own investigations. It shall have primacy over national courts of South Sudan and shall have jurisdiction over genocide, crimes against humanity, war crimes and other serious crimes under international law and relevant South Sudanese laws, including gender-based crimes and sexual violence.

Concluding remarks

In every society, not all criminals are brought to face justice. Many *coup* leaders, their accomplices and collaborators have found safe haven outside their respective countries.[167] Some *coup* leaders are never prosecuted because the power is transferred to those loyal to them although the latter subsequently stay in office via democratic elections.[168] Justice sometimes comes too late, with the usurpers having died before being punished.[169]

There is a sliding scale of criminal responsibility in the case of *coups*. There are a few instances where *coups* were staged apparently to end national crises, with the usurpers stepping back in due course and ceding power to civilian governments after general elections, as mentioned in Chapter 1 and as in the case of the February 2010 military *coup* in Niger referred to earlier in this chapter. If a usurper and his regime do not violate fundamental rights and freedoms or commit crimes apart from the crime of high treason or unlawful rebellion for their unconstitutional usurpation of power, a blanket amnesty, pardon, immunity or statute of limitations during the transitional justice phase may be more objectively justifiable and generally acceptable to the populace. However, the more serious violations of fundamental rights and freedoms the usurper and his regime have committed, the more difficult it is to justify any amnesty, pardon, immunity or statute of limitations which would, after a regime change, benefit the usurper and those working to sustain his repressive regime. As for perpetrators of crimes of international concern, they must be prosecuted and duly punished since there is simply no place for amnesties, pardons, immunities or statutes of limitations to shield them from criminal justice in post-*coup* societies. This happened, for example, in Greece after the right-wing military junta which came to power by the military *coup* on 21 April 1967 collapsed and was replaced by a civilian government on 23

167 As in the cases of, e.g., Mengistu Haile Mariam, who led the military *coup* in Ethiopia in February 1977, Joseph Mobutu Sese Seko who staged two *coups* in DR Congo in 1960 and 1965, Tunisia's Ben Ali, Paraguay's General Alfredo Stroessner who staged the *coup* in August 1954 and ruled Paraguay as a dictator for 34 years and 6 months, and Pakistan's Musharraf.

168 France-Albert René is one such example. He was installed by the junta as Seychelles' President after the June 1977 military *coup*. René remained in that post until July 2004, when he stepped down in favour of his Vice President and long-time loyalist, James Michel. Michel was President until October 2016 when he himself stepped down in favour of Vice President Danny Faure, less than a year into Michel's third term of Presidency. René passed away in February 2019, when Faure, Michel's protégé, was still President.

169 As in the cases of Türkiye's General Kenan Evren and Air Force General Tahsin Sahinkaya.

July 1974. Colonel Georgios Papadopoulos, who led the 1967 *coup*, and 19 other co-conspirators of the military junta were arrested in January 1975 on charges of high treason and insurrection. Papadopoulos and three of his leading henchmen were sentenced to death for high treason, which sentences were later commuted to life imprisonment for humanitarian reasons. In another trial, Papadopoulos and 19 others were convicted and sentenced to long-term imprisonment for their ruthless suppression of student demonstrators against the regime at the Athens Polytechnic in November 1973, leaving a large number of civilians dead or seriously injured. General Dimitrios Ioannides, who staged the *coup* to topple Papadopoulos on 25 November 1973, was given seven life sentences, the heaviest sentence of all those convicted in the Athens Polytechnic uprising case. There were also a series of separate trials involving torture by the regime.[170] In December 1990, due to universal condemnation by the overwhelming majority of the Greek people the Greek Government, citing the need to avoid 'political tension', backed down from its plan to pardon and release from prison Papadopoulos and the other former members of the military junta, except Ioannides, who were still remaining in prison.[171]

The laws of some countries specifically include members of the Judiciary among those benefiting from amnesties, pardons, immunities or statutes of limitations post-*coups*. The laws of other countries broadly refer to government officials who are protected against prosecution for their respective roles in repressive regimes, and judges are, of course, 'government officials'. This book should raise international awareness of the parts played by judges of domestic courts in such regimes, as well as seriously question whether they deserve protection from criminal prosecution, either in domestic courts of their own country after a regime change or abroad. Like anyone else working under a repressive regime, judges are subject to a sliding scale of criminal responsibility in this regard, as evident from the *Justice* case[172] discussed at length in Chapter 4. That is to say, some judges deserve heavier punishment than other judges, and in order to be fully exonerated judges must conscientiously discharge their judicial responsibility post-*coups* by exerting their utmost efforts to safeguard the fundamental rights and freedoms of citizens as well as to ensure abuses by the regimes do not go unpunished, bearing in mind also the international legal obligations binding on their country as well as best practices from other jurisdictions.[173] As the IACtHR in *Gomes Lund et al.* reminds us, judges

170 Amnesty International, *Torture in Greece: The First Torturers' Trial 1975* (Amnesty International Publications 1977).

171 Neil Kritz, *Transitional Justice: How Emerging Democracies Reckon with Former Regimes*, vol II (United States Institute of Peace 1995) 264–82. See also Evanthis Hatzivassiliou, 'The Ghost of Trials Past: Transitional Justice in Greece 1974–1975' (2022) 31 Contemporary European History 286.

172 *In re Josef Altstoetter and Others*, Military Tribunal III Case 3, Report of the Trials of War Criminals before the Nuremberg Military Tribunals under Control Council Law No 10, October 1946–April 1949, vol III.

173 See also Alexander Orakhelashvili, 'Between Impunity and Accountability for Serious International Crimes: Legal and Policy Approaches' (2008) 55 Netherlands Int'l L Rev 207.

of domestic courts are required to exercise 'control of conventionality' between the domestic norms and international obligations under international law binding on their country.

With respect to transitional justice as applied to domestic judges, one study, focusing specifically on Nigeria, demonstrates that the purview of transitional justice mechanisms should, as a matter of policy, be extended to scrutiny of public accountability of the Judiciary through the mechanism of a truth-seeking process as a necessary component in securing comprehensive accountability in a post-conflict society for the judicial role in the past.[174] This should be the case in every country which has experienced a *coup*.

An amnesty, pardon, immunity or statute of limitations under the domestic law or constitution of one country is completely inapplicable at trials before a competent international criminal court, a competent ad hoc or hybrid court, or a domestic court of another country that exercises universal jurisdiction over crimes of international concern, as will be explained in Chapter 6.

174 Hakeen Yusuf, *Transitional Justice, Judicial Accountability and the Rule of Law* (Routledge 2013).

6

INTERNATIONAL OR EXTRA-TERRITORIAL CRIMINAL PROSECUTION OF *COUPS*-RELATED CRIMES OF INTERNATIONAL CONCERN

This chapter examines the potential international and extraterritorial prosecution of unconstitutional usurpers of power, their accomplices and collaborators, which may include judges of domestic courts, for acts that are *coups*-related crimes of international concern. The prosecution may be before the International Criminal Court (ICC), an ad hoc international criminal tribunal, a hybrid criminal court or a criminal court of a foreign State that exercises universal jurisdiction.

Prosecution before the International Criminal Court, ad hoc international tribunals and hybrid courts

The ICC is the permanent court set up under 1998 the Rome Statute of the International Criminal Court[1] to try individuals accused of the most serious crimes of international concern. Besides the ICC, the international community has set up ad hoc international criminal tribunals such as the International Criminal Tribunal for the former Yugoslavia (ICTY) and that for Rwanda (ICTR) as well as special or 'hybrid' courts with foreign judges and chief prosecutors working side by side with national judges and prosecutors to render criminal justice in particular States, as in the case of, for example, the Special Court for Sierra Leone, the Extraordinary Chambers in the Courts of Cambodia (or the Khmer Rouge Tribunal), the Serious Crimes Panels in the District Court of Dili (East Timor), the extraordinary chambers operating under the auspices of the Dakar municipal courts in Senegal to try former Chadian dictator Hissène Habré, and, since 22 October 2018, the Special Criminal Court of the Central African Republic (CAR) which is cooperating closely with the ICC to bring to justice perpetrators of serious violations of

1 2187 UNTS 3, in force 1 July 2002.

DOI: 10.4324/9781003358428-6

TABLE 6.1 States that are parties to the Rome Statute of the ICC at the time of unconstitutional usurpation of power

Date of ratification/accession	*Date(s) of usurpation of power*
Burkina Faso: 16 Apr 2004	30 Oct 2014; 24 Jan 2022; 30 Sept 2022
Chad: 1 Jan 2007	Apr 2021
Central African Rep: 3 Oct 2001	15 Mar 2003; 24 Mar 2013
El Salvador: 3 Mar 2016	1 May 2021 (Legislative Assembly's removal of several judges of the Supreme Court and the Attorney-General who were opposed to the President of El Salvador was considered a *coup* by the President's opponents)
Fiji: 29 Nov 1999	19 May 2000; 5 Dec 2006
The Gambia: 28 Jun 2002	22 July 1994 (the *coup* leader in power until 19 Jan 2017)
Guinea: 14 July 2003	24 Dec 2008; 5 Sept 2021
Honduras: 1 July 2002	28 June 2009
Madagascar: 14 Mar 2008	17 Mar 2009
Mali: 16 Aug 2000	22 Mar 2012; 18 Aug 2020; 24 May 2021
Niger: 11 Apr 2002	18 Feb 2010
Tunisia: 24 June 2011	25 Jul 2021

international human rights law and international humanitarian law committed in CAR since 1 January 2003.[2]

Usurpers of power together with their accomplices and collaborators may be held accountable under the Rome Statute, which, as of this writing, has 123 parties. Table 6.1 lists the States Parties to the Rome Statute that have experienced *coups* since their ratification of or accession to the Statute.

Crimes proscribed by international criminal law

Crimes proscribed by international criminal law are codified in Articles 5 through 8 *bis* of the Rome Statute. By becoming party to the Rome Statute, a State accepts the ICC's jurisdiction with respect to the crimes listed in Article 5 thereof; namely, genocide, crimes against humanity, war crimes and, where applicable, the crime of aggression.

The crime of aggression is not relevant to our discussion. Aggression is defined by Article 8 *bis* (1) of the Rome Statute as the planning, preparation, initiation or execution, by a person in a position effectively to exercise control over or to direct the political or military action of a nation State, of the use of armed force against the sovereignty, territorial integrity or political independence of another nation

2 See also Juan-Pablo Pérez-Léon-Acevedo, 'UN-Backed Hybrid Criminal Tribunals (HCTs): Viable Options in International Criminal Justice?' (2022) 22 Int'l Crim L Rev 641.

State, or in any other manner inconsistent with the UN Charter which, by its character, gravity and scale, constitutes a manifest violation of the UN Charter.[3]

Pursuant to Article 6 of the Rome Statute, 'genocide' means any of the following acts committed with intent to destroy, in whole or in part, a national, ethnical, racial or religious group, as such: (a) killing members of the group; (b) causing serious bodily or mental harm to members of the group; (c) deliberately inflicting on the group conditions of life calculated to bring about its physical destruction in whole or in part; (d) imposing measures intended to prevent births within the group; or (e) forcibly transferring children of the group to another group.

Article 7(1) of the Rome Statute defines a 'crime against humanity' as any of the following acts when committed as part of a widespread *or* systematic attack directed against any civilian population, with knowledge of the attack: (a) murder; (b) extermination; (c) enslavement; (d) deportation or forcible transfer of population; (e) imprisonment or other severe deprivation of physical liberty in violation of fundamental rules of international law; (f) torture; (g) rape, sexual slavery, enforced prostitution, forced pregnancy, enforced sterilization or any other form of sexual violence of comparable gravity; (h) persecution against any identifiable group or collectivity on political, racial, national, ethnic, cultural, religious, gender or other grounds that are universally recognized as impermissible under international law, in connection with any act referred to in this paragraph or any crime within the ICC's jurisdiction; (i) enforced disappearance of persons; (j) the crime of apartheid; or (k) other inhumane acts of a similar character intentionally causing great suffering or serious injury to body or to mental or physical health. Article 7(2)(a) adds that, for the purpose of paragraph 1 of Article 7: 'attack directed against any civilian population' means a course of conduct involving the multiple commission of acts referred to in paragraph 1 against any civilian population, pursuant to or in furtherance of a State or organizational policy to commit such attack.

A war crime may be committed when the junta and those who oppose the junta are engaged in armed conflicts. By virtue of Article 8(1) of the Rome Statute, the ICC shall have jurisdiction in respect of war crimes in particular when committed as part of a plan or policy or as part of a large-scale commission of such crimes. Article 8(2)(c) enumerates as war crimes in an armed conflict not of an international character[4] serious violations of Article 3 common to the four Geneva Conventions of 12 August 1949;[5] namely, any of the following acts committed against

3 See further, Mark Klamberg (ed.), *Commentary on the Law of the International Criminal Court* (Torkel Opsahl Academic EPublisher 2017) 152–60; Meagan Wong, 'Aggression and State Responsibility at the International Criminal Court' (2021) 70 ICLQ 961; Carrie McDougall, *The Crime of Aggression under the Rome Statute of the International Criminal Court* (2nd edn, CUP 2021); Andrew Clapham, *War* (OUP 2021) 156–61, 444.

4 See also Rogier Bartels, 'The Classification of Armed Conflicts by International Criminal Courts and Tribunals' (2020) 20 Int'l Crim L Rev 595.

5 Convention for the Amelioration of the Condition of the Wounded and Sick in Armed Forces in the Field (75 UNTS 31); Convention for the Amelioration of the Condition of the Wounded, Sick and

persons taking no active part in the hostilities, including members of armed forces who have laid down their arms and those placed *hors de combat* by sickness, wounds, detention or any other cause: (i) violence to life and person, in particular murder of all kinds, mutilation, cruel treatment and torture; (ii) committing outrages upon personal dignity, in particular humiliating and degrading treatment; (iii) taking of hostages; or (iv) the passing of sentences and the carrying out of executions without previous judgment pronounced by a regularly constituted court, affording all judicial guarantees which are generally recognized as indispensable.[6] Article 8(2)(d) clarifies that Article 8(2)(c) applies to armed conflicts not of an international character and thus does not apply to situations of internal disturbances and tensions, such as riots, isolated and sporadic acts of violence or other acts of a similar nature.

Article 8(2)(e) additionally lists the following acts as war crimes in an internal armed conflict: (i) intentionally directing attacks against the civilian population as such or against individual civilians not taking direct part in hostilities; (ii) intentionally directing attacks against buildings, material, medical units and transport, and personnel using the distinctive emblems of the Geneva Conventions in conformity with international law; (iii) intentionally directing attacks against personnel, installations, material, units or vehicles involved in a humanitarian assistance or peacekeeping mission in accordance with the UN Charter, as long as they are entitled to the protection given to civilians or civilian objects under the international law of armed conflict; (iv) intentionally directing attacks against buildings dedicated to religion, education, art, science or charitable purposes, historic monuments, hospitals and places where the sick and wounded are collected, provided they are not military objectives; (v) pillaging a town or place, even when taken by assault; (vi) committing rape, sexual slavery, enforced prostitution, forced pregnancy, enforced sterilization and any other form of sexual violence of a gravity comparable to that of a serious violation of Article 3 common to the four Geneva Conventions of 1949; (vii) conscripting or enlisting children under the age of 15 years into armed forces or groups or using them to participate actively in hostilities; (viii) ordering the displacement of the civilian population for reasons related to the conflict, unless the security of the civilians involved or imperative military reasons so demand; (ix) killing or wounding treacherously a combatant adversary; (x) declaring that no quarter will be given; (xi) subjecting persons who are in the power of another party to the conflict to physical mutilation or to medical or scientific experiments of any kind which are neither justified by the medical, dental or hospital treatment of the person concerned nor carried out in his or her interest, and which cause death to or seriously endanger the health of such person or persons; and (xii) destroying or seizing the property of an adversary unless such destruction

---

Shipwrecked Members of Armed Forces at Sea (75 UNTS 85); Convention Relative to the Treatment of Prisoners of War (75 UNTS 135); and Convention Relative to the Protection of Civilian Persons in Time of War (75 UNTS 287). All of them entered into force on 21 October 1950.

6 See Knut Dörmann, *Elements of War Crimes under the Rome Statute of the International Criminal Court: Sources and Commentary* (CUP 2003) 382–438; David Elder, 'The Historical Background of Common Article 3 of the Geneva Convention of 1949' (1979) 11 Case Western Reserve JIL 37.

or seizure be imperatively demanded by the necessities of the conflict. Article 8(2)(f) clarifies that Article 8(2)(e) applies to armed conflicts not of an international character and thus does not apply to situations of internal disturbances and tensions, such as riots, isolated and sporadic acts of violence or other acts of a similar nature. Furthermore, Article 8(2)(e) applies to armed conflicts that take place in the territory of a State when there is protracted armed conflict between governmental authorities and organized armed groups or between such groups.[7]

Article 8(3) stipulates that nothing in paragraph 2(c) and (e) of Article 8 shall affect the responsibility of a Government to maintain or re-establish law and order in the State or to defend the unity and territorial integrity of the State, by all 'legitimate means'.

Trigger of jurisdiction

By virtue of Article 13 of the Rome Statute, the ICC's jurisdiction is triggered by: (a) referrals by its States Parties; (b) the UN Security Council acting under Chapter VII (Action with respect to threats to the peace, breaches of the peace and acts of aggression) of the UN Charter to refer a situation in which one or more of the crimes enumerated in Article 5 appears to have been committed;[8] or (c) the ICC Prosecutor initiating investigations on his or her own initiative on the basis of information on crimes within the ICC's jurisdiction.

In the case of Article 13(a) or (c), Article 12(2) of the Rome Statute stipulates that the ICC may exercise its jurisdiction *only if* one or more of the following States are parties to the Rome Statute *or* have accepted the ICC's jurisdiction in accordance with paragraph 3 of Article 12 on an ad hoc basis: (a) the State on the territory of which the conduct in question occurred or, if the crime was committed on board a vessel or aircraft, the State of registration of that vessel or aircraft; (b) the State of which the person accused of the crime is a national. Pursuant to Article 12(3), if the acceptance of a State which is not a party to this Statute is required, that State may, by declaration lodged with the ICC Registrar, accept the exercise of jurisdiction by the ICC with respect to the crime in question, in which case the accepting State shall cooperate with the ICC without any delay or exception.

As for ad hoc or hybrid courts/tribunals, their jurisdiction is triggered by the conditions stipulated in their respective statutes.

Complementarity

The ICC operates on the principle of 'complementarity', deferring to national criminal jurisdiction.

7 See Dörmann, *Elements of War Crimes under the Rome Statute of the International Criminal Court* 439–86.

8 See further Alexandre Skander Galand, *UN Security Council Referrals to the International Criminal Court: Legal Nature, Effects and Limits* (Brill 2018); Stefano Marinelli, *The International Criminal Court and the Responsibility to Protect* (Routledge 2022).

Pursuant to Article 17(1) of the Rome Statute, the ICC shall determine that a case is inadmissible where: (a) the case is being investigated or prosecuted by a State which has jurisdiction over it, unless the State is unwilling or unable genuinely to carry out the investigation or prosecution; (b) the case has been investigated by a State which has jurisdiction over it and the State has decided not to prosecute the person concerned, unless the decision resulted from the unwillingness or inability of the State genuinely to prosecute; (c) the person concerned has already been tried for conduct which is the subject of the complaint, and a trial by the ICC is not permitted under Article 20(3); or (d) the case is not of sufficient gravity to justify further action by the ICC. Article 20 (*Ne bis in idem*) provides in paragraph 3 that no person who has been tried by another court for conduct also proscribed under the Rome Statute shall be tried by the ICC with respect to the same conduct unless the proceedings in the other court: (a) were for the purpose of shielding the person concerned from criminal responsibility for crimes within the ICC's jurisdiction; or (b) otherwise were not conducted independently or impartially in accordance with the norms of due process recognized by international law and were conducted in a manner which, in the circumstances, was inconsistent with an intent to bring the person concerned to justice.

Article 17(2) of the Rome Statute stipulates that, in order to determine unwillingness in a particular case, the ICC must consider, having regard to the principles of due process recognized by international law, whether one or more of the following exist, as applicable: (a) the proceedings were or are being undertaken or the national decision was made for the purpose of shielding the person concerned from criminal responsibility for crimes within the ICC's jurisdiction; (b) there has been an unjustified delay in the proceedings which in the circumstances is inconsistent with an intent to bring the person concerned to justice; or (c) the proceedings were not or are not being conducted independently or impartially, and they were or are being conducted in a manner which, in the circumstances, is inconsistent with an intent to bring the person concerned to justice.

Article 17(3) of the Rome Statute adds that in order to determine inability in a particular case, the ICC is to consider whether, due to a total or substantial collapse or unavailability of its national judicial system, the State is unable to obtain the accused or the necessary evidence and testimony or otherwise unable to carry out its proceedings.

With respect to ad hoc and hybrid courts/tribunals, complementarity is not a precondition for the exercise of their jurisdiction since they are set up because the domestic courts in the States concerned have failed to discharge their function. For instance, Article 8 of the Statute of the Special Court for Sierra Leone[9] provides that although the Special Court and the national courts of Sierra Leone shall have concurrent jurisdiction, the Special Court shall have primacy over the national courts of Sierra Leone and, at any stage of the procedure, the Special Court may formally request a national court to defer to the competence of the Special Court.

9 S/RES/1315 (2000).

Modes of commission of international crimes

According to the law of complicity, he who participates in a crime or plays a consenting part therein is guilty of the crime.[10] The remit of 'complicity' is quite wide in its scope. For example, according to the ruling of France's Court of Cessation (Criminal Chamber) on 7 September 2021, one can be complicit in crimes against humanity even if one does not have the intention to participate in or approve of the crimes committed. In the case at bar, knowingly paying money to an organization whose sole purpose was exclusively criminal sufficed to constitute complicity in such crimes, so long as one had *precise knowledge of the actions of the organization, which were likely to constitute crimes against humanity*. Otherwise, numerous acts of complicity would go unpunished if courts adopted a more lenient interpretation.[11]

The unconstitutional usurper of power of government and those playing roles in the usurper's repression amounting to international crimes will be subject to punishment if they engage in any of the modes of participation in criminal acts or omissions stipulated in Rome Statute of the ICC, where it has jurisdiction, or the statute of an ad hoc or hybrid tribunal set up to try such persons.

In the case of the ICTY set up by the UN Security Council, Article 7(1) of its Statute[12] reads: 'A person who planned, instigated, ordered, committed or otherwise aided and abetted in the planning, preparation or execution of a crime [under the present Statute], shall be individually responsible for the crime'. This is copied verbatim in Article 6(1) of the Statute of the ICTR, another ad hoc tribunal set up by the UN Security Council.[13]

The ICTY Appeals Chamber has held that its Statute does not exclude those modes of participating in the commission of crimes which occur where several persons having a *common purpose* embark on a criminal activity that is then carried out either jointly or by some members of this plurality of persons. Whoever contributes to the commission of crimes by the group of persons or some members of the group, in execution of a *common criminal purpose*, may be held to be criminally liable, subject to certain conditions.[14] Acting in pursuance of 'a common purpose' or design to commit a crime is distinguished from aiding and abetting as follows.

(i) The aider and abettor is always an accessory to a crime perpetrated by another person, the principal.

10 *US v Ernst von Weizsaecker et al.*, Trials of War Criminals before the Nuremberg Military Tribunals under Control Council Law No 10, quoted in *Prosecutor v Tadic*, Case no IT-94-1-A, ICTY App Ch, Judgment of 15 July 1999 para 264.

11 *Life for Paris Association v Lafarge SA Society and Others*, Judgment No 886, Court of Cassation (Criminal Chamber) (7 September 2021). Charges were brought against cement giant Lafarge for complicity in crimes against humanity in Syria's civil war by paying nearly 13 million euros to armed groups, including the terrorist Islamic State group, to keep its cement factory in northern Syria running through the early years of the ongoing civil war. On 18 May 2022, the Paris Court of Appeal confirmed the indictments of Lafarge for complicity in crimes against humanity and endangering the lives of its employees in Syria.

12 S/RES/808 (1993).

13 S/RES/995 (1994) Annex.

14 *Tadic*, ICTY App Ch, Judgment of 15 July 199 para 190.

> (ii) In the case of aiding and abetting no proof is required of the existence of a common concerted plan, let alone of the pre-existence of such a plan. No plan or agreement is required: indeed, the principal may not even know about the accomplice's contribution.
>
> (iii) The aider and abettor carries out acts specifically directed to assist, encourage or lend moral support to the perpetration of a certain specific crime (murder, extermination, rape, torture, wanton destruction of civilian property, etc.), . . . By contrast, in the case of acting in pursuance of a common purpose or design, it is sufficient for the participant to perform acts that in some way are directed to the furthering of the common plan or purpose.
>
> (iv) In the case of aiding and abetting, the requisite mental element is knowledge that the acts performed by the aider and abettor assist the commission of a specific crime by the principal. By contrast, in the case of common purpose or design more is required (i.e. either intent to perpetrate the crime or intent to pursue the common criminal design plus foresight that those crimes outside the criminal common purpose were likely to be committed), as stated above.[15]

The ICTY Appeals Chamber has also developed the doctrine of 'joint criminal enterprise' to facilitate prosecution in the ICTY of crimes committed by a large number of groups of people in different geographical locations. When a plurality of persons acts in unison to put into effect a 'joint criminal enterprise', all the participants in a joint criminal enterprise are equally guilty of the committed crime irrespective of the part played by each in its commission. Specifically, the objective elements (*actus reus*) of this mode of participation in one of the crimes provided for in the ICTY Statute are as follows. First, there is a plurality of persons who need not be organized in a military, political or administrative structure. Second, there exists a common plan, design or purpose which amounts to or involves the commission of a crime provided for in the Statute. It is not necessary for this plan, design or purpose to have been previously arranged or formulated. The common plan or purpose may materialize extemporaneously and be inferred from the fact that a plurality of persons acts in unison to put into effect a joint criminal enterprise. Third, the accused's participation in the common design involves the perpetration of one of the crimes provided for in the Statute and this participation need not involve commission of a specific crime under one of those provisions (e.g., murder, extermination, torture, rape), but may take the form of assistance in, or contribution to, the execution of the common plan or purpose.[16] The mental element (*mens rea*) differs according to the category of common design under consideration. The first category requires the intent to perpetrate a certain crime (this being the shared intent on the part of all co-perpetrators). With regard to the second category, personal knowledge of the *system* of ill treatment is required

15 Ibid para 229.
16 Ibid paras 195–203, 227.

(whether proved by express testimony or a matter of reasonable inference from the accused's position of authority), as well as the intent to further this common concerted system of ill treatment. As for the third category, what is required is the intention to participate in and further the criminal activity or the criminal purpose of a group and to contribute to the joint criminal enterprise or in any event to the commission of a crime by the group. In addition, in this third category, responsibility for a crime other than the one agreed upon in the common plan arises only if, under the circumstances of the case, (i) it was *foreseeable* that such a crime might be perpetrated by one or other members of the group and (ii) the accused *willingly took that risk*.[17] The ICTY considers a joint criminal enterprise, as a form of commission of a crime, has been established in customary international law since at least 1992.[18]

The ICTR and hybrid tribunals such as the Special Court for Sierra Leone, the Iraqi High Tribunal set up to try former President Saddam Hussein and his co-defendants under international and Iraqi law and the extraordinary chambers operating under the auspices of the Dakar municipal courts in Senegal to try Habré have followed the ICTY in applying the doctrine of joint criminal enterprise,[19] although the Khmer Rouge Tribunal has refused to apply the third category—the so-called extended form of joint criminal enterprise—on the ground that this did not reflect customary international law at the time of the Khmer Rouge members' commission of the crimes under the Khmer Rouge Tribunal's Statute.[20]

17 Ibid para 228. See also the summary of these three categories of joint criminal enterprise in ibid para 220. For criticisms of this doctrine, see Jens Ohlin, 'Three Conceptual Problems with the Doctrine of Joint Criminal Enterprise' (2007) 5 J Int'l Crim Justice 69; id, 'Joint Intentions' in François Tanguay-Renaud and James Stribopoulos (eds), *Rethinking Criminal Law Theory: New Canadian Perspectives in the Philosophy of Domestic, Transnational, and International Criminal Law* (Hart 2012) ch 14.

18 *Prosecutor v Jadranko Prlić et al.*, ICTY App Ch, Judgment, 29 November 2017 para 587. See also Mark Osiel, *Making Sense of Mass Atrocity* (CUP 2009) 48–90; Darryl Robinson, *Justice in Extreme Cases: Criminal Law Theory Meets International Criminal Law* (CUP 2020) Annex 2.

19 Ian Ralby, 'Joint Criminal Enterprise Liability in the Iraqi High Tribunal' (2010) 28 Boston U ILJ 281, 310–26; Simon Meinsenberg, 'Joint Criminal Enterprise at the Special Court for Sierra Leone' in Charles Jalloh (ed.), *The Sierra Leone Special Court and Its Legacy: The Impact for Africa and International Criminal Law* (CUP 2014) 69–95; Michael Scharf, 'Joint Criminal Enterprise, the Nuremberg Precedent, and the Concept of "Grotian Moment"' in Tracy Isaacs and Richard Vernon (eds), *Accountability for Collective Wrongdoing* (CUP 2011) 119–39; Kerstin Bree Carlson, 'Joint Criminal Enterprise before the Chambres Africaines Extraordinaires' (2017) 2017 African J Int'l Crim Justice 7; Pedro Caeiro and Joana Costa, 'Joint Criminal Enterprise on the Decline: A Step Further in the Self-Becoming of International Criminal Law' (2019) 19 Int'l Crim L Rev 214; Gerhard Werle and Florian Jessberger, *Principles of International Criminal Law* (4th edn, OUP 2020) 241 (n 214); Victoria Bo Wang, 'A Creative Case for Abolishing the Doctrine of Extended Joint Criminal Enterprise' (2019) 83 J Crim Law 144; Elinor Fry and Elies van Sliedregt, 'Targeted Groups, Rape and *Dolus Eventualis*: Assessing the ECCC's Contributions to Substantive International Criminal Law' (2020) 18 J Int'l Crim Justice 701, 717–20.

20 *Prosecutor v Ieng Sary et al.* (Decision on the Appeals Against the Co-Investigative Judges Order on Joint Criminal Enterprise (JCE)), Extraordinary Chambers in the Courts of Cambodia, Pre-Trial Chamber, Case no 002/19-09-2007-ECCC/ OCIJ (PTC38), 20 May 2010 para 83. See also *Prosecutor v Noun Chea and Khieu Samphan*, Extraordinary Chambers in the Courts of Cambodia, Appeal Judgment, Case no 002/19-09-2007-ECCC/SC, 23 November 2016 para 773 ff. Cf. Muhsina Farhat Chowdhury, 'In Search of Joint Criminal Enterprise in the International Crimes (Tribunals)

The advantages of joint criminal enterprise are obvious since crimes under international criminal law are mostly of a systematic, large-scale and collective character. By contrast, domestic criminal law mainly deals with less complex crimes normally committed by individuals who can easily be linked to the crime.[21] Where the doctrine of joint criminal enterprise is applied by domestic courts it is not necessarily the same as the one applied by ad hoc or hybrid international courts.[22]

Although joint criminal enterprise and conspiracy are often seen as one and the same, they are in fact distinguishable, both in their elements and form as well as in their treatment in domestic law of several countries, such as the United States, and in international case law. Conspiratorial liability extends liability to individuals who entered into an agreement to commit a particular offence, in instances where the planned event was in fact executed by at least one of the co-conspirators.[23] No distinction is made in the case of conspiracy between direct perpetrators and indirect perpetrators, perpetrators and co-perpetrators or perpetrators and accomplices: all the participants are associated in the framework of a common plan and have jointly decided to commit the crime.[24] The prerequisite elements under domestic law

---

Act 1973' (2015) 3 Legal Issues J 1, contending that the doctrine of joint criminal enterprise should be applied by the International Crimes Tribunal, a domestic tribunal set up by Bangladesh under the International Crimes (Tribunals) Act, 1973 (Act no XIX of 1973) to prosecute heinous crimes committed during the 1971 Liberation War, including genocide, crimes against humanity, war crimes and other crimes under international law.

21 Kai Hamdorf, 'The Concept of a Joint Criminal Enterprise and Domestic Modes of Liability for Parties to a Crime' (2007) 5 J Int'l Crim Justice 208. On the allocation of criminal responsibility to individuals who are members of delinquent or criminal organizations under domestic criminal law, see Christopher Harding, *Criminal Enterprise: Individuals, Organisations and Criminal Responsibility* (Routledge 2007) chs 1 through 5 and ch 10.

22 See, e.g., the doctrine of joint criminal enterprise as applied by the UK Supreme Court in *R v Jogee* [2016] 2 WLR 681 and by the Privy Council on appeal from Jamaica in *R v Ruddock* [2016] 2 WLR 681. However, even among the Common Law countries, their respective courts do not approach joint criminal enterprise in the same way. On the application of extended joint criminal enterprise by Australian courts which is different from the UK Supreme Court in *Jogee*, see Timothy Smartt, 'The Doctrine of Extended Joint Criminal Enterprise: A "Wrong Turn" in Australian Common Law' (2018) 41 Melbourne U L Rev 1324. Domestic law of non–Common Law countries, such as Germany, divides all parties to a crime into two main groups: principals and accessories—the person who commits the criminal act himself (the direct perpetrator) or through another person (the indirect perpetrator) will be punished as a perpetrator/principal and if several parties commit the criminal act jointly on the basis of a common plan, each of the co-perpetrators contributing to the fulfilment of the plan will be punished as a perpetrator/principal (co-perpetrators) (Hamdorf, 'The Concept of a Joint Criminal Enterprise and Domestic Modes of Liability for Parties to a Crime' 210–18, 224–5). For a comparison between German law and US law in this matter, see Michael Heyman, 'Losing All Sense of Just Proportion: The Peculiar Law of Accomplice Liability' (2013) 87 St John's L Rev 129, 138–42.

23 Anna Sanders, 'New Frontiers in the ATS: Conspiracy and Joint Criminal Enterprise Liability after Sosa' (2010) 28 Berkeley JIL 619.

24 Report of the International Law Commission Special Rapporteur on the Draft Code of Crimes against the Peace and Security of Mankind, *Yearbook of International Law Commission*, ii (1990) pt II at 16.

for criminal conspiracy by more than one person differ from one legal system to another.[25]

As for the modes of commission of international crimes punished by the ICC, Article 25(3) of the Rome Statute[26] provides that a natural person who commits a crime within the ICC's jurisdiction shall be individually responsible and liable for punishment in accordance with this Statute if that person:

> (a) Commits such a crime, whether as an individual, jointly with another or through another person, regardless of whether that other person is criminally responsible;
>
> (b) Orders, solicits or induces the commission of such a crime which in fact occurs or is attempted;
>
> (c) For the purpose of facilitating the commission of such a crime, aids, abets or otherwise assists in its commission or its attempted commission, including providing the means for its commission;
>
> (d) In any other way contributes to the commission or attempted commission of such a crime by a group of persons acting with a common purpose. Such contribution shall be intentional and shall either:
>
> (i) Be made with the aim of furthering the criminal activity or criminal purpose of the group, where such activity or purpose involves the commission of a crime within the jurisdiction of the [ICC]; or
>
> (ii) Be made in the knowledge of the intention of the group to commit the crime;
>
> (e) In respect of the crime of genocide, directly and publicly incites others to commit genocide;
>
> (f) Attempts to commit such a crime by taking action that commences its execution by means of a substantial step, but the crime does not occur because of circumstances independent of the person's intentions. However, a person who abandons the effort to commit the crime or otherwise prevents the completion of the crime shall not be liable for punishment under this Statute for the attempt to commit that crime if that person completely and voluntarily gave up the criminal purpose.

For its part, the ICC does not consider it is legally bound to adopt the joint criminal enterprise doctrine applied by several ad hoc and hybrid tribunals. The ICC Appeals Chamber notes that Article 25(3) of the Rome Statute has a different

25 See, e.g., Mark Summers, 'Attribution of Criminal Liability: A Critical Comparison of the U.S. Doctrine of Conspiracy and the ICTY Doctrine of Joint Criminal Enterprise from an American Perspective' (2011) 18 Croatian Annual Crim L & Practice 171, 177–82.

26 See further Klamberg (ed.), *Commentary on the Law of the International Criminal Court* 261–73.

structure than the relevant provisions of the Statutes of the ICTY and other ad hoc international criminal tribunals. The terms 'commits [. . .] jointly with another' under Article 25(3)(a) of the Rome Statute is to be interpreted to the effect that in circumstances where a plurality of persons was involved in the commission of crimes under the Rome Statute, the question of whether an accused 'committed' a crime—and therefore not only contributed to the crime committed by someone else—requires a normative assessment of the role of the accused in the specific circumstances of the case. The most appropriate tool for conducting such an assessment is an evaluation of whether the accused had 'control over the crime', by virtue of his or her essential contribution to it and the resulting power to frustrate its commission.[27] The essential contribution can be made not only at the execution stage of the crime, but also, depending on the circumstances, at its planning or preparation stage, including when the common plan is conceived. At the core of this approach is the assumption that a co-perpetrator may compensate for his or her lack of contribution at the execution stage of the crime if, by virtue of his or her essential contribution, the person nevertheless had control over the crime. This approach applies objective criteria to determine whether a person is a perpetrator rather than an accessory and does not rely primarily on subjective criteria.[28] It has been argued that, compared to the doctrine of joint criminal enterprise, the 'control-over-the-crime' approach as applied to cases involving senior perpetrators of international crimes: (a) allows a clearer differentiation between principals and accessories to the crimes; and (b) in its manifestation as perpetration through another person using an organized structure of power, is more suitable to appropriately determine criminal liability of those most responsible in large criminal enterprises.[29]

The involvement by the ICC and hybrid courts in post-coup situations

Of the States listed in Table 6.1, the situations in CAR and Mali are currently under investigation by the ICC Prosecutor. They have been referred by these two States Parties to the Rome Statute.

CAR first referred its situation the ICC in December 2004 for alleged war crimes and crimes against humanity committed in the context of an armed conflict in CAR between the government and rebel forces since 1 July 2002, with the peak of violence in 2002 and 2003. This reference, known as CAR I, has produced one

27 *Prosecutor v Lubanga Dyilo*, ICC App Ch, Judgment, 1 December 2014 paras 472–3.

28 Ibid paras 445–7, 458, 463, 469, 472–3. Cf. *Prosecutor v Ntaganda*, ICC App Ch, Judgment, 30 March 2021 paras 879–80.

29 Juan-Pablo Pérez-Léon-Acevedo, 'Bringing the Bosses to International Criminal Trials: The Problems with Joint Criminal Enterprise and the "Control over the Crime" Approach as a Better Alternative' (2019) 32 Pace Int'l L Rev 1. Cf. Elies van Sliedregt, *Individual Responsibility in International Law* (OUP 2012) 83–8; Laura Ausserladscheider Jonas, *Individual Criminal Responsibility for the Financing of Entities involved in Core Crimes* (Brill 2022) 51–128.

main case, *Prosecutor v Jean-Pierre Bemba Gambo*. The defendant was President and Commander-in-chief of the Movement for the Liberation of Congo at the time of the arrest warrant issued on 10 June 2008. He was charged with two counts of crimes against humanity (murder and rape), and three counts of war crimes (murder, rape and pillaging), allegedly committed between 2002 and 2003 in CAR. On 8 June 2018, the ICC Appeals Chamber decided, by majority, to acquit him of these charges.[30]

In March 2013, the so-called Séléka rebels,[31] who were Muslims, deposed the then CAR President François Bozizé, who himself came to power in a *coup* in 2003, and engaged in widespread human rights abuses. After losing power in January 2014, the former Séléka coalition split into armed militia groups with various military capabilities, dispersed into the countryside and committed mass atrocities against Christians who account for 80 per cent of CAR's population. In response, Christian militia groups under the name 'anti-balaka'[32] were formed to fight back under the leadership of Patrice-Edouard Ngaïssona, Maxime Mokom and others such as Alfred Yekatom. In May 2014 CAR once again referred to the ICC the situation in the country (CAR II). The ICC's investigation in CAR II focuses on alleged war crimes and crimes against humanity committed in CAR since 1 August 2012 by both Muslim Séléka and Christian anti-balaka groups leading to thousands of deaths and leaving hundreds of thousands displaced, with the United Nations also issuing warnings of the high risk of genocide in CAR. In opening the investigation in September 2014, the Office of the ICC Prosecutor stated that the information available provided a reasonable basis to believe both groups had committed crimes against humanity and war crimes including murder, rape, forced displacement, persecution, pillaging, attacks against humanitarian missions and the use of children under 15 in combat. As of this writing, four accused CAR nationals are in the ICC's custody. Yekatom, arrested in CAR, and Ngaïssona, arrested in France, are being tried by the ICC for these offences. The trial by the ICC of Mahamat Said Abdel Kani, a Séléka commander, started in September 2022, whereas Maxime Mokom was surrendered to the ICC by Chadian authorities on 14 March 2022.

As for Mali, in July 2012 it referred to the ICC the alleged war crimes committed in Mali since January 2012, mainly in three northern regions, Gao, Kidal and Timbuktu, with certain incidents in Bamako and Sévaré, in the south. According to the Office of the ICC Prosecutor, the situation in Mali in 2012 was marked by two main events: first, the emergence of a rebellion in the north on or around 17 January 2012, which resulted in northern Mali being seized by armed groups; and, second, a *coup d'état* by a military junta on 22 March 2012, ousting President

30 *Prosecutor v Jean-Pierre Bemba Gambo*, ICC App Ch, Judgment, Case no ICC-01/05–01/08 A, 8 June 2018.

31 *Séléka* means 'coalition' or 'alliance' in Sango, one of CAR's two official languages.

32 The name 'anti-balaka' has two popular meanings: ability to resist a machete attack and ability to resist bullets.

Toure shortly before presidential elections could take place on 29 April 2012. The rebellion in the north involved deliberate damaging of shrines of Muslim saints in the city of Timbuktu, attacks on a military bases in Gao, Kidal and Timbuktu, alleged execution of between 70 and 153 detainees at Aguelhok, and incidents of looting and rape. Separately, incidents of torture and enforced disappearances were reported in the context of the military *coup*. The ICC Prosecutor has decided to open an investigation into the 'Situation in Mali' since January 2012. The ICC has convicted Ahmad Al Faqi Al Mahdi of being a co-perpetrator of the war crime consisting in intentionally directing attacks against religious and historic buildings in Timbuktu in June and July 2012. He was sentenced to nine years' imprisonment on 27 September 2016, which was subsequently reduced on 25 November 2021 by two years. He was also ordered to pay reparations in the amount of 2.7 million euros.[33] On 14 July 2020, Trial Chamber X of the ICC started its trial of Al Hassan Ag Abdoul Aziz Ag Mohamed Ag Mahmoud, a Malian national who was allegedly a member of a movement associated with Al Qaeda and the de facto chief of the Islamic Police. He was also alleged to have been involved in the work of the Islamic court in Timbuktu and to have participated in executing its decisions. Al Hassan was accused of the following crimes against humanity allegedly committed in Timbuktu between 1 April 2012 and 28 January 2013: torture, rape, sexual slavery, other inhumane acts, including, inter alia, forced marriages, persecution; and the following war crimes allegedly committed in Timbuktu during the same period: torture, cruel treatment, outrages upon personal dignity, passing of sentences without previous judgment pronounced by a regularly constituted court affording all judicial guarantees which are generally recognized as indispensable, intentionally directing attacks against buildings dedicated to religion and historic monuments, rape and sexual slavery.

With regard to Guinea, Captain Moussa Dadis Camara staged a military *coup* and became Guinea's President from 23 December 2008 until 15 January 2010 after being shot in the head in an assassination attempt on 3 December 2009, forced to leave Guinea for medical treatment in Morocco and prevented by the then acting President from returning to Guinea. He lived in exile in Burkina Faso. On 14 October 2009, the ICC Prosecutor announced that his Office would carry out the preliminary examinations of the situation in Guinea, focusing on alleged Rome Statute crimes committed in the context of the 28 September 2009 events at Conakry Stadium in the capital city. According to Human Rights Watch, several hundred members of Guinea's security forces burst into the stadium and opened fire on tens of thousands of opposition supporters peacefully gathered there, leaving no fewer than 150 Guineans dead or dying in and around the stadium complex. Dozens of women at the rally suffered particularly brutal forms of sexual violence at the hands of the security forces, including individual and gang rapes

33 Al Mahdi was an alleged member of Ansar Eddine, a movement associated with Al Qaeda in the Islamic Maghreb, head of the 'Hisbah' until September 2012, and associated with the work of the Islamic Court of Timbuktu.

and sexual assault with objects such as sticks, batons, rifle butts and bayonets. No fewer than four women and girls were murdered during or immediately after being raped. For several days, additional abuses—including murder, rape and pillage—were committed by members of the security forces who had deployed throughout the neighbourhoods where the majority of opposition supporters came from. Scores of other opposition supporters were arbitrarily detained in army and police camps where many were subjected to serious abuses including torture.[34] The ICC Prosecutor's preliminary examinations explored whether crimes under the Rome Statute including the crimes against humanity of murder, imprisonment or other severe deprivation of liberty, torture, rape and other forms of sexual violence, persecution and enforced disappearances might have been committed. The preliminary examinations also focused on the existence and genuineness of national proceedings in Guinea in relation to these crimes. The panel of Guinean judges investigating the 28 September 2009 incidents concluded their investigation on 9 November 2017. This domestic investigation, which commenced in February 2010, progressed slowly due to political, financial and logistical obstacles. On 28 September 2022, a trial commenced under Guinean law in which 11 accused including Captain Moussa Dadis Camara, who had voluntarily returned to Guinea from exile 'to clear his name', were charged for their alleged crimes at Conakry Stadium, with alleged killing or disappearance of between 156–200 people and the rape or infliction of sexual violence against 109 women. The ICC Prosecutor attended the opening of the trial, after which he signed a memorandum of understanding with the leader of Guinea's September 2021 *coup*. Pursuant to the Memorandum, Guinea, in close collaboration with the Office of the ICC Prosecutor, committed to, among other things, supporting this trial to ensure accountability of all those involved as well as provide, in collaboration with its international partners, support and assistance to victims and witnesses participating in the trial. Having regard to the principle of complementarity, the preliminary examinations by the Office of the ICC Prosecutor were closed but if the Office discerned any attempt to shield the accused or if Guinea's judicial process was not consistent with Rome Statute obligations, the preliminary examinations would be re-opened.

In the case of Myanmar, the Independent Investigative Mechanism for Myanmar (IIMM) has been set up by the UN Human Rights Council on 27 September 2018 to collect, consolidate, preserve and analyze evidence of the most serious international crimes and violations of international law committed in Myanmar since 2011, in order to facilitate and expedite fair and independent criminal proceedings, in accordance with international law standards, in national, regional or international courts or tribunals that have or may in the future have jurisdiction over these crimes, in accordance with international law.[35] By early November 2021, the

34 Human Rights Watch, *Bloody Monday: The September 28 Massacre and Rapes by Security Forces in Guinea* (17 December 2009), https://www.hrw.org/report/2009/12/17/bloody-monday/september-28-massacre-and-rapes-security-forces-guinea.

35 A/HRC/RES/39/2 (3 October 2018).

IIMM had received more than 200,000 communications since the military *coup* in Myanmar on 1 February 2021 and collected more than 1.5 million items of evidence that led to the IIMM's preliminary conclusion that the *coup* was followed by widespread and systematic attack by the military regime on the civilian population who opposed the *coup* to the extent it amounted to crimes against humanity. There were patterns of violence—a measured response by security forces to demonstrations in the first six weeks or so after the *coup* followed by an uptick in violence and much more violent methods used to suppress the demonstrators in different places at the same time, indicating a central policy behind them. Particular groups were also targeted especially for arrests and detentions without due process of law.[36] Myanmar is not party to the Rome Statute and the alleged crimes took place within Myanmar's territory and the persons suspected of perpetrating these crimes were Myanmar nationals. Therefore, unless Myanmar accepts the ICCs jurisdiction on an ad hoc basis, only by the UN Security Council referring the Myanmar situation to the ICC may the ICC exercise jurisdiction over the said crimes and persons involved.

The UN Security Council has referred to the ICC Prosecutor the situation in Darfur, Sudan, which is not party to the Rome Statute, after determining that 'the situation in Sudan continues to constitute a threat to international peace and security', and authorized the ICC to exercise its jurisdiction over crimes listed in the Rome Statute committed on the territory of Darfur or by Sudanese nationals from 1 July 2002, when the Rome Statute entered into force, onward.[37] President Omar al-Bashir who staged the *coup* to topple the Government of Sudan on 30 June 1989 and ruled Sudan with iron fists until toppled by the Sudanese armed forces on 11 April 2019 has been under an arrest warrant issued by the ICC for alleged war crimes, crimes against humanity and genocide in Darfur.[38] Ahmad Muhammad Harun, Sudan's Minister of Interior in 2007, has been under the ICC's arrest warrant for crimes against humanity and war crimes in Darfur. So has Abdel Raheem Muhammad Hussein, Minister of National Defence at the time of the ICC's arrest warrant in March 2012. In June 2020, after 13 years on the run and as a result of the regime change in Sudan that ousted al-Bashir, Ali Muhammad Ali Abd-Al-Rahman (a.k.a. Ali Kushayb), alleged leader of the Janjaweed militia fighting for the Sudanese

36 'Attacks on Civilians in Myanmar "Crimes against Humanity": UN' *Al Jazeera* (6 November 2021), https://www.aljazeera.com/news/2021/11/6/attacks-on-civilians-in-myanmar-crimes-against-humanity-un.

37 S/RES/1595 (31 March 2005).

38 The issue of personal immunity of the Head of the State not party to the Rome Statute who is subject to the ICC's arrest warrant has been extensively dealt with elsewhere by the present author (Kriangsak Kittichaisaree, *The Rohingya, Justice and International Law* (Routledge 2021) 197–204) and will not be analyzed here. With respect to the ICTY, it has dealt with this issue in *Prosecutor v Radovan Karadžić (Decision on Accused's Second Motion for Inspection and Disclosure: Immunity Issue)*, Case IT-95-5/18-PT, ICTY Trial Chamber, 17 December 2008 paras 17–18. So has the Special Court for Sierra Leone, in *Prosecutor v Charles Taylor* (Decision on Immunity from Jurisdiction), Case SCSL-2003-01-I, Special Court for Sierra Leone App Ch, 31 May 2004 paras 44–53. See also Charles Jalloh, *The Legal Legacy of the Special Court for Sierra Leone* (CUP 2020) 214–76.

Government in Darfur, surrendered himself to CAR authorities and was taken into the ICC's custody to stand trial for of 53 counts of crimes against humanity and war crimes in Darfur.[39] A lesson to be learned is that even though the usurper of power like al-Bashir and his henchmen may not be brought to stand trial before domestic courts of their country, the ICC can step in to punish them for their atrocities.

Besides the ICC, *coup* leaders, their accomplices and collaborators have been tried before hybrid criminal court/tribunals.

In March 1997, members of Sierra Leone's Army overthrew the Government of President Kabbah and installed a new government under the name the Armed Forces Revolutionary Council (AFRC), which ruled Sierra Leone from May 1997 to February 1998. Brima, Kamara and Kanu, who were high-ranking members of the AFRC, were convicted by Trial Chamber II of the Special Court for Sierra Leone of war crimes and crimes against humanity, in particular by ordering, committing planning or being responsible as superiors for the murders, beatings, mutilations, rapes, forced marriages, abductions, looting, collective punishments and recruitment of child soldiers perpetrated by the AFRC forces. Brima and Kanu were sentenced to 50 years' imprisonment, and Kamara to 45 years in prison. The Appeals Chamber upheld their convictions and sentences.[40] A fourth individual, Johnny Paul Koroma, who had been 'Chairman' of the AFRC was also indicted, but he was believed to have been killed before he could be arrested for surrender to the Special Court in March 2003.

A special hybrid tribunal was set up to try Hissène Habré who came to power as Chad's President by a *coup* in June 1982 until he himself was toppled by another *coup* on 1 December 1990. His one-party regime was condemned for its repression and widespread serious human rights abuses and atrocities. On 15 August 2008, a Chadian court sentenced Habré to death *in absentia* for war crimes and crimes against humanity. On 19 February 2009, Belgium filed an Application instituting proceedings in the International Court of Justice (ICJ) against Senegal relating to Habré who had been living in exile in Senegal since 1990. In particular, Belgium submitted that, by failing to prosecute Habré for certain acts he was alleged to have committed during his Presidency, including acts of torture and crimes against humanity, or to extradite him to Belgium, Senegal violated the obligation to prosecute or extradite[41] provided for in Article 7 of the Convention against Torture

39 Of those war lords in Darfur who were enemies of the Sudanese Government under al-Bashir, Abdallah Banda Mohammed Jerbo Jamus, chief of Staff of the Sudan Liberation Army, who stood trial before the ICC on charges of war crimes in Darfur, is now dead. Abdallah Abakaer Nourain, commander-in-chief of the Justice and Equality Movement Collective Leadership, is wanted by the ICC to stand trial for war crimes in Darfur. As for Saleh Bahr Idriss Abu Garda, leader of the United Resistance Front, a rebel group fighting the Sudanese Government in Darfur and a commander of the Justice and Equality Movement, in 2010 the ICC declined to confirm the charges against him due to insufficient evidence.

40 *Prosecutor v Brima, Kamara and Kanu*, Case SCSL-2004-16-A, Special Court for Sierra Leone, App Ch, Judgment (22 February 2008).

41 See further Kriangsak Kittichaisaree, *The Obligation to Extradite or Prosecute* (OUP 2018) passim.

and Other Cruel, Inhuman or Degrading Treatment or Punishment,[42] to which both Belgium and Senegal were parties, and in customary international law. The ICJ held that the obligations in Article 7(1) of the Convention required Senegal to take all measures necessary for its implementation as soon as possible, in particular once the first complaint had been filed against Habré in 2000. Having failed to do so, Senegal had breached and remained in breach of its aforesaid obligations and, consequently, Senegal had engaged its international responsibility. Therefore, Senegal was required to cease that continuing wrongful act and to take, without further delay, the necessary measures to submit the case to its competent authorities for the purpose of prosecution, if it did not extradite Habré.[43] On 22 August 2012, or 33 days after the ICJ's judgment in that case, Senegal and the African Union, which considered this matter 'an African affair', signed an agreement to set up 'Extraordinary African Chambers' within the Senegalese court system to try Habré. On 19 December 2012, the Senegalese National Assembly enacted the Extraordinary Chambers Statute setting up the Chambers composed of the trial chamber and the appeal chamber to try 'the persons most responsible for international crimes committed in Chad between 7 June 1982 and 1 December 1990'. Each Chamber is composed of two Senegalese judges and one non-Senegalese judge who presides over the proceedings. On 8 February 2013, the Chambers officially opened pre-trial investigations. Habré was arrested by the Senegalese authorities on 30 June 2013. His trial by the trial chamber commenced on 20 July 2015. On 30 May 2016, he was found guilty of rape, sexual slavery and ordering the killing of 40,000 people during his Presidency and was sentenced to life imprisonment. His life sentence was upheld on appeal on 27 April 2017. So were all his convictions against him except rape because of some procedural issue. He was also ordered to pay more than £100 million to 7,396 named victims in reparations, and a trust fund set up by the AU would search for his assets to this end.[44] Habré died on 24 August 2021 at the age of 79 after falling ill with COVID-19.

In tandem with the ICC, a Special Criminal Court has been set up in CAR in 2015 and become operation in 2018 as a domestic tribunal made up of national and international judges and prosecutors, with a mandate to investigate, prosecute and

42 1465 UNTS 85, in force 26 June 1987.

43 *Questions relating to the Obligation to Prosecute or Extradite (Belgium v Senegal)* [2012] ICJ Rep 422.

44 The African Union allocated US$5 million to the trust fund, which has not yet started to provide reparations as of this writing. In Chad, the Chadian Court of Appeal awarded approximately US$119 million in reparations to 7,000 victims, ordering the Chadian Government to pay half and the convicted agents of the Habré regime the other half. It ordered the Chadian Government to erect a monument 'in not more than a year' to honour those killed under Habré and to create a museum in the former police headquarters where detainees were tortured. The Government has not complied with any of these orders, however. The victims and their representatives filed a case in 2017 before the African Commission on Human and Peoples' Rights against Chad for failing to provide reparations to the victims. That case is still pending as of this writing. See also Sharon Weill, Kim Thuy Seelinger and Kerstin Bree Carlson (eds), *The President on Trial: Prosecuting Hissène Habré* (OUP 2020); Margaret deGuzman and Charles Jalloh, *The Habré Effect? How an African Trial Shaped Justice Norms* (CUP 2022).

judge serious human rights violations and grave breaches of international criminal and humanitarian law committed in CAR since 1 January 2003. This hybrid court, which is supported by the UN, has a mandate for five years (from October 2018), renewable only once, for a maximum of ten years. On 19 April 2022 the Court commenced its first trial, for war crimes and crimes against humanity committed in May 2019 allegedly by the three defendants, Issa Sallet Adoum, Ousman Yaouba and Tahir Mahamat, members of the Return, Reclamation, Rehabilitation rebel group which emerged in late 2015 to protect the minority Peuhl population in north-western CAR from attacks by anti-balaka militia.

In The Gambia, in late November 2021 after two years of hearings, the Truth, Reconciliation and Reparations Commission (TRRC) submitted a 14,000-page report with recommendations concerning human rights violations by the regime of President Yahya Jammeh, who came to power by a *coup* in July 1994 and stayed in power until he lost the 2016 presidential election and went to live in exile in Equatorial Guinea. Among other things, the report concludes that up to 250 persons were killed in State-sanctioned abuses, while the death squads' use of rape and torture as punishment was rampant. The TRRC has recommended that Jammeh face prosecution for murder, torture and rapes before a special international court to be set up to try Jammeh and others elsewhere in West Africa, outside The Gambia.

Although the Gambian Supreme Court in *The State v Yankuba Touray*[45] has ruled that the self-immunity granted under the 1997 Constitution of The Gambia to the members of Jammeh's junta is invalid, prosecuting Jammeh in Gambian courts would risk causing political stability in The Gambia where Jammeh still has many loyal supporter. Besides, The Gambia may not have adequate financial resources as well as a sufficient number of trained prosecutors and judges for this purpose. The personal safety of witnesses testifying against him at his trial in The Gambia is also a major concern. It would, therefore, be better to have Jammeh prosecuted elsewhere, as in the case of Chad's Habré. In this regard, the UN Working Group on Enforced Disappearances in its report presented to the UN Human Rights Council in 2021[46] supports prosecution of crimes committed during Jammeh's Presidency. It has also proposed that there be a new international inquiry into the massacre of West African migrants in July 2005 when more than 50 West African migrants bound for Europe were arrested by Gambian security forces on suspicion of involvement in a *coup* attempt against Jammeh after their boat landed in The Gambia. Evidence produced before the TRRC showed the migrants were arrested in a coastal settlement and transported to Banjul, The Gambia's capital city, where they were reportedly tortured at a naval base and transported to various police stations and safe houses outside of Banjul before being killed. The massacre victims included one Gambian, approximately 44 Ghanaians, nine Nigerians, two Togolese

45 Case No SC Co CR/001/2020, Supreme Court's Judgment, 19 March 2021.
46 A/HRC/48/57/Add.1 (16 September 2021).

and nationals of the Côte d'Ivoire and Senegal.[47] The Working Group's recommendation for the establishment of hybrid national/international courts with specialized judges to process the cases referred for prosecution to the Gambian Ministry of Justice by the TRRC may prompt the countries whose nationals were killed in the 2005 massacre to cooperate with The Gambia to set up such courts which will, in turn, put pressure on Equatorial Guinea where Jammeh has been living in exile to surrender him to the courts or at least stop providing him with a safe haven.

Prosecution in foreign courts exercising universal jurisdiction

Several States exercise 'universal jurisdiction' over a crime of international concern, or 'an international crime',[48] which has no connection (*nexus*) with these States at all. In other words, the crime is committed outside their respective territories, does not have any effect therein and neither the perpetrator nor the victim is a national of the State exercising universal jurisdiction.[49] Universal jurisdiction exercised by a foreign criminal court becomes a viable alternative when prosecution of the accused is not feasible in the State where the crime is committed because that State does not have adequate human and financial resources and/or the necessary political will to prosecute the accused.

The Princeton Principles on Universal Jurisdiction,[50] adopted in January 2001 by a group of eminent scholars and jurists,[51] posit, inter alia, that serious crimes

47 Mustapha Darboe, 'Gambia's ex-leader involved in migrants' killings' *Anadolu Agency* (26 February 2021), https://www.aa.com.tr/en/africa/-gambias-ex-leader-involved-in-migrants-killings-/2157854. See also Human Rights Watch, *Gambia: No Justice for 2005 Massacre of Migrants—International Inquiry Needed* (21 July 2020), https://www.hrw.org/news/2020/07/21/gambia-no-justice-2005-massacre-migrants.

48 Kevin Jon Heller, 'What Is an International Crime: (A Revisionist History)' (2017) 58 Harvard ILJ 353; Margaret deGuzman, *Shocking the Conscience of Humanity: Gravity and the Legitimacy of International Criminal Law* (OUP 2020) 1–60.

49 *Arrest Warrant of 11 April 2000 (DR Congo v Belgium)* [2002] ICJ Rep 3, 75 [42] (Joint Separate Opinion of Judges Higgins, Kooijmans and Buergenthal). See also Kittichaisaree, *The Obligation to Extradite or Prosecute* 204–18; id, *The Rohingya, Justice and International Law* 216–37; Alexander Orakhelashvili, *Peremptory Norms in International Law* (OUP 2006) 288–306; Aisling O'Sullivan, *Universal Jurisdiction in International Criminal Law: The Debate and the Battle for Hegemony* (Routledge 2017).

50 The 14 Principles are reproduced in Stephen Macedo (ed.), *Universal Jurisdiction: National Courts and the Prosecution of Serious Crimes under International Law* (U Pennsylvania Press 2006) 18–25.

51 Adrian Arena, Lloyd Axworthy, Gary Bass, M Cherif Bassiouni, William Butler, Hans Corell, Param Cumaraswamy, E.V.O. Dankwa, Richard Falk, Tom Farer, Cees Flinterman, Mingxuan Gao, Menno Kamminga, Michael Kirby, Bert Lockwood, Stephen Macedo, Stephen Marks, Michael O'Boyle, Diane Orentlicher, Stephen Oxman, Vesselin Popovski, Michael Posner, Yves Sandoz, Jerome Shestack, former President of the International Court of Justice Stephen Schwebel, Kuniji Shibahara, Anne-Marie Slaughter, Turgut Tarhanli and Wang Xiumei. Although Lord Nicholas Browne-Wilkinson of the UK House of Lords participated in the project, he did not join in the adoption of the Principles.

under international law which are subject to universal jurisdiction include: piracy, slavery, war crimes, crimes against peace, crimes against humanity, genocide and torture as well as 'other crimes under international law'.

England and Wales, for example, exercise universal jurisdiction over torture, grave breaches of the four Geneva Conventions of 1949[52] and other war crimes as defined by the Rome Statute of the ICC, genocide, crimes against humanity and enforced disappearance.[53] Belgium exercises universal jurisdiction over genocide, crimes against humanity, war crimes, enforced disappearance and torture.[54] With regard to the United States, genocide, torture and the recruitment or use of child soldiers are criminal offences under US federal law, regardless of where the acts were committed or the nationalities of the victims and perpetrators, as long as the alleged offender is present in the United States.[55]

Indeed, where a crime violates a norm of *jus cogens*, universal jurisdiction over the perpetrator may be acceptable by the international community of nations. A case in point is the *Zimbabwe Torture Docket Case* decided by the Constitutional Court of South Africa, holding that the South African Police Service (SAPS) has a duty to investigate crimes against humanity committed in Zimbabwe by Zimbabweans against Zimbabweans.[56] While South Africa is a State Party to both the Convention against Torture and the Rome Statute of the ICC, Zimbabwe is party to neither. It was alleged that six Cabinet Ministers and Directors General and the ruling party in Zimbabwe itself were implicated as suspects in the commission of these crimes. The Court explains:

> We have found that our applicable legislative scheme, understood in light of international customary law and other international obligations, places an obligation on our country through the SAPS to investigate crimes against humanity, including torture, committed outside our territory. However, the universal jurisdiction to investigate international crimes is not absolute. It is subject to at least two limitations. The first limitation arises from the principle

52 Wilful killing; torture or inhuman treatment, including biological experiments; wilfully causing great suffering or serious injury to body or health; extensive destruction and appropriation of property, not justified by military necessity and carried out unlawfully and wantonly; compelling a prisoner of war or a protected person to serve in the forces of the hostile Power; wilfully depriving a prisoner of war or a protected person of the rights of fair and regular trial; unlawful deportation or transfer or unlawful confinement; and taking of hostages.

53 Open Society Justice Initiative, TRIAL International and REDRESS, *Briefing Paper: Universal Jurisdiction Law and Practice in England and Wales* (May 2022) 4–8.

54 Open Society Justice Initiative and TRIAL International, *Universal Jurisdiction Law and Practice in Belgium* (May 2022) 4–9.

55 As for war crimes, US law requires that the defendant or victim be a US national or member of the US armed forces (Open Society Justice Initiative, TRIAL International, CJA and CIVITAS MAXIMA, *Briefing Paper: Universal Jurisdiction Law and Practice in the United States of America* (May 2022) 5–12).

56 *National Commissioner of the South African Police Service v. Southern African Human Rights Litigation Centre and Another* (CCT02/14) [2014] ZACC 30.

> of subsidiarity. It requires that ordinarily there must be a substantial and true connection between the subject-matter and the source of the jurisdiction. And once jurisdiction is properly founded, the principle of non-intervention in the affairs of another country must be observed; investigating international crimes committed abroad is permissible only if the country with jurisdiction is unwilling or unable to prosecute and only if the investigation is confined to the territory of the investigating State. Simply put, we may not investigate or prosecute international crimes in breach of considerations of complementarity and subsidiarity.[57]

The second limitation is that of practicality, whereby 'it must be considered whether embarking on an investigation into an international crime committed elsewhere is reasonable and practicable in the circumstances of each particular case . . . in light of all the relevant circumstances', particularly 'whether the investigation is likely to lead to a prosecution and accordingly whether the alleged perpetrators are likely to be present in South Africa on their own or through an extradition request . . .'.[58]

The inclusion of genocide as a crime over which States may exercise universal jurisdiction is interesting. The European Court of Human Rights (ECtHR) in *Jorgić v Germany* upheld the jurisdiction of German courts under German Criminal Code to try persons charged with genocide committed abroad, regardless of the defendant's and the victims' nationalities. The German domestic courts had therefore established jurisdiction in accordance with the clear wording of the pertinent provisions of the German Criminal Code. The ECtHR observed:

> In determining whether the domestic courts' interpretation of the applicable rules and provisions of public international law on jurisdiction was reasonable, the [ECtHR] is in particular required to examine their interpretation of Article VI of the Genocide Convention.[59] It observes that . . . the Contracting Parties to the Genocide Convention, despite proposals in earlier drafts to that effect, had not agreed to codify the principle of universal jurisdiction over genocide for the domestic courts of all Contracting States in that Article VI. However, pursuant to Article I of the Genocide Convention, the Contracting Parties were under an *erga omnes* obligation to prevent and punish genocide, the prohibition of which forms part of the *jus cogens*.

57 Ibid para 62.

58 Ibid paras 63–4 See also Mia Swart, 'Towards a Multi-Layered System of International Criminal Justice' in Evelyn Ankumah (ed.) *The International Criminal Court and Africa: One Decade On* (Intersentia 2016) 139, 150–2; Angela Mudukuti, 'Complementarity and Africa: Tackling International Crimes at the Domestic Level', ibid 489, 499.

59 78 UNTS 277, in force 12 January 1951. Art VI of the Genocide Convention stipulates that persons charged with genocide or any of the other acts enumerated in Article III of the Genocide Convention 'shall be tried by a competent tribunal of the State in the territory of which the act was committed, or by such international penal tribunal as may have jurisdiction with respect to those Contracting Parties which shall have accepted its jurisdiction'.

> In view of this, the [German] national courts' reasoning that the purpose of the Genocide Convention, as expressed notably in [Article I], did not exclude jurisdiction for the punishment of genocide by States whose laws establish extraterritoriality in this respect must be considered as reasonable (and indeed convincing). Having thus reached a reasonable and unequivocal interpretation of Article VI of the Genocide Convention in accordance with the aim of that Convention, there was no need, in interpreting the said Convention, to have recourse to the preparatory documents, which play only a subsidiary role in the interpretation of public international law (see Articles 31(1) and 32 of the Vienna Convention on the Law of Treaties of 23 May 1969).[60]

The ECtHR also noted that this interpretation of Article VI of the Genocide Convention in light of Article I of that Convention and the establishment of universal jurisdiction to try the applicant on charges of genocide was 'widely confirmed by the statutory provisions and case-law of numerous other Contracting States to the [1950 European Convention on Human Rights] and by the Statute and case law of the ICTY'.[61] Furthermore, Article 9(1) of the ICTY Statute was held to have confirmed the German courts' view, providing for concurrent jurisdiction for genocide of the ICTY and national courts, without any restriction to domestic courts of particular States.[62]

Several persons involved in violation of human rights after unconstitutional usurpation of power have been prosecuted under the principle of universal jurisdiction. For example, some members of Jammeh's regime in The Gambia have been arrested and prosecuted in Switzerland, the United States and Germany in addition to those prosecuted in The Gambia.[63]

Ousman Sonko, Jammeh's Minister of Interior from 2006 to 2016, was apprehended in Switzerland in January 2017 after TRIAL International, a human rights NGO, lodged a criminal complaint with the prosecution authorities in Bern where Sonko was applying for asylum following his dismissal from office in September 2016. He was accused of taking part in acts of torture, including in detention centres, while still in office. The charges against Sonko were subsequently reclassified as crimes against humanity. On 19 October 2017, the Swiss Federal Tribunal confirmed the seizure of Sonko's assets, worth approximately US$14,000, to be

60 *Jorgić v Germany*, App no 74613/01 para 68, ECHR 2007-III.

61 Ibid paras 53–4. The ECtHR cited the relevant law of the following States authorizing the exercise of universal jurisdiction over the crime of genocide: Spain, France, Belgium (at least until 2003), Finland, Italy, Latvia, Luxembourg, the Netherlands (since 2003), Russia, Slovakia, the Czech Republic, Hungary, Austria, Denmark, Estonia, Poland, Portugal, Romania, Sweden and Switzerland (since 2000).

62 Ibid para 69.

63 On 13 July 2022 a Gambian court convicted and sentenced former intelligence chief Yankuba Badji and four other members of the intelligence service to death for the killing of an important member of the opposition United Democratic Party during Jammeh's rule in April 2016.

used to cover the case's expenses in Switzerland. In tandem with the proceedings in Switzerland which is still pending as of this writing,[64] in January 2022 Sonko faced new charges formulated by The Gambia's Truth, Reconciliation and Reparations Commission for his involvement in the repression under the Jammeh regime. In particular, he was accused of having participated in the concealment of the massacre of 56 West African migrants in July 2005 by the 'Junglers' paramilitary death squad set up by Jammeh in the mid-1990s to serve and protect Jammeh as well as planning, in collaboration with Jammeh, the execution of several detainees in 2012 and committing multiple other acts of sexual violence, including numerous rapes from the 2000s.

In June 2020, Michael Sang Correa, an alleged former member of the Junglers death squad who went to the United States in December 2016, was indicted before the US District Court of Colorado on charges of, inter alia, committing, attempting to commit, aiding and abetting the torture of at least six people in 2006, following an attempted *coup* against Jammeh.[65] The crime is punishable under the United States' 1994 federal extraterritorial torture statute.[66]

On 16 March 2021, Bai Lowe, another alleged former member of the Junglers, was arrested in Germany on charges of crimes against humanity, murder and attempted murder in The Gambia. Bai Lowe who was living in Hanover, Germany, at the time of his arrest was accused of driving Junglers members to carry out three 'liquidation orders' between December 2003 and December 2006, targeting Jammeh's critics and those opposing the regime, and of participation in the murder of 59 West African migrants in 2005.[67]

With regard to atrocities committed in Afghanistan, on 16 February 2022 the criminal proceedings under the principle of universal jurisdiction commenced in the Hague District Court in the Netherlands against Abdul Razaq Arif, a 76-year-old man suspected of committing a number of war crimes in Afghanistan in the 1980s. From 1983 to 1990, the defendant was the commander and head of political affairs in the Pul-e-Charkhi prison, where putative opponents of the then ruling communist Afghan regime that had come to power by a bloody *coup* in December 1979 were imprisoned for years without fair trial and subjected to inhumane treatment, in appalling conditions. This prison in Kabul was Afghanistan's largest prison and was notorious for torture and mass executions after an earlier *coup* in April 1978 and throughout the 1980s. The defendant was arrested in 2019 in a Dutch city where he had been living after he had left Afghanistan in 2001 as a refugee and later acquired Dutch nationality. On 14 April 2022, he was convicted of serious violations of international humanitarian law, consisting of arbitrary deprivation of liberty, cruel and inhumane treatment and assault on the personal dignity of at least

64 TRIAL International, https://trialinternational.org/latest-post/ousman-sonko/.

65 www.justice.gov/opa/press-release/file/1284531/download.

66 18 USC §2340A.

67 Human Rights Watch, 'Gambia: Alleged "Death Squad" Member Arrested in Germany' (17 March 2021), www.hrw.org/news/2021/03/17/gambia-alleged-death-squad-member-arrested-germany.

18 persons in the period 1983–7 at the said prison. He was sentenced to 12 years' imprisonment.[68]

Bringing usurpers of power to justice can be a long, winding and time-consuming process. Such is the case of General Khaled Nezzar, who was Minister of Defence in Algeria and one of the military leaders who staged the *coup* on 11 January 1991. Considered to be the most influential person within the junta between 1991 and 1994, he is suspected of having authorized and incited the army and public officials to commit countless crimes within the context of the 'dirty war', which resulted in approximately 200,000 dead and 20,000 disappeared persons in Algeria.[69] In September 2005, the Charter for Peace and National Reconciliation was put forth by the Algerian Government for national referendum which approved it by 97.36 per cent of the voter turnout of almost 80 per cent. The Charter grants amnesty to the members of armed groups who turned themselves in to Algerian authorities before the end of August 2006, except those who were involved in offences such as mass killings, rape or attempts to set off explosives in public places. The Charter implicitly exonerates the security services for the 'disappearance' of thousands of Algerians during the dirty war, but it provides financial and other compensation to the families of the dead and disappeared.[70] In August 2019 while Nezzar was in Spain, the Algerian military justice issued an international arrest warrant against him following the investigation against Said Bouteflika, the brother of deposed Algerian President Abdelaziz Bouteflika. Said Bouteflika and Nezzar are accused of 'conspiracy against the State and breach of public order', punishable by death penalty under Algeria's Penal Code. On 25 September 2019, following a three-day trial, Said Bouteflika was sentenced to 15 years' imprisonment, while Nezzar and the other defendants were sentenced *in absentia* to 20 years' imprisonment. In December 2020, Nezzar returned to Algeria apparently after obtaining guarantees for a retrial and suspension of the international arrest warrant issued against him. On 2 January 2021, an Algerian military appeals court overturned the convictions and sentences of Said Bouteflika and two former Presidential security chiefs for plotting against the army and the State, but Said Bouteflika remained in custody awaiting a separate trial over alleged corruption during his brother's rule. As of this writing, Nezzar is being sought for prosecution in Swiss courts exercising universal jurisdiction over his alleged crimes in Algeria. After more than ten years of investigation, in early February 2022 the Swiss Public Ministry of Confederation conducted the final hearing in this case, opening the way for Nezzar's next

68 Case no 09/748011–12, Judgment of the Hague District Court, 14 April 2022, https://uitspraken.rechtspraak.nl/inziendocument?id=ECLI:NL:RBDHA:2022:3410.

69 For a narrative about the dirty war, see Aïcha Madi, 'Analysing Long-term Impacts of Counter-insurgency Tools in Civil Wars: A Case Study of Enforced Disappearances in Algeria' (2021) 31 Torture J 83.

70 Valerie Arnold, 'Amnesty, Peace and Reconciliation in Algeria' (2007) 7 Conflict, Security & Development 227; Jessica Mecellem, 'Misfortune or Injustice? The Political Work of Postconflict Narrative in Contemporary Algeria' (2018) 12 Int'l J Transitional Justice 237.

committal for trial before the Federal Criminal Court for having participated as an accomplice in the commission of multiple war crimes and crimes against humanity between January 1992 and January 1994, when he was Minister of Defence and de facto head of the military junta.

For universal jurisdiction to have significant impact on international criminal justice, it is crucial for interested States to provide each other with active judicial and prosecutorial assistance[71] as well as set up a specialized task force in their respective countries. In this connection, the European Union has established a network of investigators and prosecutors working on cases involving crimes under international law, the European Genocide Network, to enhance cooperation and facilitated the sharing of best practices among EU Member States. Several EU Member States, including the Netherlands, Belgium, Denmark, Sweden, France and Germany, have set up specialized war crimes units comprising police and prosecutors with specific expertise and focus on these cases.

Since 2011, the United Nations has established various mechanisms to probe serious violations of international human rights, humanitarian and, increasingly, international criminal law. They include the International, Impartial and Independent Mechanism to assist in the investigation and prosecution of persons responsible for the most serious crimes under International Law committed in the Syrian Arab Republic since March 2011, the Independent Investigative Mechanism for Myanmar, and the UN Investigative Team to Promote Accountability for Crimes Committed by Da'esh/ISIL. Evidence gathered by means of these mechanisms can immensely assist States exercising universal jurisdiction in their prosecution of those accused of crimes of international concern.[72]

The obligation to either extradite or prosecute those accused of crimes of international concern has become crucial. The ICTY Appeals Chamber has held that national courts of any State are under 'a customary-law obligation to try or extradite persons who have allegedly committed grave breaches of international humanitarian law'.[73] This is also the case of the offence of torture, where there is a growing willingness by States to recognize an obligation to either extradite or prosecute someone accused of torture that exists independently of the Convention against Torture itself.[74]

According to the Princeton Principles on Universal Jurisdiction, a State shall comply with all international obligations applicable to, inter alia, prosecuting and

71 See further Kittichaisaree, *The Obligation to Extradite or Prosecute* 204–30.

72 Federica D'Alessandra, Stephen Rapp, Kirsty Sutherland and Sareta Ashraph, *Accountability for Mass Atrocities: The Permanent Support Needed to Fulfil UN Investigative Mandates* (Oxford Institute for Ethics, Law and Armed Conflict 2022).

73 *Prosecutor v Tihomir Blaskic* (Judgment on the Request of the Republic of Croatia for Review of the Decision of Trial Chamber II of 18 July 1997), ICTY App Ch, Judgment of 29 October 1997 para 29.

74 Claire Mitchell, *Aut Dedere Aut Judicare: The Extradite or Prosecute Clauses in International Law* (Graduate Institute of International and Development Studies 2009) 30. See also UN International Law Commission, *Final Report of the International Law Commission on the Topic 'The Obligation to Extradite or Prosecute (*aut dedere aut judicare*)'*, UN Doc A/69/10 at 139–65.

extraditing persons accused or convicted of crimes under international law. However, a State or its judicial organs shall refuse to entertain a request for extradition based on universal jurisdiction if the person sought is likely to face a death penalty sentence or to be subjected to torture or any other cruel, degrading or inhuman punishment or treatment, or if it is likely that the person sought will be subjected to sham proceedings in which international due process norms will be violated and no satisfactory assurances to the contrary are provided. A State which refuses to extradite on the aforesaid ground shall, when permitted by international law, *prosecute* the individual accused *or extradite* such person to another State where this can be done without exposing him or her to the aforementioned risks. A State exercising universal jurisdiction may, for the purposes of prosecution, seek judicial assistance to obtain evidence from another State, provided that the requesting State has a good faith basis and that the evidence sought will be used in accordance with international due process norms. Prior criminal or accountability proceedings conducted in good faith in accordance with international norms and standards shall be recognized by other States, so that there can be no multiple prosecutions or punishment for the same conduct. Where more than one State has or may assert jurisdiction over a person and where the State that has custody of the person has no basis for jurisdiction other than universal jurisdiction, that State or its judicial organs shall, in deciding whether to prosecute or extradite, base their decision on an aggregate balance of the following criteria: (a) multilateral or bilateral treaty obligations; (b) the place of commission of the crime; (c) the nationality connection of the alleged perpetrator to the requesting State; (d) the nationality connection of the victim to the requesting State; (e) any other connection between the requesting State and the alleged perpetrator, the crime or the victim; (f) the likelihood, good faith and effectiveness of the prosecution in the requesting State; (g) the fairness and impartiality of the proceedings in the requesting State; (h) convenience to the parties and witnesses, as well as the availability of evidence in the requesting State; and (i) the interests of justice. Where there is a dispute concerning the exercise of universal jurisdiction, States should settle it by all available means of peaceful dispute settlement and in particular by submitting the dispute to the International Court of Justice. Pending the determination of the issue in dispute, a State seeking to exercise universal jurisdiction shall not detain the accused person nor seek to have that person detained by another State unless there is a reasonable risk of flight and no other reasonable means can be found to ensure the person's eventual appearance before the judicial organs of the State seeking to exercise its jurisdiction.

According to the Princeton Principles on Universal Jurisdiction, amnesties for serious crimes under international law are generally inconsistent with the obligation of States to provide accountability thereto and the exercise of universal jurisdiction with respect to serious crimes of international law shall not be excluded by amnesties which are incompatible with international legal obligations of the amnesty granting State.

Indeed, amnesties and pardons purportedly granted by the States where *coups* are staged are not recognized by the foreign State exercising universal jurisdiction over the crimes and persons concerned. This is because the foreign State applies its own domestic criminal law to prosecute and punish the crimes in question, although its courts may draw upon decisions of international criminal courts or tribunals, be they the ICC, ad hoc tribunals or hybrid ones to reach decisions in the cases before them.

Moreover, statutes of limitations are those stipulated under the law of the forum State exercising universal jurisdiction, and not the law of the State where the crime is committed. Under the law of England and Wales, for example, there is no statute of limitations for the crimes subject to universal jurisdiction. Under Belgian law, there is no statute of limitations for genocide, war crimes and crimes against humanity, whereas torture that does not amount to a war crime or crime against humanity is subject to a limitation period of 20 years. In the United States, genocide is not subject to any statute of limitations. In the case of torture resulting in death or creating a foreseeable risk of death or serious bodily harm to the victim, no limitation period applies; otherwise, the statute of limitations for torture is eight years. The US statute of limitations for recruitment or use of child soldiers is ten years from the date of commission of the offence.

As for immunities, serving Heads of State and foreign ministers are immune from civil and criminal suits whilst in office.[75] This is known as immunity *ratione personae* (or personal immunity). Once they leave office, immunity from criminal prosecution remains intact only for acts performed in an official capacity—this is immunity *ratione materiae* (or functional immunity). Immunity *ratione materiae* is enjoyed by State officials in general, irrespective of their position in the hierarchy of the State.[76] Where the act proscribed by a treaty can only be committed on behalf of the State, there can be no immunity *ratione materiae*. This is the case of torture as defined by Article 1(1) of the 1984 Convention against Torture as an act 'inflicted by or at the instigation of or with the consent or acquiescence of a public official or other person acting in an official capacity'. Therefore, the UK House of Lords rules in *Pinochet (No 3)* that former Chilean President Augusto Pinochet enjoys no immunity for torture committed after the UK has become party to the Convention against Torture and torture is a crime under UK law.[77] The same reasoning applies to offences under the 2006 International Convention for the Protection of All Persons from Enforced Disappearance,[78] Article 2 of which defines 'enforced disappearance' as 'the arrest, detention, abduction or any other form of deprivation of liberty by agents of the State or by persons or groups of persons acting with the authorization, support or acquiescence of the State'.

75 *Arrest Warrant of 11 April 2000* [2002] ICJ Rep 3, 20–1 [51]. Affirmed by the ICJ in *Certain Questions of Mutual Assistance in Criminal Matters (Djibouti v France)* [2008] ICJ Rep 177, 236–7 [170].

76 *The 'Enrica Lexi' Incident (Italy v India)*, PCA Case 2015–28, Award of 21 May 2020 para 848 and see also ibid paras 856, 859.

77 *R v Bow Street Metropolitan Stipendiary Magistrate and others* ex parte *Pinochet Urgarte (Amnesty International and others intervening) (No 3)* [1999] 2 All England Law Reports 97.

78 2716 UNTS 3, in force 23 December 2010.

Under no stretch of imagination can conduct amounting to crimes of international concern be considered acts performed in an official capacity; hence, no functional immunity is available in a foreign criminal court to shield perpetrators of these crimes. Therefore, in 2017 the UN International Law Commission provisionally adopted, in light of the relevant treaties and emerging State practice, Article 7 of the draft Articles on Immunity of State Officials from Foreign Criminal Jurisdiction, pursuant to which immunity *ratione materiae* from the exercise of foreign criminal jurisdiction shall *not* apply 'in respect of the following crimes under international law: crime of genocide; crimes against humanity; war crimes; crime of apartheid; torture and enforced disappearance'.[79]

79 A/CN.4/L.893 (10 July 2017) and Statement of the Chairperson of the Drafting Committee on the topic 'Immunity of State Officials from Foreign Jurisdiction', 20 July 2017; International Law Commission, 'Report on the work of its 69th Session (1 May–2 June and 3 July–4 August 2017'), UN Doc A/72/10 at 164–5, 177–91.

7
EPILOGUE

Coup instigators and their supporters normally insist there is no one-size-fits-all formula for government and the Western liberal democracy originating from the Age of the Enlightenment in Europe in the 18th century is not always appropriate to the society where the *coups* are staged in modern days.

The *Oxford English Dictionary* defines 'liberal democracy' as '[a] democratic system of government in which individual rights and freedoms are officially recognized and protected and the exercise of political power is limited by the rule of law'. Liberal democracy is manifested in genuinely free and fair elections at regular, periodic intervals; universal suffrage; the rule of law; separation of powers among the Executive, Legislature and the Judiciary; and political and civil liberties—as guaranteed under a written or unwritten constitution. Whatever its shortcomings, democracy is generally expected across the globe to be much better than other systems of government, such as those under autocratic rulers and dictators who remain accountable to only narrow segments of their societies, if at all.

In an oft-recounted Oriental parable, anyone who stages a *coup* is a person who 'rides on a tiger's back'. To get off the back of this ferocious beast, the *coup* leader must be firmly convinced he will never be bitten by the tiger. Hence, the self-amnesty, self-pardon, self-immunity and other mechanisms to save the usurper from unwanted perils after relinquishing power, or else he will fight to the death to stay in office indefinitely. Besides, unconstitutional usurpation of power puts the usurper in a very complex maze from where he finds it hard to exit. Those benefiting from the regime installed by a *coup* naturally make suggestions or give advice to the usurper to take the directions inside the maze which will keep him there as long as possible, so that they will continue to gain from the regime. Regarding the usurper's personality, he may be an opportunist who seizes power when a golden opportunity arises, a megalomaniac, a person with a superiority complex who considers only he can save the nation in dire straits, or an altruistic idealist

DOI: 10.4324/9781003358428-7

who genuinely and selflessly wants the best for his country and its people. Some usurpers may have more than one of such personalities at the same time or at different times. Not infrequently, the usurper expresses his frustration there is no other 'equally qualified' person to take over from him to deal with any remaining 'unresolved businesses' the *coup* intends to put an end to. What has just been said does not happen in a true democracy. People in countries where *coups* take place are almost always caught between a rock and a hard place in which the alternative is equally untenable since there is no lesser of the two evils between national crises preceding *coups* and deleterious effects on fundamental rights, freedoms and democracy post-*coups*. Some optimists might cling to a glimmer of hope of seeing the light at the end of the deep dark tunnel out of the crises cited as the rationale for the *coup*, but that light may turn out to be from an incoming high-speed train on a direct collision course. Judges of domestic courts, therefore, have judicial responsibility as independent and impartial referees to ensure the usurper take the right direction and in the best interests of the country, to tell the usurper when the time has come for him to go and to punish excesses and abuses during his regime committed by the usurper and/or by other persons. *Coup* instigators should also be barred from holding government offices after, or even during, the country's transition to democracy.

Since post–Cold War *coups* are staged in the Global South, most practices alluded to in this book apart from the works of competent international organizations come from the non-Western world and should, hopefully, not arouse any suspicion that such practices are efforts by the West to maintain its ideological hegemony over, and pursue a hidden neo-imperialist agenda against, the Global South.

One study published in 1994 examines judicial responses to *coups d'état* in post-colonial Common Law settings in Bophuthatswana, Cyprus, Ghana, Grenada, Lesotho, Nigeria, Pakistan, Seychelles, Southern Rhodesia (now Zimbabwe), Transkei and Uganda, where there are diverging opinions among judges in their reactions to *coups d'état* and other forms of abrupt and unconstitutional changes to the pre-existing legal order. The author of the study finds four clear options open to judges in response to such unconstitutional usurpation of power: (i) validation/legitimation of the usurpation, (ii) strict constitutionalism in the sense of judging the change according to the pre-existing constitutional order, (iii) resignation of office or (iv) judicial abdication by declining to assume jurisdiction on the ground that the issue is a non-justiciable political question. That author strongly recommends the last option as the only feasible one dictated by realism and prudence.[1] Another author, who responds to the aforesaid author in 1996 and writing mainly from a Nigerian perspective, contends that there are only two options open to a judge when confronted with *coups d'état: either* accommodating herself to the facts, which entails accepting the changes and becoming part of the usurper's regime, *or*

1 Tayyab Mahmud, 'Jurisprudence of Successful Treason: Coup d'Etat & Common Law' (1994) 27 Cornell ILJ 49, 100–40.

refusing to accommodate the overthrow of a government and the constitutional order, which entails refusing to accept the authority of the usurper regime. The first option will almost inevitably diminish the judge's stature while the second option will normally lead to the judge's resignation or dismissal. Judicial abdication practically equates to the first option of accommodation to the changes and this might not be appropriate in all situations; for example, when the usurpers violate fundamental rights guaranteed under the constitution the judge has taken an oath to protect. Although the choice between the two options presents an ethical dilemma, the resolution of which should in large part depend upon the conscience of the particular judge, the second author proposes that the option of refusing to accommodate the changes might be the preferable and more appropriate choice in the interest of political stability and the enhancement of democratic culture in which judges have a pivotal role in the promotion of the rule of law and constitutional governance and the protection of individuals' rights. Above all, whatever the doctrinal or theoretical appeal the option of judicial abdication might have, the ultimate result is that it, like the validation/legitimation option, confers legitimacy on an event that is manifestly unlawful and would, in most countries, amount to treason.[2]

The present author does not completely subscribe to either view of the two aforesaid authors since there are nuances in the responses by judges of domestic courts to the vexing moral and pragmatic dilemma of either condoning or denouncing *coups*. The analysis in the preceding chapters of this book leads to the conclusion that, in reality, after unconstitutional usurpation of power in a country, judges of the domestic courts of the country can fall into one of the following categories.

First, they are installed by the usurper specifically to uphold the regime's legitimacy, or they may toe the line with the regime for the sake of their career advancement. The judgment and reasoning of the Post–Second World War US Military Tribunal sitting in Nuremberg in the *Justice* case[3] should shed light on the accountability of these judges.

Second, judges may adopt a pragmatic approach by according *formal* recognition of the regime's legitimacy as a *fait accompli*, but subjecting the regime to strict scrutiny by the Judiciary so as to uphold the rule of law and fundamental rights and freedoms of citizens, as in the case of the Pakistan Supreme Court during the dying days of General Pervez Musharraf's Presidency.

Third, judges may pursue an idealistic crusade, denying the usurper's legitimacy right from the outset of the usurpation of power.

Fourth, in-between the aforesaid three categories are judges who balance all relevant factors in light of the circumstances prevailing at the time of their deliberation of the cases before them.

2 Ambrose Ekpu, 'Judicial Response to Coup D'Etat: A Reply to Tayyab Mahmud (From a Nigerian Perspective)' (1996) 13 Arizona J Int'l & Comp L 1.

3 *In re Josef Altstoetter and Others*, Military Tribunal III Case 3, Report of the Trials of War Criminals before the Nuremberg Military Tribunals under Control Council Law No 10, October 1946–April 1949, vol III.

In whichever category a judge may fall, the judges must abide by international legal obligations binding upon their country under treaties and customary international law as well as bear in mind the developments elsewhere that set best practices or international standards for them to emulate. Since judges may not always be able to subjectively determine whether a *coup* is or is not a 'good' one, they can discharge their judicial oversight functions by ascertaining the reaction of the international community, including decisions of global and regional human rights mechanisms, to determine whether the regime commits unforgivable abuses—the information on which may be censored inside the country. During the transition from a repressive regime to democracy, the risk of angering the still powerful military establishment by prosecuting its members is one oft-cited reason why human rights violators and perpetrators of crimes of international concern under the previous regime are not brought to face justice. But once they are arrested and brought to stand trial in court, there is no *lawful excuse* why judges cannot discharge their judicial responsibility to mete out justice.

Some of the salient points in the judgment in the *Justice* case may be repeated here. First, the defendants were charged with, inter alia, *enforcing statutes, decrees and orders of an essentially criminal nature* and with working with German Security Police organizations *for essentially criminal purposes*, in the course of which, by *distortion and denial of judicial process*, they committed crimes against the victims.[4] Second, the defendants were charged with *crimes committed in the name of the law and in the guise of legal process* by 'consciously and deliberately' suppressing the law, engaging in an unholy masquerade of brutish tyranny disguised as justice and converting the German judicial system into an integral part of dictatorship.[5] Third, the defendants were not called to account for participation in and responsibility for the killings, tortures and other atrocities which resulted from, and which the defendants knew were an inevitable consequence of, the conduct of their offices with all its methods of terror and its cynical and open denial of the rule of law.[6] Phrased differently, the defendants were not charged with specific overt acts against named victims—they were charged with and convicted of *criminal participation in government-organized atrocities and persecutions in the name of the law*.[7]

A question may be asked whether the *Justice* case which was decided pursuant to Control Council Law No 10,[8] its constituent instrument, could serve as a precedent of general application.[9] Chapters 3 through 6 of this book should convince readers that the answer to this question is in the affirmative.

Then comes a question of policy. *Should every single individual, including a judge, be held criminally responsible and punished for his or her role in sustaining the regime*

4 Ibid 17–18, 311.
5 Ibid 31.
6 Ibid 32–3.
7 Ibid 1177.
8 (1946) 3 Official Gazette Control Council for Germany 50–5.
9 A pointed raised by Otto Kirchheimer, *Political Justice: The Use of Legal Procedure for Political Ends* (Princeton U Press 1961) 341.

installed by unconstitutional usurpation of power that entails violation of fundamental rights and freedoms or even commission of crimes of international concern?

An 'on the ground' review by one author of the sentencing of perpetrators of genocide and crimes against humanity in Rwanda, Bosnia, East Timor and other places afflicted by atrocity leads to his conclusion that the international community's preference for prosecution and imprisonment may not be as effective as we hope. Instead, he calls for a broader-based response to atrocity that welcomes bottom-up perspectives, including restorative, reparative and reintegrative traditions that may differ from the adversarial Western criminal trial.[10] In his opinion, there are limits to the ability of judicialized determinations of individual criminal culpability to attain post-conflict and transitional justice since atrocity is the product of 'collective violence', in which individual participation is deeply conformist—motivated by 'collective obedience' than by individual transgression. As atrocity becomes more widescale in nature, and more popular, it becomes more difficult to construct participation therein as deviant—most perpetrators are ordinary people caught up in extraordinary circumstances. Even less deviant is the complicity and acquiescence of the bystander, which fall outside of the criminal law paradigm but constitute an essential prerequisite for violence to become truly massive in scale. The criminal law does not reach bystanders, so how could it ever deter them, stigmatize their involvement or accord them their just desserts? The courtroom and the jailhouse make modest gains in terms of actualizing retributive, rehabilitative, reconciliatory and deterrent goals following atrocity; they do somewhat better at actualizing expressive goals of looking at the messaging effect of trials, verdict and punishment to affirm the value of law, strengthen social solidarity and incubate a moral consensus among the public. In the aggregate, however, these modalities arguably fall short of their penological objectives. This may be because these objectives are too ambitious. It may also be because the criminal law, standing alone, simply is not enough—nor can it ever be enough. Collective determinations of criminal guilt, in which individuals whose conduct did not affirmatively contribute to the crime are indiscriminately imprisoned, executed or otherwise denied their liberty, arguably run afoul of customary international law. In that author's view, these limitations suggest that adequately redressing collective violence requires a discursive shift to other accountability mechanisms, including collective forms of responsibility—something quite different from collective guilt or collective punishment dependent on criminal law. Collective responsibility entails non-criminal sanctions that attach to groups whose conduct is supportive of, acquiescent in, causally connected to or necessary for serious violations during the repressive regime. Collective responsibility in the forms of sanctions such as civil liability, community service and public reintegrative shaming has powerful impact and does not entail mass imprisonment, execution or destruction of property. Collective responsibility schemes can also

10 Mark Drumbl, *Atrocity, Punishment, and International Law* (CUP 2007).

permit a much larger number of victims to be validated and vindicated as victims of wrongdoing.[11]

This present author begs to differ. Although this book may seem punishment driven,[12] it does not propose the imposition of criminal punishment upon 'bystanders' who are 'ordinary people caught up in extraordinary circumstances'. Nor does it recommend 'collective determinations of criminal guilt, in which individuals whose conduct did not affirmatively contribute to the crime are indiscriminately imprisoned, executed or otherwise denied their liberty'. The present author wishes to ensure that each individual committing a crime as part of a repressive regime after unconstitutional usurpation of power be held criminally responsible according to the principle of legality and the rule of law. The International Criminal Court as well as modern-day ad hoc international criminal tribunals and hybrid courts do not distinguish between those in the leadership positions and their minions, unless their respective statutes stipulate otherwise.[13] It would be morally arbitrary to draw a line between such individuals.[14]

As Trial Chamber I of the International Criminal Tribunal for the former Yugoslavia (ICTY) has explained in *Jelisic*, in order for the ICTY to discharge its mission of contributing to the restoration of peace in the former Yugoslavia, it needs to identify, punish and pursue the political and military leaders responsible for the atrocities committed there since 1991. However, if the crimes committed during the armed conflicts could be attributable especially to these persons, such persons could not have achieved their objective without the enthusiastic cooperation or the direct or indirect contribution from individuals like Goran Jelisic, a Bosnian Serb former police officer and commander of a prison camp charged with participation in 1992 in the illegal confinement, illegal treatment and killings of Muslims and Croats at the Luka camp, a makeshift detention facility in Brcko, northern Bosnia, following the takeover of the city by Bosnian Serb forces. Therefore, Jelisic could not be heard to say it would be unjust to punish small fry like him instead of punishing the big fish.[15]

Some countries, like Argentina and South Korea, may find it more practical for the reasons explained in Chapter 5 to focus their prosecution on perpetrators who

11 Id, 'Collective Responsibility and Postconflict Justice' in Tracy Isaacs and Richard Vernon (eds), *Accountability for Collective Wrongdoing* (CUP 2011) 23–60.

12 Cf. Karen Engle, 'Anti-Impunity and the Turn to Criminal Law in Human Rights' (2015) 100 Cornell L Rev 1069.

13 As in the case of the crime of aggression punishable under the Rome Statute of the International Criminal Court (2187 UNTS 3, in force 1 July 2002), Art 8 *bis* (1) of which provides that a person who may be punished of this crime must be 'in a position effectively to exercise control over or to direct the political or military action of a State'.

14 See also Mark Osiel, 'Why Prosecute? Critics of Punishment for Mass Atrocity' (2000) 22 Human Rts Quarterly 118, 125–8; Hans Petter Graver, *Judges Against Justice: On Judges When the Rule of Law Is Under Attack* (Springer 2015) 115–23, 189–201, 205–13.

15 *Prosecutor v Goran Jelisic*, Case no IT-95-10-T, ICTY Trial Chamber I, Judgment, 14 December 1999 para 133.

played leading roles under the repressive regimes. However, this is not the same thing as postulating as a general principle or a best practice that those not in the national leadership positions or those 'ordinary people caught up in extraordinary circumstances' who have committed crimes should not be punished for their crimes. Also, according to another study which utilizes qualitative comparative analysis to assess the impact of transitional justice initiatives in Latin America, trials come closest to being a necessary condition for successful democratic consolidation.[16]

It could be argued that Nazi Germany was where mass atrocities were mostly committed by 'ordinary people caught up in extraordinary circumstances'. According to a report commissioned by the German Government which was published in 2016, between 1949 and 1973 some 53 per cent of Germany's Federal Ministry of Justice's staff born before 1927 were former members of the Nazi party, and, more disturbingly, 20 per cent were former members of the Nazi Party's original paramilitary wing Storm Troopers or Brownshirts. Only six individuals were members of the SS, the elite Nazi Party paramilitary organization, representing 3.5 per cent of all the individuals surveyed. Overall, former SS memberships played only an insignificant role among the staff of the Federal Ministry of Justice after 1949.[17] Nevertheless, the German judicial system in the post–Second World War era, with the exception of the *Justice* case which took place under Allied leadership, avoided being prosecuted itself almost entirely in spite of the fact that thousands of judges and public prosecutors had helped to enforce Nazi ideology in ordinary courts, special courts, courts martial or the notorious People's Court and were directly or indirectly involved in the crimes of the Nazi regime. They had been supplied with the methodological tools of the trade by many university teachers and the 'Academy of German Law' founded in Munich in 1933 as a central academic agency for restructuring German law in line with the Nazi world view and as an instrument of judicially enforced conformity. The Reich Ministry of Justice prepared laws and decrees and also meticulously monitored compliance with the new ideology by the Judiciary. Following completion of their training and the start of their working life, practically a whole generation of jurists had fitted into this framework in the 1930s. Partly out of conviction and partly out of opportunist careerism, they had devoted themselves to the Nazi Party and the 'Führer'. Yet, hardly any judges and public prosecutors in the Federal Republic of Germany after 1949 were held accountable for unjust judgments in the Third Reich. In the Soviet Zone of Occupation/East Germany, the attempt was at least made to remove public prosecutors who were tainted by their association with the Nazis and to replace former judges by so-called People's Judges who had undergone short-term training. In the Federal Republic of Germany, on the other hand, countless jurists who had supported the Nazi regime returned to their posts largely unrepentant, tacitly adapting to the

16 Geoff Dancy and Eric Wiebelhaus-Brahm, 'Timing, Sequencing, and Transitional Justice Impact: A Qualitative Comparative Analysis of Latin America' (2015) 16 Human Rts Rev 321.

17 Manfred Görtemaker and Christoph Safferling, *The Rosenburg Files—The Federal Ministry of Justice and the Nazi Era* (German Federal Ministry of Justice and Consumer Protection 2016) 30.

new constitutional order, often sustained by the will to cover the past with a veil of silence and to let the inconceivable extent of the crimes be forgotten. Although this did not seriously endanger democracy in the Federal Republic of Germany, tainted former Nazi lawyers thus continued to exert an influence in important government and social positions and repeatedly helped each other to evade a Judiciary operating under the rule of law. The failure of the Judiciary in the Federal Republic of Germany in dealing with the Nazi legacy is denounced by the authors of the report since the failure concerns primarily the professional group of jurists themselves, who had a special responsibility for upholding the law, especially in the period after 1949, when a critical assessment of the past was possible without any personal risk or at least without any danger to one's own life. The authors consider this failure anathema to the ruling in the *Justice* case, in which no fewer than nine of the 16 accused had held a senior position in the Reich Ministry of Justice and consciously participated in a system of brutality and injustice that was spread throughout the whole country and was organized by the government—they were convicted of having not only violated laws of war, but also laws of humanity in the name of justice, under the authority of the Ministry of Justice and with the assistance of the courts.[18]

In 1950, the German Parliament (Bundestag) passed a general amnesty law for former Nazis, followed by another amnesty law in 1954, the latter being applicable specifically to crimes committed at the very end of the Second World War, including the massive forced transfers of prisoners from one Nazi camp to another and mass killings of concentration camp inmates as the Allies advanced into Germany. It has been estimated that 200,000 and possibly close to a million people were at one point or another actively involved in carrying out the Holocaust against Jews in Nazi Germany, but, between 1945 and 2005, only 140,000 cases were brought against Nazi criminals in German courts, resulting in 6,656 convictions for Nazi crimes and 75 per cent of those convicted received prison sentences of up to two years. East Germany convicted many more Nazi criminals than West Germany did but with equally light sentences.[19] In 1968, the West German Government passed a statute of limitations law, with retroactive effect, barring most Nazi crimes except for murder, proving which is quite onerous due to the long passage of time and disappearance of evidence.[20] The situation in Nazi Germany and immediately post–Second World War Germany may be likened to the apartheid regime in South Africa and its aftermath. Yet, while the transitional justice model in post-apartheid South Africa has been widely praised internationally, the one in Germany has not.

18 Ibid 13–18.

19 Mary Fulbrook, *Reckonings: Legacies of Nazi Persecution and the Quest for Justice* (OUP 2018). Cf. David Cohen, 'Transitional Justice in Divided Germany after 1945' in Jon Elster (ed.), *Retribution and Reparation in the Transition to Democracy* (CUP 2006) 59–88; Devin Pendas, *Democracy, Nazi Trials and Transitional Justice in Germany, 1945–1950* (CUP 2020).

20 Zachary Simon, 'Germany's Culture of Acquittal' *Tablet* (22 January 2022). Cf. Sanya Romeike, *Transitional Justice in Germany after 1945 and after 1990* (International Nuremberg Principle Academy 2016) 11–42.

Therefore, the best practices identified throughout this book is to be preferred to the path taken by Germany in this regard.[21]

That judges are not impervious to individual criminal responsibility related to a *coup* may be seen in the example of the Turkish Government's purge and prosecution of thousands of members of the Turkish Judiciary accused of being members of the Gülen Group, which has been blamed for the attempted *coup* on 15 July 2016 and designated as a terrorist organization by the Turkish Government.[22] If, *arguendo*, these judges could be prosecuted for their role in the failed *coup*, there is no justifiable reason not to hold judges criminally responsible for their role in sustaining a successfully staged *coup* that results in violation of fundamental rights and freedoms of citizens or even commission of crimes of international concern.

Those brought to face justice after the transition to democracy may be extremely aged, looking frail and being of poor health. Their prosecution is not feasible earlier due to many factors. The wheel of justice may turn slowly, but justice delayed is still better than no justice at all. The many years taken to bring them to justice can be well used to collect evidence leading to their convictions although it may be increasingly difficult to obtain evidence after such a long time.[23] Their ages and state of health do not mean they do not deserve punishment for their past wrongs[24] although these factors may be taken into consideration in mitigation of their sentences.[25]

21 *Contra*: Giovanni Capoccia and Grigore Pop-Eleches, 'Democracy and Retribution: Transitional Justice and Regime Support in Postwar West Germany' (2020) 53 Comparative Political Studies 399, posing a question: How harshly should perpetrators of past abuses be punished, to reinforce the legitimacy of a new democracy? Drawing on socio-psychological theories, the authors conclude that when defendants are largely seen as co-ethnics and their guilt is contested, like in the West German case, pro-democratic attitudes are likely to be strengthened by lighter punishments and undermined by harsher sanctions.

22 For detailed accounts of this prosecution, see *Alparslan Altan v Turkey*, App no 12778/17, ECtHR, Judgment, 16 April 2019; *Baş v Turkey*, App no 66448/17, ECtHR, Judgment, 30 March 2020; *Tercan v Turkey*, App no 6158/18, ECtHR, Judgment, 29 June 2021; *Turan and Others v Turkey*, App nos 75805/16 and 426 others, ECtHR, Judgment, 23 November 2021.

23 As in the case of Radovan Karadžić and Ratko Mladić, the war-time Bosnian Serb leaders (Iva Vukušić, 'Later Rather Than Sooner: Time and Its Effects on the Karadžić and Mladić Trials' (2022) 22 Int'l Crim L Rev 189). See also Samuel Matsiko, 'Optics, Aged Witnesses and Aged Defendants: Habré at the Extraordinary African Chambers' ibid 244.

24 Mark Drumbl and Caroline Fournet, 'The Visualities and Aesthetics of Prosecuting Aged Defendants' (2022) 22 Int'l Crim L Rev 1; Kirsten Fisher, 'The Expressive Value of Prosecuting Aged Defendants: A Rebuke of Ageism' ibid 63. Cf. Konstantinos Tsinas, 'Prosecuting Asymmetrically: On Some "Preconditions" of Criminal Liability of Aged Defendants for Atrocities' ibid 43; Lior Zylberman and Adriana Taboada, 'The Age-Impunity Rhetoric in Trials for Crimes Committed during the Argentinian Genocide (1975–1983)' ibid 109; Caroline Davidson, 'Of Old Men, Country Clubs, and Atrocities: The Visualities and Externalities of Detaining Elderly Human Rights Violators in Chile' ibid 142. *Contra*: Shannon Fyfe, 'Negative Aesthetic Experiences of Prosecuting the Barely Alive' ibid 23; James Burnham Sedgwick, 'An Age-Old Question: Optical (A)llusions, (In)Decency, and (In)Justice in the Trial of Japanese War Criminals' ibid 86.

25 Hikmet Karcic, '"The Court is Accommodating our Murderers": Prosecuting Aged Defendants in Domestic Courts in Bosnia and Herzegovina' (2022) 22 Int'l J Crim L Rev 209, 218–24.

Glaringly inadequate in most of the debates about accountability in the aftermath of unconstitutional usurpation of power and consequential atrocities is the perspective of female victims. There are even oppositions to those voicing grievances of female victims of repressive regimes or dictatorships.[26] While most of the usurpers and the members of their apparatus as well as those taking up arms against them are male, an inordinate number of victims are female, especially in the context of sexual crimes such as rape and other sexual abuses based on the victims' female gender as part of the regime's strategy of repression against political opponents.[27] For example, during The Gambia's 22-year dictatorship, women were the most adversely impacted since they not only suffered torture and brutality from State agents but also encountered State-sanctioned sexual and gender-based violence, leaving them with deep psychological scars for the rest of their life.[28] As noted by the International Court of Justice in the context of an armed conflict, victims of sexual violence often experience psychological trauma and social stigma, and, therefore, such violence is frequently under-reported and notoriously difficult to document to the extent it is impossible to derive even a broad estimate of the number of victims of rape and other forms of sexual violence from the reports and other data available to it although the rape and other forms of sexual violence in question were undoubtedly committed on a large and widespread scale.[29]

Because women face challenges in accessing justice due to patriarchal structures and ongoing discrimination in the political, economic, social and legal spheres, and because of the gendered nature of the crimes and harms they experience, a gender-transformative approach to transitional justice that focuses on transforming psycho-social, socio-economic and political power relations in society is needed in order to attain human rights for women and build a sustainable peace.[30] This is fully

26 Ariana Awad, *Women against Dictatorship and Repression: A Comparative Study of the Women's Organizations Formed in Chile and Argentina Respectively between 1973–1990 and 1976–1983*, Honours thesis (Union College, Schenectady, NY 2011).

27 See, e.g., María Elena Acuña Moenne and Matthew Webb, 'Embodying Memories: Women and the Legacy of the Military Government in Chile' (2005) 79 Feminist Rev 150; Mariana Joffily, 'Sexual Violence in the Military Dictatorship of Latin America: Who Wants to Know?' (2016) 13 Int'l J Hum Rts 165. For the widespread nature of the problem of gender-based violence as a form of discrimination and regional treaties dealing with this problem in the Americas, Africa and Europe, see Rosa Celorio, *Women and Human Rights in Modern Times: A Contemporary Casebook* (Edward Elgar Publishing 2022) 38–68.

28 International Center for Transitional Justice's report, 'Women's Experiences of Dictatorship in The Gambia: A Submission by Women from Sintet, Janjanbureh, and Basse to the Truth, Reconciliation and Reparations Commission' (December 2019); Isatou Bittaye-Jobe, *The Impact of State Violence on Women During the 22 Years of Dictatorship in The Gambia*, Master's thesis (City U New York 2021).

29 *Armed Activities on the Territory of the Congo (DR Congo v Uganda)*, Judgment of 9 February 2022 on the Question of Reparations [2022] ICJ Rep paras 188–93.

30 Wendy Lambourne and Vivianna Rodriguez Carreon, 'Engendering Transitional Justice: a Transformative Approach to Building Peace and Attaining Human Rights for Women' (2016) 17 Human Rts Rev 71. See also Catherine O'Rourke, *Gender Politics in Transitional Justice* (Routledge 2015); Lia Kent, 'After the Truth Commission: Gender and Citizenship in Timor-Leste' (2016) 17 Human Rts Rev 51; Natasha Teresa Jolly, 'Transformative Justice: Exploring the "Relational" in Transformative

acknowledged by the UN Security Council in its Resolution 1325 of 31 October 2000, which addresses, inter alia, how women and girls are disproportionately impacted by violent conflict and war. The Resolution recognizes the critical role women can and already do play in peace-building efforts, and affirms that peace and security efforts are more sustainable when women are equal partners in the prevention of violent conflict, the delivery of relief and recovery efforts and in forging lasting peace.[31]

For its part, the 1998 Rome Statute of the International Criminal Court criminalizes in a comprehensive manner all gender-based crimes that constitute genocide, war crimes or crimes against humanity.[32] Several States Parties to the Rome Statute have criminalized these crimes under their respective domestic laws. As can be seen from Chapter 6, only a few countries that have experienced a *coup* are parties to the Rome Statute. Furthermore, even where gender-based crimes under the Rome Statute are now criminalized in domestic law, where unconstitutional usurpation of power took place before such domestic criminalization, these crimes might not be punishable as such at the time of their commission. This is because of the principle of legality—no one may be accused or convicted of a criminal offence on account of any act or omission which did not constitute a criminal offence at the time it was committed; nor may a heavier penalty be imposed than that which was applicable at the time the criminal offence was committed.[33] On some rare occasions, domestic courts determine that even in the absence of statutory proscriptions certain crimes were somehow (e.g., under customary law or Common Law) criminalized and with appropriate punishment at the time of their commission. For example, the Supreme Court of The Gambia has held that customary international law is part and parcel of the Common Law of The Gambia insofar as it is not inconsistent therewith or with local statute law, and that The

---

Gender Justice' in Katerina Standish, Heather Devere, Adan Suazo and Rachel Rafferty (eds), *The Palgrave Handbook of Positive Peace* (Palgrave Macmillan 2022) 455–71.

31 S/RES/1325 (2000). See also Christine Chinkin and Hilary Charlesworth, 'Building Women into Peace: The International Legal Framework' (2006) 27 Third World Quarterly 937; Chile Eboe-Osuji, *International Law and Sexual Violence in Armed Conflicts* (Brill 2012) 1–10, 257–69, 312–4; Christine Chinkin, *Women, Peace and Security and International Law* (CUP 2022).

32 Tathiana Flores Acuña, 'The Rome Statute's Sexual Related Crimes: An Appraisal under the Light of International Humanitarian Law' (2004) 39 Revista IIDH 169; Fatou Bensouda, 'Gender and Sexual Violence under the Rome Statute' in Emmanuel Decaux, Adama Dieng and Malick Sow (eds), *From Human Rights to International Criminal Law* (Brill/Nijhoff 2007) 401; Valerie Oosterveld, 'Gender-Based Crimes against Humanity' in Leila Nadya Sadat (ed.), *Forging a Convention for Crimes against Humanity* (CUP 2011) 78–101; Rosemary Grey, *Prosecuting Sexual and Gender-Based Crimes at the International Criminal Court: Practice, Progress and Potential* (CUP 2019) 30–321; Tanja Altunjan, 'The International Criminal Court and Sexual Violence: Between Aspirations and Reality' (2021) 22 German LJ 878.

33 See, e.g., the decision of 15 September 2021 by the Spanish Constitutional Court dismissing a complaint alleging tortures committed by a member of the secret police in 1964, 1967 and 1974 against the complainant during the Franco dictatorship on the grounds of the principle of legality against retroactive application of criminal law, the statute of limitations, and the Law 47/1977 on Amnesty (*Auto 80/2021*, Boletín Oficial del Estatdo, no 251, 20 October 2021 at 128154).

Gambia's treaty obligations not yet enacted into local statute law may also create a legitimate expectation on the part of the beneficiaries of the treaties or even pass into the realm of customary international law.[34] Were female victims' views taken more seriously, punishment of perpetrators of abuses and atrocities might be more severe; judges, particularly female judges, would take a less compromising attitude towards the usurpation and its consequences; and the process of inclusive gender transitional justice might be more victim-oriented.[35] A positive development in this regard is the judgment of a Chilean court in November 2020 convicting, for the first time, three agents of the Pinochet military junta for 'sexual torture', thereby recognizing the gender-based aspect of torture.[36]

On the whole, this book aims to inspire and encourage judges in countries experiencing unconstitutional usurpation of power to discharge their judicial responsibility to protect fundamental rights and freedoms of citizens as well as punish perpetrators of international crimes. A series of *coups* in Africa in recent years show how the sense of impunity among *coup* instigators emboldens potential usurpers to depose the incumbent government, as in the case of the attempted military *coup* in Guinea-Bissau on 1 February 2022 following the *coup* in Guinea on 5 September 2021 or that of the September 2022 *coup* in Burkina Faso that toppled the junta installed by the January *coup* of the same year. This kind of *coup d'état* contagion effect or copycatting[37] can be halted or at least alleviated by judges' ending the said impunity and preventing their respective countries from sinking deeper into an intractable and unfathomable quagmire of tyranny. Discharging judicial responsibility by judging against unconstitutional usurpation of power can, therefore, be more effective than trying to pre-empt threats from national armed forces by organizing presidential guards, militarized police and militia to counterbalance the regular military. As shown by one empirical study drawing on an original dataset of State security forces in 110 countries over a span of 50 years as well as case studies of *coup* attempts in Asia, Africa, Latin America and the Middle East, even where

34 *The State v Yankuba Touray*, Case no SC Co CR/001/2020, Gambian Supreme Court's Judgment, 19 March 2021. See further, Anne-Marie de Brouwer, Charlotte Ku, Renée Römkens and Larissa van den Herik, *Sexual Violence as an International Crime: Interdisciplinary Approaches* (Intersentia 2013).

35 Cf. Martha Albertson Fineman and Estelle Zinsstag, *Feminist Perspectives on Transitional Justice* (Intersentia 2013); Fionnuala Ní Aoláin, 'Advancing Feminist Positioning in the Field of Transitional Justice' (2012) 6 Int'l J Transitional Justice 205; Philipp Schulz, 'Towards Inclusive Gender in Transitional Justice: Gaps, Blind-Spots and Opportunities' (2020) 14 J Intervention & Statebuilding 691; Karen Engle, *The Grip of Sexual Violence in Conflicts: Feminist Interventions in International Law* (Stanford U Press 2020); Laura Martin, '(En)gendering Post-conflict Agency: Women's Experiences of the "Local" in Sierra Leone' (2021) 56 Cooperation & Conflict 454; Tiina Pajuste, 'Inclusion and Women in Peace Processes' in Marc Weller, Mark Retter and Andrea Varga (eds), *International Law and Peace Settlement* (CUP 2021) 291–312.

36 Alberto Peña, 'Slow Justice for Women Abused by Chile's Dictatorship' *AFP* (5 March 2021), https://sg.news.yahoo.com/slow-justice-women-abused-chiles-015003875.html.

37 Cf. Ellen Ioanes, 'How to Understand the Recent Coups in Africa' *Vox* (5 February 2022), https://www.vox.com/2022/2/5/22919160/coup-guinea-bissau-africa-burkina-faso-sudan-why, where the author explains that despite some commonalities there are different circumstances among these *coups*.

such counterbalancing helps to prevent *coups*, the resentment generated by it within the regular military can provoke new *coup* attempts. Also because counterbalancing changes how soldiers and police perceive the costs and benefits of a successful overthrow of government, it can create incentives for protracted fighting between them that may result in the escalation of a *coup* into a full-blown civil war.[38]

It is hoped that this book will enlighten judges and the general public around the globe about the best judicial practices from various jurisdiction as well as applicable rules of international law in cases of unconstitutional usurpation of power. Let's start an international movement to consign *coups d'état* anywhere on earth to the dustbin of history, never to be recycled in anyway whatsoever.

38 Erica de Bruin, *How to Prevent Coups d'État: Counterbalancing and Regime Survival* (Cornell U Press 2020).

INDEX

Abdülsamet Yaman v Turkey 192–3
Additional Protocol II to Geneva Conventions 176–7
Adejumo v Johnson 31
ad hoc tribunal 13, 123, 126, 208, 214, 218, 219, 223–5, 228, 229–30, 246, 253
Afghanistan 3, 85, 148, 184, 189–91, 242–3
African Charter on Democracy, Elections and Governance 56–61, 64
African Charter on Human and Peoples' Rights 104, 146
African Commission on Human and Peoples' Rights 104, 167, 108, 212–13, 236n44
African Court of Justice 64
African Court of Justice and Human Rights 64–5
African Court on Human and Peoples' Rights 64, 145–6, 147
African Governance Architecture 57
African Union 56–65, 147, 178, 183, 215, 236
aggression 52, 65, 87n23, 101, 123, 220–1, 223, 253n13
aid and abet 135, 136, 225–6, 242
al-Bashir, Omar 6, 60, 234–5
Algeria's *coup* 82, 83, 85, 243
Almonacid Arellano et al. v Chile 170n31, 172
Alvarez, Gregorio 174–5
American Convention on Human Rights 66–8, 98–103, 114, 143–4, 172–3, 176–7, 184, 193, 195–6, 200–1, 207, 212–13
American Declaration on Rights and Duties of Man 66, 185
amnesty 4, 11, 23–4, 156, 162–84, 189–202, 206, 213–18, 243, 245–6, 248, 255
amparo 100, 102
apartheid 87, 139, 165–7, 189, 221, 247, 255
Arab Spring 91
Argentina's *coup* 4, 68, 197–9, 201, 253–4
Arif, Abdul Razaq 242–3
ASEAN 68–70, 183
ASEAN Charter 69
ASEAN Declaration 68–9
Athens Polytechnic case 36, 178–9, 217
Attorney-General of the Federation v Guardian Newspaper Limited 30
Aung San Suu Kyi 10, 46, 52, 126, 143
Azanian Peoples Organization (AZAPO) case 165–7

Bainimarama, Frank 32, 73, 128–9
Baker v Carr 119–20
Baldy v Hunter 19–20
Bangalore Principles of Judicial Conduct 141
Bangladesh Italian Marble Works Ltd v Bangladesh 35, 169
Bangladesh's *coups* 35, 168–70, 207
Barbosa de Souza et al. v Brazil 177–8
Barrios Altos v Peru 170n31, 172–3, 213

Barrios Altos and La Cantuta v Peru 173
Basic Principles of Independence of Judiciary 139–41, 158
Basic Principles on Use of Force and Firearms 114–18
Bemba case 231
Ben Ali 192, 193n98, 216n167
Bhutto v Chief of Army Staff 23, 27n30, 30, 44, 150n65
Bignone, Reynaldo 198–9
Bolivia's *coup* 35, 185
Bordaberry, Juan María 174–5
Bouterse, Dési 195–7
Brazil's *coup* 199
Brima, Kamara and Kanu case 235
Burkina Faso's *coups* 49, 60, 63, 82, 85, 207–8, 220, 259
Burundi's *coups* 178
Buyoya, Pierre 178

Castillo Petruzzi v Peru 112–13
CCPR 37, 77, 78, 83, 93, 95–6, 108, 113, 115, 118, 164, 174, 183
Central African Republic, Special Criminal Court of 219–20, 236–7
Central African Republic's *coup* 193n98, 231
Chad's *coups* 61, 82, 83, 220, 236
Chaudhry, Iftikhar Muhammad 147–9, 153
child, right of the 77, 78, 80, 98, 108, 118–19, 164, 213, 215
child soldier 235, 239, 246
Chile's *coup* 4, 82, 120–1, 127–8, 171–2
Chocrón Chocrón v Venezuela 143n50, 144
Chun Doo Wan 186–7, 205–6
Civil Law 141, 156–7
Colombia's Final Peace Agreement 214–15
Common Law 17, 21, 32, 141, 156–7, 210–11, 228n22, 249–50, 258–9
common plan 226–30
common purpose 225–6, 229
Commonwealth 70–2
Compaoré, Blaise 60, 207–8
compensation *see* remedy
complementarity 223–4, 240
complicity 178, 198, 225, 252
conspiracy 130–1, 134, 228–9, 243
Constitutive Act of African Union 56
Control Council Law No 10 129n13, 131n19, 251
control of conventionality 201, 218
control over the crime 230
Correa, Michael Sang 242
corruption 25, 42–3, 58, 65, 105, 106, 126, 142–3, 147–8, 153, 180, 206–7, 243
crime against humanity 11, 47, 60, 65, 86–7, 88, 94, 111, 130–1, 135, 154, 155, 156, 159, 163, 171–3, 175–7, 184–5, 187, 189–91, 194–5, 200, 213–16, 220–1, 225, 230–5, 237, 239, 241–2, 244, 246–7, 252, 258
crimes of international concern 3, 13, 14, 74, 75, 78, 159, 165, 191, 194, 208, 214, 215, 216, 218, ch 6, 251, 252, 256
customary international law 10–11, 13, 37, 75, 86, 88, 122, 183, 187, 194, 210–11, 227, 236, 251–2, 258–9
Cuya Lavy et al. v Peru 144–5
Cyprus's *coup* 44, 82, 249

Daokrajai Lilamian v Ministry of Finance 28
Darfur, Sudan 88, 234–5
death penalty 79, 95, 105, 111, 243, 245
Decaux, Emmanuel 107–12
defences 11, 13, 17, 36, 104, 110, 120, ch 4, 179, 198, 212
democracy (generally) 2, 25, 65–7, 248–9
derogable rights 213–14
derogation 7n22, 37, 55, 86, 89–104, 108, 212
Dosso case 29–30
dualist approach to international law 123, 124, 211
due process 6, 12, 39, 130, 143, 148, 167, 224, 234, 245
duress 13, 18, 127, 155–8

ECOMIG 64
ECOWAS 62–4
Ecuador's *coups* 5, 67, 82, 83, 161–2, 191–2
effectiveness 15, 28–34, 41, 74, 159, 250
effet utile 124n135, 201
efficacy *see* effectiveness
Egypt's *coup* 58–60, 82
El Salvador's *coups* 67n155, 166, 175–7, 220
emergency, state of 4, 7n22, 13, 17, 20, 21, 28, 29, 32, 37, 51, 53, 55–6, 78, 86, 89–104, 106–7, 112, 117, 128, 149, 151, 153, 180, 212
enforced disappearance 77, 87, 127, 148, 187, 195, 221, 239, 243, 246, 247
Enforced Disappearance Convention 77, 85–6, 163, 246
enforcement of international law (in general) 76, 123

Erdemovic case 156–8
erga omnes obligation 240
Ergin v Turkey (No 6) 113
Ershad, Hussain Mohammed 35n54, 168–9, 207
eternity clause 182–3
EU Charter of Fundamental Rights 145
European Convention on Human Rights 37, 54–6, 97, 212, 241
European Court of Human Rights 37, 54, 113, 115, 116, 122, 144, 164, 192–3, 240–1, 256n22
European Court of Justice 145
European Genocide Network 244
European Union 37, 49, 54, 145, 244
Evren, Kenan 192–3, 216n169
extradite or prosecute 89, 235–6, 244–5

female victims' perspective 257–9
Fiji's *coups* 11, 32–4, 45, 47, 71–2, 73, 128–9, 179–80, 181, 220
Francisco v House of Representatives 120
Fujimori, Alberto 3, 124, 125, 172–3
fundamental rights and freedoms 3, 4, 6, 10, 11, 12, 13, 36, 44, 61, 66, 69, 70, 73, 74, ch 3, 125, 138, 143, 147, 152, 158, 160, 164, 172, 173, 177, 183, 191, 207, 211, 212, 216–17, 249, 250, 256, 259
Furundzija 88–9

Gambia's *coup* 82, 83, 208–10, 220, 237–8, 241–2, 257
Garcia v Executive Secretary 119
Garcia Lucero et al. v Chile 172
Gelman v Uruguay 170n31, 193
gender-based crime 66, 78, 87, 216, 221, 258, 259
general principles of law 12, 196
Geneva Conventions (1949) 171, 221–2, 239
genocide 60, 65, 67n155, 87, 88, 94n41, 114, 132, 135, 154, 155, 163, 164, 170–1, 172, 175, 185, 195, 214, 215, 216, 220, 221, 229, 231, 234, 239, 240–1, 246, 247, 252, 258
Genocide Convention 79, 87n24, 94n41, 185, 240–1
Gomes Lund et al. v Brazil 37n58, 68n158, 124n135, 170n31, 184n77, 200–1, 217–18
Gonzales-Vera v Kissinger 121
Greece's *coups* 4, 36, 55–6, 178–9, 216–17
Greek Case 55–6, 97n47
Grenada's *coups* 26, 45, 50, 161, 249
Guatemala's *coups* 170–1, 194–5
Guidance on Less-Lethal Weapons in Law Enforcement 118
Guinea-Bissau's *coup* 58, 63, 82, 259
Guinea's *coups* 5, 58, 62, 82, 83, 127, 220, 232–4, 259

habeas corpus 89–90, 98–100, 102, 109, 120, 127
Habeas Corpus in Emergency Situations, Advisory Opinion 98–100
Habré, Hissène 219, 227, 235–6, 237
Haiti's *coups* 52–3, 82
Hitler, Adolf 3, 130, 133–5, 155
Honduras' *coup* 7, 21, 51, 67, 82, 83, 101–4, 183n74, 220
Horn v Lockhart 18–19
humanitarian intervention 76
Human Rights Council 107, 141, 142–3, 233–4, 237
hybrid court 13, 126, 183, 208, 214, 215–16, 218, 219–20, 223–5, 227–30, 235–8, 246, 253

ICCPR 37, 78–84, 91–7, 98, 107–8, 110, 111n88, 113, 117, 119n115, 164, 174, 177, 183, 207
ICRC 187
ICTR 154, 209, 219, 225, 227
ICTY 88, 154, 156–8, 209, 219, 225–7, 230, 241, 244, 253
illiberal democracy 57, 58
immunity 11, 13, 36, 106, 121, 127, 140, 158–9, 162–3, 166, 170, 177–80, 190, 192, 208, 210–13, 216, 218, 234n38, 237, 246–7, 248
implicit unamendability of constitution 183
impunity 103, 107, 108, 112, 125, 167, 170–4, 177, 180, 184, 189–90, 194, 199, 208, 211, 212, 214, 259
independence of judiciary 13, 24, 38–9, 70, 102, 107, 109–10, 112–14, 125, 127, 130–1, 133, 139–53, 155, 158–60
Independent International Fact-Finding Mission on Myanmar 142
Independent Investigative Mechanism for Myanmar 233–4, 244
individual complaint mechanisms 55n116, 69, 77, 85, 104
Inter-American Commission on Human Rights 68, 101–3, 117–18, 200
Inter-American Court of Human Rights 68, 98–101, 108, 112–14, 115, 116, 122, 124, 143–5, 155, 170–3, 175–8,

184n77, 188, 193–6, 200–2, 213, 217–18
Inter-American Democratic Charter 66–7, 103
international acceptance/approval 12–13, 16, 47–74
International Court of Justice 76, 78, 88, 235–6, 245, 257
international crimes *see* crimes of international concern
International Criminal Court 11, 60, 65, 86–7, 88, 123, 126, 153–6, 187, 208, 214, 215, 218, 219–24, 225, 229–37, 239, 246, 253, 258
international criminal law 3, 114, 126, 138, 209, 220–3, 228, 244
international humanitarian law 87n23, 88, 94, 107, 157, 175–7, 214–15, 220, 242–3, 244
international human rights law 3, 115, 118, 138, 146, 173, 209, 210, 215, 220
International Military Tribunal *see* Nuremberg Tribunal
Ioannides, Dimitrios 217
Iraqi High Tribunal 227

Jammeh, Yahya 64, 208, 237–8, 242
Janata Tower case 207
Jasmine Revolution 192
Jelisic case 253
Jilani v Government of Punjab 21–3, 30, 44, 73
joint criminal enterprise 226–30
Jorgić v Germany 240–1
judges' roles in *coups* 7, 8, 75, 120, 123, 128, 152, 183, 218, 250, 251–2, 256
judicial immunity 13, 127, 158–9
judicial independence *see* independence of judiciary
jurisdiction trigger 223
jus cogens 13, 75, 86–8, 165, 187, 208, 214, 239, 240
Justice case 13, 123, 129–39, 155, 158, 217, 250, 251, 254–5

Kelsen, Hans 29–30, 41
Khan, Ayub 21, 29
Khan, Yahya 21–2
Khmer Rouge Tribunal 219, 227
Khondker Delwar Hossain case 169
Knaul, Gabriela 112–14

Lakanmi v Attorney-General, Western State 30–1
law enforcement measures 75, 114–19, 122
legality principle 6–7, 12, 37–8, 81, 92, 95, 99, 114–15, 131, 186, 187, 253, 258
legal vacuum 12, 15, 40–1
Lesotho's *coups* 31–2, 47, 249
Liasi v Attorney-General 44, 45, 73
liberal democracy 58, 248
Liberian civil wars 167–8
limitation of rights 36, 92–3, 97, 183
Los Josefinos Village Massacre v Guatemala 171n35
Lowe, Bai 242

Madagascar's *coup* 51, 57, 58, 82, 83, 220
Madzimbamuto v Lardner Burke 20, 21, 160
Malabo Protocol 64–5
Mali's *coups* 40, 49, 57, 58–9, 62–4, 82, 83, 85–6, 220, 230–2
Manitoba Language Rights 40
Marcos, Ferdinand E. 3, 5, 90–1, 120, 203–5
Marcos, Jr v Republic 204
Marcos v Manglapus 203
Marcos Estate v Republic 204
Marguš v Croatia 164
martial law 3, 21–3, 25, 29, 32, 35n54, 89, 90–1, 105–6, 107, 120, 151, 168–9, 186, 204
Massacres of El Mozote case 175–6
Matovu case 30, 31, 44, 48, 73
Meza case 35–6, 38, 183, 185–6
military tribunals 13, 75, 104–14
mistake of fact 154–5
mistake of law 135, 154, 155
Mitchell case 26–7, 44, 45, 73
modes of commission of international crimes 225–30
Moiwana Community v Suriname 195–6
Mokotso case 31–2, 45
Mugabe, Robert 5, 61
Musharraf, Pervez 24–5, 27, 91, 147–9, 152–3, 216n167, 250
Myanmar's *coups* 2, 9, 10, 46–7, 49, 51–2, 53, 68–70, 73–4, 88, 105, 126–7, 180, 233–4, 244

Nachova and others v Bulgaria 116, 213
National Council for Peace and Order 7n22, 28–9, 36n56, 106, 181
national reconciliation 14, 53, 72, 163, 164–7, 170, 188–92, 195, 196–7, 203, 205, 207, 208, 237, 242, 243
Nazi regime 89, 130–8, 155, 158, 254–6
ne bis in idem 80, 224, 245
necessity 12, 15–27, 30, 32–3, 40, 46, 73, 89, 100–1, 108, 112, 115–16, 153

Nezzar, Khaled 243–4
Nibia Sabalsagaray case 37n58, 175n53, 184–5, 188
Niger's *coups* 5, 58, 82, 83, 191, 216, 220
Nigeria's *coups* 5, 30–1, 82, 202–3, 218, 249
non-derogable rights 93–5, 99, 172, 212–14
non-intervention in internal affairs 68–70, 240
Nuremberg Tribunal 185, 187

OAS Charter 66, 99
Ocampo Enriquez 205
Operation Condor 42, 174
Organization of American States 65–8, 90, 98, 183

Pacific Islands Forum 72n164
pacta sunt servanda 124n135, 196, 201
Pakistan's *coups* 21–6, 29–30, 34–5, 71, 73, 91, 126, 147–53, 159–60, 183, 249, 250
Palamara Iribarne v Chile 112–13
Papadopoulos, Georgios 36, 178–9, 217
Paraguay's *coup* 5, 89, 90
Park Geun-hye 206
pardon 4, 10, 11, 14, 158, 161–2, 164, 173, 174, 179, 185, 191–2, 198, 205–6, 215–18, 245–6, 248
Pasrawalee Thanakijvibulpol case 96–7
peace agreement 163, 167, 170, 214–16
Peace and Security Council of African Union 57–9, 61
peremptory norm *see jus cogens*
Peru's *coup* 3, 82, 83, 125
Philippines' *coup* 3, 90–1, 204–5
Pinochet, Augusto 96n43, 121, 123, 128, 177, 246, 259
Pinochet (No 3) case 246
plebiscite *see* referendum
political climate 195–207
political crime 163, 166, 175, 191, 199, 215
political offence exception 89
political question 119–22, 249
political will 58, 174n48, 202, 238
popular acceptance 12, 16, 27, 31, 33, 44–7
practicality principle 240
Princeton Principles on Universal Jurisdiction 238–9, 244–5
prosecute or extradite *see* extradite or prosecute
Punsak Sritape case 40–1, 180–1, 183

Qarase v Bainimarama 73, 129
Questions relating to the Obligation to Prosecute or Extradite (Belgium v Senegal) 235–6

realpolitik 73, 208, 209
referendum 4, 7, 106, 128, 186, 191–3, 243
remedy 7n22, 18, 24, 78–9, 83, 84, 85, 86, 91, 94, 99–100, 103, 109–12, 118, 145, 151, 165, 167, 170, 171n35, 172, 173, 176, 178, 184, 186, 188, 192, 193, 196, 199–200, 204, 209, 211, 212, 213
reparation *see* remedy
Republic of Fiji v Prasad 11, 27n26, 32–4, 45, 47–8, 73
restorative justice 188–9
restriction of rights *see* limitation of rights
retributive justice 188, 252
revolution 3, 5, 26, 30–1, 33, 41, 45, 47, 55, 192
Ríos Montt, José Efrain 170–1, 177
Roh Tae Woo 186, 205–6
Rome Statute of International Criminal Court 86–7, 88, 153–4, 155, 156, 163, 187, 215, 219–25, 229–30, 232–4, 239, 258
rule of law 12, 15, 32, 37–40, 54, 56, 69–71, 95, 99, 101, 107, 126, 128, 130, 141, 145, 146, 151, 159–60, 177, 248, 250, 251, 253, 255

SADC 51
Saied, Kais 106–7, 146–7
salus populi suprema est lex 17, 24, 34, 43–4, 101, 153, 183
sanction 47–74, 172, 176, 180, 205
Sandiganbayan case 204
Santiago Commitment to Democracy 65
São Tomé and Príncipe's *coup* 60–1, 162
Schmitt, Carl 89
Schneider v Kissinger 120–2
Senegal's municipal courts' extraordinary chambers 219–20, 227, 236
separation of powers 107, 144, 146, 151, 175, 248
Seychelles's *coup* 44–5, 216n168, 249
Siddique Ahmed v Bangladesh 35n54, 169–70
Sierra Leone, Special Court for 154, 155, 219, 224, 227, 235
Sierra Leone's *coup* 82, 83, 168, 235
Sindh High Court Bar Association v Federation of Pakistan 153
sliding scale of criminal responsibility 216, 217

soft law 122–3
Sombat Boon-ngamanong case 28–9, 34
Sonko, Ousman 241–2
South Africa 139, 165–7, 189, 239–40, 255
South Korea's *coup* 4, 186–7, 205, 253–4
South Sudan's Revitalized Agreement on Resolution of Conflict 215–16
sovereignty 12, 15, 20, 24, 34–7, 40–1, 44–5, 50, 150–1, 152, 183
Special Rapporteur on independence of judges and lawyers *see* Knaul, Gabriela
statutes of limitations 13, 14, 86, 89, 161, 165, 170, 184–8, 196, 197, 205, 208, 216–18, 246, 255, 258n33
Stroessner, Alfredo 5n15, 89–90, 216n167
subsidiarity 240
Sudan's *coups* 2, 6, 9, 53–4, 58, 60, 82
superior orders 13, 36, 127, 153–6, 182, 198
Suriname's *coups* 82, 83, 195–7

Tañada v Cuenco 119–20
Taylor, Charles 167
Texas v White 18
Thailand's *coups* 7n22, 8, 28–9, 36n56, 40–3, 69
torture 7, 11, 47, 55, 68, 77, 78, 79, 83–5, 87–9, 91, 92, 100, 105, 108, 110, 111, 114, 118, 121, 127, 130, 155, 164, 170, 172, 175, 176, 192, 195, 196, 197, 198, 204, 205, 212, 213, 214, 215, 217, 221, 222, 226, 232, 233, 235–6, 237, 239, 241, 242, 244, 245, 245–7, 251, 257, 258n33, 259
Torture, Convention against 77, 83–5, 109, 164, 235–6, 244, 246
Touray case 184–5, 208–13, 237, 258–9
transitional justice 3, 14, 90, 188–209, 214, 216, 218, 252, 254–60
treason 20, 29, 105, 157, 168, 186–7, 216–17, 250
treaty monitoring bodies (generally) 76–8
TRIAL International 241–2
Truth, Reconciliation and Reparations Commission 208, 237–8, 242, 257n28
truth commission 166, 167–8, 189, 191, 200–3, 205, 208, 237–42
Tunisia's *coups* 61, 82, 83, 85, 106–7, 146–7, 192
Türkiye's *coups* 8–9, 192–3, 256

Uganda's *coup* 5, 31, 249
UN General Assembly 50–1, 54, 58, 85, 86n18, 112, 114n99, 139, 142, 163n10, 185
UN International Law Commission 10n32, 12, 87n23, 247
Universal Declaration of Human Rights 37, 117, 211–12
universal jurisdiction 13, 123, 126, 183, 208, 218, 238–47
UN Security Council 52–4, 63–4, 73–4, 88, 105, 123, 209, 214, 223, 225, 234, 258
Urrutia v Chile 143n47, 155n81
Uruguay's *coups* 82, 83, 174–5, 184, 193, 194, 201

Valabhaji v Controller of Taxes 44–5
Videla, Jorge 197–9
Vienna Convention on Law of the Treaties 241
Vienna Convention on Diplomatic Relations 9

war crime 88, 156, 187, 221–3, 232, 246
welfare of the people 12, 16, 17, 22, 23–4, 34, 43–4, 73, 183
West African Economic Monetary Union 62
Williams v Tah 167–8

XYZ v Republic of Benin 145–6

Yassiada Island trial 8–9, 105

Zafar Ali Shah v Musharraf 24–6, 34, 44, 46, 73, 91, 149–52, 153, 159, 189
Zia ul Haq 23, 27, 150n65
Zimbabwe Human Rights Forum v Zimbabwe 167n22, 212–13
Zimbabwe's *coup* 5, 61, 82
Zimbabwe Torture Docket Case 239